GLOBAL
JOURNALISM

SECOND EDITION

LONGMAN SERIES IN PUBLIC COMMUNICATION

Series Editor: Ray Eldon Hiebert

GLOBAL
JOURNALISM

SURVEY OF INTERNATIONAL COMMUNICATION

SECOND EDITION

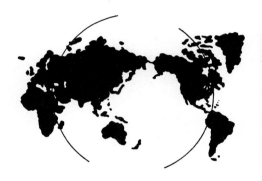

BIPOD

John C. Merrill, Editor

Longman
New York & London

Global Journalism, second edition

Longman, 95 Church Street, White Plains, N.Y. 10601

Associated companies:
Longman Group Ltd., London
Longman Cheshire Pty., Melbourne
Longman Paul Pty., Auckland
Copp Clark Pitman, Toronto

Executive editor: Gordon T. R. Anderson
Production editor: Halley Gatenby
Cover design: Kevin C. Kall
Text art: Art Directions
Production supervisor: Kathleen Ryan

Library of Congress Cataloging-in-Publication Data

Global journalism / [edited by] John C. Merrill.—2nd ed.
     p.   cm.—(Longman series in public communication)
   Includes bibliographical references.
   ISBN 0-8013-0512-8
   1. Journalism.   I. Merrill, John Calhoun, 1924– . II. Series.
PN4775.G56   1990
070.4—dc20   90-31302
                                                CIP

ABCDEFGHIJ-DO-99   98   97   96   95   94   93   92   91   90

Contents

Preface

This second edition of *Global Journalism* continues the basic plan of the first edition: to provide a survey of the issues facing world journalism and describe the broad dimensions of international mass media. It is thus a two-pronged book that introduces students to global controversies and perplexing questions while providing them with a substantive framework of the physical aspects of global mass communication.

The scope of the present edition is, however, somewhat larger than the first. For example, in the original book global issues, press theories, and attendant concerns of the Third World and UNESCO—along with some data on news agencies and news flow—were rather sketchily dealt with in Part I. In this new edition such material is treated in more depth. Part I now has four separate chapters, dealing successively with the following topics: press theories, collection of flow and world news, global news media, and prominent controversies in international communication.

More contributors are now involved in the book's preparation. Whereas the first edition had seven contributors, the present edition has fourteen, besides the editor. Because of the broad scope of such a project as this and the specialized information contained, enlarging the writing base has substantially improved *Global Journalism*.

A book such as this is needed today more than ever before. Although books abound on media systems of various countries and regions of the world and numerous tomes discuss such topics as news flow, Third World concerns, global propaganda, and news agencies, there is still a place for a survey book that attempts to pull together the highlights of all this material and to summarize it for the uninitiated student. This is what *Global Journalism* attempts to do.

This book does not pretend to be exhaustive. It is designed to give an overview, a survey of global journalism. This book should serve well in a course dealing with comparative world journalism or international communication or as a supplemental text for a basic journalism or social science course.

All journalism students need at least an introduction to the world's media so that they may better appreciate and evaluate the media system of their own country. Such an introduction should go a long way in helping students shed their provincialism and begin thinking of their own press system in an international context. Since the 1960s, the study of global communication has been growing rapidly in schools and departments of journalism and mass communication. Courses in this broad area have become important fixtures in most curricula. It is now generally recognized, for example, that an American studying journalism or communication should no more be limited to American journalism than a history student should study only American history. This present volume is presented as such an introduction to the world's journalism and, if used intelligently and creatively with collateral readings, guest lectures, and the like, should provide insights into the scope, general characteristics, and issues of global journalism.

Global Journalism should, of course, be used in concert with the professor's fresh lectures, with classroom visits by resource persons—such as foreign correspondents and on-campus persons from other countries—with information from embassies and consulates, and with special oral reports on aspects of a country's journalism by various members of the class. None of this, however, will obviate the fact that the very nature of a book like this one makes some content somewhat dated even on the day it is published. But the editor and contributors have tried to keep it as contemporary as possible and hope that both professor and students will update it as they use it.

Since this is an attempt to give a panoramic view of journalism around the world, we purposely use rather broad strokes to paint our picture. Also we eschew minor qualifiers and footnotes in order to move readers rapidly forward and to acquaint them briskly with some of the generally agreed on ideas and data relative to international journalism. We don't consider this volume a reference work so much as a panoramic picture, an introduction to communication problems and issues.

At this point, it would perhaps be helpful to mention a few key terms used in this book. It is hoped that at least some semantic clarity will be contributed by showing how we use the following terms.

- *Press* is used in a historical context, as in "press freedom or law," and the "power of the press."
- *Journalism* has a print origin but is also used here in reference to the gathering and presentation of news and information.
- *Media* is used to refer to the instruments and organizations of communication. It is used both collectively and with qualifiers such as "news," "broadcast," and "electronic."
- *Broadcast media* refers to radio, television, and the new technologies of telecommunication but not to film, video, telephones, and so forth.
- *Electronic media* includes broadcast media as well as film and video.

Quotations and statistical data, of course, are important. Although we do include some tables and figures, they have been kept to a minimum. Readers desiring to compensate for what they may see as statistical or evidential deficiencies are encouraged to consult reference works in international communication or more topical books listed in our bibliography for each chapter in the back of the book.

Information for this book has been obtained from innumerable sources—analysis of foreign publications, lectures, scholarly papers, articles, books, government pamphlets, interviews, embassy materials, journals and magazines of all types, and newspapers. The editor and the 14 authors have traveled extensively abroad and have had occasion to see press systems firsthand and to have had numerous interviews and conversations with leading journalistic figures in the media and in academia the world over.

One final note: In a very real sense, all the contributors to this work are coauthors; the chapters were all designed and written especially for *Global Journalism* and are not reprints from other publications. As editor, I would like to express my deep appreciation to, and admiration of, the contributors who have worked so diligently with me to bring out this new edition.

J. C. M.

GLOBAL
JOURNALISM
SECOND EDITION

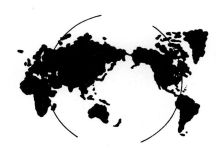

Introduction

International communication and intercultural communication have burst forth in recent years as popular courses in U.S. colleges and universities. This book is designed primarily for journalism and communications courses in this broad area of concern, for professors and students who are interested in an introductory and general survey of global media concerns and comparative communication systems.

The chapters of Part I introduce the international patterns of journalism and mass communication, the leading theories, and the most prevalent controversies and issues in contemporary global journalism.

Perhaps more important are the chapters of Part II, which present a substantive, descriptive overview of the dimensions of journalism in the main regions of the world. Thus this is a survey book, which in its broad reaches is designed as a descriptive and comparative textbook.

The media systems described in Part II of this book, as well as the more theoretical concerns dealt with in Part I, combine to give a general picture of the physical and ideational dimensions of the world's journalism that will remain useful as the reader's knowledge grows and details change. I believe that basic tendencies of press systems and underlying issues in global journalism change rather slowly. Also, even the physical dimension (leading newspapers, news agencies, structure of broadcasting, etc.) in the various world regions tends to evolve extremely slowly. The student can glean useful and meaningful concepts and patterns of world journalism from this book, even though year by year various media units (newspapers, magazines, etc.) continue to appear and disappear.

GLOBAL MEDIA PROBLEMS

Let us focus on some basic communication problems that global journalists face as they go about their work of spreading news and news-related information. Pychological and physical barriers exist in all countries; these are reinforced by a host of problems such as cultural differences, languages, definitions of journalistic concepts, educational and economic deficiencies, control mechanisms, and propaganda proclivities. Such communication barriers constantly block global journalistic progress and frustrate international understanding. Let us look at a few of these briefly.

In spite of improved international relations, distrust and misunderstanding among peoples are commonplace today; and in this climate of suspicious anxiety and unrest, the world's mass media of communication are reaching more people with more messages than ever before. All who are in positions to think about such things are aware that the world is still in crisis and that one hasty or irresponsible action might plunge the world into a disastrous, even catastrophic, war. Representatives of many nations come increasingly to conference tables to talk about the multitude of world problems and dangers, and ostensibly they wish to establish peace, allay fears, gain global justice, and improve world understanding through better communication.

But seated with these men and women at United Nations forums and elsewhere are deep-rooted prejudices and suspicions, strong national feelings, and vested interests; beneath the smooth patina of the words are long-simmering antagonisms, traditional power politics, and fundamental misunderstandings. And all the while, the media of mass communication are pouring a glut of messages over vast audiences. The global press—the giant organism holding together cultural and nationalistic groups—is busy "reporting" and "interpreting" the constant succession of world crises and the conferences dealing with them.

The global media wield tremendous power as purveyors of vital information. They have the potential to erase erroneous impressions and stereotypes and to ease tensions; they can also create fears and needlessly perpetuate anxieties. They can shake people from complacency or lull them into an unthinking and dangerous sleep. With psychological warfare raging fiercely, the media find themselves in a position of tremendous responsibility today. Modern technology has created of the world a small house, and human beings are locked together in the same tiny room where everyone is forced to share the consequences of one another's action.

Physical means of communicating news and disseminating it throughout the world are well developed and capable of providing the quantity of messages needed for proper understanding among peoples. But as messages flow more rapidly and in greater quantity than ever before, questions of quality, of impact, of significance, of balance, of truth, and of motive come to the forefront. And while on the surface adequate information appears to be moving through most parts of the world, government pressures, secrecy, censorship, and propaganda impede the free flow of news.

As governments get larger and more complex in bureaucratic structure, the problems of media access to basic and relevant information become more difficult. At the same time, sincere and normally cooperative government representatives find that with more exposure to the mass media, they are misrepresented—their statements are twisted and their meaning is distorted, all of which can lead toward a climate of suspicion and mistrust on the part of public officials and in turn to a reluctance on their part to say very much for public dissemination. As governments become more sensitive and cautious when confronted by the media, the universe of frank and open news reporting is restricted, and honest and thoroughgoing dialogue becomes more difficult.

A BASIC CONCERN: FREEDOM

On the world scene as on the national scene, truthful and unfettered media can best serve the people. Such media freedom can go far to mend differences among nationalities, classes, and groups; it can frustrate the plans of war-hungry leaders and rulers. The realization of these possibilities is a prodigious task for the media, one that requires the acceptance and application of the free-press theory; for only with a free press can people have more than a foggy or lopsided picture of what is happening around them.

Throughout the world, freedom of communication is an ideal; no country has actually achieved it. This ideal is simply on a continuum somewhere between absolute control and complete freedom. Recent surveys and studies tend to indicate that in many ways freedom of communication is not firmly entrenched worldwide. Restrictive laws are proliferating, sanctions of many kinds are hindering the free workings of the media, and groups are moving in to guide media activities.

The world is full of would-be media controllers, in both libertarian and authoritarian countries. Government leaders desire political and social stability and realize that too much communication freedom endangers this stability and the status quo. Hence it is quite understandable that the natural national tendency is toward more media regulation. Control, then, is the common—not the exceptional—state of things in the world, and relatively free media today may be highly restricted tomorrow.

In the light of the foregoing, the idea of media having free access to factual and significant information may understandably appear to many thoughtful persons as only the dream of unrealistic optimists. Certainly, few observers could fail to see the difficulties of implementing such an idea in these days when the world is divided into numerous nationalistic camps, each with its own government and press philosophy. And it might be added at this point that each nation's communication infrastructure and philosophy are usually closely in step with the nation's basic political and social system and ideology. So in one very real sense, every country's media are more often than not truly a "branch of government" or a cooperating part of the national establishment.

Even the casual observer will note that world journalism today is subjecting people's minds to a ceaseless bombardment of messages calculated to influence and control. Internally, a nation's media try to mold the state into a consolidated, smooth-running machine ready to repel any outside danger, and externally they direct their broadsides at potential enemies. This may be a practical course in times of danger, but it does not make for objective, information-oriented communication within or among countries.

Perhaps the media have come in for too great a share of blame for this situation. Responsibility to all people of all nations is a fine concept, but responsible media in an irresponsible social or government context are hardly to be hoped for except by those too uninformed or too idealistic to know better. And the individual citizen may be to blame for the bias and government propaganda that permeate large segments of world journalism today.

Many critics say that the media are actually hindering world understanding and cooperation and that they are stretching animosities among nations to dangerous dimensions and thereby worsening the international psychic crisis. This does not seem an unlikely thesis. It would imply that "exceptional" incidents are disseminated as important news; it would further imply that "eccentric" and "dangerous" people are the subject of much of the news. In short, it would imply that "unreal" and "alarmist" news dominates newspaper columns and television screens.

MEDIA AS AGITATORS

When we examine the world media today, we get the feeling that the jangled nerves of the world's populations can hardly be eased by the newspapers—and certainly not by TV. On the contrary, anxieties are created, magnified, and perpetuated; religion is set against religion, social class against social class, race against race, and nationality against nationality. Instead of being conveyors of enlightenment and harmony, the national media systems tend too often to be "press agents" for individual nations or special groups, thus doing a good job of increasing irritations and suspicions among governments and giving distorted pictures of various nations.

Very few observers would deny that the news media are involved largely in creating and destroying images. Certainly the world's communication channels have been all but choked in recent years by inflammatory and slanted messages concerning explosive situations in the Middle East, in the emerging nations of Africa, and in parts of Asia and Latin America. Readers, listeners, and viewers searching for the "real story" are often left bewildered. Contradictions in the news, discrepancies among world news agencies, and opinions creeping more and more into news columns and network newscasts puzzle them and frustrate their quest for truth.

All indications are that the world's consumers of news and views are in for a long siege of ideological messages. There have been few truces in international psychological warfare. As technology pushes mass messages into the more remote regions and saturates ever-growing populations, the world's psychosis is bound to worsen. Truth in the messages is no assurance of enlightenment or emotional stabilization; recent history has shown clearly that even the most truthful statement can boomerang, that it can appear as something quite different when viewed from the perspective of a particular audience's traditional beliefs, desires, and expectations.

The mass media should not be looked upon as a panacea for the world's problems. The most powerful radio transmitters and the most enterprising and honest newspapers and magazines will not be able to substitute for international cooperation and progress on the diplomatic level. Mass communication is obviously no substitute for direct involvement of persons and their technologies in the world crisis; international action certainly speaks louder than mass-oriented words.

Worldwide envy, resentment, suspicion, and hatred build emotional walls against the most objective and well-intentioned printed word and erect mental jamming stations against the most honest broadcast. And when one considers that in every nation the government uses news as a weapon, with little attempt at honesty or objectivity, the task of the mass media in the fight for peace and understanding takes on a dismal cast.

SIGNS FOR A BETTER FUTURE

It must be noted, however, that beginning in 1989 and 1990 the boiling cauldron of global problems cooled considerably with the advent of *perestroika* (reordering) and *glasnost* (openness) in the Soviet Union. The major powers, at least, seemed to be curbing their harsh rhetoric, and there were definite signs that the Eastern European countries were changing rapidly as they were taking the new openness and restructuring seriously. Soviet media, as well as those in such countries as Hungary and Poland, were showing surprising signs of outspoken commentary and full-disclosure news reporting.

The world was shocked in November 1989 when a spirit of freedom swept into what was considered the most entrenched of the communist Warsaw Pact countries, East Germany. Thousands of East Germans left their homes for the West, the Berlin Wall began to crumble figuratively and physically, travel restrictions were eliminated, and *glasnost* became the order of the day. Even unification of the two Germanies was a hot topic. At the same time, this same spirit permeated all of Eastern Europe, with Poland and Hungary leading the way toward a more Westernized type of market economy while retaining for their nations a core of their old ideology, which they are renaming "democratic socialism."

As the last decade of the twentieth century began, Europe's hard-line communist regimes were moderating and Central American friction was disappearing. Although the Middle East was still experiencing unrest and danger pervaded parts of Southeast Asia, there was a new optimism in the world—even in southern Africa—that portended well for the century ending on an upbeat note of world peace and harmony.

With this introductory discussion of general global journalism problems behind us, we are ready to head into the main body of this book, the substantive chapters highlighting the issues and dimensions of global journalism.

Part I will bring to the forefront some important contemporary issues and problems in international journalism and major aspects of communication developments in a worldwide context. The more specific and substantive matters of global journalism (e.g., leading newspapers and magazines, broadcast media, government-press relations, press freedom, journalism education, and media economics) will be dealt with in Part 11, the descriptive and comparative portion of the book dealing with media in the five main regions of the world—Europe, the Middle East and North Africa, Africa, Asia and the Pacific, Latin America, and North America.

PART I

The Global Perspective

The problems, issues, and controversies of international communication are many and great. Global journalism can be looked upon as a gigantic enclosure in which large numbers of varied and complex media systems are clashing and coexisting. In Part I, four authors provide the philosophical, economic, and political contexts in which the regional media systems exist.

Part I, therefore, is the macroscopic part of the book—the world overview of journalism. It seeks to answer such questions as these: What are the major nations in the global journalism picture? How are information and news gathered, processed, and disseminated worldwide? What are the main global media theories or concepts? Why are large parts of the world unhappy with the contemporary system (or order) of global communication?

Whitney Mundt of Louisiana State University in Chapter 1 deals mainly with media philosophy, the various politicocultural approaches to journalism around the world. He presents the classic four-theories typology of Fred Siebert, Theodore Peterson, and Wilbur Schramm and then proceeds to revisions and variations on these theories, all stemming from the binary concepts of authoritarianism and libertarianism. Some of the scholars who have dealt with such revisions of, and criticisms of, the four-theories approach are discussed.

In Chapter 2, Al Hester of the University of Georgia shows how international newsgathering and transmittal developed and how it operates today. He deals with the main global news agencies, including Reuters

(Britain), the Associated Press (United States), and TASS (Soviet Union), and some of the smaller national agencies and syndicates. The principal international newspapers and magazines (e.g., *New York Times, Le Monde, Time*) are introduced, and an overview of global broadcasting is presented. The important role of foreign correspondents and the fundamental problems of news flow are discussed, and some attention is given to the future of world media operations.

Lowndes (Rick) Stephens of the University of South Carolina tackles the tough assignment in Chapter 3 of surveying the world's media systems as he provides a broad view of some of the pressing problems and physical dimensions of global journalism. He emphasizes the impact of technology on world media and talks about the growth of big media conglomerates and media barons. Freedom of communication is dealt with from a global perspective, and Freedom House surveys are highlighted. This chapter conveys a broad picture of the printed and broadcast media of the world; it also delves into the importance of international advertising and the general impact of media on national development.

Finally, in Chapter 4, Robert Picard of California State University, Fullerton, reviews current controversies in international journalism. They center mainly on the economically developing nations of the Third World and the inequities that exist in global communication infrastructures. Picard discusses the evolution of these problems and shows how UNESCO and other international organizations have tried to deal with them. The "New World Information and Communication Order"(NWICO)—a restructuring of global communication—is much desired by Third World nations, and this chapter focuses on NWICO and its proponents and critics.

It should by now be apparent that one cannot embark upon the complex and arduous tour of global journalism lightly. The chapters of Part I are intended to get you accustomed to the landscape and adjusted to the climate before venturing into the more strenuous descriptive and substantive terrain of Part II.

CHAPTER 1

Global Media Philosophies

Whitney R. Mundt

Media philosophy is a term that perhaps masks the reality of the task that we are undertaking in this chapter. We do not seek to inculcate a true *philosophy*—"the love of wisdom or knowledge"—nor do we attempt to set forth a set of principles by which the media may govern themselves. Rather, we seek to describe a relationship between government and journalism in which the balance of power is forever shifting. One of the eternal conundrums with which philosophers busy themselves is where to draw the line between freedom and control: At what point may coercion be applied legitimately to define the limits of permissible conduct?

Governors and journalists put that line in various places and offer various justifications for doing so. In this chapter, we shall examine those rationales—or at least some of them, for they are as diverse as are their proponents. In reality, then, we are setting forth theories of control by which governments seek to limit the freedom of the media or, conversely, the rationales by which the media claim freedom from such restrictions. There are many such theories or rationales, and our task will be to examine each, in an attempt to illuminate these difficult relationships as they exist in various forms around the globe.

When Johannes Gutenberg introduced movable type to Europe in the early fifteenth century, he made possible the relatively inexpensive mass production of the printed word and, some might argue, loosed the winds of error to play upon the earth. It is also arguable that he assisted Truth to enter the field in order that she might grapple with Falsehood.

And who ever knew Truth put to the worse in a free and open encounter? John Milton was assured on that point, and he argued persuasively for unlicensed printing in *Areopagitica*, two centuries after Gutenberg's technological development. In the interim, the ruling monarchs had moved to control printing, having recognized the dangers implicit in mass communication. The field of battle had been defined, the forces arrayed. The victor has yet to be declared in this conflict between authoritarian repression of the word and libertarian freedom to express it.

THE "FOUR THEORIES" TYPOLOGY

In 1956, Fred Siebert, Theodore Peterson, and Wilbur Schramm sought to describe the conflict between the state and the press, or, as they phrased it, "the system of social control whereby the relations of individuals and institutions are adjusted." (Table 1.1 gives their typology.) Their little book, *Four Theories of the Press*, has been immensely influential and continues to be read by succeeding generations of aspiring mass communication scholars and practitioners. Subtitled *The Authoritarian, Libertarian, Social Responsibility, and Soviet Communist Concepts of What the Press Should Be and Do*, the book argues that there really are only two theories—the authoritarian and the libertarian—and that the other two concepts are merely developments and modifications of the first two.

Authoritarian

The oldest of these is the authoritarian, born in the age of Gutenberg. In that society, truth was revealed to the rulers, who in turn disseminated that truth to the masses through the press. In other words, the function of the press was to convey to the people what the rulers wanted them to know. In such a system, the press was naturally obligated to endorse the version of the truth supplied by the rulers. To prevent challenge to their version of the truth, the king or queen permitted the press to exist only by royal authority, although private ownership was allowed. But this permission, or license, could be withdrawn at royal whim, and the right to censor was presumed. The press was thus the servant of the state. This role was unquestioned, as it was the logical corollary of the philosophy of divine right or absolute power by which the monarchs ruled. This theory of authoritarian control has not died out, although the age of monarchs is waning; authoritarianism continues to exist in countries where strong rulers wield power.

TABLE 1.1. SIEBERT-PETERSON-SCHRAMM TYPOLOGY

Authoritarian	Libertarian	Soviet Communist	Social Responsibility
Developed in sixteenth- and seventeenth-century Europe	Arose in England in the late seventeenth century; spread to America and the European Continent	Arose in early twentieth-century USSR	Arose in the mid-twentieth-century United States out of the libertarian tradition
Stemmed from the absolute power of the monarch	Stemmed from Enlightenment thought and natural rights	Stemmed from Marx and Lenin	Stemmed from the writings of the Commission on Freedom of the Press and other critics of the libertarian press
Purpose: To support state and leadership	Purpose: To help find truth, inform, interpret, entertain	Purpose: To support the Marxist system, to serve the people	Purpose: Mainly to inform and educate, to help social progress
Licensing, censorship, autocratic power, laws	Editorial self-determination; separation of state and press	Theoretically, the people own the press, and can use it	Press should be open to anyone with something to say
No criticism or threat to the power structure is permitted	Media controlled by owners in a free market of ideas and by courts	Media controlled by the Communist Party government apparatus	Social responsibility of the press is more important than its freedom
Owned by ruler, party, or private persons	Nothing forbidden from publication prior to publication	Media cannot criticize Party objectives	Controlled by community opinion and consumer action and by codes of ethics, press councils, etc.
Forerunners: Hobbes, Hegel, Machiavelli	Private ownership	Owned "by the people"	No publishing of socially harmful information or invasion of private rights
Examples today: Iran, Paraguay, Nigeria	Forerunners: Locke, Milton, Mill, Adam Smith	Developers: Marx, Lenin, Stalin, Mao, Castro, Gorbachev	Private ownership, but threat of government interference to assure public service
	Examples today: United States, Japan, West Germany	Examples today: USSR, China, Cuba	Examples today: none; several countries tending, including the United States

Source: Adapted from Frederick S. Siebert, Theodore Peterson, and Wilbur Schramm, *Four Theories of the Press* (Urbana: University of Illinois Press, 1956).

Libertarian

Libertarianism is at the other end of the spectrum, as Siebert, Peterson, and Schramm defined and described the system of social control. In libertarian theory, men and women are no longer mere passive recipients of the truth as it is determined by the rulers. Instead, they are rational beings who are innately able to distinguish truth and falsehood. Furthermore, the *right* to search for truth may be exercised by each person. The role of the media is to assist in that search, to help the individual discover truth. It follows that in a libertarian system, the media cannot be subject to government but rather must be independent, autonomous, free to express even outrageous ideas without fear of government intervention. This belief in the primacy of the word and the destructiveness of censorship was eloquently expressed by John Milton, one of the philosophers of libertarianism, in *Areopagitica:* "Who kills a man kills a reasonable creature, God's image; but he who destroys a good book, kills reason itself, kills the image of God."

Libertarianism means that humans, as rational beings, must be free to search for truth and that the media are partners in that search. Because government may sometimes erect obstacles to that search, the media in a libertarian system must also be able to check on government—this is the so-called watchdog role of media. In turn, the media are controlled by the "self-righting process of truth." This self-righting process was described by U.S. Supreme Court Justice Oliver Wendell Holmes in *Abrams* v. *United States* (1919), when he wrote in his dissenting opinion: "The best test of truth is the power of the thought to get itself accepted in the competition of the market." The concept of a free marketplace of ideas requires, of course, that all people, minorities as well as majorities, have access to the media in order for libertarianism to succeed.

Social Responsibility

In 1919, when Holmes wrote his dissent in *Abrams,* the free marketplace concept was closer to reality than it was nearly a quarter-century later, when a commission was formed to inquire into the status of freedom of the media. Under the leadership of Robert M. Hutchins, chancellor of the University of Chicago, the commission found that freedom of the press had become endangered because of increasingly monopolistic conditions. Too few owners controlled too many media outlets. Increased concentration of ownership resulted from the growing cost of print and broadcast technology, and the effect was that fewer people had access to communication channels. The commission suggested that media owners should accept a greater responsibility to society, granting more liberal access, including a right of reply. Commission members were uneasy about the growing power of media owners and managers to control information, much as authoritarian rulers had done in Gutenberg's day.

This uneasiness, Siebert, Peterson, and Schramm argue, is the basis of the social responsibility theory, a modification of or development from libertarianism. Social responsibility differs from its roots in that the function of the press is to provide a medium for the discussion of conflict, whereas under libertarianism the press was to check on government. And whereas the libertarian theory provides that the media are available to all who have the economic means to use them, social responsibility theory holds that everyone with something to say has the right to use the media. A third distinction between the two theories is that a socially responsible press will be controlled by community opinion, consumer action, and professional ethics, whereas libertarianism relies on the free marketplace of ideas for its correction.

The Hutchins Commission (1947) suggested that if the press did not recognize and fulfill its social responsibilities, some organization must assume the task of requiring the press to do so. The commission proposed the creation of an independent agency that would review press performance and report annually.

Despite the outrage media people expressed at the Hutchins Commission's recommendations, a number of steps have been taken in the direction of a more socially responsible press. For example, several codes of ethics have been adopted, opinion pages have been added to newspapers for reader contributions, consumer-oriented programming is now regularly featured on both local and network television, and the National News Council was formed in 1973 to adjudicate complaints by media consumers and to defend media freedoms where warranted. The news council expired after about a decade of operation as a result of lack of media support and funding, but similar organizations still operate at city and state levels.

Soviet Communist

The last of the concepts described in *Four Theories of the Press* is the Soviet communist approach. It is an offshoot of authoritarianism, according to Siebert, Peterson, and Schramm, just as the social responsibility concept is a modification of libertarianism. Like the press in an authoritarian regime, the Soviet Communist press serves the ruling party. But unlike the press in an authoritarian system, the Soviet press is owned by the state. Other differences between the Soviet totalitarian system and its roots, according to Siebert, Peterson, and Schramm, are these:

1. The Soviet system removes the profit motive; the authoritarian system retains it.
2. In the Soviet system, the emphasis is on requiring certain things by the press; in the authoritarian system, the press is forbidden to do certain things.
3. The Soviet press must assist in accomplishing change; the press in an authoritarian system is charged with helping to maintain the status quo.
4. The Soviet media are integrated into the mass communication system; media in an authoritarian state retain their individual "personalities."

This litany of state controls in the Soviet communist theory would lead anyone acquainted with the libertarian system to conclude that the Soviet press is the victim of a slave-master mentality, while the libertarian press breathes free. But in fact Marxist dogma finds the reverse to be true. The Soviets would say that their press is free to express the truth, whereas the press in a so-called libertarian system is controlled by business interests.

OTHER MEDIA MODELS

The Siebert-Peterson-Schramm typology has been immensely influential. As John Merrill says in *The Dialectic in Journalism* (1989), "Almost every article and book dealing with philosophical bases for journalism alludes to this book [*Four Theories*], comments on it, or quotes from it" (pp. 97–98). But time has outstripped *Four Theories of the Press.* It can no longer be said to describe the Soviet Communist model accurately. And it does not attempt to describe various systems, such as the revolutionary theory of the press, which have flowered since publication of that little book in 1956. Consequently, a number of mass communication scholars have offered their own global media philosophies.

Ralph Lowenstein

In 1971, Ralph Lowenstein proposed a revision of the four-theory typology because he believed that the Siebert-Peterson-Schramm model was inflexible and could not be applied to all press systems. In *Media, Messages, and Men* (Merrill & Lowenstein, 1971), he suggested instead a two-tiered approach that would identify ownership types as well as philosophy. For example, media might be privately owned, supported by advertising and subscriptions, or they might be owned by competitive political parties, with subsidies from party funds or party members, or they might be government-owned, with funds provided from the treasury or from license fees. With respect to press philosophy, Lowenstein retained the terms *authoritarianism* and *libertarianism* and their meanings from the Siebert-Peterson-Schramm model, but he modified the other two terms to rid the theories of their connotative baggage. "Soviet communist" became *social-centralist* in order to remove the negative values in the original term and also to broaden it. *Social* conveys the collectivist orientation of the communist system, and *centralist* conveys the reality of the centrally guided nature of Marxist press systems. Social responsibility became *social-libertarian* in order to be rid of the ambiguity in the original term and to reflect more readily the roots of this theory in libertarianism. The new term retains the sense that some regulation of the media may be required to ensure public benefit.

In 1979, Lowenstein revised his list of press philosophies for the second edition of *Media, Messages, and Men* (Merrill & Lowenstein, 1979); it is reprinted as Table 1.2. Social-centralist now became *social-authoritarian* so as to reveal more clearly the relationship of the press

TABLE 1.2. LOWENSTEIN TYPOLOGY

Press Ownership

1. Private—Ownership by individuals or nongovernment corporations; supported primarily by advertising or subscriptions.
2. Multiparty—Ownership by competitive political parties; subsidized by party or party members.
3. Government—Owned by government or dominant government party; subsidized primarily by government funds or government-collected license fees.

Press Philosophies

1. Authoritarian—Government licensing and censorship to stifle criticism and thereby maintain the ruling elite.
2. Social-authoritarian—Government and government-party ownership to harness the press for national economic and philosophical goals.
3. Libertarian—Absence of governmental controls (except for minimal libel and obscenity laws), assuring a free marketplace of ideas and operation of the self-righting process.
4. Social-libertarian—Minimal governmental controls to unclog channels of communication and assure the operational spirit of the libertarian philosophy.
5. Social-centralist—Government or public ownership of the limited channels of communication to assure the operational spirit of the libertarian philosophy.

Source: Reprinted from John C. Merrill and Ralph L. Lowenstein, *Media, Messages, and Men* (New York: Longman, 1979), p. 164.

systems in the Eastern bloc nations with the authoritarian philosophy. Lowenstein then added a fifth term to his list: social-centralist. This term is *not* to be confused with the same term that he had earlier used to designate systems of the Soviet-bloc nations. Social-centralist press systems are those in which government or public ownership of media outlets has become necessary "to assure the operational spirit of the libertarian philosophy."

In his new book *Macromedia: Mission, Message, and Morality* (Lowenstein & Merrill, 1990), Lowenstein provides a fuller explanation of his typology, which remains fundamentally unchanged although slightly edited.

John Merrill

John Merrill found Lowenstein's model to be "more sophisticated and realistic" than the Siebert-Peterson-Schramm model but basically flawed in that Lowenstein's social-libertarian concept is logically contradictory. Merrill argues in his book *The Imperative of Freedom* (1974) that a philosophy cannot be both libertarian (that is, free) and directed (that is, controlled). The Lowenstein model and the Siebert-Peterson-Schramm model share another basic weakness, according to Merrill: They both propose a spectrum, with authoritarianism at one end and libertarianism at the other. This scheme is a "pigeonhole" model that assumes that media systems are mutually exclusive and independent, he writes. In their place he proposes a "political-press circle"—a model that places libertarianism at the top and authoritarianism at the bottom of a closed circle (see Figure 1.1). In this schema, the four theories are reduced to two (with all modifications of the two recognized to be authoritarian-tending or libertarian-tending), and the two theories are seen to be interdependent in the sense that the path from freedom to statism may proceed in either direction: left, through socialism, or right, through capitalism.

William Hachten

William Hachten made the first significant changes to the four-theory model as it had been proposed in 1956 (the Lowenstein and Merrill models were, by and large, refinements of the original typology proposed by Siebert, Peterson, and Schramm). In *The World News Prism* (1981), Hachten proposed a five-concept typology that retained the authoritarian and communist ideologies, combined libertarianism and social responsibility into what he called the Western concept, and added two new theories: revolutionary and developmental (see Table 1.3).

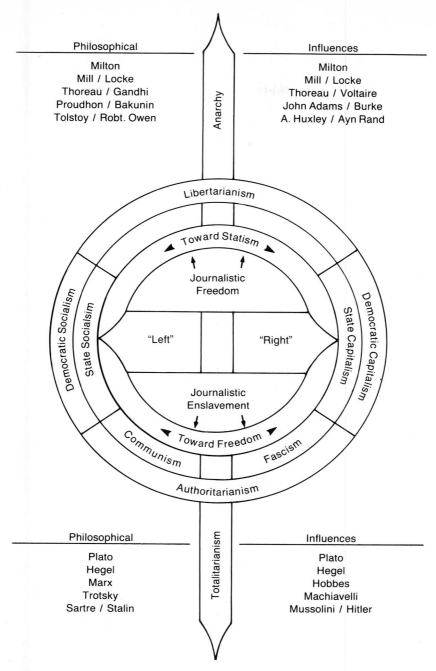

Figure 1.1. Merrill Typology: The Political-Press Circle (*Source:* John C. Merrill, *The Imperative of Freedom* [New York: Hastings House, 1974], p. 42.)

TABLE 1.3. HACHTEN'S FIVE-CONCEPT TYPOLOGY

Type	Control	Policy	Representatives
Authoritarian	Public and private, subordinate to the state	Media can operate if there is no criticism of regime or dissent; implied or actual censorship	Early European countries; modern dictatorships in Africa, Latin America, and elsewhere
Western (libertarian and social responsibility)	Private ownership of press; private and public broadcasting systems	Emphasis on freedom from governmental restraints, but obligations to perform responsibly	United States, Britain, Western Europe, Japan
Communist	Media part of the Communist Party or government; no private ownership	Stress on transmitting official views and policies; mobilizing support for national progress	Soviet Union and Communist nations of Eastern Europe; Cuba; China
Revolutionary	Illegal or subversive media; uncontrolled by government	Underground media, often from outside country; seeking to overthrow a government	Underground media in wartime occupations; colonial press in parts of Africa, India
Developmental	Government and/or party controls and directs all media	Mobilization of media to serve national goals in development; political integration; campaign against poverty, disease, and illiteracy	Nonindustrialized, noncommunist nations of the Third World

Source: Adapted from William Hachten, *The World News Prism* (Ames: Iowa State University Press, 1981).

Hachten defines the revolutionary concept as the use of illegal and subversive mass communications to overthrow a government. Samuel Adams and Thomas Paine are examples of revolutionary journalists in U.S. history. Hachten cites *Pravda,* which was founded in 1912, as "a fine example of the Revolutionary Concept." (Lenin had suggested the use of a legal newspaper as a cover for a revolutionary organization.) A contemporary example, Hachten suggests, is the use of audiocassettes and photocopiers by supporters of the Ayatollah Khomeini in the effort to overthrow the Shah of Iran.

The developmental concept, Hachten concedes, is a variation of the authoritarian theory. It posits a role for mass communication in the business of nation building. Proponents of developmental journalism believe that mass media should be mobilized to assist in economic development, eradication of illiteracy, and political education. Also, the media must support authority, lest the task of nation building be retarded. The flow of news generated by foreign journalists must be subject to the nation's sovereignty for the same reason. Because information is a national resource, it must be used to further national goals. The right of expression is necessarily subordinate to these goals.

J. Herbert Altschull

In 1984, J. Herbert Altschull published *Agents of Power*, a book written in part to honor journalists who have sought "to free themselves of their ideological straitjackets and go beyond the conflictual norms that dominate their culture" (p. xi). It is not surprising, in light of this dedication, that he rejected the terminology adopted in *Four Theories of the Press* as "value-laden." In devising his own typology, he chose "modified economic identifications," corresponding to the political designations of First, Second, and Third World. Thus the First, or Western World, becomes the "market" movement; the Second, or Eastern World, becomes the "Marxist" movement; and the Third, or Southern World, becomes the "advancing" movement (see Table 1.4).*

Altschull examines the three movements from three perspectives, the purposes of journalism, articles of faith about the press, and views on press freedom. His analysis departs from conventional wisdom in several areas. For example, Altschull believes that truth is a goal of the press in all three philosophies, as is socially responsible behavior.

Altschull also examines the three movements from the perspective of their "articles of faith," or beliefs held so passionately that they are not subject to rational analysis. For an example, Altschull cites the Western (market) journalists' conviction that their press is free of interference by advertisers and others. Within the Marxist movement,

---

*It must be evident at once that the same difficulties appear here as in other attempts to create mutually exclusive categories; facts have an exasperating ability to defy a scholar's wish to place them in neat piles. What do you do with Cuba, which is both Marxist and Southern? Or with Japan, which is both market and Eastern? Or with Saudi Arabia, which deserves its own category?

TABLE 1.4. ALTSCHULL TYPOLOGY

Market (First World)	Marxist (Second World)	Advancing (Third World)
Journalists seek truth.	Journalists seek truth.	Journalists serve truth.
Journalists are socially responsible.	Journalists are socially responsible.	Journalists are socially responsible.
Journalists inform in a nonpolitical way.	Journalists educate in a political way.	Journalists educate in a political way.
Journalists serve the people impartially and support capitalism.	Journalists serve the people by demanding support for socialism.	Journalists serve the people and government by seeking change.
Journalists serve as watchdogs of government.	Journalists mold views and change behavior.	Journalists serve as instruments of peace.
The press is free from outside interference.	The press teaches workers class consciousness.	The press unifies; it does not divide.
The press serves the public's right to know.	The press serves the needs of the people.	The press works for social change.
The press seeks to learn and present the truth.	The press facilitates effective change.	The press is an instrument of social justice.
The press reports fairly and objectively.	The press reports objectively about reality.	The press is a vehicle for two-way exchanges.
A free press means that journalists are free of all outside controls.	A free press reports all opinion, not only that of the rich.	A free press means freedom of conscience for journalists.
A free press is not servile to power or manipulated by power.	A free press is required to counter oppression.	Press freedom is less important than the visibility of the nation.
A free press does not need a national press policy to remain free.	A free press requires a national press policy in order to be correct.	A national press policy is needed to safeguard freedom.

Source: Adapted from J. Herbert Altschull, *Agents of Power* (White Plains, N.Y.: Longman, 1984).

true believers subscribe passionately to the notion that their press is educational rather than propagandistic. Altschull finds especially intriguing the idea among advancing-movement journalists that the newspaper is an instrument of two-way communication, or dialogue. Market journalists believe in the public's right to know but not in the reader's right to tell the journalist what the reader wants to know. In other words, according to Altschull, market journalists claim the right to tell the reader what the reader has a right to know. Meanwhile, in the Marxist world, journalists suffer under the delusion that the news media serve the needs of the masses by publishing letters to the editor.

From the perspective of their views on freedom of the press, the three movements also differ markedly, Altschull finds. For example, to the market journalist, a free press is not "servile" to power; to the Marxist journalist, a free press is required to counter oppression; and to a journalist in the advancing world, press freedom is not all that important—less important, certainly, than the viability of a nation. On the subject of a national press policy, there are also differences among the three movements. For example, market journalists believe, according to Altschull, that no press policy is required to ensure a free press,* Marxist journalists believe that a press policy is required to guarantee that a free press takes the correct form, and journalists in the advancing movement believe that a press policy is required in order to provide legal safeguards for freedom.

Altschull's classifications serve to dispel or at least to challenge some notions fondly held among Western journalists, who cherish with all the passion of true believers the idea that objective truth is the product of their labors and that propaganda and enslavement are characteristic of journalism elsewhere.

Robert Picard

In 1985, Robert Picard proposed a significant modification of Hachten's five-concept typology. In *The Press and the Decline of Democracy*, Picard suggests that the democratic socialist approach should be identified among the subcategories of the Western concept. Hachten, you will recall, had subsumed the libertarian and the social responsibility theories in what he called the Western theory. In addition, he had postulated the developmental and revolutionary theories, in a major contribution to scholarly thought on the issue of global media philosophies. Inasmuch as the social responsibility theory is merely an offshoot of libertarianism (and in fact the two can be seen to coexist within a single media outlet in the United States today), Hachten believed it only logical that the two be conjoined under a single heading—Western. Picard would include democratic socialism along with social responsibility and libertarianism as coequal strands in the Western theory.

The democratic socialist theory of the press, like the social responsibility theory, holds that the media have an obligation to allow diverse voices to be heard. But the democratic socialist approach, which developed in Western Europe, permits the state to intervene in media economics and ownership in order to assure the continued existence of the press and the ability of citizens to use it. Picard writes that "ultimately, ownership under such a system would be public and

---

*Perhaps Altschull should have written, "Market journalists believe that to ensure a free press, it is required that there be no press policy."

not-for-profit, through foundations, nonprofit corporations, journalist-operated cooperatives, and other collective organizations" (p. 67).

This is a significantly different concept from the libertarian and even the social responsibility philosophies as outlined in *Four Theories of the Press*. It should be identified as what it is: a sixth theory of the press. Picard acknowledges the radical differences from the traditional theories when he writes: "Under democratic socialist theory, media are viewed as instruments of the people, public utilities through which the people's aspirations, ideas, praise, and criticism of the state and society may be disseminated." In such a system, "the media are operated for the citizens' use and for the protection of the citizens' social, economic, and political rights" (p. 70).

In his schema (see Figure 1.2), Picard groups democratic socialist with libertarian and social responsibility theories under Western theories. But in the same table he places the democratic socialist theory under "Balanced or Indeterminate" tendencies, along with the revolutionary and developmental theories. And he characterizes both the libertarian and social responsibility theories as "libertarian-tending."

This plan of organization introduces a tension that cannot be reconciled easily. And perhaps any attempt at reconciliation should be rejected. It would be more logical to elevate the democratic socialist theory to coequal status with the revolutionary and developmental theories. One might also drop the "Western" heading (which is merely a geographic aid to organization as well as a way of indicating the close relationship of the libertarian and social responsibility theories), thus restoring the libertarian and social responsibility designations to coequal status. Finally, one might drop the suffix *-tending* from the "Authoritarian" and "Libertarian" designations as well as any separation of those terms from "Balanced or Indeterminate." This simple alteration in the Picard typology would eliminate the "pigeonhole" classification system, creating a continuum that suggests that these theories are fluid rather than fixed, shifting along a line in a dynamic, organic way rather than remaining static in a theoretical, mutually exclusive relationship. (This simple alteration also eliminates the illogic in a typology that categorizes "Authoritarian" under "Authoritarian-tending" and "Libertarian" under "Libertarian-tending.")

But despite the organizational and logical flaws in the Picard typology, the recognition of a democratic socialist theory fills a gap in this area.

Another gap has not been dealt with adequately in scholarly research: the relationship of broadcast to print media. Most of the literature treats both as if they were indistinguishable with respect to the system of state control imposed on them. For example, scholars and

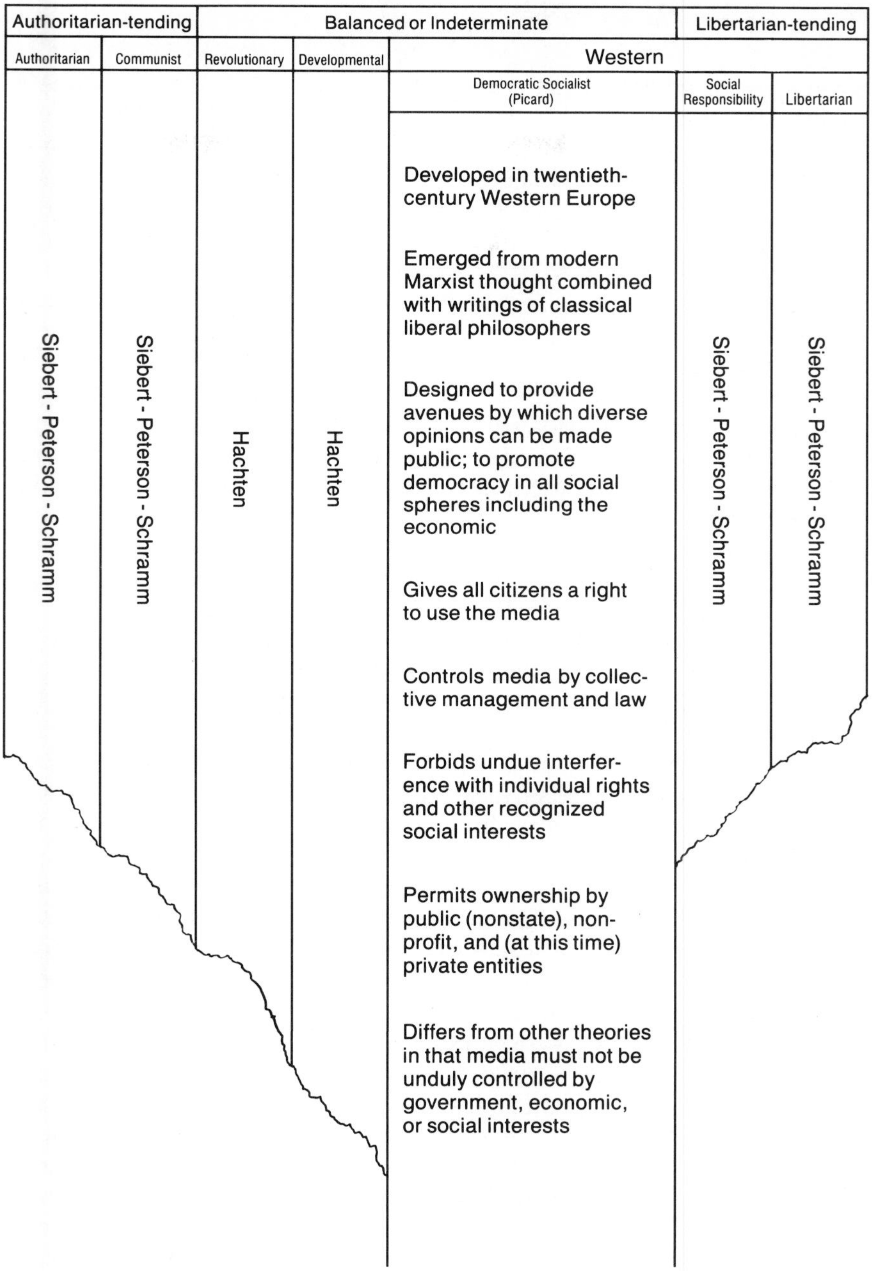

Authoritarian-tending		Balanced or Indeterminate			Libertarian-tending	
Authoritarian	Communist	Revolutionary	Developmental	Western		
				Democratic Socialist (Picard)	Social Responsibility	Libertarian
Siebert - Peterson - Schramm	Siebert - Peterson - Schramm	Hachten	Hachten	Developed in twentieth-century Western Europe Emerged from modern Marxist thought combined with writings of classical liberal philosophers Designed to provide avenues by which diverse opinions can be made public; to promote democracy in all social spheres including the economic Gives all citizens a right to use the media Controls media by collective management and law Forbids undue interference with individual rights and other recognized social interests Permits ownership by public (nonstate), non-profit, and (at this time) private entities Differs from other theories in that media must not be unduly controlled by government, economic, or social interests	Siebert - Peterson - Schramm	Siebert - Peterson - Schramm

Figure 1.2. Picard Typology (*Source:* Adapted from Robert G. Picard, *The Press and the Decline of Democracy* [Westport, Conn.: Greenwood Press, 1985].)

media practitioners both would be likely to place the United States in the libertarian category. But that would be true only of the print media; the broadcast media have been subject to extensive and relatively restrictive legislation almost since the beginning of the industry. Broadcasters in the United States must grant a right of reply to persons whose character or integrity is attacked—and do so free of charge. Under certain conditions, broadcasters must sell time to politicians at most favorable rates. "Indecent"—not necessarily obscene—programming is prohibited during certain times of the day. Certain commercial products may not be advertised. An aspiring communicator must obtain the permission of the government (a license) before he or she can begin broadcasting. And the government may withdraw that license once granted, forcing divestiture. But what government agency can enforce such rules on the print media? There is no Federal Communications Commission for newspapers.

Broadcasting: Sydney Head

None of the various typologies discussed so far deals in significant fashion with the differences between broadcast and print media, although such differences may be found in countries other than the United States. The Lowenstein concept recognized the distinction between broadcast and print media but did not apply rigorous analysis. One must look for a model in a broadcast textbook because international mass communication scholars have not devoted attention to the problem of differences between print and broadcast media.

Sydney Head, author of *World Broadcasting Systems* (1985), offers a simple and usable model of government-media relationships in international broadcasting. He observes that the United States and the United Kingdom, though closely related Western democracies, had established "quite different styles of ownership and legal oversight of their national broadcasting systems" (p. 58) and that the USSR had adopted still another pattern. The U.S. model, Head writes, left the operation and ownership of broadcast properties to free enterprise, the British model granted monopoly ownership and control of the nation's stations to a public corporation, and the USSR retained ownership and control within the government. Head characterizes the U.S. system as *permissive*, the British system as *paternalistic*, and the USSR system as *authoritarian*. A permissive system relies on market forces and consumer desires; a paternalistic system deemphasizes market forces, emphasizes consumer needs rather than desires, and prevents domination by either government or advertisers; an authoritarian system

minimizes both market forces and consumer preferences while imposing regulation in accord with official doctrine.

Using UNESCO figures published in 1982, Head calculated per-
centages of ownership in each category for 184 radio systems and 131
television systems. Of the radio systems, 49 percent were owned by
government, 21 percent by public corporations, and 21 percent by
private, commercial firms. Of the television systems, 49 percent were
owned by government, 22 percent by public corporations, and 16
percent by private, commercial firms. The remaining radio and television systems were of mixed ownership variety.

Making lists, playing with numbers, creating typologies, and clas-
sifying data are academic games that are a step away from reality. They
have informational content, and they are useful for pedagogical purposes. But the real world is that world of the media practitioner, who
must live every day within the limits imposed on him by the system in
which he works. He will find little assistance, practical or otherwise, in
these academic games. Whatever the nature of the system—free, controlled, or uncertain—the individual journalist confronts decision making firsthand. Unless theoretical constructs, such as the typologies cited
here, become the basis for informed journalistic choices, they remain
mere intellectual exercises.

CHAPTER 2

The Collection and Flow of World News

Al Hester

At the start of this final decade of the twentieth century, the profile of the people who originate, collect, and distribute the news of the world is a varied one indeed. Media users in parts of the globe have a great many more potential sources of foreign news than they had even a decade earlier. No one can keep count of the billions of words and millions of images transmitted internationally as news each year. The flood of information has reached truly vast proportions (see Figure 2.1).

But despite the great quantity of information transmitted, serious problems remain with the news presented—or not presented—to the world's media users. These problems involve who controls the news flow, the utility of such news to the world, and the unevenness of its distribution. Then, of course, there are always questions concerning how well individuals use the news resources that are available to them to make decisions to improve their lives. These are large issues. Let us begin tackling them by tracing the development of news collection and delivery.

Only a little more than a century ago, armies still fought battles after diplomats in far-off capitals had already signed the peace treaties. As far as the military commanders knew, those facing them in battle were enemies. Yet across the seas, the diplomats had designated these enemies as new friends. Even the most vital news, such as the end of war, took weeks or months to cross the Atlantic from Europe to North America.

The invention of the steamship, the railroad, and the telegraph

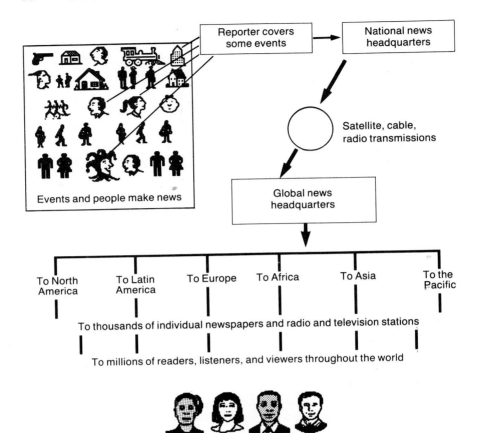

Figure 2.1. How International News Is Collected throughout the World. Reporters can cover only a fraction of the universe of world events on any given day. Editors then prepare the stories for transmission via satellite, cable, microwave relay, or radio. These are then sent to the national headquarters of the news agency, network, or syndicate, and editors there determine to which parts of the globe the stories will go. They are transmitted in various languages and sent to individual newspapers and radio and television stations. News editors there determine what stories will be put in the news columns or on the air. Finally, the media user decides what is of interest, and reads it, listens to it, or views it.

made the transmission of news miraculously faster. What had once taken months to arrive now took at first days and then, in short, hurried spurts over the wires and undersea cables, in but a few moments' time. With the invention of the telephone, the wireless telegraph or radio, television, the computer, and the communications satellite, the news comes from anywhere in the world in fractions of a second, its transmissions moving almost at the speed of light. Most of the time lapse in our knowing what occurred halfway around the world nowadays is due to the time it takes to compile the news, not the actual transmission. Nevertheless, thanks to telecommunications and computer technology, we can get news of prime importance within minutes. The main factor now is the human factor—how long it takes to cover a story and then to write it. Our machines work much faster than we do.

Perhaps the collection of international news really began with the efforts of rulers to be informed by high-quality intelligence sources about what other nobles were up to. And the merchants of the world very early learned that information is power. For instance, if they had it before other merchants, they might corner the market in a scarce commodity and make tremendous profits.

Confidential networks of intelligence gatherers came into being many centuries ago. Ancient peoples relayed priority information via smoke signals or by flashing mirrors or used runners to carry the tidings. Those who could afford to paid for private newsletters written by business correspondents in other countries to bring them news of developments in government, trade, or shipping. The Fugger newsletters of sixteenth-century Europe were examples of such international gathering and transmitting of information.

INTERNATIONAL NEWS AS A COMMODITY

Almost from the inception of the use of movable type in Europe, printers realized that people would pay for news. Less than a century after Johannes Gutenberg put his first press to work, news-sheets were being published. Frequently, foreign news was among their subjects. For example, the first news-sheet in the Americas of which we have a record was printed in Mexico City in 1542 and was a recounting of a frightful earthquake and storm that destroyed the city of Guatemala in September 1541. Other news flyers of the fifteenth and sixteenth centuries told of war, crime, the lives of royalty, and miracles. Very early, people showed a strong interest in things that were threatening or odd or appealed to basic drives and needs.

Travelers, merchants, diplomats, and sea captains were among the first reporters. The early newspapers of Europe and the Americas are full of news brought via oceangoing vessels carrying letters and word-of-mouth accounts of important events. By the eighteenth century, an early cooperative enterprise was started in colonial North America to give the latest shipping news, according to Victor Rosewater in his *History of Cooperative News-Gathering in the United States* (1930). In 1811, Samuel Gilbert at his Exchange Coffee House began compiling what he called "news books" that contained the latest shipping and other information for his customers. His young assistant, Samuel Topliff, Jr., took over the job. But he was not content to wait for the ship captains to bring the news to him. He paddled out in a small skiff to meet incoming vessels and then returned to post the news in the news books. One book was for general news, both foreign and domestic, and the other was for commercial news. It wasn't long before newspaper publishers began to reprint the news from the coffeehouse news books of Topliff and others. People using the books were charged an annual fee.

At almost the same time, Charles Havas, a young Frenchman of Hungarian extraction, decided to sell news as a commodity. His service began in 1825 in Europe, where he had correspondents in many of its capitals. Merchants and governments were among his first subscribers. Havas realized that newspapers could make good use of his news service, but they didn't begin to use his services until he speeded up his news transmissions, sometimes using semaphore signals and carrier pigeons. In 1848, Bernard Wolff, a Havas employee, began his own news agency, the Wolff News Agency, which served German and Northern European newspapers. Another Havas assistant, Paul Julius Reuter, in 1851 opened a news office in England after unsuccessfully trying to start a news agency in continental Europe. Reuter had some success getting speculators and merchants to use his financial information, but it was not until 1858 that newspapers began subscribing. The fledgling news agencies could be considered wholesalers of news to other organizations, which made a further profit from it.

Reuter, who seems to have a more developed public relations flair than his competitors, furnished free news telegrams over the recently invented electric telegraph to Queen Victoria and high officials of the British government. A close relationship grew between the Reuters agency and the British government. Reuter was even given access to telegrams the Foreign Office received from India, according to Graham Storey in his *Reuters: The Story of a Century of News-Gathering* (1951). Later on, Reuter made arrangements with English authorities to use the newly laid submarine cables linking the British Empire. His news dispatches were allowed on the cables at the reduced press rate of a penny per word between points in the British Empire.

COOPERATIVE VENTURES IN NEWS GATHERING

The scrapping and fighting "penny press" in the United States was engaged before the midpoint of the nineteenth century in a fierce competition to be first with international news. In 1846, when the

United States went to war with Mexico, these efforts reached a high pitch. News was relayed by express, steamship, and telegraph (which extended south only to Richmond, Va.). News-gathering and transmission costs were staggering, and publishers were soon combining resources to share both the news and the cost of gathering and transmitting it.

An "associated press" was formed by several New York newspapers to share the costs of bringing European news from Boston to New York. This cooperative was soon named the New York Associated Press, and it extended its services to other U.S. newspapers to lessen telegraph costs. These papers were organized into regional groups, such as the Western Associated Press.

By 1859, the Reuter, Wolff, and Havas agencies had worked out a news exchange agreement with the New York Associated Press. In 1870, the same agencies signed an agreement that set up "news preserves" for each agency. This was the beginning of the "news cartel," which was to last well into the twentieth century. Each news agency had exclusive areas for gathering and distributing the news. Havas got France, Switzerland, Italy, Spain, Portugal, Egypt (jointly with Reuters), and Central and South America. Reuters held sway in the British Empire, Egypt (with Havas), Turkey, and the Far East. Wolff's sphere of interest was Germany, Austria, the Netherlands, Scandinavia, Russia, and the Balkans. The New York AP had control of the United States.

Some newer members of the New York AP became dissatisfied, and the Western AP withdrew in 1885. It was reconstituted as the Associated Press of Illinois in 1892. Eventually the old New York AP went out of business and the AP of Illinois signed an exclusive contract with the Reuters, Havas, and Wolff agencies. In 1900, the AP of Illinois was reorganized in New York and formed the basis of the present news-gathering cooperative known as the Associated Press.

An early rival to the AP was set up by Edward Wyllis Scripps, who was building his own newspaper group. He organized a news service in 1897 to serve his own papers, disliking the AP's policy of serving only one paper in a given area. In 1907, he formed a new agency, the United Press Associations, which eventually became AP's main U.S. rival. Scripp's UP was to be a profit-making venture, not a nonprofit cooperative. It wasn't a party to the news cartel agreements and soon set up its own foreign bureaus.

Many AP officials and members were not happy with the international news contracts with the European agencies either. In the early years of the twentieth century, the AP began to set up its own overseas operations, although the cartel did not die until later. In 1909, another world news agency came into being in the United States—the International News Service, mainly serving the Hearst newspapers. It was not a party to the cartel contracts and had some overseas operations. In 1958, it was absorbed by the United Press, forming the present global news agency, United Press International (UPI), which is set up as a profit-making venture.

Another modern news agency was formed in 1918 by the government of the Soviet Union. This agency soon became the Telegraph Agency of the U.S.S.R. (TASS), which operates globally but is an integral part of the government of the Soviet Union.

THE CARTEL GOES OUT OF BUSINESS

By the 1930s, the news cartel was out of business, although some agencies are still strong in their original spheres of influence. The Wolff Agency ceased to exist in 1933. Havas, the French agency, was discredited in World War II and was transformed into the present Agence France-Presse (AFP), a global news agency that has autonomous status but receives large subsidies from the French government and parliamentary protection. The International News Service became a part of UPI in 1958. The AP is today a nonprofit cooperative. UPI, although in a very precarious financial situation, is set up to make a profit. Reuters is a small part of Reuters Holdings PLC, a huge information-furnishing, profit-making organization. The AFP is a nonprofit agency, and TASS continues as an arm of the Soviet government. The AP, Reuters, AFP, and UPI are generally considered to be the major global news agencies, with TASS sometimes given the same status because of its large international operations. Inter Press Service (IPS), a news agency founded in 1964 to emphasize gathering and disseminating news for and about the Third World, has a global news-gathering capability, although it is smaller than the other agencies mentioned. IPS is a nonprofit cooperative. More than 100 national and regional news agencies have grown up to serve the needs of the media in the twentieth century, and some operate with highly professional standards. A few of considerable importance internationally include Xinhua News Agency, operated by the government of the People's Republic of China; TANJUG, the Yugoslav news agency; Deutsche Press Agentur (DPA), the West German service; Kyodo, a Japanese agency; the Pan-African News Agency (PANA); and the Caribbean News Agency (CANA). Also of note is the Pool of News Agencies of Non-Aligned Countries, set up to circulate news of the nonaligned countries mainly in the less-developed portions of the globe. This pool depends upon several other agencies, such as IPS and TANJUG, to transmit new items from member agencies.

WHY NEWS AGENCIES ARE IMPORTANT

It has been estimated that only about one-tenth of all the information transmitted internationally is "news." The rest includes anything from computerized financial information, scientific data, personal letters, and phone calls, to television and radio entertainment. But the focus of this chapter is upon that very significant percentage of international communication that is news. A variety of organizations gathers and transmits world news, and the global news agencies are still the prime purveyors of news internationally. But what was once their near monopoly is being eroded considerably by other organizations, which include news syndicates, supplemental news agencies, foreign correspondents for television networks and print media, internationally published magazines, and specialized media networked to provide specific information to attentive publics.

The global news agencies still maintain the most complete transmission networks and capacity for widespread, rapid coverage of the international news operations. It is impossible to estimate the immense amounts of information sent by the global news agencies daily. Until a few decades ago, a typical news agency report for the day might run only a few thousand words and several score stories. The number of stories sent was limited by the speed of the teletype machines used. But we have seen transmission speeds rise from less than 100 words per minute to 9,000 words per minute or higher in international communication. Digitization of communication by computer has made this vast increase in speed possible. Teamed with the communications satellite, the computer has also increased the capacity of the channels in international news flow. And a wider variety of transmission channels is available internationally as well. Nations are now linked by signals relayed by communications satellites, transoceanic cables, fiber-optic cables, microwave relays, and high-frequency radio.

A few thousand journalists, photographers, and technicians are responsible for gathering and conveying news involving the lives of the more than 5 billion persons who live on the earth. Although the Reuters organization has grown to embrace a variety of information-gathering and transmitting activities and receives revenues of more than $1.5 billion annually, even its news-gathering resources are stretched thinly. Reuters had nearly 1,200 reporters and editors in 115 news bureaus worldwide to furnish news to more than 15,000 subscribers. Only a small percentage of this information giant's business is devoted to its traditional business of gathering general news. Most of its energy goes into furnishing and conveying business and financial information.

The Associated Press, with a budget of $300 million in 1989, had

3,500 employees and more than 10,000 foreign newspaper, radio, and television subscribers. There were 2,900 U.S. users of the AP. The AP maintains 84 foreign bureaus in 70 countries and serves news outlets in 110 countries. To gather its foreign news outside the United States, the agency had more than 480 news and photo staff members. These staffers were responsible for covering and transmitting news over English, German, French, Swedish, Dutch, and Spanish services. The news agency estimates that its news is read, viewed, or heard by more than a billion persons each day.

The resources of the other global agencies are less than those of Reuters and the AP. The French agency, AFP, in the 1980s listed 432 French clients and 1,297 clients abroad. Only about 45 percent of AFP's clients were newspapers, broadcasting stations, or national news agencies. French ministries, embassies, official missions, and other French governmental agencies made up much of the rest of the total. The agency distributed news to approximately 150 countries and maintained services in French, Arabic, English, German, Spanish, and Portuguese in the 1980s. AFP has an especially strong presence in areas that have close cultural and economic ties with France, such as portions of Africa and Asia.

United Press International went bankrupt in 1986 and has since been in a desperate struggle for survival after changing hands several times. The agency is trying to rebuild its operations and anticipates that it will again make a profit within the next few years. In 1990, nearly all of UPI's stock was controlled by Infotechnology, Inc., which holds about 99 percent of New UPI Inc., an investors' group set up to try to save the news agency. Infotechnology has interests in information and scientific ventures.

In 1989, UPI employed approximately 1,200 persons, about 800 of them engaged in international news gathering full-time. UPI has said it provides news and information to more than 3,000 media, business, and government clients from its 180 bureaus in 90 nations.

The Soviet agency, TASS, reported in 1989 that it had about 4,000 subscribers in the Soviet Union and more than 1,000 subscribers in 115 other nations, including 11 in the United States. TASS says it transmits more than 4 million words daily and sends more than 6.5 million photos yearly. It distributes its world service in Russian, English, Spanish, French, German, Arabic, Italian, and Portuguese. According to Igor Y. Makurin, TASS bureau chief in New York, his agency has more than 100 overseas bureaus.

TASS has the reputation as a "political" agency in that it is a branch of the Soviet government, and part of its job has been to create a favorable impression of the Soviet Union. In the past, TASS has been involved in several espionage cases in which certain staff members were accused of spying. In some areas of the world, TASS also charges very little for its service or gives it away. But with recent developments favoring more openness in the Soviet Union, TASS dispatches have become more closely akin to those of other global news agencies. TASS officials said in 1989, as reported by *Editor & Publisher*, that they should not be considered the official voice of the Soviet Union and that they had been given orders to become financially self-sufficient as a news agency.

OTHER PURVEYORS OF WORLD NEWS

Other important wholesalers of news to individual media include the press syndicates. These are commercial organizations devoted to marketing news and entertainment features, supplementing the basic "hard" news coverage for which global news agencies are best known. The syndicates sell the news products of various media chains or individual mass media, packaging it and sending it electronically or by mail to thousands of users throughout the world. The syndicates and other operations, sometimes known as supplemental news agencies, have their own foreign correspondents and carry the work of columnists and cartoonists.

Some of the best-known syndicates are headquartered in the United States. These include the New York Times Syndicate Sales Corp. It packages news not only from the United States but also from many of the world's elite newspapers and magazines. For instance, the NYT Syndicate transmits 25,000 words weekly from selected Spanish publications, 30,000 words from Italian media, 10,000 words from a Japanese newspaper, 50,000 words weekly from the *International Herald Tribune*, which publishes a number of editions throughout the world, 40,000 words weekly from a French paper, and stories from leading magazines in the United States and Europe. Of course, it can also call upon the resources of the *New York Times*, with its widespread network of foreign correspondents.

Another large U.S.-based syndicate is the Los Angeles Times Syndicate. Its wide range of news and other services is used in more than 50 nations.

INTERNATIONAL NEWSPAPERS

Several newspapers may be termed international, although they reach rather limited readerships. They are expensive to produce and to distribute, but frequently leaders and opinion makers in many countries read them. Perhaps the most truly international newspaper is the *International Herald Tribune*, headquartered in Paris. This highly respected paper has a small staff of its own but uses mainly stories from the *New York Times, Los Angeles Times,* and *Washington Post.* When the paper is ready to go to press, electronic images of its pages are sent by satellite and printed in Paris, London, Zurich, Hong Kong, Singapore, The Hague, Marseilles, Miami, Rome, and Tokyo. The *Wall Street Journal* also publishes international editions, as does *USA Today.*

No discussion of the international flow of news would be complete without mention of the international newsmagazines, which are steadily gaining readership throughout the world. A handful of these magazines provides more in-depth coverage of foreign news than many newspapers and news agencies can give. *Time* magazine publishes editions for the Atlantic region, Asia, Canada, Europe, Africa, the Middle East, and Latin America. Total circulation of the magazine in its foreign editions was more than 1 million in 1989, in addition to its 4.7 million U.S. subscribers. *Newsweek* publishes editions for the Atlantic and European Common Market areas, several other European editions, and editions for Latin America, the Pacific, Southeast Asia, and Japan. Nearly a million subscribers read these editions. *Newsweek*'s U.S. circulation was 3.1 million in 1989. *U.S. News & World Report* also places considerable emphasis on foreign news and has correspondents in London, Paris, the Middle East, Moscow, Tokyo, Beijing, and Miami for Latin America. Another highly respected international newsmagazine is the *Economist,* published in the United Kingdom and in several foreign editions.

A recent phenomenon is the growth of special-interest newsletters. In these international newsletters, just as in the newsletters written centuries ago, expert reporters dig out information or news of benefit to specific interests, especially businesses, bankers, and investors. An October 1989 issue of the *World Paper* carried advertisements for a dozen special-interest newsletters promising in-depth, specialized information on regional politics, economies, government policies, currency transactions, and marketing. A subscription to a typical newsletter runs several hundred dollars per customer per year. The *World Paper* itself was created recently to fill a need for what it terms "international news and views." It is published in Boston and is translated from English into Spanish, Chinese, and Russian and is used in national newspapers in countries where those languages are used. It appears biweekly or monthly, depending on the language edition.

VIDEO AND AUDIO NEWS FLOW

World news flow is by no means limited to the printed word. The visual image and the spoken word play an increasingly important role in international communication. Millions of the world's population depend mainly on visual images and spoken words to tell them about the world outside their own experience. Some resort mainly to television and radio through choice and list TV as their main source of news. This is especially true in many countries where newspaper circulation has not kept up with the growth of the population. In other nations with high illiteracy rates, radio and TV become the primary sources of media information through necessity.

Almost all the major news agencies operate news photo services that can transmit black-and-white or color photographs electronically for later use in the print and broadcast media. Many agencies also have broadcast news divisions that send stories, pictures, and audio transmissions specifically tailored to radio and TV needs.

Television is becoming an internationalized medium. Because of the communications satellite, thousands of TV stations throughout the world can carry the same live news programming simultaneously or on a delayed basis. Though national governments have tight control of electronic broadcasting systems in much of the Third World, the trend is away from depending entirely on a governmental broadcasting system. Private-enterprise systems are booming in Europe, where television airtime doubled in six years in the 1980s. More than 100 new TV stations are projected in Europe by 1995.

The vast amounts of programming needed are frequently furnished via satellite internationally. The United States' commercial TV program sources are the largest operators in the business of exporting TV programming. Recently, U.S. interests have made a direct entrance into foreign markets, putting their own news programs into many foreign countries. The U.S.-based Cable News Network (CNN) of entrepreneur Ted Turner is now viewed in 85 countries by some 200 million viewers. CNN officials say that by the end of the 1990s, half of their total advertising revenues will come from international operations.

Other large North American television programming organizations include the three U.S. commercial networks, ABC, CBS, and NBC. These networks, along with CNN, operate news bureaus throughout the world, although they cannot compete with the global news agencies in the magnitude of their news operations abroad. Typical of these operations is ABC, which has 12 U.S. domestic bureaus and 17 foreign bureaus (located in Beijing, Beirut, Bonn, Cairo, Frankfurt, Hong Kong, Johannesburg, London, Madrid, Manila, Moscow, Paris, Rome, Tel Aviv, Tokyo, and Warsaw, plus the Central American bureau in Miami).

CNN is taking the lead to develop 24-hour news programming around the world. The service already reaches 4 million households in Europe, and 250,000 in Latin America, and 16,000 in Asia. In addition, its news programs may be seen in 100,000 hotel rooms in Europe, 40,000 in Latin America, and 50,000 in Asia. It also produces "World Report," unedited English-language newscasts sent to CNN at its Atlanta, Ga., headquarters from 92 different contributing nations.

Another major source of visual images in international news flow is VisNews, a commercial venture begun in 1964. VisNews has more than 200 subscribers in 98 countries. It furnishes pictures and news video footage to television networks and stations throughout the world. They depend on VisNews for video coverage when they do not have their own cameras on the scene. VisNews is owned by Reuters, the U.S. network NBC, and the British Broadcasting Corp. (BBC). VisNews can also relay video shot by local television stations covering foreign stories back to the local stations.

The internationalizing of the TV business is not just an American phenomenon. Europe began direct broadcasting to home satellite dishes in 1989, with Luxembourg-based ASTRA satellite service beaming programs including MTV Europe and Rupert Murdoch's SkyTV and British and Scandinavian channels. France, along with West Germany, is also involved in direct satellite broadcasting.

The communications satellite business is in an almost frantic boom. In the past, satellite companies built the "birds" on speculation, hoping that users would come forward. Now users have to reserve transponders (channels) in advance before the satellites are ever launched. In 1989, there were 33 commercial satellites in orbit. In addition to these were about 15 satellites of the International Satellite Consortium (Intelsat), which furnishes services to 170 countries. Intelsat is a nonprofit cooperative with 114 members. It has available almost 100,000 half-circuits for use by television, telephone, telex, facsimile, digital data transmission, photo transmission, electronic mail and teleconferencing. Intelsat also handles entire national satellite communications systems for a number of nations.

Another rapidly developing form of international news and information flow is that of computerized and digitized graphics for use in print and electronic media over the globe. Drawings, graphs, cartoons, and other pictorial devices may be sent in a few seconds' time to anyone with satellite communication capabilities. A few of the commercial companies offering these visuals are AP Graphics Net, Knight-Ridder, MacNet, the Tribune News Graphic Network, the Copley News Service, and the New York Times News Service.

Although not so popular in the United States, listening to high-frequency (shortwave) radio broadcasts from powerful transmitters over the globe is a major way of getting news in many countries. A special shortwave receiver is necessary to receive the radio frequencies transmitted, but shortwave signals have the ability, under the right conditions, to travel thousands of miles. This form of communication depends on the reflective qualities of the electrically charged ionosphere, many miles above the earth's surface. The radio signals are aimed at the ionosphere and "bounce off" it back to earth, making possible long-distance radio communication. More than 200 nations use shortwave radio because it is a relatively cheap means of communication, carries great distances, and can be heard in mountainous terrain where regular radio or TV reception is difficult.

The popularity of international shortwave newscasts is especially high where repressive governments limit access through domestic dia. A few countries still try to jam external broadcast signals so that they cannot be heard, but almost always some broadcasts get through. Shortwave also offers governments a persuasive communication medium, since there are no "gatekeepers" to stop or change the message going to the receiver. Most major nations operate governmental external shortwave broadcasting services, as do numerous religious groups and some commercial broadcasters. The best-known shortwave broadcaster is the BBC, known for its highly credible international content. Other major international broadcasters operating in many languages include the Voice of America, Radio Moscow, Radio Beijing, Radio Cairo, Radio Nederland, Radio France International, and Radio Tirana (Albania).

The extent of shortwave radio listening can be estimated by surveys and by letters from listeners. In some countries, 20 percent of the population tunes in to the BBC daily. The Voice of America claims that more than 110 million people listen to its broadcasts around the world. Some shortwave stations transmit their signals to satellites, which then send the signal to relay stations closer to the listeners to ensure better audio reception.

Another international communication development is the recent growth of talk shows on radio and television stations throughout the world. Phone-in programs make it possible for Americans to speak with Russians, for example, through stations in both countries. As long-distance telephone rates decrease, such interactive communication becomes more feasible. Distance becomes less of a determining factor in telecommunications rates, thanks to the ease of communicating with satellites and large-capacity fiber-optic cables. The American Telephone & Telegraph Co. (AT&T), with European communications organizations, laid the first transatlantic fiber-optic cable, capable of carrying 40,000 different circuits.

FOREIGN CORRESPONDENTS

Finally, no discussion of international news flow and collection would be complete without a mention of foreign correspondents who work for one specific media organization. If a newspaper, for example, has its own stable of foreign correspondents, it can obtain foreign news tailored to its own interests. Prestige attaches to having your own staff cover events throughout the world, with the bylines of your own reporters on them. But only a handful of print and broadcast media can afford to have their own correspondents.

By the end of the 1980s, placing a foreign correspondent in the field could easily cost $250,000 annually. Approximately 200 full-time correspondents from U.S. newspapers were working abroad in 1989. Only about 25 newspapers maintained their own foreign bureaus. The *New York Times* had the most foreign bureaus—30. Some of the other U.S. papers with a major foreign presence include the *Los Angeles Times*, the *Miami Herald*, the *Chicago Tribune*, and the *Washington Post*. As mentioned earlier, the U.S. television networks operate with a few more than a dozen foreign bureaus each. Many newspapers and broadcasters supplement their own foreign full-time staffs by paying part-time "stringers" to cover major news when it breaks abroad. In addition, free-lance correspondents make significant additions to foreign coverage, staffing the news for several papers simultaneously.

H. D. S. Greenway, the national and foreign editor of the *Boston Globe*, explains another method of foreign news coverage which can save money on foreign correspondents.

> Many regional newspapers long to put their own imprint on foreign news but gag at forking over the annual $150,000 or so [considerably higher now] to set up a foreign correspondent overseas. Often, we've found, the answer is to have one or two reporters designated as "airport" correspondents who, while based at home, fly off on regular assignments,

he wrote in the October 1983 issue of the *ASNE Bulletin*, published by the American Society of Newspaper Editors.

Using such roving correspondents cuts costs on office expense, moving, housing, supplements for support of dependents, and so on, but it also has some disadvantages, he said.

> It's impossible for an airport correspondent to use time as effectively as a correspondent actually living in a foreign country; there, any casual dinner conversation, tip or small news item in the local press can lead to a story idea.
>
> Then, too, there's the danger of "parachute journalism" whereby a jack-of-all-trades-and-master-of-none drops in for the big story.

Expenses that drive the foreign news budget up include correspondents' salaries, life insurance, automobile insurance, telephone, telex and satellite costs, airfares, and translation and clerical costs.

As the costs of maintaining foreign bureaus have climbed, the number of foreign correspondents has decreased. One argument is that today the media are not nearly so dependent on just the global news agencies for foreign news. They can subscribe to various syndicated and supplemented foreign news services or purchase stories from freelancers to add dimension to foreign coverage.

Quite a few U.S. editors do not give very high priority to foreign news, believing that most readers are not consistently interested in it. This editorial judgment results in only about one-fifth to one-third of the news space in print media and in television being devoted to foreign coverage in the United States. This ratio has been borne out over many years and in many content analyses of news. Also, the print or broadcast news editor has many times more foreign news stories offered to him or her than can possibly be used. Surveys of readers and viewers, however, have indicated recently that many persons claim a higher interest in foreign news than the editors believe their publics have.

In much of the rest of the world, foreign news is given more thorough coverage, frequently at the expense of local news. Many countries are much more affected by activities of their international neighbors than the United States, which is self-sufficient in many ways. But even the United States finds its citizens strongly affected by international economic, military, environmental, and criminal activities, such as distribution of narcotics.

PROBLEMS IN THE FLOW OF INTERNATIONAL NEWS

The collection and flow of news internationally cannot be considered isolated from the developments in economics and politics. The mass media are just as much creatures of their societies as political, health, and education systems. In the past few decades, the worldwide system of collection and distribution of news and information has been widely criticized, as has the process of agenda setting to determine the kinds of news and information to be made widely available.

The criticisms of the flow of foreign news and information are in many ways similar to discussions of the faults of news gathering within a country. The debate is unceasing about the role of the mass media and how the media can best perform their information and entertainment functions. For instance, minority groups in our society question the near-invisibility of their lives as reflected in the majority-run mass media. Many black citizens, for example, note that the focus on them tends to be negative and only as black actions might adversely affect the interests of the racial majority. Since early in the history of the media, critics have questioned the widespread ignoring of cultural, educational, religious, and economic news to make way for sensational coverage of violence, crime, military ventures, and faddish personality-cult stories.

In the 1960s and 1970s, however, criticism increased as the less developed countries of the world realized that they were suffering from many faults in news coverage or in news furnished to them, or about them. (These issues will be examined in greater detail in Chapter 4.) This increase paralleled the realization by the less developed countries that they had often been shortchanged with respect to control of the natural and economic resources. Many were newly independent and could with much justice place the blame for many problems on their former colonial masters, mainly Western European nations. The United States, too, got a great share of the criticism for its vast economic power. Although the United States has had realtively few colonies, it has during its two centuries of existence strongly affected the history of other nations through its wealth and its industrial prowess.

Colonial and economic domination, however, are by no means only a Western European or U.S. characteristic. Romans, Persians, Arabs, Turks, Germans, Chinese, Russians, Japanese, and native Africans—to name only a few—have all at one time or another attempted to control foreign peoples through colonialist policies. But in the twentieth century, the economically less developed countries have rebelled against Western colonial domination, especially where the colonies were run mostly for the benefit of the Western countries.

This rejection of the yoke of colonial domination extended to communication systems in the newly independent nations of the globe, especially in Africa and Asia. Through the nonaligned-nation movement and various United Nations organizations, the less developed countries began to express criticisms of the exercise of economic and communication power. In our world, money and industrialized development spell power. Those who control the economy and the dissemination of information are frequently the shakers and movers among nations.

During the past 500 years or so, the Western nations have had the lion's share of economic and information power. The seats of modern international communication power and control are along an east-west axis linking Western Europe and the United States and now extending to Japan. The headquarters for operation of the global news agencies, the syndicates, the picture agencies, and the world satellite systems are all in capitals of the West. Communication for the past several hundred years has certainly moved more easily along the east-west axis than in a north-south direction. Also, it was more efficient and convenient for the West to be linked to its colonies by strongly developed networks of communication. Major transportation routes, telegraph, and telephone service have, for example, efficiently linked England with its colonies or former colonies in Africa. Such efficient communication is necessary for the exercise of power. Even today, it is still often easier to communicate from West Africa to East Africa via London or Paris than directly.

Because of recent history and the power structure, the organizations and individuals who control the flow and content of much of the news of the world are centralized in a handful of Western cities—New York, London, Paris, and Moscow. Tokyo is also growing into a center of communication power as Japan gains economic strength. (See Figure 2.2.)

The so-called gatekeepers—those who determine the flow of news and information and what it contains—are collected in a relatively few major communication centers. Although it is certainly technically possible to communicate between almost any two points on the face of

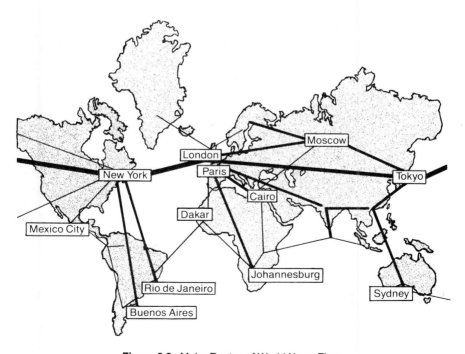

Figure 2.2. Major Routes of World News Flow

the globe, most of the communication traffic is controlled by the Western news agencies or multinational information conglomerates.

It is a fact of life that usually the person who pays calls the tune. The news agencies, for example, have to concentrate their resources on the types of coverage they perceive the majority of their customers want. If most of the customers who pay for the operation live in the United States and Western Europe, it is difficult not to pay the most attention to the needs of these media users. We also can theorize, using common sense, that most Westerners have more common interests with others of the same cultural backgrounds and ancestries. It seems likely that much of the news flow of the world links those with common cultures and political and economic interests. Perhaps we can say that citizens of the less developed countries are like minority members in the United States—they generally do not have the economic or communications power that the majority has.

But one striking violation of such a comparison is that the citizens of the less developed nations make up nearly four-fifths of the world's population—and their majority is growing (see Figure 2.3). While population growth is almost stagnant in Western Europe and slow in the

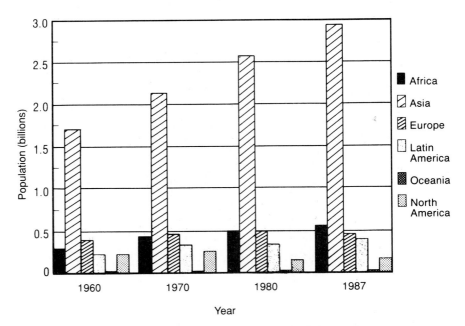

Figure 2.3. Population of the World's Regions, 1960–1987 (*Source:* U.S. Census Bureau.)

United States, it is very rapid in the rest of the world. Thus we have a majority of the population of the globe often being treated as a minority. The West is in fact the minority. Western journalists do not necessarily set out to give the less developed nations short shrift. Sometimes Western news and information may serve the needs of the world well. But it is human nature to desire to be in control of one's own destiny, whether it be in politics, in economics, or in the communication process.

The Western European and U.S. communications powers have prepared a "feast of news and information" and set it before themselves and the rest of the world. But some critics in the less developed countries say that they had no hand in selecting the menu for this banquet. Is it to their taste and to their needs? And often it is the only feast available. These critics note, too, that the banquet of news and information doesn't come free. Because they don't have enough money, they are turned away from the banquet hall.

Such criticism resulted in a call for a New World Information and Communication Order, just as international organizations have called for a New World Economic Order. Such efforts, mainly on the part of less developed and socialist nations, have focused on the serious imbalance in the distribution of news and information resources and the lack of content ideally suited to the needs of the less developed nations. The particulars of this controversy are discussed in Chapter 4.

The people controlling much of the communications power in the 1980s became somewhat more sensitive to the needs of the less developed nations, not just through altruism but through a realization that the destinies of the West are linked with Asia, Africa, and Latin America. We in the West will find it in our own self-interest to have better communication with the other peoples of the globe. Communication scholars have shown that there has been an improvement in the quantity of news about the less developed countries. But the question still remains whether the quality and content of international news best fulfills the needs of the world.

The less developed countries have banded together to sponsor a number of communications ventures, including their own communications satellite systems, the news pool for nonaligned nations, and several regional news agencies. Some Western communications organizations are working to consider the needs of Third World countries, especially in Europe. Examples of new ventures by developing countries into international communication include the launching of Arabsat to form a communications network among many Islamic nations, the Pan-African News Agency (PANA) to promote news for and about Africa, and the establishment of the Caribbean News Agency (CANA).

Although these efforts have some success, they are beset by political and philosophical problems and, above all, by a lack of financial resources.

It is extremely difficult for the "have-not" nations of the world to match the communication efforts of the "have" nations. Although the technology exists to move great quantities of news and information efficiently and rapidly, such technology is often very expensive. A commercial communications operation spends money to make money. It may not be blind to its social responsibilities, but if such a company does not make a profit, it will cease to exist. Even a nonprofit news cooperative, such as the Associated Press, cannot finance operations that do not mainly benefit the largest number of members. Subscribers must pay for services, and the more they can pay, the more communication services they can get.

Thus while newspapers and radio and television stations in Europe, the United States, and a relatively small number of other countries can finance major international news budgets, the national news agency of a small, poor country, for instance, is very limited in what it can do. Likewise the owner of a small radio station in Latin America cannot call on many international news services to help bring more foreign news to listeners.

Finally, even if the operators of the mass media throughout the world could obtain all the international news they desire, many of the more than 5 billion people in the world couldn't have access to it. To subscribe to a newspaper for a year might take the entire monthly salary of a clerk in Bangladesh. Buying a TV set is out of the question for much of the world's population. In many nations, people consider themselves lucky if they can afford a cheap transistor radio. The mere cost of buying and stringing copper telephone wire to furnish up-to-date telephone networks for India is so huge that telephone service of that nature is not likely. Hence there are immense problems in making news and information available to a majority of the persons in the world, even if the content of the communication would be of use to them.

Another problem of international news flow is the existence of a great many governments that do not believe in free access to information by news gatherers or citizens. It is a sad fact of life that many millions of persons live under authoritarian regimes in which a handful of selfish leaders set the rules of the game. It is not in the interest of dictators or tyrants to have news and information circulated if it does not serve their own ends. Even if we improve the international communication system so that it is speedy, efficient, and affordable by all, with content germane to the world's needs, efforts at better international communication will not be consistently successful without a free press and democratic governments.

THE OUTLOOK

As the twenty-first century nears, the outlook for improved international news flow and communication is mixed. The negative influences include the vast imbalance of economic resources around the globe, lack of stability in many new and developing countries, and in many nations, fantastically growing populations that outrace their resources (see Figure 2.4). Added to these minus factors can be the thrusting of high-cost technologies upon poorer countries whose needs may not always be met by high-tech solutions. For example, equipping a newsroom with computers and video display terminals may not be such a good idea if it puts clerk-typists out of work. If reporters type their own stories, what will the clerks do? In many nations today, labor-intensive newsroom practices still exist. Technology may create more jobs than it takes away in growing economies, but will this be true in countries that have a 40 percent unemployment rate?

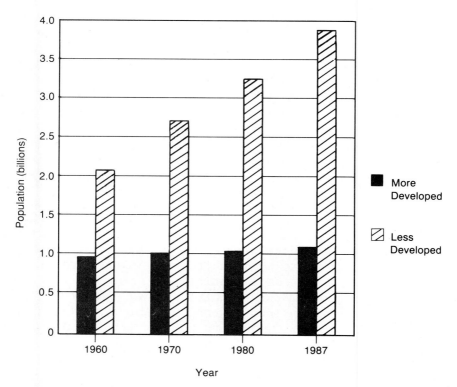

Figure 2.4. World Population Now More than 5 Billion (*Source:* U.S. Census Bureau.)

Paradoxically, while many critics of the news are asking for more news, some question whether more is necessarily better. They fear an oversupply of news and information not geared to individual cultures. Such bombardments of news and other information may serve to confuse and frustrate large segments of the world population and erode national cultures, they say.

But the positive developments in international communication should give us considerable hope for an international news flow that meets the needs of all. Developments toward more openness in what were considered hard-line authoritarian societies have already had some effect on the flow of international communication. The Soviet Union and Eastern Europe come first to mind. The Soviet legislature has implemented new press laws doing away with prior restraint, making it possible for anyone to start a publication, and protecting anonymous sources. Such developments represent a vigorous breath of hope for more press freedom.

Reporters in many countries are being given greater access. The movement is away from limited sources of governmental information through official news agencies and broadcasting systems and toward mixed systems that encourage a variety of viewpoints. The effects of some new technologies have included making it impossible for dictatorial regimes to seal off their borders to news and new ideas. Widespread availability of radio, television, video- and audiocassettes, and networked computer communication all spell trouble for despots who would throttle the flow of news and information.

We can see very graphically the great impact of the mass media in helping citizens of Eastern European nations in their rejection of repressive governments. Romanian citizens, for example, depended upon national television to keep up with the lastest events in their revolution after patriots took over the broadcasting facilities.

Privately owned and operated newspapers and magazines are springing up throughout Eastern Europe, and already a great variety of voices and opinions is being heard through a freer press. Those working in journalism feel an excitement as doors are opening wide for the dissemination of more accurate information.

Coupled to these developments is the growing feeling that the world is too small to allow selfish interests to destroy it, whether these interests work against the environment, peace, or the flow of news and information. We realize more and more fully, as John Donne did, that "no man is an island, entire of itself; every man is a piece of the Continent, a part of the main."

CHAPTER 3

The World's Media Systems: An Overview

Lowndes F. Stephens

Imagine! American and Soviet journalists engage in a two-hour seminar on press and society, during a West Coast convention of the American Society of Newspaper Editors, as part of the Center for Communication's "USA/USSR SPACEBRIDGE" project. The program originates from the Masonic Auditorium in San Francisco and a large broadcast studio in Moscow; studios in Boston and Tblisi, the capital of the Soviet republic of Georgia, are also connected by fully interactive live satellite feeds.

In San Francisco, the images and sound from a mobile production truck are transmitted via microwave to a satellite uplinking facility nearby. The signal is then transmitted to *Satcom IR,* an American domestic satellite, where it is received at the Comsat earth station near Etam, West Virginia, then uplinked to a satellite operated by the Intelsat consortium 32,000 miles above the Atlantic Ocean. The feed is received at a Soviet earth station near Dubna, 150 miles from Moscow, where the video signal is converted from the American television standard (NTSC) to the format used by the Eastern-block countries (SECAM). Finally, the signal is transmitted from Dubna to the Gosteleradio television studios in Ostenkino, Moscow.

Imagine! Television camera crews from around the world cover the release of Nelson Mandela, 71-year-old leader of the African National Congress, after 27 years of imprisonment. Ted Koppel brings ABC News "Nightline" viewers a live interview with South African president F. W. DeKlerk, the man committed to ending apartheid.

Imagine! Soviet General Secretary Gorbachev, architect of *pere-stroika* and *glasnost,* enjoys a remarkable ticker-tape parade in New York's Times Square and soon afterward receives the highest popularity ratings of any head of state, even among Americans! Less than one year later, as three committees of the Soviet legislature approve a proposed press law allowing any citizen or group to publish newspapers, magazines, or books and forbidding government censorship or prior restraint before publication, Soviet journalists involved in drafting the legislation call it the most important broadening of press freedom in Soviet history.

Imagine! The Global Technology Foundation in Boulder, Colorado, ships $2 million of outmoded computers to needy recipients in developing countries—a boys' home in Honduras, a food cooperative in Belize, and a high school on Grenada. Kenya's Friends College Kaimosi will build a model office for accounting and secretarial students around old Morrow desktop computers given to it by the foundation.

Imagine! Business reporters for the *Wall Street Journal* and the *Asahi Shimbun,* the largest-circulation dailies in the United States and in Japan, respectively, scramble for background information regarding Sony's $3.4 billion cash buyout offer for Columbia Pictures Entertainment (Sony bought CBS Records in 1988). They log on to Dow Jones News Retrieval and download company reports from the Disclosure II databases, manipulate the files with their word processors, and merge background information from these reports into their news stories. Depending on when they called, the baud rate (speed) of their phone modems, and other technical factors, the cost for 40 manuscript pages of information is about $100.

Rushworth Kidder, senior columnist of the *Christian Science Monitor* and author of *An Agenda for the 21st Century* (1987), reminds us that these global information technologies refuse to recognize borders, centralization, or even illiteracy, as the values of individual freedom replace those of collective obedience.

GLOBAL TECHNOLOGIES

The technologies empower governments to beam their messages to internal and external audiences, and they empower individual citizens with alternative sources of information. For example, the Soviet Union beamed 2,572 hours of radio a week in 1988 to external audiences through its Radio Moscow, Radio Station Peace and Progress, and regional stations. The United States aired 2,364 hours of radio a week in 1988 to external audiences: Voice of America (1,153 hours), Radio Free Europe (636 hours), Radio Liberty (434 hours), Radio Free Afghanistan

(14 hours), and Radio Marti (129 hours). The People's Republic of China, third most active programmer to external audiences, sent 1,513 radio program hours per week to external audiences.

Ironically, it was Gorbachev's visit to the People's Republic of China (PRC) in June 1989 that afforded students in the prodemocracy movement the opportunity to stage their demonstration in Beijing's Tiananmen Square. Foreign journalists from all over the world were there—Mikhail Gorbachev was head of state of the Soviet Union, and his *perestroika* and *glasnost* policies signaled an end to the cold war and a commitment to improving civil liberties and political rights for Soviet citizens. Deng Xiaoping, senior leader of the PRC, was not only more cautious about encouraging prodemocracy initiatives in China but was also worried that the students would take the opportunity to embarrass him, the party, and the country by calling for his resignation. Deng dismantled the prodemocracy movement, and he removed former party general secretary Zhao Ziyang for having encouraged the students.

In Iran, Poland, the Soviet Union, South Africa, and elsewhere, low-cost technologies—audiocassettes, printing presses, videocassettes, and other interactive media—have increased the opportunities for participatory democracy. These technologies run "electronic software" primarily supplied by countries in the West. Television programs and movies from the West, to the extent that they transmit Western values, may be inappropriate for audiences in developing countries whose value systems may be antithetical to the value systems of Western democracies. Some critics believe that these programs constitute a form of "cultural imperialism."

In this overview chapter, we will compare press freedom in major regions of the world, relate press freedom to media usage and economic productivity, look at the concentration of ownership of news media institutions, and provide overviews of the newspaper press, broadcasting, and telecommunications.

PRESS FREEDOM

Countries are ranked according to political rights and civil liberties by Freedom House, a New York–based organization interested in strengthening democratic institutions that has conducted an annual Comparative Freedom Survey since 1972. The Associated Press, the Inter-American Press Association, and the International Press Institute also conduct annual assessments on gains and losses in press freedom, and some of these are published in the Stanley Foundation magazine known as *World Press Review*. Freedom House's survey is used because scholars are involved in making the assessments and the assessments include overall evaluations of changes in political rights and civil liberties.

Ratings for political rights and civil liberties are combined into a rating ranging from 2 (most free) to 14 (least free), and Freedom House determines whether political rights or civil liberties have changed since the previous year's survey. Changes in the tables are indicated by + or − for political rights (PR) and civil liberties (CL). Freedom House also makes an assessment of press freedom, rating press systems as "most free" (+), "intermediate" (0), or "least free" (−).

According to the International Bank for Reconstruction and Development, commonly known as the World Bank, about 52 percent of the world's population lives in countries where the GNP per capita per year is less than U.S. $500, mostly in the developing Third World nations of Africa and Asia. Between 1980 and 1987, there was no growth in the per capita output of the economies of 61 countries representing about 14 percent of the world's population. By contrast, growth in GNP per capita output exceeded 3 percent in the PRC (9.1 percent), Pakistan (3.3 percent), and 21 other countries representing 29 percent of the world's population. These changes in economic growth are the highest rates among 185 countries followed by the World Bank.

Let's look at how political freedom, civil liberties, and press freedom relate to media use, economic productivity, literacy, and population size. We have not attempted to include data on television, radio, and telephone use in our discussion because the data are reported differently from country to country. Furthermore, the reliability of statistical data on communication and development (e.g., on literacy) is always questionable, so we don't want to compound the problem by attempting to make inferences from such data on television, radio, and telephone use. The freedom designations are based on the Freedom House Comparative Freedom Survey, and the ordinal scale is my own interpretation of Freedom House's numerical ratings. Raymond Gastil, who supervises the preparation of the annual book that reports the results of the Comparative Freedom Survey, emphasizes that the ratings are comparative assessments. In 1988, for example, 36 percent of the 159 countries in the survey were judged to have the "most free" press systems, 12 percent were judged to have "intermediate" freedom, and 52 percent were judged to be "least free."

The Most Freedom.   Fourteen nations receive the highest ratings from Freedom House (2) and each of the countries also receives a + (most free) press rating. With the exception of Australia, New Zealand, and Japan in the Asia-Pacific region and Costa Rica in the Latin America–Caribbean region, the countries are in Western Europe and North America. As a group, these countries have the highest levels of newspaper circulation (349 per 1,000), GNP per capita ($10,214), and literacy (98 percent).

More countries in this group beam propaganda to external audiences, led by the United States. The United States is second only to the Soviet Union in the number of hours of programming broadcast for consumption by external audiences.

The countries receiving the highest ratings by Freedom House are Norway, the United States, Australia, Italy, Sweden, Denmark, New Zealand, Belgium, Japan, the Netherlands, the United Kingdom, Costa Rica, Luxembourg, and Canada.

Some recent restrictions on press freedom in these countries have infuriated professional journalism organizations. A far-reaching mutual trade agreement signed by the United States and Canada in 1988 defined the professional credentials of journalists who would be permitted to cross borders and seek employment in the other country; the provision, that journalists have a bachelor's degree and three years of work experience in the news business, was considered by Freedom House as the equivalent of a licensing requirement for journalists.

The United Kingdom uses the Official Secrets Act to limit British press coverage and publicity of the activities of paramilitary groups such as the Irish Republican Army (IRA) in Northern Ireland. Press-government tension is high in Britain, as there is no Bill of Rights, as we have in the United States, and a strong head of state, such as Margaret Thatcher, can work Parliament to favor government secrecy when national security issues are at stake. The Official Secrets Act was invoked to ban references to *Spycatcher*, a book written by a retired member of the British domestic intelligence service. The Royal Ulster Constabulary confiscated undistributed film taken by the British Broadcasting Corp. (BBC) and Britain's Independent Television News (ITN) of an IRA mob killing two British soldiers. The BBC and ITN refused to turn over the film, wanting not to be viewed as aligned with the government, thus keeping channels of communication open with all groups concerned in the conflict.

Finally, Costa Rica, whose president, Oscar Arias Sanchez, won the Nobel Peace Prize in 1987, has long licensed its journalists, though a special government commission was established in 1988 to bring the country's law into harmony with the Inter-American Court of Human Rights's 1985 covenant, which rejects the licensing of journalists.

Very, Very Free. Five Western European and two Latin American countries receive the second highest rating by Freedom House (3), and the press systems of each of these countries are judged "most free." They are

Venezuela, Argentina, Portugal, West Germany, France, Finland, and Spain.

These countries, collectively, are in the 75th percentile on GNP per capita, enjoy high levels of literacy (94 percent), and rank second in newspaper circulation (222 per 1,000).

Very Free. The countries of Uruguay, Ecuador, Israel, and Jamaica receive a ranking of 4 from Freedom House. Each country's press system is considered among the "most free" in the world. Israel, however, apparently concerned with its own survival and the court of public opinion regarding the Palestinian uprising in the West Bank, detained or arrested 36 journalists and expelled 6 more in 1988. These countries as a group rank in the top half of the 100 countries in our sample, enjoy rather high levels of literacy (87 percent), and have fairly active newspaper readers (135 per 1,000 daily circulation).

Free. India, the largest democracy in the world; the Philippines; South Korea; and six Latin American and Caribbean countries fit into this category (5). Political changes in South Korea in 1987 led to a free press in 1988 for the first time in more than half a century. Seoul hosted the Olympic Games in 1988. Bolivia and Honduras enjoy only moderate freedom of the press, while the others are judged by Freedom House to be among the "most free" press systems in the world. These countries, taken together, have an average GNP per capita rank of 62 (out of 100) and a literacy rate of 72 percent, somewhat below the median of 75. The group's average newspaper circulation of 47 per 1,000 is somewhat above the median of 41 per 1,000. Other countries in this group are Colombia, Suriname, Brazil, and Peru. The drug cartels and terrorists in Colombia have had a chilling effect on press freedom. Twenty-five journalists were killed in 1988, five of them in Colombia. Indeed, harassment of journalists was a problem in the 1980s. In 1988, some 225 journalists were arrested or detained, 24 were expelled, and 14 were kidnapped, according to Freedom House; also in 1988, the Committee to Protect Journalists in New York documented more than 800 incidents of abuse against journalists in 79 countries.

Somewhat Free. Four of the five countries with overall freedom ratings of 6 have press systems that are only moderately free; the exception is Pakistan, which made the transition from military rule to a parliamentary government in 1988. Pakistan's newspapers became largely free in 1988, though broadcasting is still heavily controlled by the government. These countries are Pakistan, Guatemala, Turkey, Thailand, and Salvador. The average GNP rank of these countries is 60. Newspaper circulation per 1,000 is 43; literacy, at 59 percent, is below the median of 75 percent.

Moderately Free. Senegal, Mexico, and Sri Lanka have moderately free press systems, though Mexico has a very high morbidity rate among its journalists (four were killed there in 1988). The media in Mexico are mostly privately owned and free from overt censorship, though they receive "guidance" from the government. The average GNP rank of these countries is 66; newspaper circulation, at 67 per 1,000, is well above the median of 41. Mexico and Sri Lanka enjoy high levels of literacy, but in Senegal only one adult in ten can read and write. These countries receive an overall freedom rating of 7 from Freedom House.

Moderately Unfree. Only the West African nation of Nigeria, with improvements in political and civil rights in 1988, is recognized among this group as having one of the "most free" press systems in the world. Still, all but two of the major newspapers in Nigeria and all television and radio are owned by federal or state governments, and the government is under the control of the military.

There are moderate controls of press freedom in Egypt, Malaysia, and the Sudan. Morocco, Uganda, Chile, Hungary, and Nicaragua are among the "least free" countries for journalists. Hungary, however, is among the Eastern-bloc countries most smitten with *perestroika* and *glasnost* and has allowed prodemocracy marches and emigration to the West.

As a group these countries have a GNP rank of 62. Newspaper circulation is 68 per 1,000, and literacy levels range from a high of 90 percent in Chile to a low of 44 percent in Egypt. The average level of literacy among these nine countries is 62 percent, below the median of 75 for the 100 countries in our sample.

Somewhat Unfree. Each of the nine countries with Freedom House freedom rankings of 10 has among the "least free" press systems in the world and literacy levels below the median of 75. The ratings predate Solidarity's assent to a position of shared power in Poland. Poland is the quintessence of the motive triangle—economic collapse and the Soviet Union's own market initiatives have encouraged Poland to experiment with a market economy and to improve the political and civil rights of its citizens.

These countries as a group are at the midpoint on GNP (rank of 50) and well above the median on newspaper readership (73 per 1,000 daily newspaper circulation). North Yemen, Indonesia, Liberia, Sierra Leone, Guyana, Qatar, Tunisia, and Bahrain are the other countries in this group.

Unfree. Unfree but comparatively well off and literate are the peoples in the nine countries from Eastern Europe, Africa, the Caribbean, and the Middle East that receive freedom ratings of 11. The Soviet Union and Yugoslavia are comparatively more free today than yesterday. The Soviet Union reports the highest newspaper circulation in the world, 726 per 1,000. Lebanon is also among the leaders in newspaper circulation. South Africa, Yugoslavia, and the Soviet Union report literacy levels of 90 percent or higher.

As a group, these countries have a per capita GNP of $2,406, almost twice the median of $1,225 (rank of 44). Other countries in this group include Panama, Madagascar, Jordan, Iran, and Swaziland. Journalists in all these countries work for among the "least free" press systems in the world.

Very Unfree. Twelve countries, including the People's Republic of China, receive freedom ratings of 12 and are judged to limit substantially the political and civil rights of their citizens. China increased its GNP per capita consistently in the 1980s and has experimented with a market economy, yet intellectuals, remembering the Cultural Revolution, are shocked at the crackdowns against student activists. Just prior to those student marches in the summer of 1989, Chinese journalists were on Ted Koppel's "Nightline" ABC-TV news program calling for reform, buoyed in part by a survey of 200 top Chinese officials, conducted by *Renmin Ribao* (the Communist Party daily newspaper), who were calling for extensive press reforms. These officials told pollsters that the press should act as a "watchdog," free to criticize the party and the government. Hong Kong residents are very uneasy about their own fate come 1997, when the United Kingdom ends its crown colony relationship and the PRC takes over.

Other countries in this category include Afghanistan, Algeria, Libya and Oman, the African nations of Zimbabwe, Ghana, Kenya, Cameroon, Rwanda, and Tanzania, and the Latin American country of Paraguay.

The average GNP rank of the group is 63; newspaper circulation averages 19 per 1,000, well below the median; and literacy averages 51 percent, substantially below the median.

Very, Very Unfree. Eleven countries are among the most repressive in the world in the sense that press freedom and political and civil rights are valued less than almost anywhere else in the world (13). In three of these countries, East Germany, Cuba, and Czechoslovakia, newspaper circulation per thousand is among the highest in the world, well above the median. But these are not newspapers that question the powers of the state or that confer status on entrepreneurs experimenting with free-market ideas but rather newspapers that convey the ideology and revolutionary zeal of the political regimes in power, motives ostensibly valued by the political culture at large.

The literacy levels of the Communist-bloc countries in this group are high, above 90 percent in East Germany, Cuba, Czechoslovakia, and Vietnam, but they are very low for Saudi Arabia and the six African nations of Mozambique, Burundi, Niger, Malawi, Zaire, and Ethiopia. Daily newspapers simply don't exist in many of these African nations, where fewer than one person in ten can read or write. The GNP ranking of this group of nations is 68, and the average literacy level is 54 percent. Newspaper circulation overall (105 per 1,000) is much higher than the median because of the high levels of circulation in East Germany (559), Czechoslovakia (284), and Cuba (140).

The Least Freedom. Eight countries are considered by Freedom House to be less free than any other countries in the world. As a group, these countries have the lowest levels of per capita GNP ($997) and among the lowest levels of newspaper circulation (40 per 1,000) and literacy (58 percent).

These countries are Iraq and South Yemen, located in the Middle East; the African nations of Angola, Benin, and Equatorial Guinea; the Eastern European country of Romania; and the Asian countries of Cambodia and North Korea.

Now that we have considered press freedom in the world today, let's turn to a consideration of how the largest (and sometimes the most distinguished) news media organizations fit into this framework.

GLOBAL MEDIA BARONS

Global media barons play in the American market big time. The largest media acquisition in 1988 was Rupert Murdoch's News Corp. purchase of Triangle Publications (*TV Guide, Seventeen, Daily Racing Form,* and *Good Food*) from founder Walter Annenberg for $3.2 billion. With that acquisition, Murdoch's News Corp., based in Sydney, Australia, reported total media revenues in 1988 of $1.68 billion, up 35 percent over 1987, making it the thirteenth largest media company.

Murdoch, known as the "Magellan of the Information Age," inherited the *News* in Adelaide at the age of 29 when his father died in 1954. He founded the first national newspaper, the *Australian,* in 1964. He outbid Robert Maxwell for the *News of the World* in 1969 and established a beachhead in the United Kingdom, adding the *Sun* in 1969, the *Times* and *Sunday Times* of London in 1981. News Corp. owns newspapers in Australia, the United Kingdom, and the United States and accounts for a daily circulation of 14 million, making it the largest newspaper group in the world. Murdoch controls two-thirds of all newspaper circulation in Australia, about half of the circulation in New Zealand, and about one-third of the newspaper circulation in the United Kingdom. Murdoch also controls William Crown books and owns 7 percent of the news service Reuters and 20 percent of Pearsons PLC (*Financial Times, Economist,* Viking Penguin books). News Corp.'s satellite channels cover the continent of Europe; its Sky Television PLC satellite system is the largest in Europe.

Murdoch publishes daily newspapers in Boston (*Herald*) and San Antonio (*Express-News*); controls Fox Broadcasting, the fourth largest U.S. television network; and the 20th Century–Fox movie studio. He also owns Harper & Row books, which he purchased in 1987.

Thomson Corp., Toronto, the seventeenth largest media company operating in the United States, owns 96 daily newspapers in that country, accounting for a combined circulation of 1.48 million. Thomson is also the fifth largest magazine publisher in the United States, specializing in technical trade journals such as *Medical Economics, American Banker,* and *Communications Engineering and Design.*

Hachette Publications, Paris, is the 48th largest media company operating in the United States, with all its U.S. media revenues in the magazine field (*Woman's Day* is the largest in terms of advertising revenues). Hachette SA is the world's largest producer of magazines— 74 in ten countries, including *Elle* and *Paris-Match.* It is also the world's largest publisher of reference books, among them the *Encyclopedia Americana,* obtained when the company purchased Grolier in 1988. This French company accounts for 30 percent of the books bought in that country, and it recently acquired Salvat of Spain, which offers the largest distribution network for printed works in the Spanish-speaking world. Media critic Ben Bagdikian (1989) believes that Jean-Luc Lagardère, the arms manufacturer who purchased Hachette in 1980, intends to combine a major television operation with the company's Europe 1, the largest radio network in Europe.

Reuters Holdings PLC, of London, is the 53rd largest media company operating in the United States, with 1988 revenues of $351.3 million. Reuters exceeds the media revenues of its American wire service rival, the Associated Press, which reported 1988 revenues of $261.6 million.

The merger of Time Inc. and Warner Communications Inc. in 1989 created the world's largest media firm, worth $18 billion, a sum that exceeds the combined gross domestic products of Jordan, Bolivia, Nicaragua, Albania, Laos, Liberia, and Mali. Time Warner is truly a global giant with subsidiaries in Australia, Asia, Europe, and Latin America. It is the world's leading direct marketer of information and entertainment and the largest magazine publisher in the United States, with a worldwide readership of 120 million. The new company is one of the world's largest book dealers—subsidiaries include Warner mass-market paperbacks; Scott Foresman; Little, Brown; Time-Life Books; and the Book-of-the-Month Club. Time Warner is the world's second largest record company (WCI). Time Warner is the second largest cable operator in the United States. Its cable subsidiaries include American Television and Communications Corporation as well as the Home Box Office and Cinemax pay channels. Its Warner Brothers division is a major player in motion picture production.

The German Firm, Bertelsmann AG, with properties in 15 countries on four continents, is another of what Bagdikian calls the "lords of the global village." Bertelsmann is probably second only to Time Warner in terms of worth. Founded in the mid-nineteenth century, Bertelsmann AG long ago exceeded the market share standards for print media set by the Federal Cartel Office of the Federal Republic of Germany, so the company has expanded elsewhere. Bertelsmann owns Doubleday, Bantam Books, Dell, and the Literary Guild book club, as well as RCA and Arista records. Gruner & Jahr, a subsidiary, publishes more than 40 magazines, including *Parents* and *Young Miss* in the United States.

Futurists Alvin and Heidi Toffler (1988) believe that the major powers of the world are vigorously pursuing master plans for survival in the next century. Opening up markets and encouraging international trade are part of the "grand designs" in Europe, the Soviet Union, the People's Republic of China, and Japan. For example, in 1992 the European Community (EC) intends to lift all customs barriers and tariffs and will convert to a single integrated economy serving some 325 million Europeans. Part of the design in Europe calls for opening postal and telecommunication services to competition and establishing EC-wide standards for products, services, and safety, which the EC believes will add 2 million jobs, result in price reductions of 6 percent, and increase GNP by 5 percent.

New information technologies such as fiber optics and satellites make it easier to publish and broadcast across borders. In many countries, especially in Western Europe, government broadcasting monopolies are turning to the private sector and advertisers are aiming at megamarkets that extend beyond country and continental boundaries.

Saatchi & Saatchi of London is the world's largest advertising agency, with offices in 80 countries, annual revenues of $5.7 billion, and a five-year earnings growth rate of 22 percent. While 80 percent of Saatchi's operating income is generated by its communication units, such as the advertising agency Backer Spielvogel Bates, the other 20 percent of Saatchi's income comes from its consulting division. This division of eight firms includes human resource consultants such as the Philadelphia-based Hay Group, Inc. Advertising spending continues to rise. Ad agency McCann-Erickson expected a 6.9 percent increase in U.S. spending and a 10 percent increase for overseas spending in 1989. Saatchi forecast a 7.2 percent increase in U.S. ad spending and a 10.9 percent increase in international ad spending for 1989. Saatchi forecast increases in ad spending for 1989 of 18.4 percent in Thailand and 15.3 percent in Taiwan; it predicted that South Korea's ad spending would reach $3 billion by 1991, making it the eleventh largest advertising nation in the world. Saatchi also expected ad spending to increase dramatically in the People's Republic of China. In Europe, Spain was its number one pick for 1989, anticipating increases in ad spending of 23 percent.

In 1989, when WPP Group of London made a hostile bid for the ad agency Ogilvy Group, one of the world's largest, Ogilvy's stock increased 53 percent. Such a merger would make WPP the world's second largest agency with billings of $13.5 billion and operations in 53 countries.

So today considerable media market power is concentrated in even fewer hands than was the case when the first edition of this book was published in 1983. Transnational corporations are the big players in this global information economy. These companies operate, for the most part, in countries where freedom of the press and political and civil rights are respected by the government.

INTERNATIONAL PRINT MEDIA

Approximately a third of the world's newspapers are published in North America and another third of them are published in Western and Eastern Europe. Europe accounts for about half the world's newspaper circulation, North America about a quarter. The cities regarded as the press centers of the world would include London, New York, Paris, Moscow, Amsterdam, Copenhagen, Stockholm, Brussels, Rome, Hamburg, Vienna, Zurich, Beijing, Tokyo, Cairo, Johannesburg, Toronto, Melbourne, Havana, Mexico City, Rio de Janeiro, Buenos Aires, and Bogotá.

Most of the world's daily newspapers are small. Only in some 25 countries can dailies be found with as many as 12 pages. More than 25 percent of the world's dailies are published in English. Chinese, German, and Spanish are the other popular print languages.

Ranking the elite papers of the world has been a scholarly interest of John Merrill's. Consult his book *The Elite Press* (1968) and the one he wrote with Harold Fisher, *The World's Great Dailies* (1980), for a thoughtful treatment of this issue. Part II of this book details the scope of publishing in each region.

Newspapers in capitalist nations normally devote 40 to 65 percent of their content to news and editorials, the rest to advertising. The news portion includes both "hard" news items (e.g., stories about the economy and the environment) and "soft" news (e.g., lifestyle features and sports). Many daily newspapers in market-oriented countries have expanded their coverage of business, consumerism, and finance, just as commercial and cable television operators have devoted more coverage to the business and consumer beats.

In countries where the dominant motive is ideology, the press tends to reflect the current regime's point of view on ideological issues. Under Gorbachev, for example, both *Pravda* and *Izvestia* have exposed the excesses of Stalin, as the current regime in the Soviet Union distances itself from the traditions of Lenin and Stalin. The presentation of news in countries following Hachten's authoritarian, communist, revolutionary, and development concepts (see Chapter 1) often includes references to the values and dominant motives that hold the political culture together. The fact-value distinction is more difficult to discern when reading newspapers from these countries. Newspapers from the West most often put opinion and argumentation copy on the "op-ed" pages, separating them from straight news stories based on the 5Ws and 1H formula. This formula, taught in the basic reporting course, emphasizes answers to the basic questions *who, what, when, where, why,* and *how.* You are more likely to see sensational news on crime, violence, sex scandals, and the like in newspapers based on the Western model. Some media barons such as Rupert Murdoch are criticized by professional journalists for sensationalizing the newspapers they own. Fleet Street newspapers in the United Kingdom were once known for publishing some pretty racy stuff! The *National Enquirer* and others like it in the United States make money selling sensational news, most of it about Hollywood stars. Some movie stars such as Carol Burnett have won libel cases against these newspapers.

The companies in free-market countries that own newspapers attempt to become full-service information providers, so they typically own other media properties, as our review of the global concentration picture indicates. For example, 92 of the 100 American media companies with newspaper properties in 1988 also made money in other media industries. Newspapers' share of the advertising dollar is eroding as cable television continues to grow and cultural literacy levels in the United States continue to decline. For example, the Cabletelevision Advertising Bureau estimates that 70 percent of America's households will have cable service by 1994, up from 55 percent in 1988. Serious readers of America's most distinguished newspapers are concerned about how developments in Tokyo affect Main Street, USA. Unfortunately, an international Gallup poll for the National Geographic Society in 1988 found that of a total of 10,000 adults in the United States, Japan, France, West Germany, the United Kingdom, Sweden, Italy, Canada, and Mexico, Americans know the least about the world, considerably less than they knew in the first such survey, conducted in the 1940s.

RADIO

Although newspapers are the oldest medium for news, radio and television have played a more important role in the modernization of new nation-states and developing countries in the Third World.

A majority of the people on earth today have access to radio; it is the lifeline to the outside world for millions of otherwise isolated people in the rural areas of many Third World countries in Africa, Asia, and Latin America. UNESCO estimates that from one-quarter to one-third of the people living in the developing Third World have access to radio. Communication and development scholars in the 1950s were buoyant about the prospects of the "transistor revolution" accelerating modernization in Third World Africa, Latin America, and the Middle East.

Researchers at the Massachusetts Institute of Technology and Stanford University thought that we could duplicate the success of our Soil Conservation Service and Agricultural Extension Agents programs, initiatives of the 1930s and 1940s that involved the use of pamphlets and "radio forums" linking agribusiness experts and farmers trying to revitalize the farm economy during the depression and after the devastation of the dust bowl in the Great Plains.

The idea emerged that developing countries could dramatically increase economic growth and political and social change and thereby move from a traditional to a modern society by making substantial investments in mass media systems. As Robert L. Stevenson notes in his thoughtful book, *Communication, Development, and the Third World* (1988), mass media, in theory, constituted the "magic multipliers" of modernization. Others, like Ralph Lowenstein in *Macromedia* (Lowenstein & Merrill, 1990), argue a stage theory of media development, believing that all media systems progress through stages of development, first "elitist," then "popular," and finally "specialized." Literacy, education, urbanization, affluence, and leisure time were antecedents to the development of mass media systems.

Remember Franklin Roosevelt's fireside chats and the admonition to a people alarmed about the Great Depression of the 1930s, "We have nothing to fear but fear itself!" Hitler's propaganda minister made effective use of radio, as did Winston Churchill in appealing to the resolve of the British and the Americans to stand tall against the menace of Nazism. Edward R. Murrow, Robert Pierpont, William Shirer, Howard K. Smith, and other famous World War II broadcasters kept Americans informed of developments in the European theater. We came to believe in the power of radio as a medium for mobilizing popular support.

So why couldn't radio work in the developing world—as a method of improving agricultural and health practices or as a method of linking change agents who might help peasants mired in a cycle of poverty? Daniel Lerner's book *The Passing of Traditional Society* (1958) was the blueprint for modernization efforts in the Third World. These efforts included projects supported by the U.S. Agency for International Development, the U.S. Peace Corps, UNESCO, and other development organizations.

In the 1970s, Elihu Katz and George Wedell examined secondary development data on 91 developing countries, conducted case studies in 11 of these nation-states, and published a report card in *Broadcasting in the Third World: Promise and Performance* (1977). The evaluation was negative in four respects:

1. Importation of the Western model of how to employ radio and television as instruments of education and development was inappropriate (both the context and content didn't fit the needs of developing countries).
2. Broadcasting was not integrated into national development planning (broadcasters should help define, not just implement, national development objectives).
3. Developing countries needed their own communication arts professionals to develop culturally relevant programming.
4. Countries needed both to encourage "group viewing" of television programs and to pool news sources.

Other scholars were troubled by the lack of progress in the developing world: No matter what quality-of-life indicators were used and despite the rapid diffusion of radio and even television in some parts of the developing world, the gap between the developed and developing countries seemed to be increasing in the 1960s and 1970s. Particularly troubling was income distribution; proportionately fewer people, "moderns" whose lifestyles and aspirations were Western in orientation—in part, some argued, because the programming emphasized materialistic values and originated in the West—garnered more and more of the wealth. In short, a few people accounted for most of the wealth.

Stevenson's 1988 book updates us regarding the contentiousness between the information-rich versus information-poor countries, between First World and Third World nations, that came to be known as the "New World Information Order" debate. UNESCO even published a documentary history of the debate in 1986.

The United States under President Ronald Reagan decided to withdraw financial support from UNESCO because it believed that this international organization had tilted in the direction of supporting the Third World claims in this debate, positions considered by many journalists as Marxist and decidedly anti-free-press. UNESCO is under new leadership these days, the United States has renewed its financial support, and the organization is not as overtly against press freedom in its rhetoric or in its financial support of efforts in the developing world.

Western democracies have come to understand why a libertarian or even social responsibility philosophy of press operations may not be appropriate for new nation-states. Others agree that the kind of entertainment fare that characterizes daytime and prime-time television in the United States is probably inappropriate and may have negative effects on the cultural identities of developing countries that choose to import it or that cannot avoid it.

Other professional news organizations like the World Press Freedom Committee have supported technology transfer and professional training programs in the Third World, under the aegis of UNESCO and the International Program for the Development of Communication.

Radio, to be sure, has been used effectively in development programs, and we will note some successes momentarily.

But we should note that radio is also a most important source of hard news and propaganda throughout the world. The BBC estimates that more than 60 countries broadcast programming for external consumption. The USSR, the United States, the People's Republic of China, the United Kingdom, India, Albania, Iran, Australia, Spain, the Netherlands, France, Turkey, Bulgaria, Poland, Czechoslovakia, Canada, Sweden, Italy, Romania, Portugal, Yugoslavia, and Hungary have all been doing so since at least 1950.

Hobbyists and citizens in closed-information societies tune in on shortwave radio to the Voice of America, Radio Free Europe, Deutsche Welle, Radio Cairo, BBC's World Service, Radio Australia, Radio Beijing, Radio Moscow's World Service, Radio Nederland Wereldomroep (the Dutch International Service), Swiss Radio International, and similar broadcasts to hear alternative points of view on world affairs or information they don't get from domestic news sources. The BBC's World Service, broadcast in English and 36 other languages, reaches an estimated 10 million listeners in Eastern Europe and the Soviet Union and is especially well regarded as a source of objective reporting that often infuriates the prime minister and Parliament. For example, the prime minister and Parliament believed that the BBC should have been more partisan in its coverage of Britain's war with Argentina over the Falkland Islands. All a person needs is less than $75 to buy a shortwave radio and a copy of *World Radio TV Handbook*, published annually in Denmark, which provides program schedules and guidance on how to tune in more than 3,800 shortwave stations around the globe.

TELEVISION

Radio evolved in the 1920s; television became a mass medium in the United Kingdom, France, and the United States in the 1950s. The British Broadcasting Company was formed by the government in 1922, aired its first experimental television program in 1929, and offered the world's first high-definition television service in 1936. King Edward VIII's abdication was broadcast on November 2, 1936. The European Broadcasting Union was formed in February 1950, and the first live television from the continent of Europe was aired August 27, 1950.

By summer 1954, eight European countries had exchanged television programs.

In the United States, the first regularly scheduled network television news program was *CBS-TV News* with Douglas Edwards in 1948.

Though broadcasting has always been more heavily regulated than print media in the United States, commercial broadcasting predates public radio and television in the United States. By contrast, in the United Kingdom, Parliament did not allow commercial competition for the BBC-TV until 1955. British adoption of commercial television prompted other countries with government-owned broadcasters to experiment with privately owned systems. British citizens pay a license fee of about $39 a year for the BBC's services: two national TV networks, four radio networks, regional television and radio, and 35 local radio stations. In 1988, BBC Television had income of $488 million versus Independent Television (ITV) advertising revenues of $883 million.

Just as public broadcasting stations in the United States have used advertising and fund-raisers to augment government and foundation support, so did television evolve in other more developed countries in the 1960s with combinations of private and public support.

The BBC served as the model for France, Italy, and several other European and Commonwealth nations. The governmental broadcasting systems of the Soviet Union and the People's Republic of China have been adopted with modifications by many African and Asian countries. The U.S. commercial broadcasting model has influenced the development of commercial broadcasting in Britain (ITV), and the BBC model has influenced public broadcasting in the United States. The Dutch co-op system, whereby listener societies own stations, is yet another model.

Since most nations have only one television service, usually government-controlled, there is considerable dependence on the syndication of television news film and videotapes. The news film of networks like the U.S.-based NBC, ABC, CBS, and CNN (Cable News Network) and the BBC is syndicated or distributed through two Anglo-American companies, Visnews and WTN (World Television News), by way of videotape and satellite.

It was explained in Chapter 2 how the Intelsat consortium has expanded the distribution of journalism. A wide variety of programming can be picked out of the air with an inexpensive backyard satellite dish. From the *Westar 5* satellite, for example, one transponder may bring X-rated movies, another the Financial News Network, yet another a sports channel, and so on. An early-generation satellite, *Comstar*, had a capacity of 18,000 two-way telephone circuits, or 24 television channels. As larger-capacity satellites are launched by developed nations seeking larger markets, cries of cultural imperialism by Third World nations may get louder because their citizens can easily pirate the programming using cheap backyard dishes.

In the developing world, television systems were often initially sought as status symbols; the lack of indigenous programming led to dependence on First World countries for content. As we have seen, the new technologies make it easier for citizens to circumvent the protective hands of Big Brother. Interestingly, the call for relaxed immigration laws—because the demand for emigration from East bloc to West bloc and from Southern Hemisphere to Northern Hemisphere countries is increasing—may be tied to the exportation of television programs and movies. Many countries welcome skilled workers, especially those who are able to contribute to the information economy. A public diplomacy argument may be the reason why the United States and other developed countries have objected to any calls for the International Telecommunication Union to tighten its regulation of the geostationary orbit.

WORLD ADVERTISING

The messages that travel across borders are not just news stories, propaganda, and entertainment programs. Advertising messages help pay the freight, and advertising has become a transnational affair. Some advertising agencies, such as N. W. Ayer, Inc., have entered into joint ventures that have the ad agencies producing TV movies and miniseries. Ayer clients (e.g., American Telephone & Telegraph, Gillette, General Motors) help finance and sponsor TV movies. Ayer has a joint venture with World International Network (WIN), an organization representing TV networks in 106 countries. WIN's member stations would pay to air the movies in their countries, thus spreading production costs around, because the movies would be shown in the United States as well as other countries.

WWP Group—parent company of J. Walter Thompson and Ogilvy Group—is the world's largest advertising group, recently overtaking Saatchi & Saatchi. Ogilvy Group was already the fifth largest international company providing advertising and related marketing services, with major operations in the United States and clients in 53 countries. About 53 percent of its revenues and 55 percent of its net income in 1988 came from foreign operations. Commissions account for about 47 percent of its operating income, and television and radio generate 22 percent. This transnational corporation provides worldwide advertising, public relations, direct marketing, promotion, and market research services. It has clout. For example, in 1989, the company signed an agreement with Omnicom's BBDO and DDB/Needham for a joint media-buying venture primarily in Europe. Individual investors have recognized the company as an industry leader; its shares have been trading at 24 times earnings and 10 times book value since WPP Group made its bid. Standard and Poor gives the stock an "A" rating.

BBDO Worldwide has 121 overseas agencies in 50 countries. J. Walter Thompson Co., already in the WPP fold, reported that 1988 non-U.S. billings rose to $2.1 billion, up 31 percent. Leo Burnett Co., Chicago, had 1988 non-U.S. billings of $1.1 billion, up 20.6 percent. D'Arcy Masius Benton & Bowles, New York, has a majority interest in 43 foreign agencies and reported non-U.S. billings of $1.6 billion in 1988, up 34.8 percent. McCann-Erickson Worldwide, New York, whose foreign billings increased 34.5 percent to $3.1 billion in 1988, has 144 agencies in 67 countries. Young & Rubicam, New York, with 127 offices in 44 countries, had non-U.S. billings of $2.6 billion in 1988, up 13 percent.

MEDIA AND DEVELOPMENT

Before closing, we should note the channels of mass communication that have been used successfully for development efforts. Some of these efforts have been widely publicized one-shot campaigns such as rock concert fund-raisers for famine victims in Ethiopia. Significant case studies are reported in a 1988 UNESCO-sponsored report by Hamid Mowlana and Laurie J. Wilson, *Communication Technology and Development.* Development specialists know that multimedia presentations are most effective in stimulating community action. For example, posters, pictures, and flannelboards accelerated adoption of an experimental nutrition project in Brazil.

In a Basic Village Education Project conducted during a three-year period in Guatemala, researchers found that a combination of radio and facilitator-led discussion showed the highest correlation to increased crop yields (rural farmers are encouraged to adopt improved corn seeds, fertilizers, etc.). Radio is also used in Sierra Leone to stimulate the agricultural sector and to encourage self-sufficiency among farmers. Teleclubs and group viewing, as recommended by Katz and Wedell, are working in India and elsewhere to close the information gap between well-connected farmers and farmers who have weak ties with change agents.

The most dramatic and successful telecommunications satellite project in the Third World is *Insat,* the satellite built by scientists in India and launched in 1983 by the United States from the *Challenger* space shuttle. Since that time, more than 200 space stations have been built in India. The satellite cost $130 million, considerably less than what a ground-based system would have cost. The satellite empowers India to put in place the infrastructure necessary to launch other development projects—8,000 telephone circuits, continuous weather reporting, early warning systems for floods and other disasters, government office links, and computerized hotel and transportation links for the tourist industry. *Insat*'s primary role is to provide instructional television broadcasts to rural areas. *Insat* broadcasts teacher-training programs, and plans are under way to establish a university of the air like that in the People's Republic of China.

Other technologies are also being used in development efforts in the Third World, including telephone and narrowband technology, computers, and mobile audio and visual media, in addition to folk and traditional media.

So technologies and channels of communication are means of mass communication used by news media organizations to disseminate hard and soft news and by nation-states to educate and expand the horizons of their citizens. Information is power, and the issues surrounding the global transfer of news, entertainment, and education are complicated. In Part II your journey takes you into particular regions of the world. The contexts developed in this chapter will sharpen your expectations of what the similarities and differences in the practice of journalism might be among countries of the First, Second, and Third Worlds.

CHAPTER 4

Global Communications Controversies

Robert G. Picard

The growing internationalization of communications during the twentieth century, combined with the emergence of new nations in search of autonomy and identity, has resulted in extensive discussions and criticisms of the roles of media and other communications systems in domestic and international life worldwide.

Previous chapters have mentioned the criticisms leveled at the control of communication technologies and international communications systems by developed nations and by private and public policies that have disadvantaged smaller countries when they need access to those technologies and systems. We will now look more closely at the participants in this debate and the controversy surrounding the new world information order.

Much of the criticism from emerging and developing nations in Africa, Asia, and Latin America has focused on the preponderance of information and its control by firms from developed nations, especially private companies in Western nations. These criticisms began to spread rapidly as the breakdown of the colonial system progressed in the three decades after World War II, spurred by independence and nationalist movements in Africa, Asia, and Latin America. The success of such movements brought about the establishment of scores of new countries whose government structures, as well as educational, communications, and other cultural institutions, had been established during colonial times to serve the interests of the colonizing country and its citizens.

The newly emerged countries faced the choice of continuing existing institutions, altering and expanding those institutions to meet new needs, or establishing entirely new institutions to meet government, educational, communications, and cultural needs. Because media are social institutions that help create and perpetuate social norms, provide significant means for educating the public, and help preserve and develop culture, their importance was rapidly recognized by the leaders of these new nations. Leaders of both existing and emerging nations also recognized the important role that media could play in national development and the need to develop communications systems, or to adapt previously established systems, for such purposes.

EMERGING NATIONS AND THE NWICO

As governments began to attempt to use communications systems to carry out national social, political, and economic goals, it became evident that significant hurdles lay in their paths. Problems included the lack of necessary communications technology, the lack of frequencies for broadcast communications because they were already occupied by communications systems in developed countries, the inability of existing media to meet the new needs of the nations, and the overwhelming nature and effects of external communications systems. Differences in ideology about the roles and functions of various media in society, the financial support available for communications systems, and the nature of government and social controls worldwide also became apparent.

At the same time, the actual and potential applications of increasingly sophisticated electronic technology worldwide concerned both developing and developed nations. The ability to transmit communications across borders using shortwave and other frequencies and to reach large regions from direct-broadcast satellites gave all with access to technology the ability to engage in significant external and internal broadcasting. National sovereignty and other international issues relating to rights to send such broadcasts, to control their reception, to regulate propaganda, and to interfere with other broadcasts arose as a result of the new capabilities.

Such problems set off significant discussions in the International Telecommunication Union (ITU), the United Nations Educational, Scientific, and Cultural Organization (UNESCO), and other organizations. These issues were subsumed in discussions of proposals that are now known as the New World Information and Communications Order (NWICO), the New International Information Order (NIIO), or the New World Information Order (NWIO), and these discussions have included vociferous debates involving news gathering and dissemination by media as well.

BASIC CRITICISMS OF THE PRESENT ORDER

The primary criticism of journalistic information contained in the NWICO has been the near monopolization of international information by the Associated Press, United Press International, Reuters, and Agence France-Press. Because of the unavailability of other news services, or their inability to provide sufficient information about events worldwide, media across the globe were forced in the 1950s, 1960s, and 1970s to subscribe to the services of the major news agencies. A similar dominance existed in television news, where two major Western suppliers provided news video worldwide. Visnews, owned by the British Broadcasting Corp. and Reuters, and UPITN, owned by Independent Television News and United Press International, provided most of the world's television with video for use in news shows.

Developing world media and newly independent governments have been highly critical of this situation, arguing that coverage from the major services contains ethnocentric occidental values that affect its content and presentation. Coverage from these media most often include political, economic, Judeo-Christian religious, and other social values that are not universal. Thus, critics argued, news from these services became a form of cultural imperialism. In addition, developing world media and governments have argued that Western ethnocentrism creates an unequal flow of information by providing a large stream of information about events in the developed world but only a very small flow from the developing world.

A related criticism has been that when news is conveyed from the developing world, it invariably conveys negative images because it focuses on the unusual, on disasters, on corruption, or on conflict. Critics argued that little information was conveyed on progress in national development, and most nations never appeared in the news. Observers in developing world nations argued that Western definitions of news and the emphasis on reporting isolated events thus created perceptions and images of nations and citizens that did not accurately portray reality and harm efforts to improve economic and social life. These critics argued that this problem was especially critical because of the developing nations' dependence on the major wire services for news about themselves and their neighbors.

At the same time, news media and others in Western nations voiced their own criticism of international communications. A primary complaint was that Western journalists' abilities to cover much of the developing world and developed communist nations has been impeded by the lack of access resulting from government restrictions and by direct efforts to censor reports. Attacks on journalists, arrests and detentions, visa denials and expulsions, and harassment have been, and continue to be, common means used by governments worldwide to halt or restrict coverage deemed harmful to their interests.

The increasing reliance of developed world media on high-technology communications systems, such as satellite uplinks, cellular telephones, and computer systems requiring data-quality transmission lines, has also created tension between foreign media and governments worldwide. Because every government has its own national policies and regulations on the use of electromagnetic spectrum and electronic technology, conflicts occur over the use and control of such equipment as journalists move about the world. Western media, which have had the opportunity to adopt these technologies faster than media in other parts of the world, have been especially critical of governments that have restricted the use of such equipment.

ACTIONS TO ADDRESS CRITICISMS

A variety of national and international efforts, both public and private, have been instituted in response to some of the difficulties and problems plaguing communications in developing and developed nations.

A result of the criticisms of dependence on Western news organizations has been the growth of interest in and use of non-Western news services and news exchanges. Two news services created specifically to overcome the objections of developing nations are the Non-Aligned News Agency (NANA) and Inter-Press Service (IPS). NANA was created in 1976 to link the national news agencies of nonaligned nations into a news pool that provides news with non-Western perspectives and values. The agency is operated for the nonaligned nations by Tanjug, the national news agency of Yugoslavia. Its staff gathers material from the participating national news agencies, translates stories, and then distributes the combined worldwide news back to participating news agencies. IPS was started in 1964 by Latin-American media interested in gaining information on government programs and policies worldwide, especially those dealing with development issues. Similar efforts to promote new exchange among television systems have developed, including an exchange program operated by the Broadcasting Organization of the Non-Aligned Countries.

As noted in Chapter 2, a significant number of regional news exchanges similar to the NANA and IPS have developed, including the Pan-African News Agency (PANA), Caribbean News Agency (CANA), and Asian-Pacific News Network (ANN). Many joint efforts have resulted from international regional broadcasting organizations such as the Arab States Broadcasting Union (ASBU), Asian Broadcasting Union (ABU), European Broadcasting Union (EBU), International Radio and Television Organization of Eastern Europe (OIRT), and Union of National Radio and Television Organizations of Africa (URTNA). A number of existing news agencies in the developed and developing world have also benefited from the increased interest in non-Western media, including TASS, the agency of the Soviet Union; Xinhua, the Chinese news agency; and the Egyptian-based Middle East News Agency (MENA). Several Western agencies that had not previously been widely used also have benefited from the criticism of news control by the so-called Big Four agencies. Agencia EFE, the Spanish news agency, has become a major supplier of news throughout Latin America, and Deutsche Presse-Agentur of West Germany has also been well received worldwide.

Although the development and maturation of new types of news agencies and news exchanges have provided alternative sources of material based on and containing some different values and news definitions, thus altering and increasing information worldwide, these new services have tended to provide coverage that focuses on hard news events and political stories, just as traditional news agencies have. In addition, the major criticisms of major Western and developed-world media continue to be voiced, and their norms and types of coverage have changed very little. As a result, international communications continues to provoke controversy and generate efforts to affect the flow of information.

MAJOR PARTICIPANTS IN COMMUNICATIONS DEBATES

A variety of international organizations and journalistic associations have played, and continue to play, important roles in the discussions about international communications and journalism. Organizations representing journalists, publishers, and broadcasters have been deeply involved, and groups representing various ideologies have also been active. Although each group has had its own purposes, much of their involvement in international communication issues has revolved around efforts by UNESCO to deal with criticism and problems in the developing world for the past two decades.

Important participants in these international communications discussions have included the Inter American Press Association, International Federation of Journalists, International Federation of Newspaper Publishers, International Organization of Journalists, International Press Institute, ITU, Movement of Non-Aligned Countries, UNESCO, and World Press Freedom Committee.

Inter American Press Association (IAPA). The IAPA grew out of meetings between Western Hemisphere publishers in the mid-1920s and promoted Anglo-American philosophies relating to the role of the press and press freedom, bringing the organization into significant conflicts with many Latin American governments. The development of nationalist, independent, and communist opposition in Latin America during the 1950s and early 1960s led to extensive disputes and a power struggle within the organization. By the mid-1960s, the IAPA was firmly in the hands of U.S. and Western-oriented publishers in Latin America and the Caribbean.

The organization's primary functions today are to promote press freedom, to support publishers and journalists who are persecuted by Latin American governments, and to provide scholarships for the training of journalism students. The organization is headquartered in Miami, Florida.

International Federation of Journalists (IFJ). This international association located in Brussels, Belgium, represents more than two dozen national journalism unions, mainly in Western nations. It has played an active role in promoting collective bargaining and the work-related interests of journalists worldwide. It also takes actions to protect journalists from being deliberately attacked or harassed while carrying out international assignments. The IFJ was formed in 1962 when its members left the International Organization of Journalists because of that organization's dominance by unions affiliated with communist parties.

International Federation of Newspaper Publishers (FIEJ). This organization represents the international interests of newspaper publishers' associations in more than two dozen mostly Western nations. Founded in 1948, the group promotes interests of conservative, commercially based publishers and a Western, liberal press philosophy. Among its main interests is the promotion of international marketing of commercial newspapers. The group is headquartered in Paris.

International Organization of Journalists (IOJ). This international organization representing about two dozen national journalists' unions worldwide was founded in 1946 and succeeded a similar group, the Federation of Journalists, that had existed prior to World War II.

The group originally represented both Eastern and Western journalists' unions. Western members broke away and formed the International Federation of Journalists in 1962, during the height of the cold war, when Eastern groups grew to dominate the organization.

Today, the group represents mainly Eastern European national unions, but also some unions in developing nations with strong links to the Eastern bloc. The group conducts communications development and training programs in the developing world to improve media capabilities and practices.

International Press Institute (IPI). The International Press Institute was founded in 1950 to promote Western liberal ideals of press freedom and to help developing nations to improve journalistic practices. The institute's headquarters are located in London.

One of the most active groups in international journalism development, the IPI has been highly successful in gaining financial support for its activities from private media companies worldwide. Early efforts included touring consultants who conducted seminars and in-house training for newspaper staffs in Asia. That program evolved into a team of specialists who toured to teach journalism techniques and management practices used by European and North American newspapers. The organization also worked to turn political papers into commercially based papers.

The IPI became highly active in Africa, helping to establish journalism training centers in Nairobi and Lagos and helping Africans to take over and operate existing media after decolonization and to establish new papers and broadcasting operations. Later, the IPI begin offering specialized journalism training in economic, health, and agricultural journalism.

International Telecommunication Union (ITU). Founded in 1932 by the merger of intergovernmental organizations concerned with telephone, telegraph, and radio communication, the ITU became a special agency of the United Nations in 1947. Its purpose is to coordinate electromagnetic frequency allocation among nations, to reduce transmission interference, to improve telecommunication equipment and compatibility, and to promote telecommunications development worldwide.

A major function of the ITU is carried out by its World Administrative Radio Conferences, which establish standards and allocate frequencies for satellite, broadcast, mobile, marine, and aeronautical communications worldwide. Other important functions of the union are carried out by the International Frequency Registration Board (IFRB), which records spectrum use worldwide and performs the task of keeping users from interfering with one another. In addition, the ITU operates consulting committees that study and make recommendations on international television, radio, telephone, telegraph, and satellite issues and technology.

Movement of Non-Aligned Countries (MNAC). This is an organization made up of new and developing nations formed to provide self-help and to create an economic and political bloc of nations alternative to the East-West bloc. The MNAC members, through a number of international conferences and communications development efforts, became the instigator of what became known as the new world information and communication order.

Throughout the 1970s and 1980s, MNAC and its members and supporters have played an active role in getting other international organizations, especially UNESCO, to deal with communications issues. Other activities of this group of nations have included the establishment of the Non-Aligned News Agency (NANA) and communications training and improvement programs in member nations.

UNESCO. The United Nations Educational, Scientific, and Cultural Organization was established in 1946 with the support of Western nations, led by the United States, to promote the flow of information and development of communication and educational facilities and exchange. As its major funder and supporter, the United States was instrumental in promoting the organization's agenda in such matters based on liberal, Western philosophy.

After significant efforts to help redevelop communication, cultural, and educational facilities destroyed in the Second World War, UNESCO began addressing the needs of nations in other parts of the world, particularly new nations emerging from the decolonization process. It provided extensive assistance in developing basic communications facilities and international satellite communications systems.

Nations that were assisted by or needed assistance from UNESCO rapidly joined and became active in its operations. Because the agency operated differently from the main United Nations structure, it gave the decolonized nations power equal to that of the developed nations and superpowers through a "one nation, one vote" system. It had no balancing structure like the Security Council, in which the large nations control operations and can exercise veto power. As the last quarter of the twentieth century approached, developing nations joined together to use UNESCO as a sounding board and agent for their concerns and tipped the balance of voting power away from the developed nations. Many of the conflicts that have arisen in UNESCO in recent years were brought about by the growing power of nonaligned countries that combined to promote their national interests and to assert that they need not be identified with either the Western or Eastern blocs of the developed countries. UNESCO is headquartered in Paris.

The organization established the International Programme for the Development of Communications (IPDC) in 1978, as a quasi-independent effort to provide assistance to nations in studying, planning, and improving domestic and international communications needs, coordinating assistance in developing systems among nations, and providing financial aid.

World Press Freedom Committee (WPFC). This group was formed in 1976 to help coordinate the activities of nearly three dozen Western journalists' and publishers' groups and media companies regarding the NWICO. Principal organizers were the International Press Institute and the Inter American Press Association.

The group declared its intentions "to be a watchdog for the free world media" by opposing government interference, censorship, attacks on journalists, and efforts by international bodies that would restrict press freedom.

The committee also recognized the validity of many of the complaints and problems outlined by developing nations and set up a program of on-the-job training, seminars, and visiting consultants to help media in the developing world. In addition, it provided assistance to journalism training programs. The WPFC headquarters is at the Newspaper Center, Reston, Virginia.

THE KEY CONTROVERSY: NWICO

No international communication issue has generated more controversy in the past two decades than efforts by members of MNAC and UNESCO to promulgate the New World Information and Communication Order. NWICO is not a unified, well-defined program for change in communications but rather a philosophical approach to the role of communications that has become manifest in various international discussions and documents. It is based on the idea that unless communication capabilities are significantly improved, less developed nations cannot accomplish meaningful economic, political, and social development that will improve the standard of living of their citizens. Proponents of the concept have argued that successful development is dependent on improvements in two areas, international communications and domestic communications.

Proponents of the NWICO argue that the economic interdependence of nations, recognized only in the second half of the twentieth century, gives advantages to nations that have strong international communications capabilities involving telephone, data transmission, and satellite communications. The ability of citizens of nations rapidly to gather and transmit information of all kinds, including news, affects their ability to participate in world commerce and political and cultural life.

Leaders of the nonaligned nations began studying needs and objectives. Because of policies of developed nations and private ownership of much communications technology worldwide, they quickly understood that access or equal access to international communications technology and capabilities was required.

Development officials also understood the need to develop internal communications capabilities, ranging from telephone to broadcasting systems. A significant focus of MNAC and international development discussions soon became developing broadcast and print media that would be used primarily for educational and informational purposes, rather than entertainment. In addition, they envisioned use of these media to help build national unity and a sense of community.

The basic philosophical tenet of NWICO is that each nation must become self-reliant in communications capabilities so that it is not dependent on other nations and thus cannot be held subservient. The NWICO also adheres to the ideal that in developing domestic communications capabilities, each nation has the right to determine what the communications system within its boundaries will be, what should be communicated, and to what end. Implicit in this ideal is the view that there are differences in communications functions in nations and that the differences are particularly evident in less developed nations that wish consciously to use media as tools to promote national economic growth, to develop and preserve national culture, and to create a cohesive national identity among diverse and often antagonistic ethnic, tribal, and religious groups.

Efforts by MNAC to draw UNESCO into efforts to promote and achieve such international communications changes have resulted in an international struggle in that worldwide organization that has pitted many Western nations against nations in MNAC and the Eastern bloc. The concept of using media and communications systems in such a fashion conflicted with Western liberal views of press freedom and desires to limit government influence on and control of communications. As a result, Western nations, especially the United States and others with highly commercialized, nongovernmental communications systems, responded to some NWICO ideas and developments negatively.

During the late 1970s and early 1980s, much of the discussion became couched in cold war rhetoric that included charges that the NWICO was Soviet-inspired and -supported. The Soviet Union and its allies admittedly supported the concepts behind the NWICO and provided assistance to MNAC nations in helping to make it a significant UNESCO issue. It is clear, however, that MNAC was the instigator of the concept. Support from the Soviet Union, Eastern bloc nations, China, and other communist nations came because communist philosophy embraces the use of communications as an agent for social change and ideological development. These nations were also unwilling to oppose the NWICO's philosophy of self-determination, which they, along with the United States, support but have rarely followed.

The outlines of the NWICO began to emerge in the 1960s as the decolonized nations were established. By the early 1970s, the director general of UNESCO, Amadou-Mahtar M'Bow of Senegal, suggested that the organization begin supporting the MNAC efforts to formulate national communication policies. When the general conference of UNESCO was held in 1972, the Soviet Union presented the "Draft Declaration on the Use of the Mass Media," which supported the use of media as a tool of the state instead of its operation as an independent institution. In 1974, discussion of the issue became highly politicized, and the United States and three dozen nations, mostly Western, boycotted discussions when UNESCO delegates voted to place in the preamble to the declaration language equating Zionism with racism.

Action on the declaration was delayed for several years as the leadership of UNESCO consulted and mediated disputes between the West and the developing and Eastern nations. The result was the establishment of UNESCO's International Commission for the Study of Communications Problems, popularly known as the McBride Commission because it was led by the respected Irish diplomat Sean McBride.

UNESCO's 1978 Declaration

While the commission's work was under way, UNESCO's general conference in 1978 agreed on the "Declaration of Fundamental Principles concerning the Contribution of the Mass Media to Strengthening Peace and International Understanding, to the Promotion of Human Rights, and to Countering Racialism, Apartheid and Incitement of War." The declaration was viewed as a victory by Western, Eastern, and nonaligned nations alike. Western nations were pleased that it removed earlier indications that the press should be controlled by the state. Eastern and communist states were pacified because it did not contain criticisms of the use of journalism to promote political agendas. Nonaligned nations supported the declaration because it included promises of technical assistance in the development of communications.

News of UNESCO's efforts gained the attention of Western news agencies and publishers' organizations, especially the International Press Institute and International Federation of Newspaper Publishers, which began organizing and pressuring their governments for not taking a strong stance against certain elements emerging from the discussion of international communication policy. Western journalists' groups argued that UNESCO's activities were merely a means of legitimizing government control of media and that the organization was paying too much attention to the power and use of the press and not enough attention to freedom of the press. Leading these critics was the International Federation of Journalists. In order to monitor developments and organize opposition more effectively, the publishers', broadcasters', and journalists' organizations joined together to form the World Press Freedom Committee.

The McBride Commission Report

In 1980, the general conference of UNESCO in Belgrade, Yugoslavia, heard the findings of the McBride Commission on contemporary communications problems and international and domestic communications issues. The report made 82 recommendations related to the human right to communicate, needs for diversity of opinion, free flow of information, and access to news. It included recognition of the need for each nation to develop comprehensive national communication policies and structures including news agencies, broadcasting networks, book publishers, and communications training institutions, and warned nations against dependence on foreign information sources.

Some Western nations, led by the United States, were troubled by elements in the report that urged governments to set up communications agencies and showed a bias against private communications media. Although agreeing that concentration of ownership and media mortality due to the competitive economic system were undesirable elements of commercialized media, representatives of some Western nations argued that these negative elements were balanced by the political freedom obtained by not having a state monopoly on media.

Despite such reservations, the Belgrade conference unanimously passed a resolution that set down the principles of the NWICO. The resolution called for media to be responsible and for a balanced flow of information worldwide. The resolution and NWICO are based on the view that the major Western news services dominate coverage of the world, set the world news agenda, and distort the picture of the world by focusing on news in developed nations. In addition, it embraced the view that dominance of the world's communication by Western information and entertainment media threatens national identity and slows development because it is based on Western attitudes and interests. The NWICO also criticizes the definition of news used by Western media for its focus on negative developments such as political instability, natural disasters, and policy failures. This emphasis, NWICO supporters argued, harms efforts to foster social, economic, and political values that promote development and to convey information on domestic and international programs designed to improve education, family planning, agricultural practices, and industrialization.

Western Reactions

Although the Belgrade resolution received wide support, few people were happy with it in its entirety. Western diplomats, especially those from the Federal Republic of Germany, the United Kingdom, and the United States, disagreed with phrases that the developing world and Soviet bloc interpreted as giving UNESCO the right to regulate news organizations and acknowledging news as a commodity that governments could control. They also perceived the concept of a balanced flow of information as conflicting with the free flow of information. Developing nations and the Soviet block were unhappy with watered-down provisions that did not provide funds for procurement of communications technology for developing nations or provide significant cost advantages in the use of international communications systems.

The unease of Western nations about UNESCO's efforts increased in 1981 when the organization sponsored a meeting to discuss a proposal for a commission for the protection of journalists. Although representatives of the West were concerned about attacks on journalists worldwide and agreed that international standards for identifying and protecting journalists might be helpful, they disagreed with proposals that the commission set regulations for journalists, be empowered to investigate reporters' conduct, and revoke identification cards of journalists not adhering to international standards.

Concern about the possible creation of such a commission led representatives of news media and journalistic organizations from Western nations and their supporters to meet in Talloires, France, at the invitation of the WPFC and Tufts University to organize opposition to

UNESCO plans. As part of their meeting they issued the "Declaration of Talloires," which upheld press freedom and the right to be informed as basic human rights, expressed concerns about censorship, and indicated opposition to international and national efforts that elevated government interests above individual interests by requiring journalists to obtain licenses or to adhere to codes of ethics or behavior.

The Western media groups involved in the NWICO discussions gave heavy coverage to the declaration, as they had to UNESCO meetings dealing with the concepts during the late 1970s and early 1980s. The coverage focused significantly on perceived threats to their abilities to cover world events and press freedoms. Several reviews of coverage, including one by the U.S. National News Council, revealed that the coverage of UNESCO's activities was highly distorted and biased.

Efforts to counteract the Western media attack on NWICO were launched by journalists' organizations in countries associated with MNAC and the Eastern bloc. The International Organization of Journalists, Federation of Arab Journalists, Federation of Latin American Journalists, and others asserted that the NWICO and its provisions were not intended to support censorship or control of communications but to improve communications. The campaign did not comfort or dissuade opponents from their positions, however.

The news coverage and pressure from Western media and journalists' groups soon gained significant support from the Reagan administration in the United States and the Thatcher administration in the United Kingdom, due in part to their strong antigovernment ideologies. Concurrently, criticism of the growth of the bureaucracy of UNESCO and the unwillingness or inability of its leadership to control its expenses was rising within the international community. In 1983, the United States responded by withdrawing from UNESCO, followed by the United Kingdom in 1984, citing the body's ideological outlook on communications as inappropriate and the failure of the organization to manage its finances. The withdrawal cost the organization more than $50 million annually; the United States had been its largest financial contributor.

The financial crisis created by the departure of the two Western members and other pressing matters held the attention of UNESCO's staff through the mid-1980s, and implementation of the International Programme for the Development of Communications (IPDC) kept staff and others interested in communications from reviving the NWICO debate significantly. By the late 1980s, the impetus for using UNESCO to promote NWICO had waned, and the new secretary general, Federico

Mayor, promulgated a communication plan that did not include most of the elements that have disturbed Western nations and journalists. Whether supporters of the concepts will revive significant UNESCO activities aimed at establishing the NWICO in international policies and programs remains to be seen, but their will and ability to do so appears limited at this time.

PART II

The World's Regions

Now that we have surveyed the world's journalism from a panoramic perspective, let us turn to more specific details. The authors featured in Part II, all of whom have personal experience with their parts of the world, provide a multitude of facts and figures from various sources. Certain aspects of their regions' media systems may be covered in more or less detail; such variability is unavoidable in a world survey book. Nevertheless, the material in these chapters is more than ample to provide a thorough introduction to the journalism of the world.

Six main regions of the world are highlighted in the six chapters making up Part II: Europe, Middle East and North Africa, Africa, Asia and the Pacific, Latin America and the Caribbean, and North America. The most advanced media systems of the world just happen to be in the first of these regions (Europe) and the last (North America). In between, the reader will be introduced to the Middle East and North Africa (a sprawling region that has the common ingredient of being predominantly Arabic), then to Africa (sub-Saharan or the mainly black African nations), then to the other side of the world to Asia and the Pacific, then back to the last big regions—Latin America and the Caribbean and North America (Canada and the United States).

Some of these chapters are more detailed than others because of the relative differences in regional media development. For example, Chapter 5 by Manny Paraschos undertakes the giant task of describing the media and media problems of Western and Eastern Europe. Journalistic development in Europe is old and well developed, and Chapter 5 attempts to convey the richness and complexity of the media scene in Europe, especially Western Europe. The political and economic situation in Eastern Europe was changing rapidly at the time of this book's publication; nevertheless, the basic information about the media in Chapter 5 should not change substantially in the next half dozen years.

Europe has the world's most diversified media system, with a staggering range of publications and broadcasting alternatives in various stages of development. Media from the most serious to the gaudiest and most sensational reach huge audiences. Attitudes toward press freedom, media financing, social responsibility, and press-government relations vary substantially from one region to another. Indeed, Europe is a fascinating mosaic of media options and philosophies.

Christine Ogan of Indiana University deals, in Chapter 6, with a colorful and potentially explosive part of the world where religious and nationalistic forces clash around the eastern and southern fringes of the Mediterranean Sea. Arabic media systems prevail in the sprawling area from North Africa to the Middle East. Instability in the region has given the media a propagandistic cast different from other regions of the world. Chapter 6 explores the various forces affecting journalism in this region.

Chapter 7, by L. John Martin of the University of Maryland, details the struggles of the media in Central Africa and the well-developed but politically troubled journalism of southern Africa. It examines the problems of the ex-colonial nations, their struggles for nationhood and a sense of nationalism, their largely broadcast menus of media material, their problems with press freedom, and their attempts to establish a viable system of journalism education. The journalistic media range from the primitive, as in Chad, to the more sophisticated ones emerging in black African countries such as Kenya in the east and the Ivory Coast in the west. The most advanced media system in Africa, in the Republic of South Africa, is described in considerable detail.

Two journalism scholars with long experience in Asia have teamed up in Chapter 8, on Asia and the Pacific. Anne Cooper Chen of Ohio University and Anju Grover Chaudhary of Howard University divide Asia into two basic areas, east and south, and provide excellent overviews of journalism there. Of all the continents and world regions, Asia has the most pluralistic journalistic systems. Rather primitive media like those in Thailand or in Nepal coexist with some of the most sophisticated, literate, and progressive media in the world, like those in Japan, Hong Kong, and Singapore. As in the Middle East and North Africa, many ideologies, languages, and religions contribute to the patchwork of the media quilt in Asia.

Chapter 9 returns the reader to the Western Hemisphere, to Latin America, the vast area from the Rio Grande south. Latin America's media systems are more homogeneous than those found in Asia or Africa, due largely to a combination of direct European and North American influences and the old, print-oriented traditions of Europe's Iberian peninsula. Of course, one important factor in Latin America is the dominance of a single language, Spanish. A few other languages (Portuguese, French, English) make minor inroads in the region's journalism, but Spanish-language broadcast and print media have significant impact across national borders. Consequently, audiences are large both for radio and television and for magazines and newspapers. Three specialists in Latin America have collaborated on this chapter: Michael Salwen and Bruce Garrison, both of Florida's University of Miami, and Robert Buckman, of the University of Southwestern Louisiana.

In Chapter 10, Paul Adams, of California State University at Fresno, and Catherine McKercher, of Carleton University in Canada, deal with the journalism of North America. Adams surveys the journalism of the United States, while McKercher deals with Canadian journalism. This last chapter, on the world's most dynamic media markets, fulfills the promise of *Global Journalism* to cover the entire world.

CHAPTER 5

Europe

Manny Paraschos

WESTERN EUROPE

Western Europe today is largely a media-rich, high-technology continent with its own traditions in journalism, its own standards and practices, and its own press heroes and villains. Although Europeans follow American media developments closely and often adopt modified versions of them, they have their own journalistic style and priorities that determine news and news writing and presentation, radio and television programming, press-government relationships, advertising types and function, media entertainment, media access, and even media technology.

HISTORICAL HIGHLIGHTS

From the days of Johannes Gutenberg's movable type in 1440, Central Europe was destined to become the birthplace of the mass-circulation newspaper as we know it today. *Avis Relation oder Zeitung* of Augsburg in 1609 was followed by the *Gazette de France* in 1631 and the *London Gazette* in 1665.

The second generation of newspapers was inspired by the ideas of the American and French revolutions and appeared in the late eighteenth century. Switzerland's *Neue Zürcher Zeitung* was founded in 1780, the *Times* of London in 1788, and the *Allgemeine Zeitung* of

93

Tübingen and later Frankfurt in 1798. Nineteenth-century newspapers, aided by the invention of the telephone and the telegraph, became sensation and circulation seekers. France's *La Presse* in 1836 cut its price to half that of the others and started the "penny press" era of Western European newspapers. In the meantime, newspapers appeared and disappeared all over Europe from Norway to Greece.

The first part of the twentieth century, despite two world wars and economic upheaval, was a time of growth for most of the Western European press. Newspapers in West Germany and Italy were held back by Hitler and Mussolini but survived. The postwar era saw the greatest expansion in the history of the Western European press, followed by a readjustment in the 1950s, which marked the beginning of contemporary publishing and the integration of the electronic media into the daily lives of Western Europeans.

Western Europe's high literacy rates (approximately 98 percent) and historically rooted print orientation have yielded the world's highest newspaper and magazine readership; different lifestyles have resulted in different, compartmentalized viewing and listening patterns; and differences in culture and media appreciation have produced a press system that is quite different from that of the United States.

Although the democracies of Western Europe tend to guarantee freedom of expression and of the press in a variety of legal ways, their press does face more legal obstacles than the American press. Furthermore, since the government watchdog function of the media is neither conceived nor exercised in Western Europe as it is in the United States, the role of the press in those societies is different.

In comparison to American newspapers, newspapers in Western Europe tend to be more political and more openly partisan, to be more analytical even in news stories, to have fewer pages, to use smaller type, to feature more foreign news, and to carry less advertising and hence earn less advertising income. In most countries, the newspapers of the capital city dominate the national press.

Regardless of the standards used to evaluate newspaper quality, however, some of the world's best newspapers can be found in Western Europe—the *Times* and the *Guardian* of Great Britain, France's *Le Monde* and *Le Figaro*, West Germany's *Frankfurter Allgemeine Zeitung* and *Süddeutsche Zeitung*, Switzerland's *Neue Zürcher Zeitung*, Italy's *Corriere della Sera* and *La Repubblica*, Denmark's *Berlingske Tidende*, Sweden's *Svenska Dagbladet*, Norway's *Aftenposten*, and *Die Presse* in Austria are all examples of newspapers practicing superb journalism.

Danger signs for Western European newspaper publishing multiplied in the 1980s as television commercialization and privatization

became legally possible and profitable and newspaper consolidation and chain acquisition gained unprecedented prominence. As the Western European advertising budget started seriously to slip away from newspapers (from 76 percent in 1975 to 64 percent in 1984), the tabloid wave, with its emphasis on sensationalist and soft news angles, followed, and news-entertainment, as practiced by television and by American newspapers, most notably *USA Today*, became a concept that Western European editors could no longer afford to ignore.

Television, by contrast, in both broadcast or cable form, is flourishing in Western Europe. Although much of the talent still comes from the newspapers, European television in the 1980s hit new heights of maturity and dynamism. Almost all European countries have their own radio and television broadcast services, and the European Broadcasting Union serves as the linking network for all of them. Satellites today connect Eurovision (the television network of the EBU) with other similar networks worldwide, and CNN (Cable News Network) is fast becoming a household word on the Continent.

A couple of interesting aspects of Western European television are that broadcasting services operate only part of the day, normally in the afternoon and evening (the average viewing time in Western Europe is less than three hours daily) and that it is not unusual for the news shows (normally two per day) to run longer than the allotted time, depending on the day's news load. In most systems, advertisements are grouped together and shown at the start or end of programs.

PRINT MEDIA

Scandinavia

Noncommunist Europe's highest newspaper readership can be found in Scandinavia, where Finnish, Swedish, Norwegian, Icelandic, and Danish daily newspapers average sales of 474 copies per 1,000 persons. The United States average is 267, and the world figure is 110.

The strong democratic and populist traditions in these countries have nurtured a newspaper system whose freedom of expression, access to government, source protection rights, and self-regulation practices have earned it worldwide respect. It was in Scandinavia, for example, that the right of reply was institutionalized, press councils were refined, and the press ombudsman (watchdog) concept originated.

Furthermore, the egalitarian nature of the political system of these countries has produced an elaborate scheme of press subsidies in order to ensure the preservation of voice pluralism, the survival of newspapers in remote regions, and/or a measure of continued employment in an industry facing revolutionary technological changes and the threat of chain acquisitions. These subsidies range from tax, postal, and transportation rate discounts to direct payments through grants, government advertising, and production improvement incentives.

However, the biggest difference a casual American observer would notice is likely to be the relative absence of "adversarial" press-government relationships in Scandinavia. This is mainly due to the general public's trust in the institution of government in that part of the world and to a well-established spirit of respect for individual rights and for the government's obligation to be socially responsible to its citizens.

Because of historic ties between newspapers and political movements, today's Scandinavian newspapers have, in varying degrees, obvious partisan outlooks on news and views, but recent economic trends have toned down some of these practices. The most apparent party press in Scandinavia is the labor press.

With minor exceptions, newspapers published in the capital cities of these Nordic nations predominate in their respective countries in both influence and circulation. In the 1980s, a trend toward tabloids gained momentum and most of the Scandinavian circulation leaders today publish in that format. The publishing technology revolution created considerable animosity between management and the labor unions in the early 1980s, but due to participatory management techniques and government-industry retraining projects, little of that is evident today, and state-of-the-art equipment can be found even at the smallest of newspapers.

In spite of its elaborate press subsidy system, mainly supported through advertising taxes, the number of dailies in Sweden declined from 114 in 1970 to 99 in 1989. Nevertheless, Sweden still has the highest number of dailies in Scandinavia, and its press is considered one of the most dynamic and respected in Europe.

Sweden's highest-circulating newspaper is Stockholm's afternoon tabloid *Expressen* (circ. 565,000), a postwar publication that supports the Liberal party and is interested in popular topics and national news displayed through the use of bold typography, graphics, and photos. Its main competitor is another Stockholm afternoon tabloid, *Aftonbladet* (circ. 391,000), one of Sweden's oldest newspapers, a Social Democratic party supporter, more sensational than *Expressen*. The more serious and influential part of the Swedish press consists of two Stockholm morning broadsheets, *Dagens Nyheter* (circ. 413,000), a well-edited, financially successful, liberal paper with several zone sections and a balance of local, national, and international news, and *Svenska Dagbladet* (circ. 226,000), a well-designed, national and international news publication with conservative leanings that many consider the nation's newspaper of record.

Most notable of Sweden's regional papers are Gothenburg's *Göteborg-Posten* (circ. 281,000), a major morning paper that devotes part of its front page to advertisements; and Malmö's *Arbetet Skåne/Arbetet Vast* (circ. 115,000) a Social Democrat supporter and *Sydsvenska Dagbladet/Snallposten* (circ. 113,000), a well-laid-out paper with a good regional, national, and international news balance. Because most of the large papers have very successful weekend editions, the weekly press is not well developed in Sweden.

The second highest number of dailies can be found in Norway, where the number of daily newspapers has remained stable (82 in 1989) in spite of recent national economic difficulties and the rise in chain ownership. Norwegian circulation figures are some of the highest in

Europe, 501 copies per 1,000 people. One important characteristic of the Norwegian press is that most of the dailies have circulations of less than 20,000 copies.

The country's most prestigious newspaper is the Oslo morning broadsheet *Afterposten* (circ. 251,000), a serious, contemporary-looking paper with a wide variety of interests, a global perspective, and conservative leanings. The national circulation leader is Oslo's *VG* (*Verdens Gang*) (circ. 317,000), a liberal morning tabloid with emphasis on popular culture and sensational topics, typography, and visuals. *VG*'s main competitor is *Dagbladet* (circ. 188,000), another Oslo tabloid with sensational appearance and emphasis on popular culture. *Arbeiderbladet* (circ. 58,000), Oslo's third major tabloid and the official organ of the nation's Labor party, has a modern appearance and offers extensive coverage of national and regional news of interest to the working class.

Regional leaders, all located in different geographic areas of the country and serving distinctly different populations, are Bergen's *Bergens Tidende* (circ. 98,600), Trondheim's *Adresseavisen* (circ. 87,000), Stavanger's *Stavanger Aftenblad* (circ. 66,000), Kristiansand's *Faedrelandsvennen* (circ. 45,000), and Tromsö's *Nordlys* (circ. 32,000).

Probably because the Finns are avid newspaper readers (they lead all Western Europeans with sales of 532 copies per 1,000 persons, and in Europe they are second only to the East Germans), the Finnish press has shown remarkable stability in the past quarter century, varying little from the 68 published dailies. It, too, is characterized by a plethora of small papers but also by its bilingualism (approximately 20 percent of its dailies are published in Swedish, Finland's second language).

The nation's most prestigious newspaper, Helsinki's broadsheet *Helsingin Sanomat* (circ. 443,000), is a conservative publication with serious news and editorials, but its front page usually is covered with ads! Second in national circulation is the tabloid *Ilta-Sanomat* (circ. 205,000); third is Tampere's broadsheet *Aamulehti* (circ. 141,000), the organ of the National Coalition party; fourth is the Turku (Åbo) independent broadsheet *Turun Sanomat* (circ. 131,000); and fifth is the Helsinki broadsheet *Uusi Suomi* (circ. 94,000). The leader of the Swedish-language dailies is Helsinki's broadsheet *Hufvudstadsbladet* (circ. 66,000). In addition to the Tampere and Turku dailies already mentioned, other leading regional dailies are Oulu's *Keleva* (circ. 91,000), Kuopio's *Savon Sanomat* (circ. 87,000), and Jyväskylä's *Keskisuomalainen* (circ. 78,000).

The Danish daily press has lost some ground since 1970 (58 dailies shrank to 46 by 1989), but it continues to foster a dynamic and prosperous group of Copenhagen dailies with national appeal and diverse quality. The country's most prestigious daily is Copenhagen's morning broadsheet *Berlingske Tidende* (circ. 133,000), a serious, conservative newspaper with strong interest in financial, political, and cultural news. It contrasts with the country's most popular newspaper, *Ekstra Bladet* (circ. 232,000), a crusading, sensational, liberal tabloid. Between these two leaders, there are the Copenhagen tabloid *Aktuell* (circ. 115,000), the world's oldest continuously published labor paper, which is associated with the Social Democratic party; *B.T.* (circ. 209,000), the sensational evening tabloid sister to *Berlingske Tidende*; *Politiken* (circ. 157,000), a serious, well-designed, and well-written liberal morning broadsheet; *Information* (circ. 31,000), an issue-oriented, liberal newspaper with a clean, modular appearance and analytical pieces on national and international news; and *Borsen* (circ. 43,000), a tabloid version of the *Wall Street Journal.*

Distinguished among the regional papers are Århus's *Jyllands-Posten* (circ. 128,000), the first regional paper with a national marketing strategy, which offers a wide variety of news in a well-designed, contemporary package; Ålborg's morning *Ålborg Stiftstidende* (circ. 74,000), the oldest provincial Danish paper (established in 1767); Århus's evening *Århus Stiftstidende* (circ. 72,000); and Odense's evening *Fyens Stiftstidende* (circ. 72,000).

Iceland's main daily is *Morgunbladid* (circ. 40,000), a conservative, serious, clean-looking morning broadsheet that emphasizes national and international news. *DV*, the nation's main afternoon paper, is another conservative broadsheet, but its layout and news coverage are less serious than its competitor's. Political opposition to these two newspapers is provided by *NT* (*Nu Timmin*) (circ. 18,000), a morning broadsheet that features sensational typography and supports Progressive party policies, and *Althydubladid* (circ. 3,000), the organ of the Social Democratic party of Iceland.

The periodical press, much like the weekly press, is not as well developed in Scandinavia as in the other Western European nations. Although some quality special-interest magazines, mainly business publications, can be found in Sweden, Norway, and Finland, most tend to be of moderate quality in writing, content selection, reproduction, design, and size. Finland leads in periodical production with more than 4,000 titles, closely followed by Norway and Sweden.

Britain

Although in the 1980s its newspaper readership declined by about 5 percent, the United Kingdom continues to have one of the world's highest newspaper circulation figures—411 copies per 1,000 persons. The aggressiveness and diversity—in content, appearance, and marketing—of London's dailies, which dominate the national press, are the main reasons. The competition among both individual papers and newspaper groups, the result of a strong chain acquisition trend in the 1970s and 1980s, is very keen and often embarrassing for the competitors as sloppiness and carelessness reign over sound news judgment and accuracy. London, however, where one can find some of the best and some of the worst newspapers in the Western world, continues to be an extraordinary newspaper town.

London is home to 12 general-interest dailies, 3 special-interest dailies, and 9 major weeklies. The notorious, sensational London tabloids, which circulate in the millions, are led by Rupert Murdoch's *Sun* (circ. 4.2 million) and followed by the *Mirror* (circ. 3.1 million), the *Daily Mail* (circ. 1.7 million), the *Daily Express* (circ. 1.6 million), the *Daily Telegraph* (circ. 1.1 million), and the *Daily Star* (circ. 1 million). The world-respected morning papers—the *Times*, a serious, analytical, gray-looking publication with a conservative bent, and the *Guardian*, a lively, thoughtful, liberal paper—have circulations of 441,000 and 447,000, respectively. The only major remaining evening paper, the *London Evening Standard*, which was born from the merger of the old *Evening News* and *Evening Standard*, is one of few London papers still being headquartered on famed Fleet Street and has a circulation of 470,000. Two of London's newest arrivals, Rupert Murdoch's *Today* and the *Independent*, both contemporary-looking morning dailies, sell 502,000 and 378,000 copies, respectively.

The most significant specialty London dailies are the *Financial Times* (circ. 282,000) and *Sporting Life* (circ. 95,000). The weeklies are dominated by another Murdoch paper, the very sensational *News of the World*, which boasts a circulation of 5.3 million. Important weeklies are the quality *Sunday Times* (circ. 1.3 million), the *Observer* (circ. 730,000), and the *Sunday Telegraph* (circ. 706,000). In addition, most of the city's successful dailies have Sunday editions. London is also home to the country's main communist newspaper, the *Morning Star* (cir. 29,000).

Most of the successful regional papers have managed to compete well with the London national papers by simply publishing in the afternoon. The most notable of the regional papers are the *Birmingham Evening Mail* (circ. 235,000), Bristol's *Evening Post* (circ. 110,000), Leeds's *Yorkshire Post* (circ. 93,000), the *Liverpool Echo* (circ. 204,000), Newcastle's *Evening Chronicle* (circ. 148,000), Edinburg's *Evening News* (circ. 114,000) and *Scotsman* (circ. 90,000), the *Belfast Telegraph* (circ. 147,000), Dublin's *Irish Independent* (circ. 151,000), and Cardiff's *South Wales Echo* (circ. 97,000).

The strength of the weeklies may be the reason for the absence of

American-style newsmagazines in Britain. However, the *Economist,* the *News Statesman and Nation,* and the *Spectator* are three quality magazines that command international respect. Enjoying an outstanding international reputation is *Punch*, Britain's humor magazine, whose caustic barbs entertain readers worldwide.

Switzerland

Another of Europe's great newspaper-reading nations is Switzerland, where newspapers sell 387 copies per 1,000 persons and where one can find two of the world's most respected dailies, the German-language *Neue Zürcher Zeitung* (circ. 156,000) and the French-language *Journal de Genève* (circ. 20,000), both serious morning tabloids. Swiss newspapers, most of which appear in German or in French, offer a good mixture of local, national, and international news, editorials, and serious cultural material. The German-language press tends to be more conservative in appearance than the French-language press. Although Zurich is the nation's press capital with eight dailies, several Swiss cities have more than two competing dailies, and the press, in general, appears to be decentralized and made up of many medium-to-small publications evenly spread around the country.

The country's circulation leaders are German-language, Zurich-based dailies: *Blick* (circ. 365,000), *Tages Anzeiger* (circ. 260,000), and *Tagblatt der Stadt Zürich* (circ. 196,000). Other major dailies are Bern's *Berner Zeitung* (circ. 122,000), Basel's *Basler Zeitung* (circ. 113,000), and Lucerne's *Luzerner Neueste Nachrichten* (circ. 57,000), all in German. The largest French-language papers are Lausanne's *24 Heures* (circ. 97,000) and *Le Matin* (circ. 53,000) and Geneva's *La Suisse* (circ. 70,000) and *La Tribune de Genève* (circ. 64,000). A segment of the Swiss daily press represents the views of the Catholic church. The most notable of these newspapers is Fribourg's *La Liberté* (circ. 33,000). The dominant weekly is Zurich's *Neues Sonntags Blatt* (circ. 440,000).

Austria

In spite of a strong regional press, the Viennese dailies *Neue Kronen Zeitung* (circ. 1.3 million) and *Kurier* (circ. 402,000), with left- and right-of-center orientations, respectively, dominate the Austrian newspaper scene. Vienna is also the seat of one of Europe's oldest and most respected papers, the conservative *Die Presse* (circ. 69,000). Notable regional papers are Graz's *Steirerkrone: Neue Kroner Zeitung* (circ. 135,000) and *Kleine Zeitung* (circ. 155,000) and Salzburg's *Salzburger Nachrichten* (circ. 67,000). Austria also has a number of Catholic and foreign-language newspapers as well as several socialist newspapers. Vienna also has a communist daily, *Volksstimme* (circ. 40,000).

West Germany

One of the most dynamic and best-quality press systems in the world is that of West Germany. The healthy geographic decentralization of the nation's approximately 1,200 dailies is counteracted by their great economic centralization in the hands of just 300 publishers, many of whom, utilizing skeleton staffs, market the same paper to several towns by localizing its first few pages.

The nation's leading daily, one of Europe's best, is *Frankfurter Allgemeine Zeitung* (circ. 420,000), a gray, old-fashioned-looking newspaper with a conservative inclination and serious writing on a variety of elitist topics from politics and economics to books and culture. Another equally respected daily is Munich's *Süddeutsche Zeitung* (circ. 408,500), a contemporary-looking, easy-to-read, well-written liberal publication. Normally considered the third leading national daily, Hamburg's *Die Welt* (circ. 275,000) is a serious-looking, conservative paper with strong coverage of Bonn and a good mixture of national and international news. The country's circulation leader is another Hamburg publication, *Bild Zeitung*, a sensational tabloid that publishes 22 different regional editions and has Western Europe's highest circulation, 5.9 million.

West Germany has an American-style pluralistic, albeit more openly partisan, press system. It includes several foreign-language dailies, labor dailies, and special-interest dailies, most notable of which are the nationally distributed business and financial dailies, *Handelsblatt* (circ. 136,000) of Düsseldorf and the health professionals' daily, *Die Neue Ärztliche* (circ. 61,000) of Frankfurt. Other popular dailies (mostly sensational tabloids) are West Berlin's *Berliner Zeitung* (circ. 303,000), Essen's *Westdeutsche Allgemeine WAZ* (circ. 1.3 million), Hannover's *HAZ-Total* (circ. 533,000), Cologne's *Express* (circ. 521,000), Düsseldorf's *Rheinische Post* (circ. 420,000), Nuremberg's *Nürnberger Nachrichten* (circ. 353,000), and Stuttgart's *Stuttgarter Zeitung* (circ. 243,000). Some of the most important weeklies are *Bild am Sonntag* (circ. 2.9 million) of Hamburg, *Sonntag Aktuell* (circ. 1 million) of Stuttgart, and *Die Zeit* (circ. 411,000) of Hamburg.

West Germany also has a very dynamic group of magazines, the most important of which are *Der Spiegel* (circ. 1.2 million), a newsmagazine, and three illustrated magazines, *Quick, Bunte*, and *Stern* (circ. over 1.5 million each). Much like their American equivalents, West German magazines rely on specialization for their success, so it is not surprising that some of the most popular of these magazines are on such topics as sports, consumerism, women's interests, cars, business, and entertainment.

The Netherlands

In spite of a recent decrease in the number of its dailies, the Netherlands continues to have high newspaper circulation—310 copies per 1,000 people. A strong tradition of partisan journalism dominates the press in both media centers, Amsterdam and Rotterdam. In the former, the conservatively inclined morning *De Telegraaf* (circ. 720,000) competes with the quality liberal evening *Het Parool* (circ. 114,000) and the Catholic morning *De Volkskrant* (circ. 311,000). Similarly, in Rotterdam, *Algemeen Dagblad* (circ. 417,000) publishes the evening *NRC Handelsblad* (circ. 215,000), which competes directly with *Het Vrije Volk* (circ. 154,000). Other quality dailies are The Hague's *Haagsche Courant* (circ. 177,000) and Houten's *Utrechts Nieuwsblad* (circ. 104,000).

Belgium

The Belgian press, Europe's second two-language press (Flemish and French), has lost approximately 20 percent of its newspapers and 10 percent of its circulation since 1970 and therefore finds itself on Europe's lower circulation end—224 copies per 1,000 people. The situation seems to be particularly alarming for the French-language dailies, which in the 1980s lost six times more circulation than the Flemish dailies. The country's most prominent dailies are Brussels's Dutch-language *De Standaard/De Nieuwe Gids* (circ. 376,000), a conservative, Christian Democrat paper; *Het Laatste Nieuws* (circ. 303,000), a liberal paper; and Ghent's *Het Volk* (circ. 105,000), another Christian Democrat supporter. The French-language papers, including the circulation leader, the independent *Le Soir* (circ. 213,000) of Brussels, are continuing to lose readers. The most notable of the regional newspapers are Antwerp's *Gazet van Antwerpen* (circ. 175,000) and Liège's *La Meuse/La Lanterne* (circ. 133,000).

France

Although home to some of Europe's, and perhaps the world's, best newspapers as well as a very successful regional press system, France does not have the high circulation figures of some its neighbors. French newspapers sell 212 copies per 1,000 people. Recent economic pressures have given rise to serious ownership concentration and are threatening the country's most important journalistic institution, *Le Monde* (circ. 343,000), whose circulation has been declining steadily. A serious, analytical, gray-looking tabloid with thoughtful commentary and left-of-center leanings, *Le Monde* appeals to an elite, intellectual audience but seems to be out of step with contemporary trends. It was established after World War II by a group of resistance journalists who were encouraged by General de Gaulle to establish a quality daily to replace the prewar *Le Temps*, in whose offices the new daily settled and on whose staff the new daily was built. An advisory board, which excludes businessmen and politicians, closely allied with the founding group, controls 40 percent of the company's stock; another 40 percent is controlled by its editorial staff, and the rest belongs to management.

Capitalizing on *Le Monde*'s troubles is the conservative *Le Figaro* (circ. 453,000). Changes made by the new owner, leading-chain president Robert Hersant, have made it the nation's circulation champion. Hersant also owns *France-Soir* (circ. 405,000), which makes him the owner of the two circulation leaders of the 11 Paris political dailies. He also owns 16 of the nation's 87 political dailies, and his papers account for 20 percent of the nation's daily circulation.

Other important Paris papers are *Le Parisien* (circ. 340,000); *Le Matin du Paris* (circ. 178,000); *L'Humanité* (circ. 117,000), the Communist party paper; and *Libération* (circ. 116,000). Many of the successful Parisian papers have weekend editions, but two very good American-style newsmagazines have managed to establish themselves in competition: *L'Express* (circ. 520,000) and *Le Nouvel Observateur* (circ. 334,000). Another successful Paris weekly is the humor magazine *Le Canard Enchaîné* (circ. 460,000). Paris is also home to many other strictly partisan political dailies as well as dailies that deal with finance, sports, medicine, and the media. Two American entities are also published there: the *International Herald Tribune* (circ. 179,000), a pan-European daily published jointly by the *New York Times* and the *Washington Post*, and *Sélection du Reader's Digest* (circ. 1.2 million).

France's major regional papers are Grenoble's *Le Dauphiné Libéré* (circ. 408,000), Rennes's *Ouest-France* (circ. 724,000), Lille's *La Voix du Nord* (circ. 374,000), Bordeaux's *Sud-Ouest* (circ. 364,000), Lyon's *Le Progrès* (circ. 359,000), Nice's *Nice-Matin* (circ. 297,000), and Strasbourg's *Les Dernières Nouvelles d'Alsace* (circ. 219,000).

The large and diverse French general magazine market is led by *Paris-Match* (circ. 900,000), an illustrated weekly that is a cross between *Time* and *Life*. Other important magazines are *Le Pélerin Magazine* (circ. 427,000), *Le Point* (circ. 337,000), and *L'Evènement du Jeudi* (circ.

115,000). Two weekly television guides, *Télé 7 Jours* and *Télépoche* have circulations of 3 and 1.8 million, respectively.

Greece

One of the most newspaper-rich countries in Europe is Greece, where more than 100 dailies are published, almost half of them in Athens. In spite of this, however, Greece has one of the lowest circulation figures (121 copies per 1,000 people) and one of the lowest-quality press systems in Europe. A fiercely partisan press, whose circulation is divided by party lines, the Greek press, with few notable exceptions, is scandal-seeking, sensational, and colorful (both in language and in appearance). Most of the national Athens dailies are tabloids, led in circulation by *Eleftheros Typos* (circ. 145,000), an unabashed rightist. The more responsible *Ta Nea* (circ. 125,000) and *Eleftherotypia* (circ. 121,000), both left of center, manage to stay away from excesses, but the well-respected and internationally known broadsheet *Kathimerini* (circ. 18,000) is having financial difficulties. The same was true of another well-recognized Greek paper, the thoughtful *To Vima* (circ. 75,000), which had to switch to weekly publication in the mid-1980s to survive. Other dailies of interest are *To Ethnos* (circ. 90,000), Greece's first tabloid, a sensational left-of-center daily; and *Apogevmatini* (circ. 113,000), an old-guard conservative. Greece has several communist, sports, and financial dailies and weeklies and is witnessing the birth of many specialized magazines.

Italy

Since Italian dailies are usually eclipsed by colorful and sensational weeklies, their circulation figures are some of Europe's lowest—82 copies per 1,000 people. Nevertheless, Italy has worldwide respected dailies: Milan's *Corriere della Sera* (circ. 800,000) and Turin's *La Stampa* (circ. 430,000). Other important papers are Rome's *La Repubblica* (circ. 700,000), a relatively young, lively written and edited paper; the Vatican's serious, official global mouthpiece, *L'Osservatore Romano* (circ. 70,000); Milan's *L'Unità*, Western Europe's most influential Communist party paper and probably the world's only communist paper to regularly run stock market quotations, and Rome's *Il Messagero* (circ. 282,000). The most notable newsmagazines are *L'Espresso* and *Panorama.*

The Italians' love for magazines explains why so many are published there—8,000. Since most readers buy more than one, the average magazine circulation figure is 1,361 copies per 1,000 people. Milan is the nation's magazine capital, as Italy's most popular magazines are published there: *Domenica de Corriere, Epoca, L'Europeo, Gente,* and *Oggi.* Most of them are sensational, colorful, gossipy, and prosperous.

In the 1980s, Italian journalists expressed serious concerns about the independence of their profession as they saw their country's industrial giants go on a media acquisition spree. Today, under various corporate names, Fiat's Giovanni Agnelli owns *La Stampa, Corriere della Sera,* and *Gazetta dello Sport;* Olivetti's Carlo de Benedetti owns *La Repubblica, L'Espresso,* and *Panorama;* Montedison chemical company's Raul Gardini owns *Il Messagero* and *Italia Oggi;* and tycoon Silvio Berlusconi, who owns businesses involved in everything from construction to insurance to movies, also owns Milan's *Il Giornale.* Critics say that such ownerships have lessened the sharpness of journalistic inquiry, especially on subjects that are dear to the owners.

Iberia

Spain and Portugal have Western Europe's weakest circulation figures—80 and 59 copies per 1,000 people, respectively. The Spanish press, however, is showing signs of strength, and quality journalism is emerging in some publications. Madrid's *El País,* the country's circulation leader with 348,000 copies sold daily, and Barcelona's *La Vanguardia* (circ. 195,000) are two respectable publications. Others of note are Madrid's old-guard *ABC* (circ. 235,000) and *AS* (circ. 153,000) and Barcelona's *El Periódico* (circ. 150,000). *Cambio,* a publication similar to *Time,* is the country's leading newsmagazine.

Portugal's leading newspapers are Lisbon's *O Seculo* (circ. 150,000), *Diario de Noticias* (circ. 100,000), and *Correiro da Manha* (circ. 78,000) and Oporto's *Jornal de Noticias* (circ. 78,000).

ELECTRONIC MEDIA

In Western Europe, as in much of the world, radio and television used to be controlled by government, but recent technologies, especially satellite and cable technologies, have opened the doors to privatization and commercialization. This unprecedented deregulation has caused in most of Western Europe something close to anarchy, which has forced even the poorest European countries into a period of adjustment as new radio and television stations emerge or die according to the marketplace. The 1980s signaled a period of historic realignment for the industry, the governments, and the publics they serve.

Almost every person in Western Europe, especially in the industrialized nations, owns a radio receiver. Britons have the most (1,157 sets per 1,000 people), followed by the Scandinavians, while those of the Iberian peninsula (Spain and Portugal) have the fewest (295 and 211 sets per 1,000 people, respectively). A similar pattern emerges in television—the United Kingdom has the most sets (534 per 1,000 people) and Portugal the fewest (157 per 1,000 people). All industrialized European countries have at least some cable service, especially in their largest cities or remotest areas.

As technology allowed the decentralization of television broadcasting, issues of politics, geography, and language prevailed, and today the majority of the Western European nations are served by more than three television networks. Most of them (20) can be found in the Federal Republic of Germany, which also has 28 different television program services and 213 stations. Italy has 15 networks, 15 program services, and 941 stations, three-quarters of which are private and regional. The United Kingdom has 13 networks, 16 program services, and 61 stations. France has seven networks, seven program services, and 246 stations. Sweden's geography requires the operation of 112 stations, although the country has only three networks, which originate four program services. At the other end of the spectrum, Austria, Ireland, Portugal, and Luxembourg have one network each, but their citizens can easily receive signals from their television-rich neighbors.

Under the slowly expiring system of government monopoly of the electronic media, countries financed their electronic media by annual fees paid by owners of television and radio sets. Commercials were banned, but when they were allowed as an effort by government to increase its media's income, they were likely to be grouped and shown in 15- to 20-minute intervals during intermissions between programs.

Today, no Western European country is without a private or commercially supported radio or television station. Most of these stations are operated either by professional commercial broadcasters for profit but in the spirit of public service or by print media, political, religious, or industrial concerns for their own purposes. Minority broadcasting has been a major point of contention of late, and national networks, especially in Scandinavia, have made serious efforts to address the issue. Under their regulations, broadcast time is reserved for minority groups, which can apply for governmental grants to fund programming expenses. Multilingual radio and television services are in operation in Belgium, the Netherlands, Finland, and Switzerland.

Government interference in broadcast news has always been a major concern in the countries with government-controlled electronic media, and hence many of them have produced elaborate systems of access to the media. The Netherlands, through the Nederlandse Om-roep Stichting (the Dutch Broadcasting Foundation), for example, uses a "pillarization" formula that allots broadcast time according to the size of nonprofit "broadcasting associations" that have been formed for that purpose.

Other countries like the United Kingdom (through the British Broadcasting Corporation), the Scandinavian countries (through Denmark's Danmarks Radio, Finland's Oy Ylesiradio AB, Iceland's Rikisut-varpid-Sjonvarp, Norway's Norsk Rikskringkasting, and Sweden's Sveriges Television AB), Belgium (through Belgische Radio en Tele-visie), and West Germany (through Arbeitsgemeinschaft der öffent-lichrechtlichen Rundfunkanstalten der Bundesrepublik Deutschland) have created largely autonomous, decentralized systems supervised by independent government bodies that have managed to remain relatively untainted over the years. France (through Radio-Télévision Française) and Greece (through Elliniki Radiophonia-Tileorasi) have systems that are highly centralized and politicized, and each new government regime usually means, automatically, a new regime at the helm of the national broadcast agency.

The best-known European broadcasting service is the veteran British Broadcasting Corporation, respected internationally not only for the high quality of its programming (radio and television) but also for the independent spirit and the integrity it has exhibited as a news organization since its inception in 1936. The corporation, which is required to broadcast "an impartial day-by-day account prepared by professional reporters of the proceedings in both houses of Parliament, is supervised by a board of 12 governors, appointed by the monarch, who in turn appoint a director general to manage the agency. Britain's Independent Broadcasting Authority was founded in 1954, when it was authorized to operate radio and television stations commercially as an alternative to the BBC.

Although Western European radio and television normally offer a larger percentage of public-affairs, cultural, informational, and educational programming than their American counterparts, entertainment is the key component of daily programming. American programs from "I Love Lucy" reruns to "Kojak" to "Dallas," "Falcon Crest," "The A-Team," and "The Cosby Show" are very popular in Europe, where they are shown mostly dubbed, except for Scandinavia, where they are shown in English, the region's second language. A more recent phenomenon is the imitation or importation of American television game shows. One of France's most popular game shows is "La Roue de la Fortune," in which a skinny brunette equivalent of Vanna White turns letters for the French equivalent of Pat Sajak. The set is the same, the rules are the same, and so are the show's ratings.

European broadcasters like the steady and relatively inexpensive flow of American programs, but as the 1992 European market integration approaches, the voices of protectionist nations such as France and Italy are strengthening. These two countries, which have the Continent's largest entertainment industries, have proposed that quotas be placed on foreign program imports in order to minimize the hazards of "cultural contamination" from abroad and to encourage locally produced programming, thus increasing employment. France has managed to establish its own import quotas, but the British and the West Germans favor the position taken by the European Community, which resists firm quotas in favor of programming subsidies. Broadcasting executives in most countries agree that it is much cheaper to buy American programs, to the tune of approximately $1 billion in 1989, than to produce locally.

One of the main beneficiaries of broadcast decentralization is the cable industry. The biggest user of cable services is Belgium, which is home to 46 cable networks with 2.8 million subscribers and 90 percent home penetration. Sweden, Norway, and Finland are the next biggest users, mainly for geographic reasons. More than 100 cable companies serve 2.5 million homes in these countries. France is the next heaviest user of cable, with 24 companies and 1 million subscribers. The United Kingdom, Austria, and Switzerland are also heavy users of cable, and the rest of the European countries are increasing their subscriber population rapidly.

In order for some national governments to keep some control over the establishment of these independent and commercial networks and stations, they have devised an application system that requires that the applicant meet certain technical and public-service standards. The result is often the subjugation of the process to partisan politics. The most notorious such instance in Western Europe was the battle for the franchise of France's La Cinq channel. La Cinq was originally awarded by the Socialists in power to leftist French millionaire Jérome Seydoux and Italian television magnate Silvio Berlusconi, but a year later, new elections yielded a Conservative government, which proceeded to cancel the original award and to give it to a consortium led by right-wing publisher Robert Hersant. Such partisan confrontations seem to be unfolding also in Greece, which awarded its first private franchises in December 1989 and January 1990.

Some of the most prominent trends in Western European radio are FM broadcasting and talk shows. Radio talk shows have become popular, especially in the highly politicized Mediterranean countries, where private radio stations are created very much in the same spirit as newspapers—to promote a political point of view.

Shortwave radio programs are sponsored by almost all Western European nations, using a variety of languages and aimed at areas where nationals of those countries reside or where there might be a strategic or market interest for them (Greece, for example, broadcasts heavily to the Arab nations, where it conducts much business). West Germany, France, the Netherlands, and the United Kingdom have elaborate foreign-language shortwave programs and a long tradition in this kind of broadcasting. These services are often the only source of news for audiences under authoritarian and communist regimes. The BBC's External Services department leads all national Western European networks with 756 hours of weekly broadcasting abroad in 38 languages. Spain is second with 319 hours, the Netherlands third with 316 hours, France fourth with 302 hours, and Sweden fifth with 209 hours.

NEWS SERVICES

Except for the smallest, all Western European nations have their own news services. Usually with the help of government, these national news agencies are limited in scope, function, and independence and are often little more than government mouthpieces (hence the commonly used qualifier "official" or "semiofficial" news agency) that serve as exclusive news agents only to the most disadvantaged members of their media system.

Western Europe's two major news agencies, Reuters of Great Britain and Agence France-Presse (AFP) of France, enjoy extraordinary international respect and popularity. Each has regional strengths (both in reporting and clientele) loosely corresponding to each country's colonial past. Reuters, founded in 1851, is owned mainly by British newspapers, has 28,126 subscribers in 158 countries, and maintains 115 bureaus in 74 countries.

AFP is run by three boards of directors, some of whom are journalists and others are parliamentary representatives and members of the judiciary. AFP has 12,500 clients in 160 countries. It maintains bureaus in 129 countries and uses six languages in its news distribution. The agency was originally started as Agence Havas by Charles Havas in 1835, and in 1940 the French government bought and used it as a propaganda agent at Vichy. During the occupation, the Germans incorporated it into their own news agency, Deutsches Nachrichten-Büro.

The agency emerged from World War II as AFP and was reorganized in its present form in 1957.

Deutsche Presse-Agentur (DPA) is West Germany's main news service. It is one of several such services (two of which are for religious media) and by far the largest and most important. DPA, which was founded in 1949, is owned by a variety of mass media, which are forbidden by agency rules to gain a controlling interest in it. It has 1,200 subscribers and correspondents in more than 70 countries.

Spain's Agencia Efe was founded in 1938 and today has a stronghold in the Spanish-speaking world. It is controlled by a combination of media and government agencies and has more than 2,000 subscribers worldwide.

Proximity to Eastern Europe and access to the smaller Communist-bloc news operations lends considerable importance to Österreichische Presse-Agentur (APA), the official agency of Austria, which disseminates more material from the Big Four (the Associated Press, United Press International, Reuters, and AFP) than it generates on its own.

Other notable Western European news services are Denmark's Ritzau, founded in 1866; Belgium's Agence Belga, founded in 1920; and Italy's Agenzìa Nazionale Stampa Associata (ANSA), founded in 1945.

GOVERNMENT-MEDIA RELATIONS

The constitutions or basic documents of all Western European countries guarantee either freedom of expression in general or freedom of the press in particular. From the laconic, seven-word Article 55 of the Swiss constitution ("The freedom of the press is guaranteed") to the verbose, 301-word Article 14 of the Greek constitution, there is great diversity in expressing a nation's commitment to the principle of press freedom. Usually a lengthy constitutional provision means that several exceptions are made to the normal standard freedom guarantee.

Like the Swiss, the Swedish, Dutch, and Belgian constitutions set no qualifications on the freedom they guarantee. Some limiting qualifiers appear in the constitutions of Finland, Austria, and Denmark and in France's Declaration of the Rights of Man (the oldest press reference clause, predating the approval of the First Amendment of the U.S. Constitution by two years). These documents are likely to guarantee press freedom "within the limits of legal regulations" (Article 77, Danish constitution). More specific qualifiers are contained in the constitutions of West Germany, Portugal, Luxembourg, Norway, Ireland, Malta, Spain, and Greece. Those qualifiers generally refer to the protection of a person's honor or reputation, national security, public morality, and public order. The most specific of the constitutions also protect religious beliefs and the head of state.

Libel laws are the most common legal restrictions on the press. Some countries have elaborate definitions of defamation, such as France's four-parter (*diffamation, injure, offense,* and *outrage*). It is also not uncommon that the accused be burdened with the proof of unintentionality. An interesting aspect of the Greek and French defamation laws is that public officials are protected better than private citizens.

Such respect for the rights of the people in power is also found in countries where the laws allow the banning of sale or actual confiscation of publications. West Germany, Austria, Finland, France, and Greece have such laws. In Great Britain, the Official Secrets Act (updated in 1989) requires that editors not publish material on subjects cited in the Defense Department's D-notices. The act also prohibits the dissemination of security information damaging to international relations. British contempt of court legislation prohibits the dissemination of any trial information until the trial is over and of any information that would undermine public confidence in the judicial system. National security was the reason given in October 1988 by the Thatcher administration when it prohibited British radio and television from broadcasting interviews with members and supporters of the outlawed Protestant and Catholic paramilitary groups in Northern Ireland. British broadcasters, however, were allowed to quote members of these groups indirectly.

The Scandinavian countries are known for their strong freedom-of-information laws, which give them virtually unlimited access to public documents, and for their laws protecting the confidentiality of sources. Source protection in Sweden, for example, which dates to 1766, prohibits journalists from disclosing the identity of a source without the source's consent, and public officials are forbidden to ask that identity. Similar is the protection afforded journalists by Finnish and Norwegian laws.

Several European countries monitor and publicly evaluate the performance of their press systems through press councils. The councils, which tend to be composed of journalists and lay people, have no punitive powers but rely on public pronouncements to accomplish their purpose. The Swedish Press Council is the oldest in Europe, founded in 1916, but the British Press Council, which was established in 1953, is known internationally for its dynamism, fairness, and integrity. Denmark, Finland, West Germany, and Norway also have press councils. Sweden has also popularized worldwide its concept of press ombudsman, a government-appointed official, normally from the judicial branch, who evaluates and processes public complaints against the press.

Regardless of many nations' press laws defining the rights and responsibilities of news personnel, most European journalists do not enjoy the same rights vis-à-vis their governments as their American colleagues do. For that reason, investigative reporting is not as developed in Western Europe. In addition to imprisonment and fines, a common press crime punishment in Western Europe is the suspension of a publication's duty-free import license for newsprint, a penalty of significant severity for small papers in countries that import all their newsprint or in protectionist countries with high import duties.

CONCEPTS OF MEDIA FREEDOM

Within each nation's peculiar cultural and political limits, the Western European press, very much like the American press, functions freely. The limits set forth by legal or other informally institutionalized means still leave plenty of room for the emergence of a high-quality as well as a second-class, sensational press system. The cacophony created by its obvious partisanship gives it much of its character and is equally determinant of its credibility and respectability.

Generally, the press of Western Europe has been founded on the tenets of pluralistic libertarianism as advanced in the works of John Milton, John Stuart Mill, and John Locke, among others. Its dedication to the rules of the "marketplace of ideas" and to independence from government have been tested for.decades, especially through the totalitarianism of the Nazi period, during which many of Western Europe's newspapers and journalists fought the aggressor from underground. The lessons learned during that period have been incorporated into political and legal institutions that today make up the societal framework within which the press functions.

Because Western Europeans in general lack the American mistrust of institutionalized government and their press lacks the spark of the adversarial press-government relationship, press freedom tends to be defined more in terms of professional conduct liberties (e.g., a journalist's right to write with impunity and to keep sources confidential) than in terms of the government's duty to operate in the open (e.g., access to documents, meetings laws).

It should also be noted that although many countries have laws that allow them to confiscate papers, or otherwise intervene, all Western European countries make special efforts to accommodate the press and to ensure press pluralism. These pro-newspaper policies, however, as well as the politically tainted licensing systems of the electronic media, are practices not free of potential hazard to press independence and justifiably raise serious questions.

MEDIA ECONOMICS AND SPECIAL PROBLEMS

The Western European printed press has been facing financial difficulties since 1970. Circulation has not kept up with population growth, and advertising budgets are spent more and more in the electronic media. The problems of the elite French and British newspapers epitomize those of the other nations. For that reason, all European governments, to varying degrees, have taken steps to assist their press and to ensure the survival of weak newspapers and the voice pluralism they represent. Some of these steps range from government advertising placement to postal cost relief to direct subsidies, all of which are widely used in the Scandinavian countries and Belgium.

These economic problems have given rise to press ownership concentration. The Hersant and Hachette chains in France, the Bonnier group in Sweden, the Springer group in West Germany, the Schibsted group in Norway, the Het Volk group in Belgium, the News Group Newspapers (owned by Rupert Murdoch), the Thomson Newspapers group in the United Kingdom, and the Agnelli and Benedetti groups in Italy are some of Europe's better-known newspaper chains. To ensure their future economic viability, many of them are expanding rapidly into broadcast and cable television acquisition. In fact, most large European newspaper proprietors are already owners or partners in ownership of television stations or program services.

The expansion of these chains and the growth of the broadcast chains such as Berlusconi's are forcing many European nations to put limits on the kinds and numbers of media these conglomerates may own in one area. France and Italy are two countries that recently instituted such laws to guarantee the survival of smaller media enterprises.

The European economic integration that is envisioned for 1992 has also spurred international activity among advertising agencies, which are gearing up for pan-European advertising. Most of this activity has been between France and England, as top agencies from each country try to aquire smaller and potentially profitable agencies in the other. This has generated a war of words and charges of cultural chauvinism.

JOURNALISM EDUCATION AND TRAINING

Since 1970, Western Europe has seen the development of a variety of types of formal journalism education. One, most prevalent in the United Kingdom, is the apprenticeship method, which requires students to go through a specialized program offered by the National

Council for the Training of Journalists and then work for a newspaper. France and West Germany have a number of journalism schools. Strasbourg, Lille, Paris, Bordeaux, Tours, Dijon, and Toulouse have higher education journalism programs that mostly resemble American undergraduate journalism programs, although the universities at Paris, Bordeaux, and Toulouse are involved in mass communication research. At least a dozen West German universities offer undergraduate and graduate studies in mass communication.

Traditional universities in the smaller countries in Western Europe are beginning to look into mass communication as a discipline, and several already have instituted courses in it. The skills component of journalism education is not part of that curriculum, which focuses on mass communication research and theory, especially from the sociological and political science perspectives. Universities in the Scandinavian and Mediterranean countries largely view journalism education from that vantage point.

Furthermore, the Scandinavian countries also have a very strong continuing education program for journalists. Supported mainly through union fees and contributions from the government and the unions of publishers and editors, these "institutes" offer short-term courses for working professionals on paid leave from their media. The topics of these courses may range from environmental coverage and newspaper management to newspaper design and database use. The largest of these schools is the Norwegian Institute of Journalism (NIJ), which has a full-time staff of 20 faculty, state-of-the-art print and broadcast equipment, and its own dormitory and restaurant facilities. NIJ, which accepts journalists from all Scandinavian countries, operates specialized programs in the United States, the United Kingdom, and West Germany.

PROSPECTS FOR THE FUTURE

Newspapers in Western Europe, like newspapers everywhere, will face difficult times ahead. Penetration and circulation are down, and the new generation of readers is growing up in the electronic era. The continuation of consolidation and chain ownership trends seems inevitable. This will be a great challenge for the loudly partisan press, and some signs already are pointing toward more widely appealing newspapers. At the same time, signs are pointing toward a more sensationalist "popular press" and a more visually attractive, albeit bland, elite press.

One of the biggest questions facing Western European publishers is their business posture vis-à-vis the economic challenges of the integration of 1992. Although there have been no big waves of transnational acquisitions on the print side, there are strong signs of such activity on the electronic side and among advertising agencies. The latter is likely to generate pan-European advertising practices that are bound to affect all media profoundly.

Current expectations are that the Western European advertising budget will soon be divided equally between print and electronic media before it begins to favor the electronic media, and the length of this transitional period may well determine the success of all these new networks and stations that almost daily develop in Western Europe. Nevertheless, broadcasting and cablecasting seem to be destined to succeed, although after the initial euphoria, a period of adjustment and attrition will be necessary. Finally, one major player in the electronic media arena may very well end up being the Eastern European resident whose market potential is still untested but may be available for tapping in the near future if the reforms that are being debated today are implemented.

EASTERN EUROPE

Although they are next-door neighbors, Eastern and Western Europeans have developed vastly different press systems, based historically on completely different, and mutually suspicious, ideas about the role of mass communication or journalism in their societies. Yet the main reason for their differences, the political system (its apparatus and ideology), is today under an unprecedented challenge and in some quarters overhaul, radically changing the Communist bloc as the world has known it since World War II.

Dictatorships of the proletariat see mass media as organs of the state, protectors, promoters, and guarantors of the Communist system. Lenin viewed the Western press as a servant of the dominant class and another profit-making institution that would have a divisive effect in a socialist society. He saw the Communist press's role as that of "agitator, propagandist and organizer," functions that could be performed only at the direction of the Party.

Two factors have affected the performance of Eastern European print and broadcast media: their country's cultural heritage or physical proximity to the West and fundamental Communist doctrine. Thus the least "Western" of the Eastern media can be found in Bulgaria, Romania, and Albania. In varying degrees, newspapers in other Eastern European nations look "Western," may include advertisements, and occasionally "evaluate" the system and its personnel. Most Communist nations have two major dailies—the Party organ and the government organ, both of which serve as the key informants of the public and are hence likely to have national and extremely large circulations. When private press ownership was prohibited, only unions and other Party agencies or institutions (e.g., the Communist Youth) were allowed to publish.

HISTORICAL HIGHLIGHTS

The first daily newspaper of the region appeared in Leipzig in what is now East Germany. Unfavorable political conditions hampered the long survival of the early press, and the only success story was Johann Cota's *Allgemeine Zeitung,* published in Tübingen in 1798 (and still publishing today). Karl Marx's paper *Rheinische Zeitung* lasted from 1848 to 1849. Censorship was abolished in 1874, but Bismarck managed to keep tight control of the press including Wolff's Telegraphic Bureau. The nineteenth century saw the press expand and turn partisan, but the more than 7,000 pre–World War I dailies and weeklies were severely hurt by the Nazis and two world wars. The first Soviet-inspired paper in Germany, *Tägliche Rundschau,* was published in May 1945. That summer saw the establishment of the political parties that generated many of newspapers in existence today.

Peter the Great published the first Russian newspaper, *Vedomosti Moskovskogo Gosudarstva,* in 1703 in Moscow and later at St. Petersburg. The paper ceased publication in 1727 and was succeeded by *Sankt Peterburskie Vedomosti,* published by the Academy of Sciences in 1728. It became a daily in 1815. The press saw its greatest growth under Catherine the Great—with her encouragement, many monthly publications and satirical journals appeared. She decreed freedom to publish privately in 1783 but withdrew it 16 years later as the writings from the French and American revolutions were gaining momentum in her country. Alexander I relaxed controls in 1801, and many new political, scientific, and literary journals appeared. Government started publishing its own newspapers, such as *Guberniskiye Vedomosti* and *Pochta* in the 1830s. *Iskra* ("The Spark") was the first important Communist movement newspaper. It was founded in 1900 in Stuttgart and addressed the conditions in Russia. *Pravda* was established by Lenin in St. Petersburg in 1912, and *Izvestia* appeared in 1917.

Czechoslovakia's first newspaper was Prague's *Prazske Noviny* in 1719, followed by Bratislava's *Prespurske Noviny* in 1783. Frantisek Palacky, a well-respected historian, political leader, teacher, and journalist, published *Slovenskyi Narodne Noviny* in 1845, the most significant newspaper of its time. The birth of modern Czech journalism, however, started with the abolition of censorship by the Hapsburgs in 1848.

Poland's first newspaper was *Merkurjusz Polski* (1661), Hungary's *Mercurius Hungaricus* (1705), Romania's *Curierul Romanescu* (1829), and Albania's *Taraboshi* (1913). For political reasons, Bulgaria's first newspaper appeared in Leipzig, Germany, in 1846, and Yugoslavia's *Sebrskija Novini* was published in Vienna, Austria, in 1791.

PRINT MEDIA

Eastern European newspapers look serious, and their content, intended to further state goals, is written in verbose, polysyllabic, colorless, bureaucratic language. Party instructions, Party news, educational articles, and life management hints are the most common stories printed. Personalities are played down. Western-style hard news is rare, as is criticism of the system. Letters to the editor, the only access to the system itself, normally complain about the inefficiency of a lower public servant.

However, Soviet *glasnost* seems to be breathing fresh air on these old practices almost everywhere in the Eastern bloc. Criticisms of processes and personnel, albeit in a corrective manner, are becoming common. Reflective of this new aura, perhaps, is the new spirit exhibited by *Pravda* in the fall of 1989, when it caught the world by surprise by issuing an apology to General Secretary Gorbachev's most prominent Soviet critic for an article it had run about him two days before. Although the article was a reprint of a story from an Italian newspaper, it caused a serious negative public reaction and brought on severe criticism from the weekly *Moscow News*, an unusual development in itself.

In spite of some "astronomical" circulation figures by Western standards, the Soviet Union is only the second highest newspaper-reading nation in Eastern Europe, circulating 422 copies for 1,000 people. Geographic reasons alone necessitate the existence of several regional papers, but there are approximately 2,500 daily newspapers in the Soviet Union and approximately 8,000 weeklies and periodicals.

Moscow has 15 dailies, including 3 focused on defense, 2 on industry, 2 on unions, 2 on youth, 2 on Moscow, 1 on sports, and 1 on rural citizens. The circulation leaders are the Labor Union's *Trud* (circ. 18 million), the Young Communist League's *Komsomolskaya Pravda* (circ. 17.6 million), the government's official organ *Izvestia* (circ. 10.4 million), the Communist Party's *Pravda* (circ. 8 million), the rural-focus

Communist Party paper *Selskaya Zhin* (circ. 6.5 million), the Physical Education Committee's *Sovietski Sport* (circ. 5.2 million), and the Defense Ministry's *Krasnaya Zvezda* (circ. 2.4 million).

Some of the most notable regional dailies are Kiev's *Silski Visti* (circ. 834,000), organ of the Central Committee of the Ukrainian Communist Party, and *Pravda Ukrainy* (circ. 480,000), organ of the Ukraine Council of Ministers; Minsk's *Znamya Yunosti* (circ. 785,000), the Leninist Youth newspaper, and Riga's Communist Youth paper *Padomju Jaunathe* (circ. 257,000). The most noteworthy of Soviet magazines are Moscow's *Literaturnaya Gazeta, Inostrahnanya Literatura,* a magazine focusing on foreign literary works, the children's magazine *Pionerskaya Pravda,* and *Noviye Tovary,* which covers new products. The slick and "Western-looking" *Soviet Life,* does not circulate in the USSR.

The leader of the Eastern European press corps is undoubtedly *Pravda,* the Soviet Union's oldest newspaper (founded in 1912 by Lenin himself), which originally published in Leningrad (then St. Petersburg). It is read by the world's elite because it reflects the Soviet elite and sets the tone for the rest of Eastern Europe's newspapers. Its commitment to the ideals of the Party is probably reflected by its employment, starting in 1918, of a large number of nonjournalist worker-correspondents whose job was to help *Pravda* keep its finger on the pulse of the nation.

In spite of the multifaceted prominence of the Soviet media, the most avid newspaper readers in all of Europe are the East Germans. Although it has only 39 newspapers to serve 17 million citizens, the German Democratic Republic has a circulation of 552 copies per 1,000 citizens. In East Berlin, the newspaper center of the country, the official Socialist Unity party paper *Neues Deutschland* leads in circulation with 1.1 million and is followed by the Communist Youth party paper, *Junge Welt,* with a circulation of 1.2 million. East Berlin also has specialized dailies on trade, agriculture, and sports, with circulation ranges from 185,000 to 410,000. The most popular regional papers are Karl-Marx-Stadt's *Freie Presse* (circ. 641,000), Halle's *Freiheit* (circ. 562,000), and Dresden's *Sächsische Zeitung* (circ. 543,000). The GDR has 30 weeklies and periodicals.

The third highest newspaper-reading Eastern-bloc country is Czechoslovakia, which has 27 dailies that sell 298 copies per 1,000 people. The country's most popular newspapers are Prague's Communist Party paper *Rude Pravo* (circ. 1.1 million), Bratislava's Party paper *Pravda Bratislava* (circ. 405,000), Prague's trade union paper *Prace* (circ. 353,000), and the Youth paper *Mlada Fronta* (circ. 330,000). Czechoslovakia has 118 weeklies and periodicals.

Hungary has 27 papers that sell 254 copies per 1,000 people. Budapest's Party paper *Nepzabadsaq* leads in circulation with 727,000 and is followed by the trade union paper *Nepszava* (circ. 295,000) and the sports daily *Nepsport* (circ. 242,000). Hungary has 94 weeklies and periodicals. Bulgaria's 12 papers sell 256 copies per 1,000 and are dominated by Sofia's Party paper *Rabotnichesko* (circ. 850,000). Bulgaria has 37 weeklies and periodicals.

Poland, not a particularly strong newspaper-reading nation (it has 45 daily papers that sell 214 copies per 1,000 people), is going through some revolutionary systemic changes. Poles recently witnessed not only the creation of the first noncommunist government in a Warsaw Pact country since World War II but also the elevation of a journalist to the post of prime minister—Tadeusz Mazowiecki, former editor in chief of *Tygodnik Solidarnosc* ("Solidarity Weekly"). Before these developments, the country's circulation leaders were Party papers in Warsaw, *Trybuna Ludu* (circ. 1 million), and in Katowice, *Trybuna Robotnicza* (circ. 683,000). Although newspapers were officially censored, a small group of Catholic newspapers, led by Krakow's weekly *Tygodnik Powzechny* (circ. limited to 40,000), has made an impact. Poland has 51 weeklies and periodicals.

Yugoslavia is another Eastern European country that is undergoing serious political changes, although since World War II it has followed a path considerably more independent than that of its neighbors. Proof of that may well be that the country's most respected papers, the morning *Politika* (circ. 200,000) and the evening *Politika Express* (circ. 250,000), are privately owned. Although the paper has confronted the authorities several times since its founding in 1904, it continues to publish autonomously. It is multipage and lively (by Eastern European standards) and carries advertising.

One of Yugoslavia's most respected papers used to be *Borba*, a serious-looking broadsheet that fell on bad times in the 1960s and was rescued by the Socialist party of Yugoslavia, whose views it carries today, but its circulation is only 100,000 copies daily, less than 20 percent of the circulation it enjoyed in the aftermath of World War II. Today's circulation leader is the Party paper *Vecernje Novosti* (cir. 320,000). Zagreb's independent *Vecerni List* (circ. 294,000) outsells its Party competitor *Vjesnik* by a margin of almost four to one. Yugoslavia has a very healthy "Western-style" periodicals and weeklies industry featuring more than 3,000 publications, the most notable of which are *Illustrovana Politika, Vjesnik u Stredu, Kommunist,* and *Arena.*

Not only were Romania and Albania until recently the most closed Eastern-bloc societies, but they also had the worst newspaper readership record of the group. Romania has 36 dailies that sell 160 copies per 1,000 people, and Albania has two newspapers that sell 52 copies per 1,000 people. The most important Romanian newspaper is the Party *Scinteia* (circ. 1.4 million) and the Physical Education Council's *Sportul* (circ. 445,000), both of Bucharest. Albania's most notable paper is Tirana's Party paper, *Zeri Popullit* (circ. 105,000). The periodical press is almost nonexistent in these countries. Romania has 24 periodicals; Albania, 4.

ELECTRONIC MEDIA

It does not take a long study of television programming in Eastern Europe to conclude that the dullness, seriousness, verbosity, and bureaucratic language and topics of its newspapers are transmitted to its different national audiences in a visual form as broadcast programs. In every Eastern European country, the council of ministers controls the national broadcasting services as well through the state committees for radio and television.

However, *glasnost, perestroika,* and access to Western European television have affected Communist broadcasting, and both news and entertainment programs are getting more visually exciting. "Vremya," for example, the Soviet Union's 9 p.m., 30-minute newscast, now uses graphics, visuals, and multicamera angles in its presentation, although by Western standards its stories are still long and didactic. Party news and official pronouncements lead the newscasts and are followed by regional, national, and international news. Weather and sports close the broadcast. Many of the entertainment programs are reminiscent of American television in the 1950s and 1960s, but there was a marked improvement in program quality in the 1980s—game shows, mysteries, and musicals are now all part of the program diet in Soviet television. Sex and violence are excluded, and the positive is emphasized always. Cultural, instructional, children's, and sports shows predominate. Only half of all programming is devoted to entertainment.

Today, the Soviets have 321 television sets per 1,000 people, or more than 90 million television sets, considerably more than the 55 million they had in 1975. Three national program services originate in Moscow (one general-interest, one educational, and one entertainment-oriented) and are transmitted at times matching workers' schedules. The First Program, for example, transmits from 4:00 to 7:45 a.m. and from 1:00 to 10:15 p.m. on weekdays. The Fourth Program transmits only from 1:00 to 5:40 p.m. In addition to a local Moscow channel, the Soviet Union has 900 stations and 11 origination-capable regional television centers that transmit programs in 67 languages.

Soviet radio programming follows the same principles as television and, in fact, retransmits the audio portion of several of the major national television programs. There are 185 million receivers, or 660 per 1,000 people. Radio Moscow transmits more than 1,200 hours per week in all airwave lengths and bands, as well as 64 foreign languages. Jamming the Iron Curtain–aimed foreign broadcasts, like those of the Voice of America, Radio Free Europe, and Radio Liberty, among others, has been one of the Kremlin's favorite international communication activities, but in the Gorbachev era even that practice has been almost completely eliminated. A little more than half of radio program time is devoted to entertainment, mainly musical.

The Soviet Union generally sets the tone for the qualitative aspect of broadcasting in the Eastern-bloc countries, which explains why their systems and programming are so similar to those of the USSR. The types of programming, the hours of operation, and the approach to information are widely duplicated in the rest of Eastern Europe.

Poland has 10 million television sets, 2 national program services, and 62 stations; East Germany has 6.2 million sets, 2 program services, and 28 stations; Czechoslovakia has 4.5 million sets, 2 program services, and 77 stations; Hungary has 4.2 million sets, 2 program services, and 21 stations; Romania has 4 million sets, a single program service, and 39 stations; Bulgaria has 2.1 million sets, 2 program services, and 21 stations; Yugoslavia has 4 million sets, 10 networks, 15 program services, and 99 stations; and Albania has 246,000 sets, a sole program service, and 5 stations. Most of these countries have relay stations for Soviet television. Though most Eastern European countries match the USSR's entertainment ratio—about 50 percent of programming—Poland and Yugoslavia devote to it only 36 and 40 percent, respectively, the least in the group.

The highest radio penetration in Eastern Europe can be found in East Germany, Hungary, and Czechoslovakia (with more than 570 sets per 1,000 people), the lowest in Albania and Romania (with 160 and 143, respectively). The highest percentage of entertainment programming can be found in East Germany (71 percent) and the lowest in Czechoslovakia (47 percent). It should be pointed out that most Eastern Europeans live in areas where Western radio and television programming is accessible, which long presented the Communist authorities with a serious dilemma, about which they could do little.

NEWS SERVICES

The dominant news agency of the Communist bloc is undoubtedly the Soviet Union's TASS (Telegrafnoie Agentsvo Sovetskavo Soiuza), which since the 1970s has been operating under the the direct supervision of the Council of Ministers of the USSR. It was founded in 1925 but was officially organized as a wire service cooperative in 1935, when it was formally named the country's main information instrument. Its functions are to disseminate domestic information domestically, to control incoming foreign information, to report Soviet news to the world, and to serve as a news informant and analyst to the government itself. Its importance today equals that of *Pravda*, articles from which are widely used by TASS.

TASS has more than 200 correspondents stationed abroad and serves approximately 500 international subscribers and 10,000 domestically. It has exchange agreements with most of the world's leading wire services. Its reports are normally addressed to four different publics and vary in content as well as importance. The least important service includes material available to all subscribers; the second level, known as "White TASS," because of the color of the paper on which it is printed, contains confidential, largely background information that goes to editors; the "Red TASS" goes to the Party and government elite; and the "Special Bulletins" go only to the Party and government leadership.

A less official Soviet news agency is Novosti (Agentsvo Pechati Novosti, or APN), which was founded in 1961 and gathers and distributes mainly feature stories, photos, and other promotional material about the USSR. It also publishes books and magazines and coordinates foreign journalists' visits to the Soviet Union.

All Eastern European countries have their own national news services patterned after TASS. Czechoslovakia, Poland, and Bulgaria also have a secondary agency patterned after Novosti. Iconoclast Yugoslavia's news service, Tanjug, which was founded by the Partisans in 1943, is a truly commercial operation and has the distinction of being in charge of the Non-Aligned News Agencies Pool that serves most of the Third World nations. Many of the large Eastern European news services have news exchange agreements with their Western counterparts.

CONCEPTS OF PRESS FREEDOM

Such terms as *newspaper, press freedom,* and *journalist* mean entirely different things in the communist world. In the West, *newspapers* are independent, private vehicles of news, views, and entertainment. *Journalists* are professionals who, *free* from government interference, work for *newspapers* and other print or broadcast media to produce a marketable news-views-and-entertainment product. In the orthodox Marxist-Leninist lexicon, both *newspapers* and *journalists* are instruments and employees of the state. Western *press freedom* is rejected as a servant of plutocracy and an exploiter of the masses. The views of the masses, Lenin believed, can best be expressed only by the people's government and the Party for whom *freedom* is justifiably reserved. Furthermore, since communists believe that all citizens and all social institutions have a political purpose, the concept of value-free informants is as utopian as value-free information and therefore rejected. For this reason, even Western Europe's communist newspapers proudly state above their nameplate that they are organs of the Communist Party.

A newspaper, Lenin said, is to be a "collective propagandist," "collective agitator," and a "collective organizer." The media, in other words, exist to promote Party principles and prepare the masses to accept, perpetuate, and defend them. To ensure that Communist journalism performs its role properly, the state selects and trains citizens in journalistic practices, carefully controls printing and broadcasting equipment, provides news sources, and exercises censorship.

Little of this stern discipline of the media, however, can be detected by reading the constitutional documents of the Eastern European countries. While some of these constitutions are being reexamined and in part reworded, it is useful to study their pre-1990 statements. This is what Article 50 of the constitution of the USSR says:

> In accordance with the interests of the people and in order to strengthen and develop the socialist system, citizens of the USSR are guaranteed freedom of speech, of the press, and of assembly, meetings, street processions and demonstrations. Exercise of these political freedoms is ensured by putting public buildings, streets and squares at the disposal of the working people and their organizations, by broad dissemination of information, and by the opportunity to use the press, television and the radio.

All the other Eastern European constitutions use similar language except for that of Romania, which adds that these freedoms "may not be used for purposes hostile to the Socialist system."

The incongruity of the language of these constitutions can be explained only by looking at their words through a Communist lens—the differences obviously go beyond semantics and denotative meanings. Even in the professional codes of ethics of the Eastern European countries (except Romania and Albania), references to ethics are always preceded by the word *socialist*. The journalist's job is to encourage the development of *socialist* citizens' "cultural maturity" by helping them "develop their constructive activities." Freedom of the press or freedom of expression as understood and practiced in the West is simply not part of the Communist experience.

MEDIA ECONOMICS AND SPECIAL PROBLEMS

When media marketing in closed societies is not at issue, competition for either circulation and ratings or advertising revenue does not exist. Media, as arms of the government, are guaranteed funding for operation.

The problems that many of these countries' media leaders face today are primarily political and professional. Those whose media and audiences are physically close to the West experience daily the comparison between their media and those of their Western neighbors. Some imitative attempts have been allowed by the authorities, but the control is still tight. During the introduction of *glasnost,* the situation became even more delicate. As the institutional limits of tolerance kept enlarging, the uncertainties of those who were testing them kept multiplying. Absent any clear and concrete vision of tomorrow, their agony is destined to continue.

JOURNALISM EDUCATION AND TRAINING

Since it is the state's duty to prepare journalists, it is not surprising that all the Eastern European countries except Albania have professional training programs. Since 1950, the Soviet Union has created 22 five-year programs of higher education around the country, led by Moscow State University. Other important programs are in universities in Leningrad, Kiev, Tashkent, and Vladivostok. A good part of a Soviet journalism student's academic program is devoted to the study of Communist ideology.

Other training grounds can be found in the Academy of Social Sciences, which has two journalism chairs sponsored by the Central Committee of the Party, and in Moscow's Institute of International Relations, which has an international journalism faculty. Upon graduation, students are placed as apprentices at newspapers or radio or television stations or with TASS. Furthermore, the USSR Union of Journalists offers short training courses in cooperation with state universities.

The Czech journalism programs are at universities in Prague and Bratislava, and East Germany's are at the Journalism Institute at Leipzig and East Berlin. Poland has two 2-year, postgraduate, nondegree programs in Warsaw and Katovice, and the National Association of Hungarian Journalists offers two short-term programs in Budapest. Romania and Bulgaria offer journalism training programs at their capital universities. Yugoslavia has undergraduate training programs at the universities in Belgrade, Zagreb, Ljubljana, Novi Sad, Skopje, and Priština and postgraduate programs at Ljubljana (where the respected Center for

Research of Public Opinion and Mass Communication is headquartered), Zagreb, and Belgrade.

PROSPECTS FOR THE FUTURE

In the four decades preceding 1990, the vast majority of Eastern European media, print or broadcast, did not normally face success or failure—their goals, budgets, and audiences were guaranteed. However, the currently evolving systemic changes in these countries have fostered the establishment of new media, new formats for news and entertainment, and new professional standards and practices. Will the old generation of journalists and media be able to fight their way through a market-based system, which is governed by such forces as circulation figures and ratings? Will the new professionals be able to compete against their slick and experienced Western colleagues, whose products currently reach and soon will inundate their markets? The answer to these and other similar questions can only be speculative.

As the historic changes in Eastern Europe take place, the journalism profession there seems to evolve around these patterns:

1. The old party press is losing popularity rapidly and is desperately trying to modernize in both appearance and ideology with little success. Some of its cost-cutting efforts have included the elimination of most nonideological publications, such as those of the arts.
2. New newspapers and magazines are emerging regularly (many including the words "new" or "free" as part of their names), and their popularity is immense. First editions of *Romania Libera*, for example, sold out in minutes. Polish journalists expect that 500 new newspapers will appear in Poland in 1990 alone.
3. Journalists interested in starting new print and broadcast media and who sought space and equipment from the established media were mostly rebuffed, in spite of the efforts of the new noncommunist regimes. Bulgarian and Polish journalists, for example, were harassed by their party counterparts as they pursued their search for office space and typewriters.
4. Especially difficult has proven to be the "liberation" of the electronic media from party control. In Czechoslovakia and Romania, for example, the effort was complicated by former party journalists who claimed that they had been members of the opposition all along and refused to relinquish their posts.
5. The mixed-economy forces that seem to be shaping the media

picture in Eastern Europe are revealing serious shortages in investment capital, equipment, and media business managers. Czechoslovakia's major *samizdat* (underground) newspaper, *Lidove Noviny*, for example, had to make a mass appeal for financial support in its transition from weekly to semiweekly publication.

6. The financial revitalization of the press seems to be taking a clear capitalist flavor in countries like the German Democratic Republic and Hungary, where international media conglomerates are acquiring local media companies. In Hungary, for example, early in 1990 Rupert Murdoch acquired a 50 percent interest in the daily *Mai Nap* and the weekly *Reform*, while British publishers Lord Rothermere and Robert Maxwell were negotiating for two small Budapest dailies. Furthermore, in February 1990, MTV (Music Television) Europe claimed 20,000 subscribers in Czechoslovakia and 5,000 in Poland. Yugoslavia, Hungary, and the German Democratic Republic are scheduled to receive MTV service by the end of 1990.

7. As ideological pluralism and a market economy govern the fate of these publications, ethnic controversies become popular newspaper topics and such coverage seems to be contributing to the deterioration of minority relationships within some countries. For example, Poland's new German-language newspaper *Schlesische Nachrichten* (Silesian News), published in Silesia, formerly a part of Germany, created a stir early in 1990 with "Silesia Is a German Land" and other similar headlines.

8. Criticism of those in power still is not easily tolerated by the governing regimes. In Bulgaria, Romania, and the Soviet Union calls for press restraint were frequently issued in the early days of the political changes. In the Soviet Union, for example, the editors of the magazine *Glasnost* and the widely circulating tabloid *Argumenty i Fakty* have come under severe Kremlin attack for criticizing Soviet president Mikhail Gorbachev's policies.

These patterns of change are perhaps due mainly to the speed with which political change has occurred in the Eastern bloc, and the confusion that it has created in most segments of society. Journalists, not unlike political leaders and common citizens, still seem to be searching for their new identities, new vehicles of expression, new targets, and new audiences.

The speed of change is not expected to continue and neither is the plethora of new media or the professional euphoria of the new generation of journalists. As the realities of a market-driven economy envelop the new media, Eastern European journalists will have to face challenges to which they are not accustomed. When the first compromises become essential to the survival of their medium, these journalists will have to decide if the freedom of expression for which they longed is worth the price. They will learn the lesson that their capitalist peers know so well—that as long as there is an economic string attached to the press, its freedom is never complete. It is a lesson they have earned the right to learn on their own and from which they will draw their own conclusions. This opportunity alone goes to the heart of freedom and democracy, goals for which these journalists fought for more than 40 years.

CHAPTER 6

Middle East and North Africa

Christine Ogan

Unlike most other regions of the world, there is no consensus on the boundaries of the Middle East. The area has been defined in part by geography but also by religion and ethnicity of the population. None of these is all-inclusive.

Geographically, the countries of the Middle East span three continents—Africa, Asia, and Europe. The largest part of the region is in Asia, but Egypt is in Africa and a small part of Turkey is in Europe. Although the bulk of the residents are Muslim, the Middle East is also home to large Jewish and Christian populations. And to define the population as Arab would leave out the Persians, Turks, Kurds, and non-Arab Semitic peoples who live in the area. For our purposes, the Middle East will refer to the following countries: Bahrain, Cyprus, Egypt, Iran, Iraq, Israel, Jordan, Kuwait, Lebanon, Oman, Qatar, Saudi Arabia, Syria, Turkey, the United Arab Emirates, the People's Democratic Republic of Yemen (South Yemen), and the Yemen Arab Republic (North Yemen). (See map on page 131.)

Egypt is geographically in North Africa but is usually classified with the Middle East. Other Arab countries located in North Africa will be included at the end of this chapter since the press systems of these countries—Algeria, Libya, Morocco, the Sudan, and Tunisia—probably more closely resemble those of Arab Middle Eastern countries than those of the remainder of the African countries.

MIDDLE EAST

All Middle Eastern countries can be classified in the developing world, though the level of economic development has a wide range. The World Bank lists the economies of this region as lower middle-income (Yemen PDR, Yemen Arab Republic, Egypt, Jordan, Syria, Lebanon, and Turkey); upper middle-income (Oman, Israel, Iran, and Iraq); and high-income oil exporters (Saudi Arabia, Kuwait, and the United Arab Emirates). Because Bahrain, Cyprus, and Qatar have populations of below 1 million, the World Bank does not classify these countries. Annual income per capita for 1986 ranged from $470 for Yemen PDR to $14,680 for the United Arab Emirates.

Income is one predictor of media development and penetration, but there are others. Educational level, journalistic traditions, and the nature of the political system within which the media operate are also correlated with media development.

HISTORICAL HIGHLIGHTS

Prior to the advent of the printed press, the bazaar, coffeehouse, and mosque served as the loci of news and information in much of the Middle East. And those places still function as important traditional communication centers alongside the modern mass media. Media scholar Majid Tehranian characterizes this as dual system in Iran, but it works much the same way all over the Middle East.

The history of the modern daily and nondaily press dates to the nineteenth century in a few countries of this region; others, such as the Gulf states, had no newspapers until the mid-1970s. In spite of the fact that all of these countries (except Iran) lived under the domination of the Ottomans for more than 400 years and under the British and French following World War I, indigenous newspapers developed from an early date in several sites. The first Arab newspaper published by Arabs was the *Jurnal al-Iraq*, dating from 1816; the first Arab daily began in Beirut in 1873. According to Turkish press scholar Hifzi Topuz, the first Ottoman newspaper was the *Takvimi Vakayi*, a weekly published by Ottoman rulers in Istanbul from 1831 to 1876. The *Takvimi Vakayi* was published not only in Turkish but also in Arabic, Farsi, Armenian, and Greek. The early Arab press in the nineteenth century was primarily an official press, says William Rugh in his book *The Arab Press* (1979). That was also true of the Ottoman press of the time.

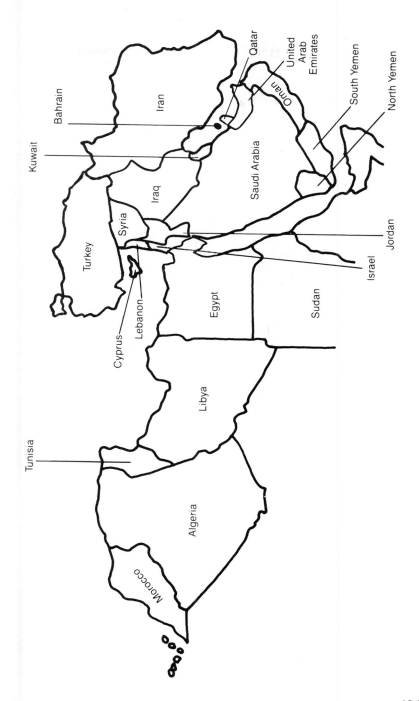

131

PRINT MEDIA

Generally, where literacy is high, the printed press has also reached an advanced state (see Table 6.1). At least 70 percent of the population in Cyprus, Israel, Jordan, Kuwait, Lebanon, and Turkey is literate, and these countries are also characterized by higher levels of newspaper penetration. By contrast, in both North and South Yemen and even in oil-rich Oman, Bahrain, and Saudi Arabia, both literacy levels and newspaper penetration are low. Literacy levels in these countries are as low as 15 percent in Yemen Arab Republic and 20 percent in Oman. Bahrain has two dailies with a total circulation of 25,000 to serve its 500,000 people (or 50 newspapers per 1,000), and Oman's 1.4 million people are served by four dailies with combined circulation of 61,500 (43 newspapers per 1,000).

TABLE 6.1. NEWSPAPERS PUBLISHED IN THE MIDDLE EAST

Country	Population (in millions)	Literacy (%)	Dailies	Weeklies
Bahrain	0.5	40	2	7
Cyprus	0.7[a]	89	19	29
Egypt	53.3	43	17	34
Iran	51.9	48	11	16
Iraq	17.6	50	7	7
Israel	4.4[b]	92	28	24
Jordan	3.8	75	5	6
Kuwait	2.0	71	7	14
Lebanon	3.3	75	38	29
Oman	1.4	20	4	3
Qatar	0.4	60	6	4
Saudi Arabia	14.2	52	11	14
Syria	11.3	45	10	11
Turkey	52.9	80	38	16
United Arab Emirates	1.5[c]	56	8	7
Yemen (PDR) (South)	2.4	39	2	9
Yemen Arab Republic (North)	6.7	15	2	5

Note: The number of dailies and weeklies listed is approximate; latest available data were used to determine actual numbers.
[a] Population is 80 percent Greek, 18 percent Turkish.
[b] Excludes population of the West Bank, Gaza Strip, and East Jerusalem.
[c] Population is 42 percent Arab, 50 percent South Asian.
Sources: 1988 Statistical Year Book (Paris: UNESCO, 1987); *Europa Year Book* (London: Europa Publications, 1988, 1989); *World Development Report* (New York: Oxford University Press, 1988); *1989 Information Please Almanac* (Boston: Houghton Mifflin, 1988).

The exception to this rule is Egypt, a country with a literate population of only 43 percent. Cairo is the largest publishing center in the Arab world, home to at least 11 dailies and 46 other publications (weeklies, magazines, journals). The 1989 *Editor & Publisher International Year Book*'s estimate of the total circulation for the 9 largest of the 17 dailies in the country was 4.2 million. The only competitors with Egypt for number of publications are Turkey and Israel. Turkey has about the same population as Egypt but a 75 percent literacy rate. For 19 of Turkey's 38 dailies, the *Year Book* reports a total circulation of 11 million in 1988. And Israel, with 28 dailies, had a total circulation of 737,000 for 20 of those papers in 1988.

Partly arising from colonial tradition and partly due to the number of foreign workers in several of the oil-rich countries, the press in each of these countries includes foreign-language newspapers alongside those in the indigenous language. Israel has the widest range of foreign-language publications because of the large immigrant population from Poland, the Soviet Union, Germany, Romania, and Hungary. There is even a publication serving newly arriving Ethiopians. In the Arab countries, the expected publications in English and French can be found. Since about half of the United Arab Republic's population is made up of South Asians, English-language dailies circulate in fairly large numbers.

The total number of dailies ranges from 2 in Bahrain and each Yemen to a high of 38 in Turkey. Turkey and Egypt are also the sites of the most influential dailies in the region.

Although Arabic is the principal language in 13 of the 17 Middle Eastern countries, no international press serves the Arab countries. Egypt's *Al-Ahram* (circ. 900,000), begun in 1875, which also publishes an international edition in London and a North American edition in New York, and *Al-Akhbar* (circ. 789,000) come closest to being international Arab newspapers. But until a change of policy in 1989, Egypt was politically separated from its Arab counterparts following Anwar Sadat's signing of the Camp David accords in 1979. The Egyptian newspapers were also probably less influential during that period, although the ban placed on all Egyptian media by other Arab countries never really held up. Other large Cairo dailies are *Al-Gomhouriya* (circ. 650,000), *Mayo* (circ. 500,000), and *Al-Misaa'* (circ. 105,000).

In spite of Lebanon's political upheaval, two of its dailies remain well respected in the Arab world. *Al-Anwar* (53,761) and *Al-Nahar* (75,000), both reportedly independent papers (although Rugh says that *Al-Anwar* has supported the Christian Lebanese Front in recent years), enjoyed a good reputation because of their ability to remain independent of government pressure. Lebanese papers try to publish daily, but in the worst of the fighting they have had to delay publication or shut down operations temporarily. A September 1989 report on the role of the news media in Lebanon's civil war indicated that 29 daily and weekly political newspapers were publishing regularly.

Turkey boasts several large-circulating dailies, a few of which also publish in West Germany to serve the large Turkish community there. Considered the only elite newspaper in Turkey, the left-of-center *Cumhuriyet*, with its 110,000 to 140,000 copies a day, is surpassed in circulation by at least seven other dailies. Those dailies are either more sensationalist, more politically mainstream, or more likely to publish pictures of scantily clad women than the serious *Cumhuriyet*. The largest of these are *Günaydin* (circ. 300,000–520,000), *Hürriyet* (circ. 450,000–700,000), *Sabah* (circ. 400,000–550,000), and *Tan* (circ. 90,000–240,000).

The most respected and influential Hebrew dailies in Israel are the independent *Ha'aretz* and the official newspaper of the General Federation of Labor, *Davar*. Both morning papers, they are surpassed in circulation by the more popular afternoon press, especially *Ma'ariv* (circ. 115,000 daily, 220,000 on weekends) and *Yedioth Aharonoth* (circ. 300,000 daily, 540,000 on Friday). The other well-known and influential Israeli daily is the *Jerusalem Post*. Providing coverage in English, the *Post* publishes a national edition (circ. 30,000 daily, 50,000 on weekends) and a weekly international edition (circ. 60,000).

In 1988, Robert Maxwell, the British publisher, bought a 30 percent stake in Modiin Publishing House, the company that owns *Ma'ariv*. Maxwell's investment is unusual in the Middle East, although Cypriot businessman Asil Nadir recently bought up several daily newspapers in Turkey (*Günaydin*, *Günes*, and *Tan*) and a publishing house that produces the weekly newsmagazine *Nokta*. Concentration of ownership within countries is also uncommon. Large publishing houses with multiple publications only exist in the publishing centers of Istanbul, Cairo, and Tel Aviv.

Weekly newspapers, newsmagazines, and other periodicals are also quite important in several countries. Israel publishes nearly 400 periodicals, including 50 weeklies and 150 biweeklies. More than half of these are published in Hebrew, the rest in 11 other languages. Aside from the international edition of the *Jerusalem Post* and *Ma'ariv Lanoar*, a weekly for youth, most of these periodicals circulate under 20,000 copies.

Egypt also publishes many periodicals, and several of them have large circulations both in Egypt and in other Arab countries. *Al-Ahram al-Iqtisadi* (circ. 65,000), the economic *Al-Ahram*, is such a publication. Others with large circulations include *Akbar al-Yaum* (circ. 1 million); *Hawa'a* (circ. 161,000), a weekly women's magazine; *Al-Wafd* (circ. 360,000), the organ of the New Wafd party; *Rose al-Yousuf* (circ. 35,000), a political weekly that circulates in all Arab countries; and the *Middle East Observer* (circ. 30,000), a weekly economic publication covering the Middle East and North Africa that also publishes supplements on law, foreign trade, and tenders.

Al-Arabi, a monthly cultural magazine published by Kuwait's Ministry of Information, is distributed to about 350,000 people in the Arab world. A weekly with political and cultural focus, *Al-Hadaf* (circ. 63,000) is also published in Kuwait, along with *Osrati* (circ. 76,000), a woman's magazine, and *Al-Yaqza* (circ. 103,000), another political, economic, and social weekly.

The circulation of dailies in the other Arab countries is much smaller. The only newspapers—dailies or weeklies—to exceed 100,000 are the *Arab News* (circ. 110,000), a daily published in Jidda by the Saudi Research and Marketing Company; *Al-Riyadh* (circ. 140,000), another Saudi Arabian daily; *Al-Thawra* (circ. 250,000), the organ of the Baath party in Iraq; and several Iranian dailies. Following the revolution in Iran, all opposition and some moderate newspapers were closed, and according to the National Union of Iranian Journalists (now an illegal organization), more than 75 percent of all journalists left the country, were jailed, or no longer work in journalism. Some of those journalists in exile began publications from Europe or the United States in an attempt to overthrow the Islamic leaders. Since 1985, some liberalization of the press has occurred, and some constructive criticism of the government has been allowed. Of the newspapers for which circulation figures are published, two circulate more than 100,000 copies: *Ettela'at* (circ. 250,000), an evening political and literary daily, and *Kayhan* (circ. 350,000), a political daily. Both papers were owned by the Mostazafin Foundation from 1979 to 1987, when they were placed under the direct supervision of Wilayat-e-Faqih (religious jurisprudence). In addition to Farsi, *Kayhan* publishes editions in English, Arabic, Persian, and Turkish; it also publishes a religious paper, one for Iranians abroad, a woman's weekly, a children's weekly, and a cultural monthly.

The Cypriot press and the Palestinian press are worthy of attention because of their unique nature. Cyprus, a country politically divided into Greek and Turkish factions since 1974, publishes dailies, weeklies, and other periodicals for both groups in their native languages. In spite of the small population (700,000), the Greek sector publishes 12 dailies, 15 weeklies, and 22 other periodicals. The smaller Turkish sector publishes 7 dailies, 12 weeklies, and 8 other periodicals. Cyprus also serves as a communication center for the Middle East. It is used as a monitoring post for journalists who are barred from entry to Iran and are concerned for their physical safety in war-torn Lebanon. As the war worsened in Lebanon in 1988 and 1989, Cyprus became a temporary home for fleeing Lebanese citizens. Palestinians have also chosen to set

up publications in Cyprus because of the relative freedom to disseminate information from that location.

By contrast, the Palestinian press operating out of the occupied
territories is a press in captivity, subject to the rules set up by the
government of Israel. Palestinians number 650,000 to 750,000 in the
West Bank and another 350,000 in Gaza. In spite of their small population, the Palestinians are not media-poor. As Dov Shinar points out in
Palestinian Voices (1987), few societies are served by such a wide array
of both locally printed and imported material and dozens of radio and
television stations. Three dailies have been published since the 1967
war, although *Al-Anba* has since been closed. *Al-Quds* (circ. 16,000),
which takes a pro-Jordan position, is owned by a Jaffa-born businessman
who has been a journalist since 1948, when he arrived in Jerusalem.
Al-Fajar-al-Arabi, owned by Palestinian Paul Ajlune, supports the
Palestinian Liberation Organization. It has been the target of the Israeli
censors several times in recent years. In fact, all Palestinian publications are subject to prior restraint by the Israeli government, and they
are published only with its permission. It should be noted, however, that
Israeli and foreign publications must also submit to censorship for the
purpose of determining violations of state security. Although the Israeli
press is still considered to be quite free of censorship, Palestinian
journalists would not agree that their publications enjoy much freedom.
In addition to the dailies mentioned so far, *Al-Sha'ab*, published since
1972, and *Al-Nahar*, published since 1986, also serve the Palestinian
people. All Palestinian dailies began as weeklies.

ELECTRONIC MEDIA

Radio and Television

Both radio and television broadcasting services in most Middle Eastern
countries are either government-owned and -operated (often under a
ministry of information or culture) or under government control. A few
privately owned stations exist—a radio station broadcasting in English
and run by Aramco for its employees in Saudi Arabia; a noncommercial
private television station in Dhahran, also operated by Aramco; and a
half-private television company with two stations in Lebanon. In
addition, the American Armed Forces Network has a radio station in
Turkey, and the BBC has a large transmitter for indigenous-language
programming in Oman. Several of the government-owned stations are
financed in part or in full through commercials; only Iran's Islamic
Republic of Iran Broadcasting company accepts no advertising. Other
sources of funding are licensing fees, taxes on television and audio

equipment, and surcharges on electricity bills. Advertising may be an important source of revenue for government-owned television stations, but most Arab governments are reluctant to invest in aggressive marketing or promotion. A London-based media consultant for the Middle East, Michael Metcalfe, characterizes Arab advertising as low key when compared to that of Europe (Welford, 1986). Saudi Arabia has been the most recent country to permit advertising, first for Saudi products and later for imported ones.

In line with the trend toward privatization in Europe, some Middle Eastern countries may permit privately owned companies to launch broadcasting stations in the future. The Turkish government pledged its support for private television in 1987 but has yet to make good on that promise. At least one private film producer is ready to launch a television station as soon as the government grants permission. But in Turkey, as in most government-controlled systems, it is hard for authorities to give up their monopolies.

In most Arab countries, broadcasting was initiated by the colonial governments and taken over at the time of independent rule. As Rugh notes, several of the Arab countries of the area have conceived of the mass media as mobilizing forces for political and social goals and have used radio and television extensively for this purpose. These countries include Egypt, Iraq, Syria, South Yemen, and Iran after the revolution. In the other Arab and non-Arab countries, governments have been less directly involved in programming for social and political change. Broadcasting has long been used for reaching the population with educational messages, if not political ones, even in countries with high literacy rates, such as Israel.

As with the printed press, broadcasting was generally introduced later in this region than in Europe (see Table 6.2). Cyprus inaugurated its television system in 1957, and the other countries followed suit throughout the 1960s. The last system came in 1975 in the Yemen Arab Republic. As mostly small countries with limited resources, Middle Eastern countries usually have only two separate television program schedules; North and South Yemen, Qatar, and Oman each have only one. Lebanon is reported to have four, and all have been broadcasting on a more or less regular basis throughout the war. In both Jordan and Qatar, one of the two stations is in English and the other in Arabic. But in many countries, residents can also receive stations that spill over borders. For Arabs with a common language, viewers can extend their choices beyond limited national programming.

All broadcast systems in the region produce original programming, but programs are also imported from other countries, mainly Europe, the United States, and Egypt. In the late 1970s and early 1980s, Third World countries were troubled by the effect of importing programming

TABLE 6.2. BROADCAST DISTRIBUTION IN THE MIDDLE EAST

Country	Radios per 1,000 Population	Date of TV Inauguration	TVs per 1,000 Population
Bahrain	513	1972	394
Cyprus	289	1957	133
Egypt	313	1960	83
Iran	240	1958	57
Iraq	198	1956	61
Israel	463	1965[a]	261
Jordan	232	1968	68
Kuwait	268	1962	241
Lebanon	770	1959	301
Oman	664	1974	734
Qatar	485	1970	393
Saudi Arabia	323	1965	269
Syria	229	1960	57
Turkey	163	1969	165
United Arab Emirates	323	1968	108
Yemen Arab Republic (North)	28	1975	7
Yemen PDR (South)	136	1969	20

[a] Educational programming began in 1965, general television not until 1968.
Source: Data from *1988 Statistical Year Book* (Paris: UNESCO, 1989).

from the West, and many of them made attempts to shake their dependence on imports that included content running contrary to local cultural values. In strict Islamic countries such as Saudi Arabia, some of the Gulf countries, and Iran, it is even difficult to import films and television programs from Egypt, where religion does not have such a strong influence on entertainment products. The Saudi concern for preserving cultural and moral values has led to cutting offensive sections from imported programs, such as scenes where any sexual activity is suggested. Program sales representatives report that after selection committees from Arab countries review the available television programs, they reject roughly half as unsuitable. Nature documentaries sell well, while many sitcoms run into trouble, especially in the religiously strict countries.

However, imports constitute a substantial part of the area's programming, primarily because talent and/or money for local production is lacking. According to a 1987 study of imports from a range of countries, published by the Media and Government Department of the Friedrich-Ebert Foundation in Bonn, West Germany, the largest importers are Cyprus and the United Arab Emirates, each importing at least 60 percent of all programs. Syria, Egypt, Turkey, and South Yemen import between 31 and 50 percent of their television programs. The other countries of this region were not listed, but Tapio Varis's 1983 assessment of international imports showed that 47 percent of television programming in South Yemen was imported. No other figures were provided by the remaining countries for that year, but his 1973 study showed all Middle Eastern countries imported between 31 and 56 percent of programming.

Egypt is a primary source of entertainment programming for all Arab countries. In spite of the political differences that arose between Egypt and its Arab neighbors and the Egyptians' more liberal approach to sexual morality, films and television programs produced in Cairo have been popular imports in all Arab countries. Egypt is a major international film producer, averaging about 50 films per year and netting about $200 million annually. It even supplies programs beyond the Arabic-speaking countries.

In Islamic states, religious programming makes up a large part of the broadcast schedule. Iran devotes an entire radio station to readings from the Koran and other religious discussion and broadcasts this programming in 13 languages to Europe, the Soviet Union, Africa, the rest of Asia, and parts of the United States. Since Saudi Arabian broadcasting was begun only because the late King Saud was able to convince religious leaders that it was not anti-Islam and in fact could be a prime means of disseminating Allah's word, religious programming occupies a central role on Saudi television. Citing a 1980 report, Douglas Boyd (1982) states that about 25 percent of national broadcasting is devoted to religious subjects. All of the countries of the region devote some part of their schedule to religious subjects, however, especially at religious holidays.

Other Electronic Communications Technologies

Perhaps because of the central control of the broadcast systems and the resulting lack of individual choice, and also because new technologies became available for viewing uncensored and previously unavailable content, the videocassette recorder has had a tremendous impact in this region. Saudi Arabia and some of the Gulf countries have the highest VCR penetration levels in the world, in spite of the high cost of the equipment. And since only Egypt, Turkey, Lebanon, and Israel have copyright laws, pirated films from Europe, the United States, India, and Egypt circulate widely in most countries. In fact, the pirated material is also available in the countries that protect copyright. Lebanon has become a major distributor of pirated Egyptian films. The widespread availability of content that cannot be viewed on television or at the cinema (Saudi Arabia even forbids the construction of cinemas) has reduced the popularity of broadcast programming.

Content that would naturally be censored in most of these countries is also available on video, since government-controlled access is virtually impossible. Pornographic and horror films are generally available in all countries, though governments have raided video shops to rid them of such material. Frequently, pornographic content will appear at the end of a tape of another acceptable film. Political content on videotape is also disseminated in the region. Content that would never pass the Israeli censors has frequently been viewed on videocassette by West Bank Palestinians. Increasing use of the VCR in all controlled-media countries is becoming the norm, making it much harder for governments to regulate what citizens will be exposed to. And governments have been influenced by the popularity of video. The availability of uncensored material has caused Egyptian officials to take a more liberal approach to content permitted on television in the hope that audiences will not turn to video. A study by the Egyptian National Center of Social and Criminal Research has concluded that competition brought by video will even cause television producers to improve program quality. The Saudi government, seeing that advertising was successful on tape, began to accept television advertising in 1987, and TV advertising was expected to reap more than $1.5 million by 1990.

Some communication technologies are received more positively by governments in the region, however. Satellites have allowed Arab countries to share programming and all Middle Eastern countries to extend their coverage of broadcast and telecommunication services. Though the cost of launching a satellite is extremely expensive, renting transponders from Intelsat or from regional satellites has proved to be cost-effective for many countries.

Because Saudi Arabia had the resources, it took the lead in the planning for a regional satellite system to serve all Middle Eastern and North African Arab countries. The Saudis contributed 25 percent of the total cost of Arabsat, the rest coming in smaller amounts from 21 different Arab League members. Finally, after about ten years of planning and working out the contracts while reconciling Arab countries' ban on trading with countries that also trade with Israel, *Arabsat 1A* and *1B* were launched in 1985. At a cost of about $100 million, Arabsat cannot be said to be worth the investment. Broadcasters of the Arab States' Broadcasting Union (ASBU), the regional electronic news organization, expected that the convenience of having a local satellite would promote extensive news exchange. However, the exchange has been limited to a daily half-hour news program and occasional cultural programs. Disagreements over what was politically and culturally acceptable content for viewing in each country has led to the minimal use of the satellites for broadcast, and they have therefore been used primarily to enhance telecommunications traffic. But even that has not brought use up to more than one-third of total capacity.

Non-Arab clients have been difficult to find, as Turkey has recently announced plans to launch its own domestic satellite and Iran has long had plans for a national system. But new earth stations in Iraq and Libya will increase the amount of use, and there is a strong inclination on the Arabsat board to include Egypt.

In most Arab countries, private reception of programming via satellite dish is illegal, but not so in Turkey. And since several European broadcast services are now available via satellite, urban Turks with the financial capability are purchasing dishes to receive CNN, Sky Channel, and other European programs. Often apartment building dwellers split the cost of a dish and connect individual apartments by cable.

Large cable systems are presently nonexistent in Middle Eastern countries, but Israel's national system should be in place by 1991, enabling residents to receive several neighboring national services, Soviet channels, Arabsat programming, and both European and U.S. services. To date, the high cost of cabling and the large percentage of populations living outside urban areas have prevented most countries from considering national cable systems. Israel's system is expected to cost about $400 million.

NEWS SERVICES

All Middle Eastern countries have national news agencies. Most of them have a single official agency over which the government has full control. In some of these agencies, the government simply passes on bulletins from the various ministries to be carried directly by the wire service. Turkey, Cyprus, Lebanon, and Israel all have multiple news agencies, where private and cooperatively owned services operate in addition to the official national news agency. There is even a news agency to serve the Palestinian media, the pro-PLO Palestinian Press Service. It publishes daily and weekly bulletins. According to Dov Shinar (1987), it has also conducted fact-finding tours in the West Bank and Gaza for both local and foreign press representatives.

Most of the region's news agency are relatively new, at least seven of them appearing after 1970. The impetus for the development of national news agencies in recent years has been the international discussion over a New World Information and Communication Order (NWICO; see Chapter 2). One of the main purposes of the newly established agencies is to present a positive picture of local events to the outside world. Most of the region's agencies serve to disseminate domestic and international news within the borders of their countries and to supply domestic news to the outside world through other domestic agencies or international agencies. Several of the national agencies are the sole suppliers of international news to domestic media, thereby having the capability to serve as editors and interpreters of certain unwanted international stories.

The only news agencies in the region to attempt to function beyond their borders as international agencies are the Middle East News Agency (MENA) of Egypt and the Jewish Telegraphic Agency of Israel. These agencies attempt to cover a range of international stories for domestic consumption and for sale to news organizations in other parts of the world. MENA is the only Arab agency subscribed to by at least one news organization in every other Arab nation. William A. Rugh (1979) reports that the agency employs nearly 300 journalists. Begun as a joint venture of the largest publishing houses in 1950, MENA has correspondents in all the principal capitals and exchanges news and photographs with both Arab and Western news organizations. The Jewish Telegraphic Agency has bureaus in at least four international capitals and stringers all over the world. It sells news to a large number of U.S. and Canadian publications.

GOVERNMENT-MEDIA RELATIONS

Whether newspapers are government-owned or private, they are subject to considerable influence, and even censorship, by authorities. In *The Arab Press* (1979), William A. Rugh discerns press-government relationships of three types: mobilization, loyalist, and diverse. Extending Rugh's classification system to include the non-Arab countries of the region, the countries with a mobilization press include Egypt, Iraq, Syria, and South Yemen; the loyalist press can be found in Bahrain, Jordan, Qatar, Saudi Arabia, and the United Arab Emirates; and the diverse press countries include Cyprus, Israel, Kuwait, Lebanon, and Turkey. Rugh decided not to include North Yemen and Oman in his classification, primarily because of their late media development, making it difficult to determine any long-term direction. Iran might be considered to have a mobilization press, but in the early years following the revolution, Majid Tehranian (1982) characterized it as having a revolutionary press. We will discuss that country separately.

In Rugh's view, the function of the mobilization press is to mobilize support for the government's social and political programs. In countries with this press system, a single power rules with no real organized opposition. The press is expected to support government campaigns, to avoid criticism of government policies and personalities, and not to serve as a forum for the expression of diverse opinions on issues. Criticism is permitted only for local government services, and local bureaucrats are held responsible for the problems. If not actually government-owned, as in Egypt and Iraq, newspapers must, as in Syria, obtain licenses from the government to operate.

Criticism is not encouraged in loyalist press systems either, but neither is active support of government campaigns. The loyalist press is characterized by its loyalty to the regime in power, its passive response to critical issues, and its failure to attack national policies or leaders' personalities. The press in these countries is privately owned, and government controls content through press law and subsidies of various kinds, leaving it with little financial or editorial independence. These countries have no independent parliament or institutionalized opposition.

Private ownership and reduced government pressure have led to more independence of opinion in the diverse press. Countries with such a press have a longer tradition of criticism, and opposition parties are well established. Cyprus, of course, is different because each ethnic group has a press to serve its own interest, but even within each system, diversity of opinion is expressed.

Since the war, Lebanon's particular form of diversity has developed in interesting ways. It appears today primarily as a partisan press. The Christian Lebanese Forces militia operates the Lebanese Broadcasting Corporation television station, the Free Lebanon radio station, and *Al-Massira*, a weekly political magazine. The Christian Phalange party controls the Voice of Lebanon radio station and the daily newspaper *Al-Amal.* And the Druze Progressive Socialist party, headed by Walid Jumblatt, operates the Voice of the Mountain radio station and that party's weekly, *Al-Anba.*

CONCEPTS OF MEDIA FREEDOM

The media in all these countries face a continual battle with government over freedom of expression, no matter what the particular media-government relationship. The International Press Institute (IPI), which attempts to monitor what it considers infractions of press freedom in various countries, writes an annual assessment of the situation on a country-by-country basis. In 1988, the organization was concerned over the following problems: The total lack of press freedom in Iraq and

Syria, where the government continues to use it as an instrument of party propaganda and where a ban on the free sale of foreign publications exists; the continued policy of not allowing foreign publications to circulate or foreign correspondents to visit the Gulf region (with the exception of Saudi Arabia, which places restrictions only on visas); the new practice of applying censorship rules for the Kuwaiti media; the closure of the only English-language publication, the *Star,* in Jordan by a state-appointed board; the dismissal of three major editors of Jordanian dailies by the government; the arrest of 50 Palestinian journalists by Israeli authorities and the periodic closure of Palestinian publications; the closure (for the first time since Hosni Mubarak came to power) of an Egyptian opposition newspaper; and the increases in the price of newsprint levied against the Turkish press for political rather than economic reasons.

No press in the world exists in a political vacuum, and the examples from 1988 serve to illustrate the fragility of press freedom in the Middle East in the face of government pressure. Nowhere is this more evident than in the recent history of the Iranian press. Prior to the revolution, the print press of Iran was primarily in the hands of leftists and liberals, but following the change of power, many publications were closed, and journalists went underground or began publishing from exile. Majid Tehranian reported in 1982 that at least 40 to 50 periodicals and several radio stations were operating outside Iran, all editorially opposed to the traditionalist view of governing Iran. The two major dailies, *Kayhan* and *Ettela'at,* were nationalized, and the government requires licensing of all newspapers and magazines. Imprisonment is the penalty for insulting senior religious figures, although the 1979 constitution declares that the press is free—except with respect to morality and religious issues or slandering individuals. The good news from Iran, as reported by the IPI in 1988, was that for the first time in nine years, no journalists were among the 279 people executed in the country for so-called political crimes. And the year marked the return of some previously banished journalists to work in the media with the publication of a new weekly, *Adineh.* In 1985, when the Ayatollah Khomeini announced a liberalization of the press, journalists were given permission to criticize the government if they did it constructively and did not seek to promote dissent.

The war in Lebanon has brought different problems related to press freedom. When the Arab Deterrent Forces moved into Lebanon in 1976, the Lebanese government tried to censor the press strictly, partly in response to the criticism that the press had helped cause the war. Since the war continued long after the censorship decree, the authorities eventually stopped enforcing the censorship restrictions, according to the *Middle East Times* (Dakroub, 1989). Today, the article concludes, press freedom in Lebanon has little to do with constitutional protection or benevolent leaders but is a consequence of the chaos in the country. The plight of the French-language daily *L'Orient—Le Jour* in its struggle to publish amid the chaos is an example of the difficulties of publishing in a war zone. Though the paper has been critical of both Syria's and Israel's role in the war and has been bombed by the Israelis, it has been off the streets only a few times since the beginning of the war, according to the *Middle East Times.* The paper is now forced to operate on both sides of the city in order to avoid possible staff kidnappings. Copy is sent by fax machine to printers in the West. Its most serious problem is not political but economic. Since the collapse of the Lebanese pound, the newspaper has been losing considerable sums of money since the newspaper is sold in Lebanese currency and has to pay the printers in U.S. dollars.

And on a related unhappy note, journalists from the United States (Terry Anderson) and the United Kingdom (John McCarthy and Alec Collett) are still being held hostage in Lebanon at this writing.

JOURNALISM EDUCATION AND TRAINING

Journalism education is a relatively recent phenomenon in the Middle East. Most journalists learned as apprentices on the job, and if they had university degrees, they were educated in the liberal arts. With one of the most developed press systems in the region, Egypt was the first country to begin a degree program in a university—in fact, it began two of them. The American University in Cairo began a program in 1935 and was followed by Cairo University in 1939. However, these programs were mostly theoretical until the mid-1970s, when training in print and broadcast journalism began. Since 1971, the American University has also offered an M.A. and Ph.D. in communications.

The next countries to launch university-level training in journalism were Turkey (1964), in the political science faculty of Ankara University, and Iraq (1964), with a department of journalism at Baghdad University. Today, Turkey offers degrees in print and broadcast communications at several more universities in Istanbul, Eskişehir, and Izmir and some form of training at eight institutions.

But most programs in the region were not established until the 1970s, and today degree programs exist in Syria (since 1979, a two-year program), Saudi Arabia (at three different universities), Lebanon (at two schools), and Jordan (one degree program at Yarmouk University and a two-year program at the University of Jordan in Amman). Iran has probably continued its programs, but in 1980 all journalism schools were closed for Islamization and purification. Kuwait and Qatar were considering new programs.

PROSPECTS FOR THE FUTURE

Predictions about the future of journalism in any region of the world are difficult, but since this region seems to be the site of continual war, unrest, and disagreement, it is even harder to tell what the future role of journalism might be. Iran and Iraq are no longer fighting, but the war hasn't been completely settled. The *intifada* continues in the occupied territories, and the Palestinians seem to be no closer to achieving independence. Tension and violence continue between the Israelis and their Arab neighbors. Syria still has troops in Lebanon, and the political situation there shows little sign of long-term improvement. And Cyprus remains divided, in spite of international efforts to reunite the two sectors.

Yet life goes on. A former resident who recently visited Lebanon reports that media have proliferated, not retracted, in that country, where war has prevailed for nearly two decades. In the state of upheaval, the government in Lebanon has less control over the content of the privately owned press, not more. So even in one of the most troubled states of the region, journalism flourishes, just as in more stable areas.

New communication technologies are being used in interesting ways, and more developments can be expected in the use of satellites and video, in particular. Satellite dishes are spreading throughout the region as Europe launches more satellite broadcast services. The inability of governments to control the entry and dissemination of information from the outside will lead to more freedom of access, even in the countries with the most restricted information systems.

Another economic trend that may spread beyond Turkey to countries with more competitive press systems is the increasing amount spent on newspaper promotion on television. Turkey has long been the site of keen competition in the daily press, and newspapers have used lotteries and contests for big prizes (cars, apartments, household goods) to promote sales, but the new push may drive some papers out of the market. The *Turkish Times* reported that during five months in 1989, one newspaper group spent the equivalent of $25 million on television advertisements, and competitive groups followed close behind in expenditures on commercials. Yavuz Donat, a prominent columnist for *Tercuman*, a conservative Istanbul daily, claims that readership among young people is down and that the sensationalist press is not meeting their needs for serious reading material. Depressed circulation and concern over lost readership are problems common to the West that may be spreading to this region of the world.

NORTH AFRICA

Geographically, all of the North African countries border the Mediterranean except for the Sudan, which lies to the south of Egypt. All North African countries have at least part of their landmass in the Sahara. The chief common feature of North African countries is their ethnic identity, which is predominantly Arab. Their Arab roots separate them from the rest of Africa. However, other groups of people live in the several countries—Berbers in Morocco, Algeria, Libya, and Tunisia (or Arab-Berber mixed people), and Beja, Nubians, and black Africans from several African ethnic groups in the Sudan. Arabic is the primary language in all these countries, but Berber dialects are spoken in most of the chiefly Berber-settled areas, and a number of African languages are spoken in the Sudan. French is spoken in the former French colonies of Algeria, Morocco, and Tunisia; Italian in Libya, once a colony of Italy; and English in Libya (which existed under a British protectorate for a time) and in the Sudan (which was jointly ruled by Egypt and England). Islam is practiced by the large majority in all of North Africa, though about 20 percent of the blacks and Nubians in the Sudan hold indigenous beliefs or are Christians.

All the North African economies are classified as developing economies. Oil has boosted the per capita income of Algeria and particularly Libya. The rest are chiefly agricultural economies. Per capita income ranges from a low of $330 a year in the Sudan to $5,460 in Libya, according to the World Bank.

PRINT MEDIA

As in the Middle East, communication was traditionally the province of imams, merchants, teachers, and tribal chiefs. Algeria is typical of North African countries in that the colonial press was the first press it knew. Citing Zahir Ihaddaden's history of the Algerian press, Mohamed Kirat (1987) says that prior to the Algerian independence, the press could be characterized in five forms. The government press, owned by the French government, was directed to the Algerian people; the colonial press was written for the French settlers and ignored the Algerians; the "indigenophile" press was produced by the French colonial sympathizers in the Algerian population, who expressed the French point of view; the indigenous press in Arabic and French was a political press that called for equality and justice but never challenged the French right to rule the country; and the nationalist press, a forum for Muslim reformists, challenged both the French settlers and the French government.

Under colonialism, the indigenous press developed at a rate that seemed to be correlated with the literacy level and economic status of the country, William Rugh (1979) says. This explains why the Libyan and Sudanese press developed more slowly than the others. Today, Sudan has the lowest literacy rate in North Africa. Oil income has probably allowed the Libyan government to improve education. However, the press in Libya is the least developed in the region today (see Table 6.3).

One way in which the colonial influence is still felt in the region is in the language used for publications. In Tunisia, Algeria, and Morocco, French-language dailies circulate as widely as Arabic publications. Some dailies, such as the Algerian *Al-Moudjahid* ("The Fighter"), organ of the ruling National Liberation Front (FLN), circulate in both French and Arabic. The existence of a popular foreign-language press is not surprising, since after long years of French rule in Morocco and Algeria, many people did not speak Arabic. The process of Arabization has been well supported, but French lingers in all three former French colonies. In 1989, a new Algerian press law required all newly created Algerian

TABLE 6.3. NEWSPAPERS PUBLISHED IN NORTH AFRICA

Country	Population (in millions)	Literacy (%)	Dailies	Weeklies
Algeria	23.1	52	5	4
Libya	4.1	50	1	10
Morocco	23.3	28	12	7
Sudan	23.1	20	1[a]	6
Tunisia	7.6	64	6	17

Note: The number of dailies and weeklies listed is approximate; latest available data were used to determine actual numbers.

[a] Since the overthrow of the civilian government, only one newspaper has been authorized to publish in Khartoum, *Al-Guwwat al-Mussallaha* ("The Armed Forces"), under rule of Brigadier General Omar Hassan Ahmed al-Bashir. The *Europa Year Book* listed 20 dailies prior to the coup, but those papers probably circulated at very low rates. Until their suspension in 1986 by the former Prime Minister Al-Mahdi, *Al-Ayyam* and *Al-Sahafa* had the largest circulations, 60,000 each.

Sources: UNESCO Year Book 1988 (Paris: UNESCO, 1987); *Europa Year Book*, 1989 ed. (London: Europa Publications, 1988); *World Development Report* (New York: Oxford University Press, 1988); *1989 Information Please Almanac* (Boston: Houghton Mifflin, 1988).

publications to be edited in Arabic. However, since existing French-language publications have larger circulations than those published in Arabic, the French-language publications were expected to remain in control of the country, according to the IPI.

Rugh sees differences in the press in the five countries; he classifies the Moroccan press as diverse, the Tunisian press as loyalist, and the press of the Sudan, Algeria, and Libya as mobilization. Changes that have taken place in Tunisia since the death of Bourguiba and in the Sudan since the election of Sadiq al-Mahdi in 1986 and his overthrow by Brigadier General Omar Hassan Ahmed al-Bashir in 1989 call for a reassessment of Rugh's typology in North Africa. In his study of the Algerian press, Kirat rejects the idea that the Algerian press is used as an instrument of mobilization.

Under an elected government in the Sudan, the IPI described the press as "mushrooming." Al-Mahdi's friendly attitude toward the media led many people to establish their own daily or periodical press. The last count of dailies before the 1989 coup stood at 22, and there were also 10 periodicals. The press flourished in spite of a disagreement between journalists and Al-Mahdi that led to the closure of the two largest dailies in 1986. Since Al-Bashir took power, the press has been put on hold. The constitution has been suspended, and there is no way to know whether newspapers will be allowed to print. The army's newspaper, *Al-Guwwat al-Mussallaha*, is the only authorized paper. It has a circulation of 7,500.

Under Habib Bourguiba, president of Tunisia from 1959 to 1987, when he was overthrown by Zine el-Abidine ben-Ali, the press was mostly in private hands. But Bourguiba insisted on keeping a party press as long as he was in power. *Al-'Amal* and *L'Action*, organs of the Destourian Socialist party, continued to publish because Bourguiba attributed his rise to power to the party press, according to Rugh. Since November 1987, President Ben-Ali has relaxed restrictions on the press, released five journalists from jail along with other political prisoners, and lifted a ban on two weeklies and another periodical. The IPI reports that by November 1988, two opposition papers were being regularly published without governmental interference, and full press freedom had been guaranteed in a national agreement between the government and opposition groups. The only actions unfavorable to the press were the restriction of the sale of the very popular weekly, *Jeune Afrique*, to 6,000 copies—down from an average of 24,000. The magazine is Tunisian but is published in Paris for political reasons. It claims to be the best-selling publication in ten African countries, according to the *World Press Encyclopedia*. Two previously banned Algerian weeklies (also published in Europe) are still not permitted to publish at home.

Algeria's press is of mixed type—a party press and one controlled by the Ministry of Information. Kirat notes that because the Algerian press lacks a clearly defined ideology such that it cannot be used for propaganda and agitation, journalists are confused about the role they play. Kirat says that this confusion results in a lack of criticism, investigation, and use of development journalism. Martin Ochs in *The African Press* (1986) agrees, writing that there is a sameness or monotony in the Algerian press. Kirat says that journalists are popularly characterized as "government secretaries."

The largest dailies in the region include the FLN's *Al-Moudjahid* (circ. 392,000) in Algeria, *Le Matin du Sahara* (circ. 100,000) in Morocco, and *Al-Sabah* (circ. 90,000) in Tunisia. Given the small populations, low literacy levels, and popularity of the foreign press in several of the countries, these low circulation levels are not surprising.

ELECTRONIC MEDIA

Radio and Television

As in the Middle East, broadcasting stations are mostly government-owned and -operated. Only Morocco has a private television station, introduced in 1989; jointly owned by Omnium Nord-Africain and Moroccan financial institutions (67 percent) and by foreign concerns, it broadcasts in French and Arabic. Multiple languages are used for broadcast transmission of information in all North African countries. In Algeria, broadcasting is in French, Arabic, and also in the Berber dialect of Kabyle on radio; Libya transmits primarily in Arabic but also for limited hours in English, Italian, and French; Morocco transmits in Spanish, Berber, and English in addition to French and Arabic; radio broadcasting in the Sudan (with the most diverse ethnic population) is in Amharic, Arabic, English, French, Somali, and Tigrinya; and Tunisia broadcasts in Arabic, French, and Italian.

In the former French colonies, programs of Arabization have extended to radio and television programming, with most countries having an official policy to transmit information in Arabic rather than French. The United States Information Service reports little success with that policy in Algeria, at least.

However, as Sydney Head states in *World Broadcasting Systems* (1985), the North African countries on the Mediterranean have been able to use radio to help one another in their respective liberation struggles. Kirat writes that the most important medium during the Algerian revolution was a radio station set up by the FLN in Tunis.

All the Mediterranean countries were influenced by European culture, both directly through colonization and indirectly because they could easily receive so many European broadcast signals. For example, Algeria had radio in 1937 and television in 1957, but all broadcasting was in French, intended for the French colonists and mostly received directly from France. Not until independence were the Algerians able to control the broadcasting system in their own country.

Compared with the Middle East, the penetration of broadcast media is relatively low, as can be observed in Table 6.4. Multiple channels for television exist in all but Algeria, though they are of varying type and purpose. Libya's additional channels are dedicated to foreign-language programming in English, Italian, and French. Tunisia added a second channel in 1983 but only began accepting advertising for the two channels in 1988. The Sudan has regional stations in Gezira and Atbara (central and northern regions) in addition to the central station at Omdurman. And Morocco's second channel is privately owned and operated.

All of the Mediterranean countries can receive broadcasts easily from Europe, particularly Spain, Italy, and France. And much of the programming on local channels is imported, despite the anti-American political positions in the area. Algeria and Tunisia are reported to import more than half of all their television programs.

Algeria and the Sudan have taken advantage of satellites in attempting to reach all of their people by telecommunication links. Algeria was the first nation to lease Intelsat transponders for domestic use. Head reports that the country installed a microwave relay network as a priority for interconnecting television stations. The Algerian government broadcasts in color one program over 11 high-power transmitters and 86 low-power receiver stations, covering about 97 percent of the country.

The Sudan has an earth satellite station operating on 36 channels and has plans for a nationwide satellite network with 14 earth stations

TABLE 6.4. BROADCAST DISTRIBUTION IN NORTH AFRICA

Country	Radios per 1,000 Population	Date of TV Inauguration	TVs per 1,000 Population
Algeria	223	1962 (French 1956–62)	72
Libya	228	1968	66
Morocco	205	1964	54
Sudan	253	1963	52
Tunisia	166	1966	69

in the nation. By 1983, fully 90 percent of the inhabited areas were reached by television signals.

Other Electronic Communications Technologies

The North African countries are all members of Arabsat. But because all but Tunisia have little financial incentive to make full use of Arabsat, the satellite system is operating at a minimum. Morocco, Algeria, Libya, and the Sudan all have transponder leases with Intelsat, which preceded the launch of the Arabsat system. In Simon Baker's analysis of Arabsat's financial problems in *Cable & Satellite Europe* (1989), he says that tariffing on Arabsat is similar to that of Intelsat, making the only advantage of the regional system the reduced size of earth stations.

Control over some television program content and lack of entertainment diversity has made the videocassette recorder popular in North Africa. The VCR is in 10.3 percent of Algerian TV households and 28.4 percent of those in Morocco. In *Screen Digest*'s periodic assessment of worldwide penetration, data were not available from the other countries. It is likely that pirating of video content takes place in all of these countries, since there are no copyright laws in the area.

NEWS SERVICES

All the North African countries have their own national news agencies. Algeria's news agency was begun even before the country achieved independence, operating in exile out of Tunis from 1961. The oldest in all the Arab world was begun in the Sudan in 1946. The government controls the news agencies in Tunisia, Libya, and Algeria. Agencies in those countries are also the sole importers and distributors of international wire service news. That means that news can be selected according to its favorability to the country in question. In Libya, the wire service editors go so far as to add their own interpretations to news stories.

Morocco's news agency is private and independent. Though it has contractual arrangements with international wire services, individual newspapers in the country are permitted to subscribe to those services too. In 1986, the Sudan's news agency (SUNA) also became independent, in the spirit of relaxation of government control of the press. Since the 1989 coup, however, it is likely that the government has closed or taken control of all incoming and outgoing news from SUNA, since the armed forces control the only newspaper.

JOURNALISM EDUCATION AND TRAINING

Tunisia has the best-developed education system for journalism in the region. The Institute of Press and Information Sciences at the University of Tunis has had a four-year program since 1967. Students can obtain state aid to train in journalism or in broadcasting. The University of Kar Yunis in Ben Ghazi also offers an undergraduate degree. Students studying in Tunis may also have access to publications from the Arab League Education, Cultural, and Scientific Organization (ALECSO). The Arab League's counterpart to UNESCO is based in Tunis and produces a journal, *Arab Communication.*

Algeria has the oldest program, begun in 1965 at the Institute of Political Sciences and News in Algiers. The Sudan, Morocco, and Libya also offer journalism training. Morocco's program is administered by the Ministry of Information.

But journalistic training is not necessarily sufficient. In Kirat's study of Algerian journalists, he concludes that those who had graduated from the country's journalism school expressed dissatisfaction with the quality of that training. Between 22 and 30 percent of the respondents in his study cited unnecessary courses, lack of practical training, lack of equipment and facilities, lack of internship programs, and a lack of qualified and experienced professors as problems with their education.

PROSPECTS FOR THE FUTURE

Prospects are certainly mixed for this area. Political strife in the Sudan, continued control of the media by Libya's Qaddafi, and economic problems in Algeria, Morocco, and Tunisia don't bode well for the mass media. As Kirat points out in the conclusion of his study:

> The key solution to the critical situation of Algerian journalism is in institutional and organizational changes. The political leadership should trust the media and should trust the journalists. More news organizations, more journalists, a regional press, more funds and infrastructure are needed.

This sums up the situation for all the countries of the region. Without needed changes, the future looks quite a bit like the present. And without increased literacy levels, it will be difficult for the printed press to develop much beyond its present condition.

CHAPTER 7

Africa

L. John Martin

When many current college students were born, one-third of sub-Saharan African countries were still dependencies of European powers. Among these were the five former Portuguese colonies that were given their independence in 1974 and 1975. But by far the majority of African states became independent during most students' parents' lives. The year 1960 was a particularly good one for Africa: That year alone, 17 of the 46 political entities (i.e., 37 percent) became independent states. Only two countries—Ethiopia, which existed as a monarchy in biblical times, and Liberia, which was founded in 1847 by former American slaves—had never been colonized. South Africa was given dominion status within the British Empire in 1910 as the Union of South Africa. In 1961, it cut its ties with Britain and became the Republic of South Africa.

Only two other nations gained their independence before 1960. The Gold Coast, an area in West Africa that had been colonized by Britain, became the independent state of Ghana in 1957. Guinea, also in West Africa but under French domination, granted independence in 1958. Today, all African countries are independent of foreign rule. The last African colony to become independent was Namibia (South-West Africa), in March 1990.

Because almost all of Africa achieved independence (not to be confused with freedom) so recently, it has had special problems. Africans hate to be thought of as Johnny-come-latelies, especially since many anthropologists believe that human beings evolved on that continent. Yet their economic and technological power fails to match their undeniable enthusiasm for participating as equal partners in world affairs. Yet they have plenty of political clout in international organizations because of their sheer numbers. They make up close to one-third of the 159 members of the United Nations, for example.

It is easy to dismiss Africa as a backward continent if we use Western criteria for judging progress. The African continent, for instance, has the smallest number of daily newspapers per capita in the world. As Table 7.1 shows, it has only 0.296 daily newspapers per 1 million people. This means that, on the average, there are more than 3.3 million people living on the continent for each daily newspaper that is published there. Ten years ago, it was 2.5 million Africans, so that the relative number of dailies is shrinking; but this is a global phenomenon.

Some analysts of the world's press have suggested that daily newspapers are a good indicator of development. Daily newspaper reading in the so-called developed countries tends to be high, as measured by circulation figures per 1,000 population. In fact, there appears to be a high correlation between per capita income and the number of daily newspapers read in a country, as many researchers such as Wilbur Schramm, Daniel Lerner, Raymond Nixon, and Bradley Greenberg have shown. (Incidentally, accurate circulation figures are even more difficult to come by than figures on the number of daily newspapers, and even estimates are highly suspect.) But to draw the conclusion that Africans have a long way to go before they catch up with the West on the basis of the number of newspapers or of newspaper readership would be completely misleading.

TABLE 7.1. DAILY NEWSPAPERS BY CONTINENT

	Population (in millions)	Number of Dailies	Dailies per Million	Population per Daily	Average GNP per Capita ($)
Africa	615.3	182	0.296	3,380,769	764.5
Asia	3,031.1	2,904	0.958	1,043,732	3,880.3
Europe	684.8	2,783	4.064	246,065	7,619.3
North America[a]	413.1	2,260	5.471	182,787	3,080.9
South America	282.2	740	2.622	381,351	1,623.3
Oceania	25.5	105	4.118	242,857	3,989.1

[a] Includes Central America.

Sources: *1989 Britannica Book of the Year; Africa South of the Sahara, 1989; The World Almanac and Book of Facts 1989.*

Information sources and communication habits are changing universally, and Africa has entered the comity of nations at a point where this change had begun to occur. There are many reasons why the press developed the way it did in the Western world. Commerce, science, and technology, Western political systems, and social interactions all require the kind of daily report on the details of individual and organizational activities that the Western press has come to provide and that Western publics have become used to and have come to expect of their press. People want their unadulterated facts, and both mass media and the wire services have been molded by the expectations of the public.

A variety of factors have created a totally different kind of press system in other parts of the world—the communist world, for example, and Africa, although communist mass media, too, are changing rapidly. Nevertheless, how people use and are able to use printed media as well as their needs and expectations are very different in Africa from what they were in the West at the same stage of development.

For one thing, Africa has still not emerged from its tribal disjuncture at a time when it is technologically far ahead of where the West was when it was similarly tribalized. Most tribes in Africa are both culturally and linguistically diverse. Estimates of the number of discrete languages and dialects in Africa range from 800 to 2,000, and between 80 and 95 percent of these have no written form or literature. It has been estimated that Cameroon, with 10.5 million people, has tribes speaking 100 different languages; that Nigeria, with a population of 115 million, has as many as 25 discriminable tongues and dialects; and that Gabon, with a mere million people, harbors 10 discrete languages.

Producing printed media, especially daily newspapers, for populations often as small as half a million is not economically viable. Furthermore, since most of the languages have no written form, the problem is moot. Then why not provide printed media in some lingua franca such as English, French, or Portuguese?

Actually, these are the very languages in which most African dailies are published, with the addition of Afrikaans in South Africa and Namibia. A few dailies are published in such widely spoken African languages as Swahili in the East and Hausa in the West. But they have limited readership. This is true in spite of increasing literacy. In 1980, the average literacy in French- and Portuguese-speaking (Francophone and Iberophone) African countries was about 20 percent, and in English-speaking (Anglophone) countries it averaged 34 percent. Today, it is estimated that the average literacy is 50 percent in Anglophone, 36 percent in Francophone, and 30 percent in Iberophone countries of sub-Saharan Africa. It is 55 percent in Spanish-speaking Equatorial Guinea and in South Africa (literacy among whites is 98 percent, among coloreds and Indians it is 85 to 90 percent, and among blacks, who make up the majority of the population, it is 50 to 60 percent). Literacy is 30 percent in Amharic-speaking Ethiopia and 12 percent in Somali- and Arabic-speaking Somalia.

While literacy is increasing, so is agitation for national, non-European languages, and there is much controversy about which tribal language should be raised to national language status. Often rulers belong to a tribe that is not the dominant group in the country, yet they wish to impose their particular language as the lingua franca. Tribal fragmentation and jealousies have led African journalist Frank Barton (1979) to predict that "even if national pride wins the day and 'national' languages become the pattern of the media, it is highly unlikely that English, French and Portuguese will ever totally disappear from the press" (p. 265).

Apart from the proliferation of languages and low literacy, both of which control the number and size of newspapers, Africa's colonial past has played an important role in the kind of press that has evolved on the continent.

HISTORICAL HIGHLIGHTS

The history of journalism in Africa covers a period of no more than 30 years. Most of its mass media today date from the 1960s. Whatever journalistic endeavors there were before independence were largely by and for the white community, many—though by no means all—of whom have left the continent. No one did Africans a favor by engaging in journalism on the continent of Africa. Most of the media ignored the "natives," and the few that included them were mostly out to convert them or to keep them in line.

During the colonial period, the press carried two types of content: some "home" news (although most such news was gleaned by white settlers from home newspapers that arrived by sea mail or, after the mid-1930s, was obtained from radio broadcasts) and social and official local news about the white population's social affairs, promotions, arrivals, and departures. Judging from most of these local newspapers, one would suppose that blacks barely existed.

Missionaries and church-related organizations did address themselves to the local population. As a by-product of their zeal to bring Christianity to the African peoples, they worked hard at turning oral languages into written ones, then taught as many as would learn the mysteries of reading and writing their own language. The next step was to produce some literature for Africans to read. Much of this literature consisted of translations of the Bible, but some missionaries also started newspapers often filled with church-related announcements.

Such was the first newspaper in Nigeria, *Iwe Irohin fun awon ara Egba Yorubas*, founded by the Rev. Henry Townsend of the Christian Missionary Society (CMS) in 1859. Many other missionaries, some of whose names have been forgotten, produced publications in most African countries. Thus the CMS mission published *Mengo Notes* in Uganda in 1900, and there was an unnamed mimeographed quarterly even before then in 1897, published by the Rev. A. W. Crabtree. Commercial printers were at work early in a few countries, especially South Africa, Sierra Leone, the Gold Coast, and Mauritius. Sierra Leone reputedly had the first periodical in black Africa in 1801 called the *Royal Gazette and Sierra Leone Advertiser*. But most of these publications lasted only a short time, disappearing with the changing character and needs of the population.

The few irregularly appearing African-owned and -run newspapers had a totally different mission and content. They were organs of revolution and dissent. Their goal was African independence. Many African leaders began their political careers as journalists or newspaper owners. Prior to independence, Julius Nyerere, president of Tanzania before he retired in 1985, edited *Sauti ya TANU*, an organ of what is now the only authorized party in the country. Jomo Kenyatta (formerly Johnstone Kamau), first president of Kenya, started the Kikuyu-language monthly *Muiguithania* in the late 1920s. Hastings Banda of Malawi, Nnamdi Azikiwe of Nigeria, and Ghana's Kwame Nkrumah were all newspaper proprietors before independence and became presidents of their countries. In French-speaking Africa, President Felix Houphouët-Boigny of the Ivory Coast was editor of *Afrique Noire* before independence; and President Leopold Sedar-Senghor of Senegal was editor and publisher of *La Condition Humaine* in Dakar in the 1950s. Finally, both President Mobutu Sese Seko and the late Premier Patrice Lumumba of what is now Zaire were editors of Congolese newspapers.

From the journalist's viewpoint, the heroes of the African press were not Africans but Europeans. They included men like Charles de Breteuil, who brought newspapers and magazines to Francophone Africa just before World War II. Another was Cecil King, of the London Daily Mirror Group, who influenced press developments in Anglophone West Africa. There was also the Aga Khan and his publisher, Michael Curtis, who established a newspaper empire in East Africa; and Canadian press tycoon Roy Thomson, with his close adviser, James Coltart, who operated in West, East, and southern Africa.

Among the names of journalists who had an impact on African journalism are those of both Europeans and Africans. Richard Hall trained many journalists in Zambia, where he was editor of the *African Mail* and the *Times of Zambia*. Norman Cattanach, a Scot, was active in Malawi; John Spicer, in Swaziland. Leading African journalists include Hilary Ng'weno and George Githii, both of whom worked for the *Nation* in Nairobi. Ng'weno is an independent publisher of a sophisticated newsmagazine. Peter Enahoro of Nigeria's *Daily Times* is always mentioned among leading African journalists, and there are others—not too many—including some political leaders such as Azikiwe and Nkrumah, who later became presidents of their nations. In South Africa, Tom Hopkinson, editor of the *Drum*, should be mentioned. He trained many African journalists. So should courageous newsmen such as Laurence Gandar, of the now defunct *Rand Daily Mail*, and one of his reporters, Benjamin Pogrund. They used their paper to bring South African prison conditions to the attention of the public. Their long-drawn-out trial on charges of publishing false information took a toll on Gandar's health.

Africans have never had an information press. Theirs has always been an opinion press. Advocacy journalism comes naturally to them. To the extent that they feel a need for hard news, that need is satisfied by the minimal coverage of the mass media, especially of radio. Soft news—human-interest news or what Schramm has called immediate-reward news—is equally well transmitted through the folk media, such as the "bush telegraph" or drum; the "grapevine," or word-of-mouth and gossip; town criers and drummers; traditional dances; plays; and songs.

Timeliness here, as in most African intercourse, is of secondary importance. Neither the interest nor the usefulness of a story diminishes with time. Accuracy is a frill and often a detriment, since events that are used as object lessons to make or to illustrate a point lose their didactic potency if they must conform to fact in all their details. Objectivity is seen as a red herring with which Western media attempt to arrogate truth to their viewpoint. Importance and size, other Western criteria of newsworthiness, are relative. Only proximity holds the kind of importance it has in the West, except more so. African media are highly parochial in their interests.

The need for printed media in Africa, such as have evolved in the West, might have been greater had African social, economic, and political institutions developed along with its technology. But the former were held back by Africa's colonial vassalage while it fell heir to modern technology upon gaining its independence. It moved directly into an electronic age with its communication, storage, and retrieval facilities. To expect Africa to take the long, hard road of printed media to achieve modernization is like asking a child to do long division or extract square roots manually just for the exercise when the answer lies at its fingertips on a cheap calculator. Thus Africa has traveled a different path, and comparisons with areas that have taken the long route to achieve communication sufficiency are futile and spurious. In the course of their development, African printed media may yet draw closer to Western media than they are at present. But this is not essential. To judge their stage of development by how closely they resemble the Western ideal in numbers, size, frequency, readership, or content is a meaningless exercise.

PRINT MEDIA

Of the 46 separate states or political entities in sub-Saharan Africa, 7 had no daily newspaper whatsoever at the end of the 1980s (see Table 7.2). These are mostly small countries with populations of around half

TABLE 7.2. COUNTRIES WITH NO PRINTED DAILIES

	Population (in thousands)	Literacy (%)	Dailies
Botswana	764	35	Bulletin
Cape Verde	337	37	None
Comoros	444	15	None
Djibouti	456	17	None
Gambia	643	12	None
Guinea	6,100	35	Bulletin
Lesotho	1,600	59	None
Rwanda	7,300	37	Bulletin
São Tomé e Príncipe	114	50	None
Sierra Leone	3,700	20	None

Sources: Editor and Publisher International Yearbook, 1989; 1989 Britannica Book of the Year; Africa South of the Sahara, 1989.

a million or less, but they include Sierra Leone, with a population of 3.7 million, which has had to cut back on its publications because of a newsprint shortage, and Lesotho, a country slightly larger than Maryland, surrounded by South Africa, with a population of 1.6 million and a literacy level of 59 percent. Three relatively larger countries—Botswana, population 764,000; Guinea, population 6.1 million, and Rwanda, population 7.3 million—have a daily government bulletin only. This is another indication that the reading of daily newspapers is an acquired habit rather than a need that necessarily comes with education and development.

True, all these countries are extremely poor. The GNP per capita is less than $500 except in Botswana, where it is $900. But then, other than South Africa, the Seychelles, and Gabon, no African country approaches a GNP per person of $2,000. Yet several countries in sub-Saharan Africa do have active newspaper systems, as Table 7.3 shows.

Most of the countries in Table 7.3 have a single daily, and the majority of these newspapers are government-owned. Eight countries in sub-Saharan Africa have major dailies, defined as newspapers with substantial circulations (more than 100,000), a trained staff, modern printing plants, and extensive news coverage. Six countries—Angola, Liberia, Madagascar, Mauritius, Uganda, and Zaire—have more than three minor dailies, and only Kenya, Nigeria, and South Africa have more than two major dailies, all privately owned in Kenya and South Africa, 8 of 21 newspapers privately owned in Nigeria. Among the

TABLE 7.3. NEWSPAPERS IN OTHER AFRICAN COUNTRIES

Country	Population (in thousands)	Literacy (%)	Number of Dailies
Angola	8,700	30	3
Benin	4,000	28	1
Burkina Faso	7.900	8	1
Burundi	5,000	25	1
Cameroon	10,500	60	1
Central African Republic	2,673	33	1
Chad	5,000	20	1
Congo	2,000	80	1
Equatorial Guinea	392	55	2
Ethiopia	47,700	30	3
Gabon	1,200	65	1
Guinea–Bissau	890	15	1
Ivory Coast	10,500	35	2
Kenya	23,300	50	5
Liberia	2,200	25	4
Madagascar	11,100	60	7
Malawi	8,000	30	1
Mali	8,500	15	1
Mauritania	1,900	17	1
Mauritius	1,000	80	6
Mozambique	14,300	17	2
Namibia	1,600	N.A.	3
Niger	7,200	13	1
Nigeria	115,100	42	21
Senegal	7,700	28	1
Seychelles	70	80	1
Somalia	5,000	12	1[a]
South Africa	35,200	55[b]	16
Swaziland	706	65	2
Tanzania	24,700	74	2
Togo	3,500	30	1
Uganda	16,800	52	6
Zaire	33,900	61	10
Zambia	7,800	54	2
Zimbabwe	8,880	50	2

[a] Plus bulletin.
[b] Whites, 98 percent; coloreds and Indians, 85 to 90 percent; blacks, 50 to 60 percent.
Sources: Editor and Publisher International Yearbook, 1989; 1989 Britannica Book of the Year; Country Data Papers: Africa. USIA, 1989; Africa South of the Sahara, 1989.

countries with a number of minor dailies, Madagascar and Mauritius are mostly privately owned.

The distribution of daily newspapers in sub-Saharan Africa provides a good index of the use being made of the printed media as a whole in the area. One might think of the African continent as divisible into ten groups of countries, one being the North African or Arab tier, which is discussed elsewhere in this book. In terms of the development of and dependence on printed media, South Africa, which is the only country in Africa that remains completely dominated by its white settlers, clearly stands alone as having a press that is most similar to that of the Western world.

By weighting each of the countries according to its dependence on daily newspapers, English-oriented East Africa, comprising Kenya, Mauritius, Seychelles, Tanzania, and Uganda, comes immediately after South Africa. It is followed by English-oriented West Africa with Gambia, Ghana, Nigeria, and Sierra Leone. Next come seven political entities in Southern Africa: Botswana, Lesotho, Malawi, Namibia, Swaziland, Zambia, and Zimbabwe. The 17 states that were once French colonies and are mostly in West Africa fall below the median in daily newspaper dependency. They are Benin, Burkina Faso, Cameroon, Central African Republic, Chad, Comoros (East Africa), Congo, Djibouti (East Africa), Gabon, Guinea, Ivory Coast, Madagascar (East Africa), Mali, Mauritania, Niger, Senegal, and Togo. The former Belgian colonies of Burundi, Rwanda, and Zaire follow closely. Then come formerly Spanish African Equatorial Guinea and the former Portuguese African colonies of Angola, Cape Verde, Guinea–Bissau, Mozambique, and São Tomé e Príncipe. Significantly, the two African countries that never were colonies—Ethiopia and Liberia—are the ones that have the lowest printed news media dependency on the continent. Somalia is in about the same category. This former Italian colony that merged with former British Somalia has a meager press system. Its one small government-owned newspaper, *October Star,* is published in Somali and Arabic. There is also an English-language daily bulletin published by the government.

A closer examination of these groups shows not only decreasing dependence on the printed media but increasing tendency toward advocacy and didactic journalism. Thus, on the whole, Anglophone Africa shows more developed daily newspaper systems than Francophone Africa, and Iberophone Africa has the weakest press system. This should in no way be interpreted as a reflection on the quality of the cultural, social, political, or economic development of these countries. It is merely an indication of differences in the traditions, habits, and needs of the peoples involved.

South Africa

The South African daily press is owned and edited by whites, who make up about 18 percent of the population. Although there are nine legally distinct ethnic groups in the country (the other three being black, 68 percent; colored, which includes Malay and mixed parentage, 10 percent; and Indian, 3 percent), and at least 24 languages spoken, the 16 daily newspapers in the country are published in only two languages: English (12) and Afrikaans (4), the official languages of South Africa.

While the ratio of whites whose mother tongue is Afrikaans to those with English as their mother tongue is six to four, three times as many English newspapers are sold as Afrikaans. This is both because the other ethnic groups tend to read the English rather than the Afrikaans press and because almost half of the Afrikaners themselves do not read dailies, preferring weeklies. However, among the Afrikaners who do read dailies, almost a third read English dailies, while fewer than 5 percent of English speakers read an Afrikaans daily. In the largest South African city of Johannesburg, which has three morning and one evening English-language dailies, there are twice as many nonwhite as white readers. Johannesburg also has two morning Afrikaans dailies whose readership is almost exclusively white. However, one-third of the readers of Cape Town's Afrikaans paper, *Die Burger*, are colored.

South Africa can boast of having had the first English-language newspaper in sub-Saharan Africa. It appeared in Cape Town in 1800, roughly 150 years after the Dutch first settled there. The *Capetown Gazette and African Advertiser*, as it was called, had news in both English and Dutch. The first Afrikaans newspaper was *Di Patriot* in 1875. There was an all-Dutch newspaper, *Du Zuid-Afrikaan*, published in 1830, but by 1875, the Society of True Afrikaaners had been launched, and the need was felt for a political organ that was distinctly African rather than European Dutch. The two major English-language newspaper chains in South Africa began with the *Cape Argus* in 1857 and the *Cape Times* in 1876.

Today the newspaper with the highest circulation in South Africa, and indeed one of the highest in all of sub-Saharan Africa, is the *Star* of Johannesburg, an evening paper with a circulation that has hovered around 200,000 for decades. According to a study by C. A. Giffard (1980), the circulations of evening newspapers have been dropping since the advent of TV in South Africa in 1976, while morning dailies have increased slightly. He speculates that this is because people have substituted evening TV watching for newspaper reading.

The *Star* belongs to the Argus Group, the largest newspaper publishing company in Africa, with holdings not only in South Africa but also in several other southern African states. Like most English speakers, it supports the opposition Democratic Party. The *Star* is a conservative, serious, quality daily directed mainly at the more affluent white reader.

To counteract the liberal tendencies of the English-language press, an Afrikaner industrialist, Louis Luyt, reputedly with the secret help of the government's Department of Information, launched in 1976 an English-language tabloid in Johannesburg called the *Citizen*, which has drawn some readers from other English-language papers, principally the *Star*. A third English-language daily, the *Sowetan*, began publishing in January 1981. It is aimed specifically at blacks, although it is owned by whites. It carries a large amount of crime, sex, and society news, and it steers clear of politics. It replaced the *Post*, which was banned by the government and in turn replaced the *World* in 1978, when that publication was closed down. This change in name has enabled the Argus Printing and Publishing Company, which owned all three papers, to continue to serve the mass market of blacks.

The Afrikaans press generally supports the ruling National Party. It is more knowledgeable about government policies than the English-language press and focuses more on domestic than on foreign news. It has practiced advocacy journalism from the start, viewing newspapers as instruments of political influence. Leading Afrikaans papers are the ultraconservative *Die Transvaler* (owned by Perskor), the unofficial organ of the National Party; and its chief competitor in the morning field, *Die Beeld*, owned by Nasionale Pers and published in Johannesburg. Perskor owns two small Afrikaans dailies in Pretoria, and Nasionale Pers owns a major Afrikaans paper in Cape Town and smaller papers in Bloemfontein and Port Elizabeth. Besides the *Star* and the *Sowetan* in Johannesburg, Argus owns the *Cape Argus*, a major evening paper in Cape Town and the first newspaper in the Argus empire. Natal Newspaper Ltd. owns a morning and an evening paper in Durban, and Times Media Ltd. owns a new English-language morning daily, *Business Day*, in Johannesburg and two dailies in Port Elizabeth. The remaining dailies (including the *Citizen*) are independently owned. A number of Sunday or weekend papers are published in South Africa, nine with main offices in Johannesburg. But the *Sunday Times*, for example, which has the highest Sunday circulation in Africa—about half a million—is printed simultaneously in Cape Town and Durban and distributed throughout southern Africa. While the *Sunday Times* is an English-language paper belonging to the liberal South African Associated Newspapers group, its Afrikaans counterpart is *Rapport*, with a circulation that is almost as high. It supports the government, as all other Afrikaans papers do.

There are at least 40 other weekly or semiweekly publications in South Africa catering to all interests. Notable among these for their influence, though not for their circulation, are *To the Point* and the *Financial Mail*. Several Afrikaans weeklies are published on Fridays. *Indian Opinion*, founded by Mahatma Gandhi in 1903 and still being edited and published by relatives, is a weekly addressed to Gujerati-speaking Indians in South Africa. Another weekly for Indians, the *Leader*, is in English. Both are published in Durban. Other weeklies are published in Zulu, Xhosa, and Yiddish. Surveys show that education and age are factors in weekly readership in South Africa. Weeklies are read by people in the higher education and lower age brackets.

East Africa

There is no doubt that next to South Africa, Kenya's newspaper system is most similar to that of the West. Three of its daily newspapers are widely read, privately owned, and by Third World standards uncensored. Two other dailies, one in English and one in Swahili, were owned by KANU, the sole political party. Of the three formerly British-administered territories of Uganda, Kenya, and Tanzania—which at one time had plans to form a federation upon attaining their independence—only Kenya developed along capitalist lines. Uganda came under military rule, and Tanzania is strongly socialist. Mauritius and the Seychelles Islands on the east coast of Africa, both formerly British, also have capitalist economies, and the former has a well-developed private press system. The sole daily newspaper in the Seychelles is run by the government and has a very small circulation.

Newspapers have been published in Mauritius since 1773, when the French-language weekly *Annonces* first appeared. Mauritius, which along with the Seychelles was seized from France by the British in 1810 and ceded to Britain by the Treaty of Paris in 1814, also has the second oldest continuously published French-language daily in the world—*Le Cernéen*, founded in 1832. Today it also has pages in English, as do at least five other dailies on the island. In addition, there are three Chinese-language newspapers.

Britain acquired most of its East African territories in the late nineteenth and early twentieth centuries, and the first news publication was a mimeographed missionary quarterly that appeared in 1897. The first newspaper, the *East Africa and Uganda Mail*, was published at Mombasa, Kenya, in 1899. In 1902, an Indian railway contractor, A. M. Jeevanjee, founded the weekly *African Standard, Mombasa Times and Uganda Argus*, which became the daily *East African Standard* in 1910 when it moved from Mombasa to Nairobi, the new capital. It became the leading newspaper in East Africa when it bought out its main competition in 1923. In 1977, it became a tabloid. The same company that published the *Standard* published an English-language daily in Kampala, Uganda, from 1955 to 1972 called the *Uganda Argus*, and another daily in Dar-es-Salaam, Tanzania, called the *Tanganyika Standard*, which lasted from 1930 to 1972. It was nationalized in 1969 and merged with the *Nationalist* to become the *Daily News* in 1972.

In 1959, the Aga Khan, leader of the Ismailis, a Muslim sect, established East African Newspapers (later Nation Newspapers) Ltd., which founded a Swahili daily, *Taifa Leo*, and an English-language paper, the *Daily Nation*. (He also established a Swahili weekly and a Sunday paper.) All these papers are tabloids and have rapidly developed into influential publications in Nairobi and throughout East Africa. The *Daily Nation* now has three times the circulation of the *Standard*, and people attribute its popularity to its sprightly content and layout and the fact that it has a more liberal tone than the *Standard*. As in the rest of East Africa, the daily press is an urban and elite institution. Outside the cities, people are largely ignored by the printed media, especially if they are not literate in English or, to a lesser extent, in Swahili.

Kenya, once again, has the most lively weekly publications in this English-speaking black African area. The *Sunday Nation*, 70 percent of which is owned by the Aga Khan's Nation Newspapers, has a circulation of more than 150,000. Like the *Daily Nation*, it is a tabloid and is modeled after the *London Daily Mirror*. In 1977, a Harvard-educated Kenyan, Hilary Ng'weno, started a competing Sunday paper, the *Nairobi Times*. A broadsheet, it is patterned after the more serious *London Observer* and has a low circulation. A third Sunday publication is in Swahili and is also owned by the Nation Newspapers. It is called *Taifa Weekly* and has a circulation of over 50,000. Two other Kenyan weeklies should be mentioned. The *Weekly Review*, published by Ng'weno, was founded in 1975 as a serious journal of political analysis, similar to the *London Economist*. Its circulation is said to be rising steadily, although it is still low. A popular weekly launched by Ng'weno in 1976, called *Picture Post*, failed. The *Voice of Africa* is a propaganda weekly that is believed to be supported by the Libyan government.

Tanzania has two Sunday newspapers. The *Sunday News* is in English and is owned by the government, while the ruling (Revolutionary) party-owned *Mzalendo* is in Swahili. In addition, there are five weeklies and one biweekly published in English and Swahili in Dar-es-Salaam and Zanzibar. Uganda has four weekly publications, all in Kampala, its capital. Three are in English and one is in Luganda. The small island of Mauritius boasts nine weekly or biweekly publications, including *Weekend,* which advertises itself as having the largest circulation in the Indian Ocean.

West Africa (Anglophone)

In terms of dependence on and use of printed media, the former British colonies of West Africa, taken as a whole, come after East Africa. Although Nigeria has the largest number of daily newspapers in sub-Saharan Africa at present, it also has the largest population in Africa (about 115 million). Despite fairly large circulations, this places Nigeria—with 5 per 1,000 inhabitants—somewhat lower than many other countries in newspaper readership. Anglophone West African newspapers are also less news-oriented and more didactic and polemical in their content. This is due to their origins. Unlike East Africa, where an English-language press catered mostly to white settlers and practically ignored black Africans, in British West Africa an English-language press developed quite early as a local medium. It united the African elite, for whom English became a lingua franca; it gave them outlets to vent their grievances against the colonial power and a means for fanning nationalist aspirations and building political support. "We are not clambering [sic] for immediate independence. But it should always be borne in mind that the present order of things will not last for ever," wrote the *Lagos Times and Gold Coast Advertiser* on March 9, 1881.

The first newspaper in black Africa was published in Freetown, Sierra Leone, in 1801. It was the *Royal Gazette and Sierra Leone Advertiser.* Very soon thereafter, a handwritten newspaper appeared in Accra, the Gold Coast (now Ghana). It was called the *Royal Gold Coast Gazette and Commercial Intelligencer* and was published from 1822 to 1825. The first African editor in the Gold Coast was Charles Bannerman, who founded the *Accra Herald* in 1858. The following year, *Iwe Irohin,* a church-related biweekly, appeared as the first African-language paper on the continent. The Rev. Henry Townsend, a missionary, had developed an alphabet for Yoruba and taught it to some 3,000 Nigerians.

For a few weeks, Accra had a daily in 1895 called the *Daily Express.* The first successful daily in West Africa was the *Lagos Daily News,* which appeared in 1925, published by Victor Bababunmi but taken over by the better-known Herbert Macaulay and Dr. J. A. Caulcrick in 1928 as a political party paper. In less than a year, the Lagos Chamber of Commerce raised money to start a competing paper, the *Daily Times,* which, despite several metamorphoses, is still being published; now owned 60 percent by the Nigerian government, it has the largest circulation in black Africa. But it suffered a setback in 1937, when an American-educated journalist, Nnamdi Azikiwe, who later became Nigeria's president, started a new daily, the *West African Pilot*. This hard-hitting political newspaper attracted many African readers. After World War II, Cecil King, who owned the *London Daily Mirror*, bought the *Daily Times* and turned it into a popular, somewhat sensationalistic tabloid, similar to his *Daily Mirror* but minus the sex. Despite its government connection, the *Daily Times* still attracts 28 percent of the readership in its circulation area, according to two separate 1980 surveys.

Besides its part ownership of the *Daily Times*, the federal government also owns the *New Nigerian* jointly with Kaduna State. Another ten dailies are owned by various individual states, while some states own weeklies. Of the nine privately owned dailies in 1989, four were founded in 1987 or 1988. A fifth paper, the *Mail*, founded in 1987, has since folded. Most prominent among the privately owned dailies are the *National Concord*; the *Guardian*; the *Nigerian Tribune*, published in Ibadan as well as Lagos; and the *Punch*, known for its picture of a different scantily dressed, generally white female every day. The *Guardian* is experiencing circulation problems because of its price (1 naira, or about $1.30), and the *Punch* is caught up in a feud in the Amuka family, which owns it.

In 1950, the Mirror Group that had bought the *Lagos Daily Times* founded the *Daily Graphic* in Accra. It easily outsold the *Evening News*, one of several newspapers being published in Accra, edited by another United States–educated journalist and politician, a Ghanaian by the name of Kwame Nkrumah, who also became president of his country. In 1958, the year after Ghana was established as an independent state, the *Ghanaian Times* was founded with public funds. It and the *Daily Graphic*, now also government-operated, remain the only dailies currently appearing in Ghana. A third daily was purchased by the *London Daily Mirror*'s Cecil King in West Africa in 1952. It was the *Daily Mail* of Freetown, Sierra Leone; but he sold it to the government in 1965 because it turned out to be a poor investment.

Most of the daily newspapers in Nigeria have Sunday editions and there are more than a score of other weeklies. Like its daily counterpart, the government-controlled *Sunday Times* has the highest readership. Among other Sunday newspapers with high readership are *Sunday Punch*, *Sunday Sketch*, *Sunday Tribune*, and *Sunday Observer*. The weekly magazine insert in the *Sunday Times*, *Lagos Weekend*, is also popular. Another weekly publication of the Daily Times Company, *Times International*, is a magazine of international news commentary but is not regarded as a very strong publication. Nigeria's weekly periodicals generally cater to most interest groups and are widely read by literate elements of the population. In a 1980 survey, 54 percent of a cross section of the population said they had read a newspaper or magazine. Even in rural areas, the proportion of readers was as high as 35 percent.

Yet because of newsprint shortages and lack of transportation, Ghana's periodical press is often in disarray. But a number of government, private, and religious weeklies and biweeklies are published from time to time. The *Daily Graphic* has a weekly supplement called *Mirror* that used to be quite popular but has a small circulation now. The *Spectator*, weekly supplement of the *Ghanaian Times*, has been suspended. Other weeklies that have in the past played important roles in Ghanaian journalism but have fallen on bad times include the *Echo*, a right-of-center, intellectual weekly that probably still has the highest circulation of all weeklies; *Palaver-Tribune*, given to exposés and investigative reporting, and the Pioneer, whose claim to fame is that it opposed President Nkrumah. It is privately owned and is based in Kumasi. The biweekly *Legon Observer* established a reputation for itself as a leading intellectual publication when a group of University of Ghana professors launched it in 1966.

Southern Africa

Skipping back to southern Africa, we find a group of seven countries that were colonized from the south and controlled either by South Africa or by Britain. One of them, Namibia, is still a South African mandate. This group has a somewhat lower dependence on printed media but includes two countries that have major newspaper systems, albeit owned by the government or the ruling party.

Until they achieved their independence as black African states—Zambia in 1964 and Zimbabwe in 1980—both countries had a series of newspapers produced by and for white mining interests. They were known as Northern and Southern Rhodesia, respectively, and were colonized through the aggressive entrepreneurship of British empire builder Cecil John Rhodes. In 1891, the Argus Company, which owns the *Cape Argus*, produced for the miners the handwritten *Mashonaland and Zambesian Times*, which became the *Rhodesia Herald* in 1892. In 1894, the same company started the *Bulawayo Chronicle*. These two newspapers are still being published, but in 1981, the government of Zimbabwe set up the Mass Media Trust with a $5 million endowment to purchase the two newspapers, which are now run under government supervision.

Zambia, too, has two major daily newspapers. The *Zambia Daily*

Mail was purchased by the government in 1965 from its co-owners, David Astor, editor of London's *Sunday Observer,* and Alexander Scott, a Scottish doctor turned journalist. They had started it as the weekly *African Mail* in 1960 and renamed it the *Central African Mail* in 1962; in 1967, the government called it the *Zambia Mail* when it went semiweekly; and in 1970, it became a daily. The other daily, the *Times of Zambia,* was founded as the *Zambia Times* in Kitwe, a town in copper-mining territory, in 1962 by Hans Heinrich, a South African. He soon sold it, along with other properties, to Lonrho, a British firm formerly called the London and Rhodesian Mining and Land Company, which owns newspapers throughout eastern and southern Africa.

Close by, in Ndola, the Argus Company owned the *Northern News,* a newspaper aimed at the European mining community. It had attractive makeup, plenty of advertising, and, what European readers wanted, foreign news. But the Argus Company wanted to get out of Zambia and consolidate in South Africa. So it sold the *Northern News* to Lonrho, which closed down the *Zambia Times* in Kitwe and renamed the Ndola daily the *Times of Zambia.* Lonrho appointed Richard Hall, a white Rhodesian civil servant and later a very successful editor of the *Mail,* as editor of the *Times.* Hall strongly believed in Africanization of newspapers and had soon trained an African editor in chief and a staff of reporters and copy editors to take over. In 1975, the *Times* was nationalized, and its editing came under the control of the United National Independence Party, the ruling party in Zambia. Its editorial offices were later moved to Lusaka, the capital.

Malawi (formerly Nyasaland) and Swaziland, a kingdom in the northern corner of South Africa, each have a small daily newspaper, poorly edited though balanced in coverage. Namibia, a former German colony known as South-West Africa, is a South African mandate seeking independence. It has three small dailies, one each in English, German, and Afrikaans. All these papers are privately owned, except that Malawi's *Daily Times* was sold as a semiweekly to its president for life, Hastings Kamuzu Banda, in 1972 by Canadian and British press tycoon Roy Thomson, who had bought the *Nyasaland Times* in 1962. It had been founded in 1895 in Blantyre by a Scot who named it the *Central African Planter,* a few years later renamed the *Central African Times* and finally *Nyasaland Times.*

The paper must carry a picture of Malawi's president (and its owner) every day, preferably on the front page—a practice that is common in authoritarian states throughout the Third World. Another rule is that the speeches of the head of state may not be edited or cut. The *Swaziland Times,* which was founded in 1897 as a weekly, owned, edited, and read by Europeans, was bought by the Argus Company in the late 1960s. When Swaziland became independent in 1968, it continued to be owned and edited by whites. In 1975, the Argus Company sold it to a Scot, who turned it into a daily in 1978. Another daily, the *Swazi Observer*, was established in 1982 by the royal family after the death of King Sobhiza II, who had ruled for 62 years.

The seven English-speaking countries north of South Africa have remarkably little in the way of weekly periodicals or newspapers. Zambia has a Sunday paper, the *Sunday Times*, with a relatively large circulation in the neighborhood of 65,000. In Zimbabwe, the *Herald* and the *Chronicle* each has a Sunday paper, the *Sunday Mail* and the *Sunday News*, respectively. The eastern part of the state is served by the *Manica Post*, founded by the Argus Company in 1893. It has a minuscule circulation. There also is a vernacular weekly, a farmers' weekly, and a radio and TV guide.

French Africa

"Fourteen independent states were to emerge from France's African Empire. But between them they could hardly muster a Press worth the name," writes African journalist Frank Barton. France treated its overseas dependencies as an extension of the mother country. Selectively, it educated those Africans who could absorb the education and culture of France and become "black Frenchmen"—*évolués* is the name given to this elite group. They spoke French with distinction, whereas the English spoken by most Africans in British territories was poor. However, only the elite were privileged to speak French, while in the British colonies English was taught down to the lowest levels of society.

France did not encourage newspaper or magazine publication in Africa, and until the mid-1930s, only French citizens were permitted to publish them. Several of these, intended for French settlers, appeared in Dakar, Senegal, in the late nineteenth century. Among them were *Le Réveil du Sénégalais* in 1885 and *L'Union Africaine* in 1896. In 1907, the French Socialist Party published *L'A.O.F.*, a weekly, in Dakar. In the 1920s, some nationalistic papers, such as *La Voix du Dahomey*, *Le Phare du Dahomey*, and *Le Cri Nègre*, appeared briefly in what is now Benin. During the 1930s, France admitted the Senegalese to full French citizenship, and when parliamentary elections were held, political candidates started a number of papers that closed down immediately after the elections. But some survived for several years, including *L'Ouest Africain* and *Le Journal de Dakar*. In 1935, the Ivory Coast produced its first anticolonial paper, *Eclaireur de la Côte d'Ivoire*, which was also the first French African newspaper owned and operated by Africans.

At about the same time, Charles de Breteuil, a Frenchman who had some journalist friends and also knew the French colonial minister Paul Reynaud, was encouraged to go traveling in Africa. He saw a market for newspapers in several of the colonies, especially among the French settlers, and he began publishing a weekly in Senegal in 1933. *Paris-Dakar* became a daily in 1935, changing its name to *Dakar-Matin*. In 1970, the government assumed 65 percent of the shares, with de Breteuil and a French state publishing enterprise, Société Nouvelles d'Editions Industrielle (SNEI), owning the rest. Its name was changed once again to *Le Soleil du Sénégal*. In the Ivory Coast, de Breteuil established *France-Afrique* in 1938, which became *Abidjan-Matin* in 1954. When the Ivory Coast gained its independence in 1960, de Breteuil formed a partnership with SNEI to continue *Abidjan-Matin*. In December 1964, it was renamed *Fraternité-Matin* and taken over by the government. It was placed under the control of the ruling party and received technical and editorial aid from de Breteuil and the French government. By the end of the 1970s, only the head printer was French. *Fraternité-Matin* is the only major daily in Francophone Africa.

Another newspaper started by de Breteuil was *La Presse de Guinée* of Conakry, Guinea. He started it in 1954 and it folded in 1958, when Guinea became independent, rejecting the new French constitution. Guinea became a Marxist state and today has no daily newspaper. In 1955, de Breteuil founded *La Presse du Cameroun* in Douala, the largest city in Cameroon. This was closed in 1974 when the government decided that its sole daily should be published in the capital, Yaounde. It owns 70 percent of the shares in the newspaper, which it named *Cameroun Tribune*. One day a week, the paper is published in English. De Breteuil and SNEI own 30 percent of the stock.

As for the rest of French West Africa, the government owns the only daily in Benin, *Ehuzu*, formerly known as *Daho-Express*. In Libreville, Gabon, the government has been publishing a small daily tabloid, *L'Union*, since 1975; and in Bamako, Mali, there is a government-controlled daily called *L'Essor—La Voix du Peuple*. The Togo government has published a small daily in Lomé, *La Nouvelle Marche*, formerly *Togo Press*, since 1962. It is in French, with pages in Ewe and Kabie. In 1984, Burkina Faso lost its privately owned daily, *L'Observateur* of Ouagadougou, which was founded in 1973 by a local publishing firm, Société Nationale d'Edition et de la Presse. The Ministry of Information has since been publishing a small daily, *Sidwaya*.

In East Africa, only Madagascar among Francophone countries has a developed press, and while circulations are small, the newspapers are numerous. They include the privately owned *Madagascar-Matin*, the largest of the dailies on the island, published in both French and

Malagasy, and the government-owned daily *Atrika,* founded in 1977. There are several other small privately owned dailies in both French and Malagasy.

Only 5 of the 17 countries in the former French colonies have weeklies. Probably the most noteworthy is *La Semaine Africaine,* founded in 1952 and published by the Archdiocese of Brazzaville, Congo. It is the only privately owned publication in the country and is distributed not only in the Congo but also in neighboring Gabon, Chad, and the Central African Republic. Cameroon has two French- and two English-language semiweeklies, plus a Sunday paper, the *Weekender. La Gazette,* published in Douala, is the largest French weekly and is privately owned. The *Cameroon Times* and the *Cameroon Outlook* are published in English on alternate days. They are printed in Victoria.

The Ivory Coast has no more than five weeklies, among them the Sunday edition of *Fraternité-Matin* in Abidjan. It is called *I.D.* (formerly *Ivoire-Dimanche*) and is printed in color. Its content is heavy on sports and cultural events. Another weekly is the organ of the ruling party, and its editorial director is the president of the Ivory Coast, Felix Houphouet-Boigny. It is called *Fraternité-Hebdo.*

In Senegal, the daily *Le Soleil* has a weekly tabloid supplement, *Zone 2.* It, too, focuses on sports and culture. The Catholic church supports an illustrated weekly magazine of news and features called *Afrique Nouvelle,* founded in 1947. It is distributed throughout Francophone Africa. Finally, on the east coast, the island of Madagascar supports seven weeklies or biweeklies printed in Malagasy.

Belgian Africa

The only country in the former Belgian colonies of Africa with a press worthy of note is Zaire, formerly the Belgian Congo. Neither Rwanda nor Burundi has more than daily news bulletins. The earliest publications in the colony that was to become Zaire were produced by Belgian newspapers mainly for Belgian settlers. The first on record was *Le Journal du Katanga,* which started in 1911 as a weekly and became a daily in 1919. It was succeeded in 1930 by *L'Echo du Katanga.* Other dailies were *L'Essor du Congo* (1922), *L'Informateur* (1934), *Les Nouvelles* (1934), and *Centre Afrique* (1948), which had been a monthly and became a weekly in 1931.

Catholic missionaries were the first to bring out newspapers intended for Africans as well as Europeans. Among the first was *Courrier d'Afrique* (1930), the only daily in Kinshasa before 1962, and *La Croix du Congo* (1936), which was taken over by Africans in 1958 and renamed *Horizons.* Because of its revolutionary tone, it was closed down by the government the following year. In 1956, *L'Avenir Colonial Belge,* a daily for Belgian settlers founded in 1930 in Leopoldville (now Kinshasa), produced a weekly supplement with an all-Congolese staff and called it *Les Actualités Africaines.* It invited African intellectuals to contribute letters and articles. Its first editor was Mobutu Sese Seko, later to become president of Zaire. It survived as a daily until 1960, when it became a weekly, renamed *Nkumu* in 1972. A second daily, published by Africans in 1957, a couple of years prior to a Belgian decree permitting Africans to own newspapers, also survived for several years. It was *Présence Congolaise,* renamed *Epanza* in 1972, by which time it had become a weekly.

All dailies today are government-owned and have small circulations. A 1974 survey shows that a third of the population of Kinshasa, the capital, are regular newspaper readers, while 42 percent never see a newspaper. The dailies in Kinshasa today are *Salongo,* formerly *L'Avenir Colonial Belge,* which in 1962 became *Le Progrès* and was given an African name in 1972, along with all other Congolese papers. It is a morning paper, while *Elima* (formerly *Courrier d'Afrique*) is an evening paper. In the provinces, up to seven small dailies are published. One is *Boyoma* (formerly *Le Renouveau*) of Kisangani; another is *Mwanga* (formerly *La Dépêche*) of Lubumbashi. All dailies are in French. There also is a daily bulletin produced by AZAP, the official government press service.

Only Zaire has weekly publications of any importance, although the government of Burundi publishes two weekly newspapers and a biweekly. Most important of Zairian news weeklies is *Zaire,* published by the government in Kinshasa. It claims readership outside of Zaire. There also are four French weekly newspapers and several vernacular weeklies published in Kinshasa and in the provinces.

Iberophone Africa

Of the five former Portuguese African colonies, Angola, Mozambique, and Guinea–Bissau have minor daily newspaper systems. Equatorial Guinea, which formerly belonged to Spain, has two small newspapers— *Ebano,* published in the capital, Malabo (formerly Santa Isabel), and *Poto Poto,* published in Bata on the mainland in Rio Muni.

Both Angola and Mozambique, upon gaining their independence from what had been a conservative Portuguese regime, adopted Marxist governments in 1974. Of the two, Angola has had less of a press history. Before independence, it had a morning daily founded in 1923—*A Provincia de Angola*—which was nationalized and renamed *O Jornal de Angola* in 1976. An evening paper, *Diario de Luanda,* later *Diario da*

Republica, was closed by the government, then reopened as the official government organ. *ABC Diario de Angola* is a small evening paper.

Mozambique has had a long press history. Its earliest recorded publication was the *Lourenço Marques Guardian,* founded in 1905 by the large British community in Mozambique's capital. In 1956, it was purchased by the Roman Catholic church and renamed *Diario,* publishing in both English and Portuguese. Much of the preindependence history of the press of Mozambique centers on a conflict that existed between the conservative Roman Catholic archbishop of Lourenço Marques, called Maputo since independence, and the liberal, pro-African bishop of Beira, the second port of Mozambique. In 1918, *Noticias de Beira* was started as a biweekly English and Portuguese publication by the archbishop. In 1932, the bishop supported the publication by local Africans of a weekly, *A Voz Africana.* In 1950, the bishop founded a daily in Beira, *Diario de Moçambique,* upon which the archbishop's biweekly was raised to daily status. Meanwhile, a conservative retired Portuguese army officer, Manuel Simões Vaz, founded a Portuguese-language newspaper in Lourenço Marques called *Noticias* in 1926. It became the official mouthpiece for the Portuguese in 1933 and was taken over by the Marxist government as its main publication in 1975. All other dailies folded that year, except *Noticias,* which continued as the country's second daily.

None of the countries in this area have any important weekly publications.

Independent Africa

Ethiopia and Liberia, which have never been colonies of a Western power, cannot boast of well-developed press systems. Liberia, in fact, has reverted to a mimeographed daily bulletin published by the Ministry of Information since its military coup in 1980. It did have newspapers in the past, starting in 1826 with the *Liberia Herald,* a four-page monthly, published off and on until 1862. Liberia had no daily newspaper until 1946, when the *Daily Listener* was founded by a Liberian politician, Charles Cecil Dennis. It folded in 1973. Roy Thomson of Britain published the *Liberian Star* as a daily in the 1960s (it had been founded as a weekly in 1939) but abandoned it in 1968. It was revived in 1969, toeing the government line, since it recognized that "the order of the day was 'survivalism not journalism,' " as a former assistant editor, Rufus Darpoh, put it. The *Liberian Star* was closed down before President William R. Tolbert, Jr., was deposed in the military coup. A few weekly and semiweekly publications still appear in Monrovia, and by mid-1982, Head of State Samuel Doe had begun to revive other elements of the press. Today, as many as five daily newspapers publish off and on, including the *Daily Observer*, the *Daily Mirror*, the *Standard*, and the *Liberian Post*.

Until the overthrow of Emperor Haile Selassie, Ethiopia had a fairly large number of small dailies, both in the capital, Addis Ababa, and in Asmara, capital of the former Italian colony of Eritrea, annexed to Ethiopia by the United Nations in 1952. All were published by the government to extol the emperor and his administration. As in many other authoritarian states, Ethiopian news dealt mostly with what the emperor and his ministers did and said rather than with the people affected. Among the dailies were the *Ethiopian Herald* in English (founded in 1941) and *Addis Zemen* in Amharic (founded in 1974). There was also a French daily in Addis, a Tigrinya daily in Asmara, and two Italian dailies in Asmara. When the emperor was deposed in a bloodless Marxist coup, some of these dailies ceased publication, leaving *Addis Zemen*, the *Ethiopian Herald*, and, in Asmara, *Hibret/ Al-Wadha* in Tigrinya and Arabic.

The Ministry of Information of Liberia publishes the semiweekly newspaper *New Liberian*. Six other weeklies and biweeklies in English are published from time to time.

The Ministry of Information in Addis Ababa, Ethiopia, publishes weeklies in Amharic, Arabic, and Oromigna and five biweeklies in Amharic. None of these is of major importance. The one with the highest circulation is *Ethiopia Today*, an Amharic weekly covering government activities.

Other Publications

The African magazine that probably is the most widely read by Africans is *Drum*. Founded in South Africa in 1951 by James R. A. Bailey, son of a millionaire mine owner, it was directed at a non-European, English-speaking market, although its first editors were white. Tom Hopkinson, one of these editors, extended its readership into other parts of southern Africa and into Anglophone East and West Africa. *Drum* is a slick, folio-sized monthly, featuring advice columns and personality stories about internationally renowned blacks; general topics of interest to blacks, coloreds, and Indians; and such touchy subjects as riots and the need for prison reform.

For many years, it served as the training ground for African journalists. During the late 1960s and early 1970s, *Drum's* popularity in South Africa declined in the face of the rising popularity of a sister publication. This was the *Post*, a tabloid weekly newspaper focusing on crime and sex. Special editions were published for African, colored, and Indian communities in South Africa. In 1965, the monthly *Drum* was discontinued in South Africa and made into a supplement to the more popular *Post*, but it was revived as a monthly in 1968 and given its first nonwhite editor the following year. *Drum*'s West African edition was opened in Lagos in 1954, and an East African edition was added in Nairobi two years later.

Other than *Drum*, almost the only magazines published in sub-Saharan Africa that circulate outside their country of origin in any quantity are published in Senegal. One is the French-language *Africa International* founded in 1962 as a political, social, and economic review of African affairs. It appears ten times a year and is sold throughout Francophone Africa. Another is a popular picture monthly, *Bingo*, intended for urban youth. Brought out in 1952 by de Breteuil, it was, at the time, the only publication in his empire designed strictly for Africans and was probably his most successful venture. It claims a circulation of over 100,000 throughout Francophone Africa. Other monthly or quarterly publications of importance published in Dakar are *Amina*, a women's magazine; *Ethiopique*, a scholarly journal devoted to African culture; *Sud Magazine*, an independent political journal; and *Afrique Médicale*, a medical review.

Entente Africaine is published quarterly in the Ivory Coast in French and English. Its aim is to attract foreign investment and tourists from neighboring countries.

In all of the rest of sub-Saharan Africa, only Kenya and Nigeria have internally circulated magazines of importance. *Kenya Yetu* is a Ministry of Information magazine published in Nairobi and widely read throughout Kenya. It is in Swahili. Another is the privately owned humor magazine *Joe*, which calls itself Africa's entertainment monthly. In Nigeria, Drum Publications also produces a general-interest picture monthly for internal distribution called *Trust*, and Daily Times Publications has a monthly family magazine, *Spear*, that is widely read. *Ophelia* is a cultural magazine of high quality that first appeared in October 1980. There also are several women's magazines. Ghana currently has no magazines worthy of note. In Zambia, the government publishes a number of vernacular magazines, but on the whole there are no magazines of significance in southern Africa. Other than Senegal and the Ivory Coast, no Francophone African country (including Belgian Africa), and no Iberophone or independent African country has important magazines.

Foreign Publications

One finds, in traveling around Africa, that there is no shortage of reading materials in hotel lobbies and bookstores. In English-speaking countries, the *International Herald Tribune* is readily available on the day of publication or the day after, as are several British newspapers and periodicals such as the *London Times*, the *Daily Telegraph*, the *Daily Mirror*, and the *Economist*. International editions of *Time, Newsweek*, and the *Reader's Digest* are also widely read. In French-speaking countries, Paris newspapers and periodicals such as *Le Monde, L'Express*, and *Réalités* may be purchased.

A crop of political and economic journals published in London and Paris especially for African readers also are commonly found on the newsstands. Oldest among these is the weekly *West Africa*, founded in 1917 and purchased in 1947 by Cecil King of the *London Daily Mirror*. It is an influential journal of news and opinion about Africa. The monthly *New African* has been available since 1966 and covers business and economic news, while *Africa* is a still more recent publication of economic and political news. Like *New African*, it is a monthly and is published in London.

The two most widely read French journals are *Jeune Afrique* and *Afrique-Asie*. *Jeune Afrique* is a weekly political journal originally published in Tunis in 1960. Its publishing offices were later moved to Paris. *Afrique-Asie* was founded in 1969 and also is published in Paris. It is a biweekly.

Rural Journalism

Because of persistent illiteracy in Africa, a number of African countries have made efforts both to raise literacy levels and to provide easy reading materials for new literates. UNESCO sponsored a survey of rural newspapers and newspaper needs in 11 African countries, and a team of African journalism educators made suggestions for the establishment of a rural press. Liberia had started to experiment with mimeographed rural newspapers in 1963, and Niger ran a similar experiment in 1964. Following the guidelines of the UNESCO consultants, Mali launched a rural newspaper called *Kibaru* in March 1972. It was written in the Bambara language, and its purpose was to help readers retain and improve their literacy.

Today, 16 African countries are participating in the experiment. Some, like Burundi, Ghana, Mali, and Tanzania, have a single rural newspaper, while others, like Liberia and Niger, which have used rural journalism the longest, have 10 to 15 newspapers. Most of the papers appear monthly or less frequently and are either mimeographed or printed on offset presses. Circulations range from 100 to 60,000, but the majority are in the 1,000-to-3,000 range. Many are in local languages, which has posed a dilemma, since some of the languages are spoken in very limited areas. Some are in English or French or in one of the more widely spoken vernaculars, such as Hausa or Swahili. They are all written in simple language, are generally printed in tabloid format, and concentrate on hygiene and social, cultural, and economic problems in addition to local news. Most are published by government ministries, but in some countries missionary groups help out, as does UNESCO.

In an experiment using such a newspaper in beginning classes of rural schools in Ghana, Neff Smart in 1974 found more reading improvement in the schools that used the paper *Densu Times* than in a control group of schools, especially after the second year. And there were several fringe benefits, including increased motivation of those students who read the newspapers and a favorable impact on adults, such as parents and teachers.

ELECTRONIC MEDIA

Radio

The low literacy rate, coupled with the traditionally high dependence on and respect for oral communication, make radio the ideal medium of mass communication in Africa. Unlike television, which requires expensive equipment beyond the means of most Africans and high voltages to run the equipment, radio transistor sets are cheap and can run on batteries. This puts them within reach of individuals and communities everywhere in Africa. As a medium for quickly rallying the population or for long-range mass education, radio is without peer. It is no coincidence, therefore, that one of the first things African states did upon gaining their independence was to consolidate their hold on whatever broadcasting facilities may have been left behind by the colonizing power. Furthermore, radio stations in many African states are as closely guarded as the presidential residence because they are among the first targets of insurgents. In fact, Gabon has a second studio and transmitter in the presidential compound for just such an eventuality. It is significant, as Elihu Katz and George Wedell (1977) have pointed out, that no African state has decided to do without a radio system, while several are managing quite well with only limited printed media.

There are some negative factors, however. Radio transmission on medium-wave, which is easy to tune in to and is less subject to atmospheric interference than shortwave, limits the reception area geographically in terms of both distance and terrain. A mountain or other physical barrier, for example, would interfere with reception. In Africa, where many countries cover vast areas and where obstructions abound, this is a problem. In the United States, the problem is overcome in two ways: Every town or urban area has its own stations, and wireless, telephonic, and satellite relays make network broadcasts possible. Africa lags behind both economically and technologically. Although shortwave is used by many countries to overcome the distance and obstruction dilemma, solar interference due to sunspots curtails such broadcasting, especially in the winter. Hence coverage is not 100 percent.

Cost is another factor. Producing programs is expensive, and despite the existence of license fees for radio sets, such fees have proved especially hard to collect in Africa. Besides, relative to the size of the population, there are not many set owners to collect fees from. There are many listeners per set or even community sets that bring in little revenue. As for commercials, even if people could afford to advertise in the subsistence economies of most African countries, the governments are reluctant to open up this potent medium to commercial exploitation.

Then there is the problem of the proliferation of languages. Every community wants to be addressed in its own language or dialect, which means not only more hardware but also more programming. And while it is a headache for governments to decide on how much airtime to give to each language, it is politically necessary to cater to each major language and culture. This is having a negative effect on education and development, since it is far slower and more expensive to educate a large population in many languages than to mass-produce education in a single language. Furthermore, social, political, and economic development depend on speedy interaction, and this is slowed down by a multiplicity of cultures. It has been said that the British Broadcasting Corporation is responsible for the evolution and widespread use of the "king's English." The broadcast policies of most African nations support continuing diversity of language and culture.

South Africa was the first African country to introduce radio broadcasting. It had a station operating out of Johannesburg in 1920, additional stations in Cape Town and Durban soon thereafter. In 1927, the British East African Broadcasting Company, Ltd., began relaying BBC broadcasts to British settlers in much of Africa from a shortwave station in Nairobi, Kenya. It broadcast from 1 to 2 p.m. and from 6 to 8 p.m. daily. In 1930, Imperial and International Communication, Ltd., took over this station, and the next year, the company was renamed Cable and Wireless, Ltd. In return for a monopoly on all international telegraphic traffic and a wireless license fee it collected through the Post Office (with a reduced rate for Africans), it agreed to do all the broadcasting for the colony. At first, broadcasts were in English only. During

World War II, Asian- and African-language programs were added to keep the many colonials who were contributing to the war effort apprised of the progress of the war. Cable and Wireless handled the English and Asian programs, while the Kenya Department of Information prepared programs in Swahili, Kikuyu, Kikamba, Nandi, Luo, Luhya, Kipsigis, and Arabic. Cable and Wireless was replaced by the Kenya Broadcasting Service in 1959 with the help of a grant from the British government.

In southern Africa, a broadcast service relaying the BBC out of Salisbury, Southern Rhodesia (Zimbabwe), to the entire area was started in 1932 to coincide with inauguration of the BBC's Empire Service. A monitoring station was also built in Lagos, Nigeria, that year, also providing wired service over telephone lines to Nigerians who could afford it. In 1935, Overseas Rediffusion, Ltd., a private company, was given the franchise for an extensive radio distribution service, which it ran for the Nigerian Post and Telegraph Service, the government department that owned the equipment. Similar wired service was provided in Sierra Leone in 1934 and in Ghana in 1935. In the meantime, the French had inaugurated a wired service in Madagascar in 1931, making their overseas programs available to the island.

The Jesuit Fathers started educational broadcasts in Kinshasa, Belgian Congo (Zaire), in 1937. One of their two transmitters was taken over by the Belgian government in 1940. Not until 1950 were there any broadcasts for Africans, however. All broadcasts until that year were in French and Flemish for European listeners in Africa. World War II opened up a number of additional African countries to radio. Among the ones that acquired broadcasting facilities during the war, in addition to the Belgian Congo, were Cameroon, Congo, Ethiopia, Gambia, Mauritius, Senegal, Somalia, and Northern Rhodesia (Zambia). By the end of the war, about 15 African countries had broadcasting facilities.

No African state permits its radio broadcasting to be controlled largely by commercial interests, as they are in the United States, with the state being involved mainly in allocating airwaves and licensing the operators. And while a few states like Ghana have constitutional provisions that permit broadcasting by private concerns, so far no applications for a license have been received in Ghana and no one is likely to apply because of the cost and the shortage of foreign exchange. With the exceptions that will be noted, all African governments own the broadcasting facilities in their territories and in all but seven states operate them as well. The seven countries that have broadcasting systems operated by "autonomous" public corporations modeled after the BBC are Ghana, Malawi, Mauritius, Nigeria, South Africa, Zambia, and Zimbabwe. This means that they are supported by public funds but their day-to-day operations are the responsibility of a board of directors appointed by the government or determined by statute. Of course, how much independent judgment this board is permitted to exercise varies from country to country and with the prevailing political climate at any given time.

Besides the government-owned and -operated stations, three countries have given broadcasting privileges to radio stations owned and operated by private religious organizations, three have privately owned commercial radio stations, two permit foreign governments to broadcast from their territory, and four countries allow the South West African People's Organization (SWAPO) of Namibia to broadcast revolutionary programs to Namibia.

In Liberia, station ELWA, which was founded in 1954 by United States church groups, is run by the Sudan Interior Mission. It is noncommercial and broadcasts on shortwave and medium-wave to West, Central, and North Africa in English, French, Arabic, and 42 West African languages. The Seychelles are hosts to the Far East Broadcasting Association, which beams religious programs to both India and East Africa in 21 languages. In Swaziland, Trans World Radio, an international evangelical organization that also has transmitters in Monte Carlo, Guam, Sri Lanka, Cyprus, and the Netherlands Antilles, broadcasts to East, Central, and North Africa in English, Afrikaans, Swahili, and other African languages. When Emperor Haile Selassie was still in power, Ethiopia permitted the Lutheran World Federation to run the oldest evangelical broadcasting operation out of Addis Ababa. It was called Radio Voice of the Gospel and was founded in 1941. But the station was nationalized in 1977 by the new government and renamed Radio Voice of Revolutionary Ethiopia.

In Liberia, two iron ore–mining companies operate radio stations. The Lamco firm broadcasts on station ELNR in nine African languages and English for its employees, and the Bong Mining Company operates ELCBR for a similar audience. Swazi Radio is a privately owned commercial service in Swaziland that broadcasts to southern Africa in English, Afrikaans, Portuguese, and Indian languages. Gambia has a commercial station, Radio Syd, that broadcasts mainly music. The Voice of America has a relay station in Liberia; and Deutsche Welle, West Germany's overseas broadcasting station, has relay facilities in Rwanda. SWAPO's Voice of Namibia is permitted to broadcast into Namibia on transmitters in Congo, Angola, Tanzania, and Zambia.

Most radio in Africa is financed through direct government subsidies. At least 29 of the 46 countries also allow commercial advertising. But in most African countries, this accounts for a very small proportion of the revenue. In Senegal, for example, it amounts to a mere 10 percent. Even where advertising promises good returns, as in South Africa, only

14 percent of the total expenditures on advertising in that country goes to radio. Fewer than half the countries have license fees; but these must of necessity be low, and they are hard to collect. Many radio sets in African countries go unregistered.

Broadcasting facilities have been increasing in Africa every year. Thus the number of transmitters in 1955 was 151; in 1960 it was 252; in 1964, it had gone up to 370; in 1976, it was 428; and by 1987, it was 1,059. But these figures are hard to substantiate and should be taken only as a measure of the growth of broadcasting in Africa. Remember that for every transmitter that is put into operation, hundreds of listeners tune in newly acquired sets.

Because radio is so important to the continent, even the smaller countries in Africa have extensive radio services, broadcasting many hours in an amazing number of languages. One would expect this of South Africa, of course. It has 9 full-time services broadcasting in 18 languages a total of 2,776 hours per week. One of these services is an all-night external service called Radio South Africa, which broadcasts to Africa, Europe, and North America.

The Voice of Kenya in Nairobi operates three services: national (in Swahili), general (in English), and vernacular (in 15 African languages and Hindustani). It also has an educational service for schools and a shortwave service for distant villages. The Federal Radio Corporation of Nigeria, which has replaced the Nigerian Broadcasting Corporation in 1978, operates three national networks and an external service known as the Voice of Nigeria, broadcasting to Africa, Europe, the Middle East, and the Americas. In addition, each of the 19 state governments in Nigeria has its own broadcasting corporation and originates its own broadcasts in local languages and English.

Ghana's Domestic Service has an English channel and a vernacular one. The English channel carries commercials; the vernacular channel broadcasts in six languages. The External Service broadcasts in English, French, and Hausa. Similarly, Zambia has an English channel, a vernacular channel broadcasting in seven Zambian languages, and an external shortwave channel broadcasting mainly to the south. The Zambia National Broadcasting Service has been a parastatal corporation since 1988 and may accept commercials.

In Francophone Africa, Senegal runs two networks, with a parent station in Dakar and four regional stations broadcasting 132 hours a week, mainly in six local languages. The news is carried in French simultaneously on both networks. The Ivory Coast operates three services: national, regional, and international. The broadcasts are mainly French on the national and international network, except for five daily newscasts in English for neighboring countries. The regional network broadcasts in 13 local languages. Cameroon has a national, a provincial, and an international shortwave service broadcasting in English and French. There are ten provincial stations in as many cities, each broadcasting in French, English, and a variety of local languages. The Voice of Zaire has a powerful 600-kilowatt transmitter covering most of the western area of Central Africa, and two powerful (100-kilowatt) shortwave transmitters that cover all of Zaire. It also has a number of other medium-wave and shortwave transmitters in major towns and in each region, and there is a shortwave transmitter that covers West Africa and Europe—13 stations in all. Zaire devotes 62 hours per week to news broadcasts, 41 hours of which are in French and the rest in four vernacular languages. Of its 23 hours a week of educational and cultural programs, 18 are in French; it also broadcasts 17 hours a week of entertainment. Because of inadequate transportation, phone, and postal facilities, Rwanda uses its radio, which is partly financed by West Germany, as a national bulletin board.

Adult education occupies a large proportion of the time on African radio. Serious programs, including news and current affairs programs plus educational programs on hygiene and social problems, constitute about 40 percent of total program time. Katz and Wedell (1977) found that in Tanzania and Senegal about half the programs fell into this category and that even Tanzania's commercial service devoted 40 percent of its programs to information. It may be that cost is an important factor. Many of these serious programs are talk shows that are cheap to produce. Among the most popular programs in Nigeria are request programs. These include a message program, a children's program, a traders' program, and a women's program. Letters are sent to the station from all over the state with messages to loved ones or questions to be discussed by panels of peers. A farmers' program discusses and recommends new farming methods. Talk shows are favored by almost a third of Kenyan radio listeners, next to news, which about three-fourths of the public listed as the program they enjoyed in a 1980 media survey. Significantly, 16 percent said they liked greetings programs, close to the 15 percent who liked popular music.

Despite the importance of radio on the African continent as a medium of education and social integration, it has not been able to penetrate the hinterland in many African countries. Its major audience in the smaller countries is in the urban areas. Nevertheless, it is still the most efficient and effective way to reach large segments of the population from central locations.

Nigeria, which has gone all out to use radio as an educational and political medium, has among the highest listenerships. In a nationwide survey in 1980, fully 90 percent of the population claimed to have heard radio at some time or other. Significantly, 86 percent in the rural areas said they had listened to radio, and urban listenership was 93 percent. The presence of television in the home does not decrease radio listenership, as another 1980 study showed. In this study, 92 percent of television owners claimed also to listen to radio regularly. In Lagos, the capital, regular listenership by TV owners is 97 percent. These are, of course, elite homes.

However, in Kenya, which is also very active in the use of radio for national development, only 69 percent of a cross section of the population said they had ever listened to radio, according to a 1980 media study. Urban listenership is, of course, higher. In response to the question "Do you listen to the radio?" 91 percent of the urban population said they did, as against 68 percent of the rural population. Only 42 percent listened in their own home, with 41 percent claiming to own a working radio (35 percent in rural areas). And lest anyone think that people probably listen in their cars, as they do in the United States, only 0.02 percent said they listened on a car radio. The frequency of regular (e.g., daily or weekly) listening is, of course, much lower in all cases.

Audience data are not readily available in Africa, but in Francophone Africa studies were done by a reputable French market research organization in 1980 in Cameroon, Gabon, and Ivory Coast. All available data are from major cities alone. Thus in Yaoundé and Douala, two principal cities of Cameroon, daily radio listenership is 67 percent, with an additional 25 percent claiming to listen several times a week. In Libreville, the capital of Gabon, 62 percent said they listened daily and another 19 percent several times a week. A 1977 study by the same organization showed a similar 80 percent "regular" urban listenership. In Abidjan, capital of the Ivory Coast, daily listenership was 56 percent, with another 25 percent claiming to listen several times a week.

Overall, an estimate of radio set ownership in Africa in the mid-1980s puts the figure at less than 8 percent of the population. This compares with 39 percent in South America. Incidentally, radio set ownership in the USSR was 64 percent, based on the same source, while France had 104 percent ownership, the United Kingdom 112 percent, and the United States, where most people own an average of two sets, 195 percent. To make radio more readily accessible in Africa, many countries have community loudspeakers in rural areas. These make it possible for large numbers to listen to a single set, but they limit the choice of station.

Television

Unlike radio, which even poor countries can afford and no African country is without, television often requires outlays that are beyond the means of both the potential transmitter and receiver of the service. The government that wants to make use of the medium needs capital equipment, such as transmitters, studios, cameras, and recorders; it must train the personnel; and it also has recurrent and continuing maintenance and production costs. Because film industries are absent in sub-Saharan Africa, there is not much locally produced entertainment material to feed the voracious monster. African countries are forced to go to their former colonizing countries or some other foreign power for entertainment materials (a thing many of them resent) or must resort to locally produced talk shows, political propaganda extravaganzas, or amateurish educational programs and short broadcasting hours. None of this is an efficient use of costly investments.

Of the 46 discrete political entities in the area, 36 had television at the start of 1989, up from 28 only seven years earlier. Other countries are planning to introduce television in the near future. Burundi, which had outlawed the importation or use of TV in the early 1980s, now broadcasts six hours daily. Residents of Botswana watch South African TV, and Gambia gets reasonable reception from Senegal. Equatorial Guinea now has its own television but can pick up signals from Nigeria or Gabon under favorable conditions, and 11,300 TV sets are in use in the country. The only major African country that continues to resist TV is Tanzania. But the islands of Zanzibar and Pemba, which merged with Tanganyika to form Tanzania, installed a color television system in 1973.

All African TV is state-owned and -operated except that Swaziland, which inaugurated its service in 1978, shares equal ownership with a private company under a royal charter, with the understanding that eventually it will acquire full ownership. Some foreign companies have assisted in bringing TV to Africa but in all cases have withdrawn because television was found to be a losing proposition for the foreseeable future. Africa is too poor to support it profitably. Thus a private British company helped Western Nigeria introduce the first television in sub-Saharan Africa in 1959. In 1976, the Nigerian Television Authority was constituted as the federal body responsible for television production, and it set up a federal station in each of the 19 state capitals. In 1980, Lagos State began a state television broadcasting system of its own, as have nine of the other states.

Zambia acquired a commercial system on the copper belt at Kitwe in 1961, which the state took over in 1966. The year 1963 saw a large surge of interest in television. Four Francophone states inaugurated television broadcasting in that year. They were Congo, Gabon, Ivory Coast, and Burkina Faso. The three Anglophone states of Kenya, Uganda, and Sierra Leone also introduced television that year. The following year, both Ethiopia and Liberia, the two sub-Saharan states that never were colonies, started TV broadcasting, and Senegal, with the help of UNESCO, Canada, and France, began experimenting with educational television. Ghana started its system with the help of the Japanese company Sanyo, which wanted the franchise for TV manufacturing and sales in the country. South Africa had no television until 1976, when it inaugurated a single channel, broadcasting alternately in English and Afrikaans. National Party leaders had hinted that their long-standing opposition to TV was due to their fear that it would have to depend too much on English-language imports for entertainment shows, slighting the Afrikaans-speaking elements of the population. In January 1982, two TV channels were introduced for blacks. One broadcasts in Zulu and Xhosa, the other in Sotho, Venda, and Tswana, with a heavy emphasis on soap operas and sports.

Like radio, TV is financed through direct government subsidization, commercials, and license fees. In addition, some countries, such as Burkina Faso and Zambia, receive foreign assistance. Mauritania received a $3 million gift from Iraq to build its color TV transmitter and studios. Some countries also have a stiff excise tax on receivers; it is 100 percent in Nigeria. As in the case of radio, license fees are hard to collect. In Kenya, for instance, where some 50,000 sets were in use in 1976, only 3,458 television licenses had been issued. (The actual number of sets in use can be estimated from imports and sales.)

A few countries, such as Kenya, Zambia, and Zimbabwe, introduced television mostly for their European population before independence. It was considered an expensive toy, and to the present day it is a medium for the elite. Of some 14,000 television sets in Kenya in 1968, fully 11,000 were said to be owned by Europeans and Asians, and 500 were community sets. Most of the 200,000 sets in the country today are in Nairobi and Mombasa, where a station was opened in 1970. Less than 10 percent of the population of Kenya lives in these two cities.

Countries that have introduced television since independence emphasize its educational role. Not only is this emphasis politically wise, since the benefit thus supposedly accrues to the masses rather than the elite, but it is economically the most expedient use of the medium. Educational programs are cheaper to produce than many entertainment programs, and they generally satisfy the nationalistic goal of most African countries to do as much as possible of the programming locally.

A typical day's schedule starts around 5 or 6 p.m. and runs for three to five hours. It may have between two and five newscasts of 5 to 15 minutes, at least one of which would include international news. It is likely to have a talk show, a children's educational program, local music and dancing, an adult educational program on health, art, clothing, the theater, or books, and possibly a foreign import, such as a film or a network rerun from the United States, Britain, or France. On weekends, and often on weekdays too, there is likely to be a sports event.

Sports is among the favorite television programs of many Africans. In a 1980 Kenya survey, 11 percent said their favorite program was wrestling; 4 percent said it was sports in general and football (soccer) "made in Germany"; 18 percent liked news best; while 6 percent enjoyed the "Six Million Dollar Man" most. In Kenya, as was pointed out, TV reaches a very small segment of the population. Only 3 percent of the public claim to have TV; only 12 percent have ever seen it. Many see it at a friend's home or at a community center.

TV has a larger audience in Nigeria, which, of course, has a higher per capita income than Kenya. A 1980 study there found that 68 percent of the public claimed to have seen TV, and the urban proportion was as high as 89 percent. In rural Nigeria, 41 percent had seen TV, according to the survey. But only 7 percent of the rural public say they watch it every day, as against 61 percent of the urban public. It should be noted that Nigeria has 41 transmitters, while Kenya has only four, plus two relays. A 1977 study in Libreville, Gabon, found 43 percent who claimed to view TV daily.

Overall, 1.1 percent of the African public owns television sets. The proportion of TV set ownership in Asia is 6 percent, a tenfold increase since 1975, when Africa and Asia both had 0.6 percent ownership. For purposes of comparison, 31 percent of the public owns TV sets in the USSR, 59 percent own sets in the United States, and 33 percent in the United Kingdom and France. TV remains a medium of wealthy countries. The fact that about half of all sub-Saharan African countries (24) belong to Intelsat and can potentially receive foreign programs directly via satellite does not mean that TV will bring African people closer to the rest of the world. Africa's integration in the global village must be preceded by its economic and educational development.

GOVERNMENT–MEDIA RELATIONS AND CONCEPTS OF PRESS FREEDOM

The relations between the mass media and government can range all the way from total independence of the two institutions to total control by the government of the mass media. In the former case, mass media are a true Fourth Estate, serving the public in their area of responsibility and competence with no interference from the government. In the latter extreme, mass media are an arm of the government with no purpose other than to further the goals and programs of the government. No country in Africa has a mass media system that may be characterized as pure Fourth Estate. By contrast, about a third of the countries in sub-Saharan Africa have media that either function as the mouthpiece and organizers of the public to implement government objectives or are permitted absolutely no freedom to operate outside government guidelines.

African countries were rated according to the following criteria:

1. Press free to criticize government, with full protection of the rights of individuals and of the press through an independent judicial system.
2. Varied opinions expressed in the press, but some constraints exist; strong judiciary.
3. Some censorship of the press, criticism discouraged, but some legal recourse; free speech permitted, and foreign publications readily available.
4. Press censored, no criticism of the government allowed; but private speech and assembly not inhibited.
5. Press and speech censored and no legal recourse, but media privately owned or, if government-owned, no interference with private speech.
6. Strict censorship, only government views available in mass media; military or communist dictatorship.

Using these criteria, no country in sub-Saharan Africa rates a 1. The countries that rate a 2, in the opinion of this author, are Botswana, Gambia, Mauritius, and South Africa. (The relatively high rating given to South Africa in no way condones its racial policies. Approval of the policies of a government must be divorced from an assessment of the degree of freedom of its press to criticize those policies.) In the 1983 edition of *Global Journalism*, Lesotho was also given a rating of 2, but in the aftermath of the military coup of 1986, its rating had to be downgraded to 3. It and Senegal are the only African countries that are rated at the 3 level at this time.

Nigeria is now given a rating of 4, although at the start of the 1980s it had a remarkably free press and was rated a 2. Successive military coups, however, have weakened the press, which nevertheless, once in a while, still has some spark left in it and speaks out against the abuses of power. Four countries dropped one point to the level of 4: Burkina Faso, Ivory Coast, Kenya, and Swaziland. In two other African states, Liberia and Madagascar, the press has shown signs of independent-mindedness in spite of military-dominated, authoritarian governments. The other countries that have remained at the 4 level for at least a decade are the

Central African Republic, Gabon, Malawi, Mauritania, Rwanda, Sierra Leone, and Zambia.

Ghana and Djibouti both dropped two points to the 5 level, and Zimbabwe dropped one point because its one-party, socialist government has tightened its grip on the press. Other countries at the 5 level are Cameroon, Mali, Niger, Seychelles, Uganda, and Zaire. Remaining at the bottom of the list—the 6 level—are Angola, Benin, Burundi, Cape Verde, Chad, Comoros, Congo, Equatorial Guinea, Ethiopia, Guinea, Guinea–Bissau, Mozambique, São Tomé e Príncipe, Somalia, Tanzania, and Togo.

Grouping the countries as in our earlier discussions, we find that the degree of dependence on the printed media is strongly related to an area's press freedom, as Table 7.4 shows. Note that press freedom has decreased in many areas, remained the same in some, and improved very slightly in "independent Africa" (Ethiopia and Liberia). Comparing a 1988 Freedom House assessment of freedom in the world with its 1981 ratings on a scale of 7, freedom in the 46 sub-Saharan states dropped by 14.5 points, or an average of 0.3 per country.

South Africa is one of the most controversial countries in the world. It is a white-dominated African state in which whites make up less than 20 percent of the population. It openly discriminates in its laws and practices against nonwhites. Yet its mass media are free to the extent

TABLE 7.4. FREEDOM RATING BY DEPENDENCE ON PRINTED MEDIA

Dependence on the Printed Media (least to most)	Average Press Freedom Rating (1 = highest, 6 = lowest)	
	1988	1981
1. South Africa	2	2
2. Anglophone East Africa	4.4	4.2
3. Anglophone West Africa	3.75	2.75
4. Southern Africa	3.57	3.17
5. French Africa	4.88	4.7
6. Belgian Africa	5	5
7. Iberophone Africa	6	6
8. Independent Africa	5	5.5
9. Italian Africa (Somalia)	6	6

Sources: R. D. Gastil, *Freedom in the World* (New York: Freedom House, 1989); United States Information Agency, *Country Data Papers: Africa* (Washington, D.C., 1989); author's analysis.

that it is no offense for them to oppose the policy of apartheid. The government's Bureau of Information itself distributes press comment critical of the government. South Africa has an outspoken white-owned and -operated English-language press that takes strong stands against government policies and practices. It is read by more people than read the pro–National Party, pro-apartheid Afrikaans press. Yet while the courts are independent and generally fair, the police can easily get an injunction against a newspaper if they wish to stop publication of a story they consider undesirable. And in early 1982, the Steyn Commission of Inquiry into the Media recommended to Parliament that journalists be registered and that a press council be formed with powers to suspend a reporter's registration. Broadcasting is a state monopoly, and the broadcast media, which, like the Afrikaans press, support the government, get preferential access to government news.

Despite all this, many observers, including Africans, say that the press of South Africa is still the freest in Africa. One must therefore examine the constraints on the press of other African countries. What makes the press of Nigeria, which many regard as the freest in black Africa, less free than that of South Africa? Frank Barton (1979), African director of the International Press Institute and a keen analyst of the African press, refers to the Nigerian military junta's "jungle style" treatment of journalists, including whipping and head shaving (p. 55). The chilling effect that such demeaning treatment will have on journalists and publishers can be imagined. Not that equivalent treatment, especially of blacks, in South Africa is unknown. But the press follows up acts of barbarism with vigorous investigative reporting. Not only is there less of such comeback in the relatively free press of countries such as Nigeria, Gambia, Ghana, and Kenya, but self-censorship is much stronger there so that brutal acts are less frequently reported. Nevertheless, recently in Nigeria the courts awarded punitive damages to an editor who had been whipped.

In the rest of Africa, one must distinguish between countries that actively use the press to achieve political objectives and ones that tolerate the mass media as an evil necessary for the entertainment and diversion of the public. Kwame Nkrumah was among the first type. "The truly African revolutionary press does not exist merely for the purpose of enriching its proprietors and entertaining its readers," the Ghanaian leader told the Second Conference of African Journalists in 1963. "The African press must present and carry forward our revolutionary purpose." Or, speaking of the role of radio, Jean-Jacques Kanda, former minister of information in Zaire, said: "In countries where independence is still ceaselessly being brought into question . . . how can we tolerate the radio's becoming an instrument of division, slander or controversy?. . . I am convinced that the radio should always be under public control."

Countries such as Zambia, Zimbabwe, Tanzania, and Sierra Leone are very conscious of the developmental role of the mass media and control them accordingly. By contrast, Gambia, Mauritius, Swaziland, and even Kenya are more tolerant of private ownership and profit making on the part of the press. This does not mean that they are disinterested in the educational and socializing potential of the press, but they do not use the press single-mindedly for this one purpose. The fact that it is being used by the government places the press in a manipulative role, thereby reducing its freedom status. In a truly free country, where the press is an institution of society—the Fourth Estate—people use the press to serve their needs. Using the press offensively makes it a tool of government, whereas defensive use puts the government on the alert against any possible harm the press might do to it. Both types of uses call for government controls.

No country in Africa is without press controls, as we have said. In most countries, the controls include such legal constraints as libel and sedition laws. This kind of constraint naturally exists in even the freest countries of the world. But the laws can be liberal or restrictive. They can define libel and sedition so broadly that criticism of any kind becomes a crime. Dennis L. Wilcox (1975), in a study of the African press, found that about one-fourth of African countries have highly restrictive libel and sedition laws, another fourth have fairly restrictive laws, about 30 percent have not very restrictive laws, while in one-fifth of the countries, the laws have no effect at all in the opinion of journalists, largely because the press is so heavily controlled or is government-operated.

One of the most pervasive and effective forms of press control is outright or majority ownership of printing presses or newspapers by the government. As we have seen, in at least three-fourths of the countries, the government is either the sole or the principal owner of the print media; and in all countries, government owns and operates most radio and television stations. In a few countries, such as Tanzania, Zambia, Ivory Coast, Cameroon, and the Seychelles, the political party in power also plays a major role in running the print media.

Another form of government control is through the allocation of newsprint. Except for South Africa and Zimbabwe, African countries must import newsprint and must set aside foreign exchange for the purpose. Ghana and Sierra Leone are so limited in their supply of newsprint at the present time that circulations have been drastically cut back and some publications are not now being printed. Wilcox (1975) found that 47 percent of the African countries he studied treated governmental and private publications equally, and in 44 percent of the countries, the problem of equal treatment did not arise because there was no privately owned press. Most of the remaining countries gave preference to government publications.

Censorship is another way that the government intrudes itself in mass communication. There are two types of censorship: prepublication and postpublication. It is hard to say which is the more undesirable. Wilcox (1975) found that almost six out of ten African countries had prepublication censorship. This involves submitting galley proofs or page proofs to an official censor, who often has an office in the newspaper building. The censor approves every item that goes into the paper. In the case of three-fourths of these countries, prepublication censorship is implied by the very fact that the newspapers are government-owned. About four in ten countries have no ostensible prepublication censorship. This includes some government-owned publications. Postpublication censorship means that the government can punish an editor and staff for publishing something the government objects to. Such second guessing is very unnerving, because one can never tell what the government will take exception to. Occasionally a newspaper is closed or an issue is seized, or an editor is fired without any reason being given. Wherever there is the threat of postpublication reprisal, self-censorship inevitably results. In such cases, there is a tendency toward overcautiousness on the part of journalists.

There are other methods that governments have used to control their media and their newsmen, and African countries have tried them all. In his 1975 book, Wilcox says that 44 percent of the 34 countries he studied required that journalists be licensed, and 53 percent required the registration of the print media themselves. Without proper certification, a journalist cannot have access to government news, and neither can one who represents a medium that is not registered. Even licensed journalists have a hard time getting access to government information. In almost all African countries, the government gives out the news it wants the press to have. There is no Freedom of Information Act in any African country. As Paul Ansah, a Ghanaian journalism educator, has said: "In Africa the principle is not generally accepted that the public is entitled to information about government business."

NEWS SERVICES

The idea of a news agency is very simple and obvious. If a number of individuals and organizations all need the same kinds of information on a regular basis, it makes sense to gather the information cooperatively.

This is what led to the founding of Reuters, the Associated Press, and all the other major wire services of the world. Newspapers, banks, the stock exchange, and other commercial interests wanted news fast, and they found it economically sound to share the cost of collection. The newspapers, and later radio and television stations, that subscribed to a news service seldom had overlapping readerships, and it broadened their feasible coverage immensely to be able to use wire copy. The stationing of correspondents in all the places that need to be covered from time to time is prohibitively expensive if each newspaper and other medium must have its own correspondent on location.

We are restating the obvious just to remind ourselves of the rationale for a news agency. Since the question is one of economizing by sharing expenses, the more participants who share in the service, the cheaper it is for each of them. And this is what creates a dilemma for most African countries. As we have seen, most states in sub-Saharan Africa have no more than one or two newspapers, one radio, and, possibly, a television station. Furthermore, in most cases they all belong to the same owner—the government. The cost of maintaining a staff of correspondents around the world is beyond the means of most governments. They must therefore buy the service from a major news agency with an international clientele. A national clientele will hardly suffice, because the potential number of subscribers would be too small to provide a broad enough coverage. This leaves the international news agencies—Agence France-Presse, Reuters, the Associated Press, United Press International, and TASS. None of the others can provide world-wide coverage. It boils down to taking the service or doing without international news coverage, or pirating the news from international broadcasts of the BBC, VOA, Radio Moscow, and others.

The dilemma is very real for African nations because most of them feel very strongly that the news carried by the international wire services is biased in selection and presentation. It is especially biased, they feel, against Third World countries in that the little that is carried about these countries generally deals with conflict and disaster and is distorted in presentation even on that. They would like the world to see their developmental side. This dissatisfaction has led to much discussion at Third World conferences and, after the 1973 Non-Aligned Summit conference in Algiers, the Yugoslav news agency Tanjug volunteered to set up a nonaligned news agencies pool that would provide the kind of news about Third World countries that these countries wished to see circulated. In January 1975, Tanjug began relaying Third World news under the code name "Pool," and by the following year there were 40 members. Each member is permitted to submit 500 words each day, and Tanjug incorporates the submissions unaltered in its daily file, translated into English, French, and Spanish where necessary. The member countries are asked to exercise self-censorship and to submit items "on the basis of mutual respect." Of the 41 members in 1977, only one country in sub-Saharan Africa—Ghana—was active enough to have submitted materials during eight days randomly drawn from a three-month period in a study by a United States foreign service officer, Edward T. Pinch.

Placement of Pool stories is meager because of poor translation, poor journalism, and insufficient editing. In the 1977 Pinch study, it was found that only 22 percent of the stories had a high potential for placement in Western media. The rest were too specialized or ideological (obvious propaganda). A 1980 study done at the University of North Carolina and reported in a book edited by Stevenson and Shaw (1984) showed that Third World news was carried mostly by Third World countries, Western news by the West, and communist-bloc news by the communist countries.

Many Africans recognize that Western reporters see things from their own perspective and need to do so, since their clientele demand news from that viewpoint. As one Kenya publisher put it to an American journalism professor, "If I could have a reporter in London or Washington, I would want him to be a Kenyan with a Kenyan perspective and aiming at a Kenyan audience." Not all journalists necessarily want only positive news published about their country. The editor of an Icelandic newspaper, speaking at the December 1979 Conference on Information and Human Rights in Venice, Italy, said Iceland, like many Third World countries, has to "live with a one-way information traffic." It is interested in what is going on in the world but cannot expect the world to be interested in Iceland's cod wars with Britain. He said he accepted the fact that there was not much good news about Iceland in the international media. Who, after all, is interested in a small country like Iceland? But he missed the bad news about Iceland because people in power are very sensitive to bad news in the foreign press.

There are other reasons, however, for setting up national news agencies than covering world news. One is that a country interested in monitoring all incoming news can use the national news agency as a gatekeeper to sift through all the news and to funnel only desirable news to its mass media. Some media have neither the staff and translating capabilities nor the inclination to winnow all the news and prefer to have it predigested by a national news agency knowledgeable about the country's interests. At the same time, the news agency can serve as a gatekeeper for news leaving the country. In some African states, the international wire services do not maintain a bureau or are not permitted to have one. In such cases, the national news agency serves as the main conduit of news about the country.

Of the 46 sub-Saharan countries in Africa, 31 have national news agencies, all but one of them government-owned and -operated. The sole nongovernmental national news agency is that of South Africa—the South African Press Association. Founded in 1938, it was the first national news agency in Africa. It is cooperatively owned by the English and Afrikaans newspapers, much as the Associated Press is media-owned in the United States. The agency was started by Reuters in 1912 as the Reuters South African News Agency to serve southern Africa. Not until 1957 was a black African news agency founded. This was the Ghana News Agency. President Nkrumah was eager to develop it into a pan-African news agency and established a number of bureaus, both in African countries and in London and New York. Its early start gave Ghana an advantage over other national news agencies in terms of the training of its staff and its reputation as a reliable wire service.

The pan-African news agency idea was picked up by the Organization of African Unity when Ghana proposed it at the 1963 Algiers conference. The following year, the Union of African News Agencies, comprising the 20 or so African countries that had them at the time, adopted a plan of organization at its Yaoundé, Cameroon, conference. The purpose of the agency was to project a "true image" of African countries through the exchange of news. It was felt, however, that many things were lacking for the operation of such an agency, including trained personnel, telecommunication links, political harmony among the participants and, above all, money. Although the members of the Union of African News Agencies agreed at their 1967 conference in Addis Ababa that there was a need for a pan-African news agency, ten years were to pass before a secretariat for such an agency was established in Kampala, Uganda. Then, in 1979, the Pan-African News Agency (PANA) was founded and based in Dakar, Senegal, but without any funds. Finally, UNESCO came to the rescue, and in January 1982, it agreed at a conference in Acapulco, Mexico, to allocate $100,000 to get PANA started. The Arab Gulf states said they would contribute the remaining $1.4 million that PANA requested to establish a news and features division, train personnel, and acquire and install telecommunications equipment. But in 1985, only about half of the members of the Organization of African Unity were contributing to PANA.

At the present time, government-run national news agencies are in operation in the following countries:

- Angola: Agence angolaise de Presse (ANGOP)
- Benin: Agence Beninoise de Presse (ABP)
- Burkina Faso: Agence d'Information du Burkina (AIB)
- Burundi: Agence Burundaise de Presse (ABP)
- Cameroon: Cameroon News (CAMNEWS)

- Central African Republic: Agence Centrafricaine de Presse (ACAP)
- Chad: Agence Tchadienne de Presse (ATP)
- Congo: Agence Congolaise d'Information (ACI)
- Ethiopia: Ethipian News Agency (ENA)
- Gabon: Agence Gabonaise de Presse (AGP)
- Ghana: Ghana News Agency (GNA)
- Guinea: Agence Guinéenne de Presse (AGP)
- Ivory Coast: Agence Ivoirienne de Presse (AIP)
- Kenya: Kenya News Agency (KNA)
- Liberia: Liberian News Agency (LINA)
- Madagascar: Agence Nationale d'Information "Taratra" (ANTA)
- Malawi: Malawi News Agency (MANA)
- Mali: Agence Malienne de Presse et de Promotion (AMAP)
- Mauritania: Agence Mauritanienne de Presse (AMP)
- Mozambique: Agencia de Informação de Moçambique (AIM)
- Niger: Agence Nigérienne de Presse (ANP)
- Nigeria: News Agency of Nigeria (NAN)
- Rwanda: Agence Rwandaise de Presse (ARP)
- Senegal: Agence de Presse Sénégalaise (APS)
- Sierra Leone: Sierra Leone News Agency (SLENA)
- Somalia: Somalia News Agency (SONA)
- Tanzania: Tanzania News Agency (SHIHATA)
- Togo: Agence Togolaise de Presse (ATOP)
- Uganda: Uganda News Agency (UNA)
- Zaire: Agence Zaïroise de Presse (AZAP)
- Zambia: Zambia News Agency (ZANA)
- Zimbabwe: Zimbabwe Inter-African News Agency (ZIANA)

Thirteen countries have no indigenous news agencies: Botswana, Cape Verde, Comoros, Djibouti, Equatorial Guinea, Gambia, Guinea–Bissau, Lesotho, Mauritius, Namibia, São Tomé e Príncipe, Seychelles, and Swaziland. In addition, there is a private Protestant news agency and a private Catholic news agency in Zaire.

JOURNALISM EDUCATION AND TRAINING

One of the many shortages that Africans experienced upon gaining their independence was one of trained journalists. "Some countries cannot claim a single qualified journalist," a 1961 UNESCO report stated. Good copy editors were especially hard to find, according to Frank Barton (1979), an African journalist who played an important role in helping to correct the deficiency. Except in Nigeria, where a few Africans had been working as journalists for some time, whites had been in full control of the press, so even after independence, newspapers and other media were forced to turn to Europeans for help in running their news operations. But even in Nigeria, the skill gap between editors and their staffs was abysmal. Francophone Africa was probably even worse off than the English-speaking countries. While some Africans had been sent to France for training, they returned with such an elevated command of the language and used such literary styles that they were completely out of touch with the masses.

Entering the breach were a number of organizations that attempted to do for African journalism what war departments everywhere tried to do for the war machines when World War II broke out. Just as war departments trained soldiers in a hurry, these organizations developed intensive, condensed training courses during the 1960s to produce the necessary cadres of journalists. Among the organizations that came to the rescue were the International Press Institute, with headquarters in Zurich, Switzerland; the International Organization of Journalists (IOJ), of Prague, Czechoslovakia; the International Federation of Journalists, of Brussels, Belgium; the Thomson Foundation in the United Kingdom; the American Press Institute and the African American Institute in the United States; and UNESCO. IPI was especially successful with six-month training programs in Nairobi for journalists in East and Central Africa and in Lagos for West Africa. Funded by Ford Foundation grants, these courses trained more than 300 African journalists between 1963 and 1968. UNESCO ran training programs for Francophone Africa in Dakar and one for East and Central Africans in Kampala, Uganda, while the East European IOJ conducted courses in Guinea, Mali, and Ghana.

One of the oldest permanent training institutions in black Africa is the Ghana Institute of Journalism, which was founded by Kwame Nkrumah in 1957 as a department of the Accra Technical Institute. It has a two- or three-year diploma course in journalism and a two-year specialist course in public relations. In 1973, Ghana established the School of Journalism and Mass Communications in Legon, outside Accra. It has been active in promoting literacy and rural journalism and offers a master's degree. Ghana also has the National Film and Television Institute, founded in 1978 to offer specialized training in television and film production.

In neighboring Nigeria, a department of journalism was opened at the University of Nigeria, Nsukka, in 1961 along the lines of United States schools of journalism. It was then called the Jackson College of Journalism. The university was closed down in 1967 during the civil war but reopened in 1970. Another program, leading to bachelor's and master's degrees, is at the University of Lagos, founded in 1966. Besides university programs in several Nigerian state universities, journalism training is also available at the Nigerian Institute of Journalism and at the Nigerian Broadcasting Staff Training School, both in Lagos.

On the east coast, Kenya's School of Journalism at the University of Nairobi was established in 1970 with the assistance of UNESCO, Norway, Denmark, and Austria. In 1975, the government took full financial responsibility for the school. It offered a two-year undergraduate diploma course until 1979, when the program was discontinued in favor of a one-year postgraduate program. Kenya's Ministry of Information and Broadcasting also operates the Kenya Institute of Mass Communication. This started as a training school for broadcast engineering staff in 1961. It still teaches engineering but has since added courses in production. There are also two schools specializing in Christian communication.

The All-African Conference of Churches Communication Training Centre in Nairobi was founded in 1963. It emphasizes broadcasting, while the International Institute of Christian Communications (IICC) is connected with Daystar Communications, an organization that helps churches and missions with their communication problems. Established in 1971 as a four-week seminar, the IICC expanded to a diploma and M.A. degree program in 1976. Uganda attempted a one-year diploma course in journalism at the Institute of Public Administration in Kampala in 1974. The program was closed down the following year but was reopened as a school of journalism when President Idi Amin was deposed. In 1975, Tanzania's Ministry of Information and Broadcasting opened its school of journalism in Dar-es-Salaam, offering a one-year certificate course and a two-year diploma program in a variety of journalism and mass communication fields. To be eligible for admission, Tanzanians must be members of the Revolutionary Party and have completed their national service. An older school, known as the Nyegezi Institute of Journalism at the Social Training Centre in Mwanza, does not have a college-level program. Zambia has a journalism training program at Evelyn Hone College in Lusaka, with excellent printing and photographic facilities. It also has probably the oldest church-related journalism program at the African Literature Centre in Kitwe, which now offers an annual journalism short course to students in the region.

A regional program for French-speaking Africans is offered at the École Supérieure Internationale de Journalisme de Yaoundé in Cameroon. It is part of the Federal University of Cameroon and is financed by the government, with assistance from the Central African Republic, Chad, Gabon, Rwanda, and Togo. Another French program, leading to a diploma in print or electronic journalism, is a three-year course of studies at the Centre d'Etudes des Sciences et Techniques de l'Information (CESTI). The center was founded in 1970 at the University of Dakar, Senegal, and has drawn students from Benin, Burkina Faso, Ivory Coast, Mali, Mauritania, and Niger, besides Senegal itself. An advanced diploma and the third year were added in 1978. A more limited program is offered at the Centre de Formation aux Techniques de l'Information in Niamey, Niger. In Zaire, IPI organized training programs at Kinshasa in 1962 and 1963. There had been a certificate program before independence in 1958 and 1959 at the former University of Lovanium in Kinshasa; but in 1973, a regular department of journalism was inaugurated at the National University of Zaire. Called the Institut des Sciences et Techniques de l'Information (ISTI), it offers bachelor's, master's, and doctoral degrees (*graduat, licence,* and *doctorat*) in print and electronic journalism. It has attracted students from Benin, Burundi, Chad, Central African Republic, Rwanda, and Togo.

In South Africa, the Argus Group found a need to train journalists for positions on its various newspapers and in 1956 established the Argus Cadet School of Journalism. It offered a five-month course in Cape Town at its evening paper, the *Cape Argus.* In 1968, it moved the program to Johannesburg. The morning chain of newspapers known as South African Associated Newspapers had a similar program for its staff. University training in journalism did not begin until after a 1967 report by a government-sponsored symposium in Pretoria on the study of communication. The University of Potchefstroom began offering a four-year undergraduate program and a one-year postgraduate diploma plus an M.A. in communications and journalism. Within three years, the University of South Africa in Pretoria, Rhodes University in Grahamstown, and Rand Afrikaans University in Johannesburg were also offering degrees in journalism. In the 1970s, the Department of Communication was established at the University of Orange Free State at Bloemfontein.

As is true in the United States, seasoned African journalists who worked their way up from "tea-boy" (i.e., go-fer or copy boy) to editor are skeptical about academic programs in journalism. They believe in on-the-job training for reporters and editors. Their prejudice against formal academic training in journalism is bolstered in English-speaking Africa by their British heritage. Britain continues to resist the idea of teaching journalism at a university. Many African leaders of the old school received their apprenticeship in journalism on British or French newspapers; some took correspondence courses, a very common educational alternative in England.

Illiteracy adds to the problem not only because of the competition for the few educated Africans who are available for responsible positions. That in itself means that journalism, which is poorly paid and low in social standing, frequently has to be satisfied with less than the top talent, since the best minds are attracted to better-paying, more prestigious careers. But high illiteracy adds to the problem of communication. It takes a better-trained person to get through to a population with limited education. Radio has been the most prevalent medium of communication in African homes, and it is significant that in Nigeria, for example, it is the newspapers that attempt to recruit former broadcast journalists rather than the electronic media going after print reporters. This is true despite the fact that there are many more newspaper than radio jobs and hence more opportunities for training in the print media.

PROSPECTS FOR THE FUTURE

Making a judgment about the future of African journalism is like talking about the professional contributions of a young man who is still in junior high school. Too many unpredictable influences and environmental factors could change the course of the young man's career. So it is with Africa. Literacy is being tackled by all African countries in every way possible within their limited means. Communication instrumentalities other than newspapers, radio, and television, but just as important, are being developed as fast as possible. They include roads, telephone lines, airports, electricity, schools, books, teachers, and informal communication channels.

Literacy must go hand in hand with economic development. One cannot outdistance the other very much. With literacy will come the ability, but not necessarily the desire or even the need, to read printed media. The habit of newspaper reading developed in Europe and the Americas at a time when there was no other link with the outside world. Electronic links today are faster, easier, and even cheaper than the printed media. The need for newspapers is not as pressing today as it was 50 years ago. Although the need and possibly even the desire to achieve and maintain relationships with the rest of the world are stronger than ever, radio and television are less painful channels of communication for this purpose than print.

By the time independence and self-determination came to most African nations, the civilized world had moved beyond the era of dependence on the printed media and into the age of electronics. Africans were under foreign tutelage and uninvolved in the kind of traffic that required daily printed communications. Their entry into the mainstream of international intercourse was at a time when it was possible for them to skip a stage in the development of many peoples and go straight to electronic communications.

It is therefore unlikely that African people will become great newspaper readers. Their traditions, their institutions, even their social and psychological needs have evolved beyond that stage. Use of radio and, with economic growth, television will increase. For entertainment, Africans will continue to depend on folk and traditional media, such as dances and plays. When it becomes economically feasible, videodisks and recorders will be very popular, as they already are at least in Kenya, where the *Christian Science Monitor* reports some 75,000 videocassette recorders are in use, to the great concern of movie theater owners.

CHAPTER 8

Asia and the Pacific

Anne Cooper Chen and Anju Grover Chaudhary

"The press always takes on the form and coloration of the social and political structures within which it operates," wrote Siebert, Peterson, and Schramm in 1956 (p. 1). To understand the mass media of Asia, where three-fifths of the world's people live, we must look briefly at the social and political life of the region. Asia is defined in this book as the nations and dependent territories that stretch from Afghanistan east to Japan and south to Australia and New Zealand, excluding the Soviet Union. About 15 percent of the population is urban, but because the region is so populous, that small percentage represents many millions in real terms.

The countries in the region vary widely on virtually any index. No other region shows such diverse population figures. Asia includes China, with well over 1 billion people, and India, with nearly 800 million—the two most populous nations on the earth. By 2100, India is expected to move into first place with 1.63 billion people, making China the second largest nation with 1.57 billion.

By contrast, certain independent states in the South Pacific have fewer people than Toledo, Ohio: Kiribati, for example, has about 64,000 inhabitants; Tonga, about 109,000; and Vanuatu, about 135,000. Tiny Nauru, with 8,400 people, has little in the way of mass media. Thus because of space limitations in this chapter, the following discussion will concentrate on nations with more than 500,000 people and a media system that can accurately be described as "mass."

But contrasts in population figures in themselves do not tell us much about the quality of life. The statistics commonly used to compare countries should be used with caution, but each can contribute to our understanding of the context in which mass media operate. A single measure of literacy does not tell us whether differences exist between men and women. However, we can learn from them that in all the countries of South Asia, and in Papua New Guinea, less than half the population over age 15 can read and write.

The often-used statistic to measure economic development, gross national product per capita, has limitations because of what it doesn't tell about the nonmonetary components of daily life. Infant mortality per 1,000 live births is commonly used to judge physical well-being and health care, but it does not tell us, for example, about the treatment of the elderly. According to the United Nations International Children's Fund (UNICEF), Asia includes four countries with the lowest number of children who die before their first birthday—Japan, Hong Kong, Singapore, and Australia—and four countries with the highest number—Afghanistan, Cambodia, Bhutan, and Nepal.

Even more telling is the "human suffering index," a composite figure that includes infant mortality and literacy among its ten components. According to the Population Crisis Committee's human suffering index, the people of five Asian nations—Afghanistan, Bangladesh, Bhutan, Cambodia, and Nepal—live under extremely poor conditions; by contrast, four nations (Japan, Singapore, Australia, and New Zealand) can boast of minimal suffering. Other regions of the world, notably Africa, suffer more extreme hardships overall, but no other region exhibits the marked contrasts that Asia does.

HISTORICAL HIGHLIGHTS

Invented in China, paper has been dated, using surviving specimens, back to 49 B.C. The use of ink (for making marks with brushes) started even earlier, at least as far back as 1300 B.C. Writing, in the form of graphs on pottery, has been dated back to about 5000 B.C. The Chinese began using woodblock printing extensively in the tenth century A.D., and the Koreans perfected metal movable type in the early 1400s. Thus print media have existed in Asia longer than anywhere else in the world.

Although the classical Chinese language united people in Japan, Korea, Vietnam, and other countries in Southeast Asia, only elites mastered it. Even in China itself, a mere 1 or 2 percent of the population could read and write the language in 100 B.C., and only about 5 percent as

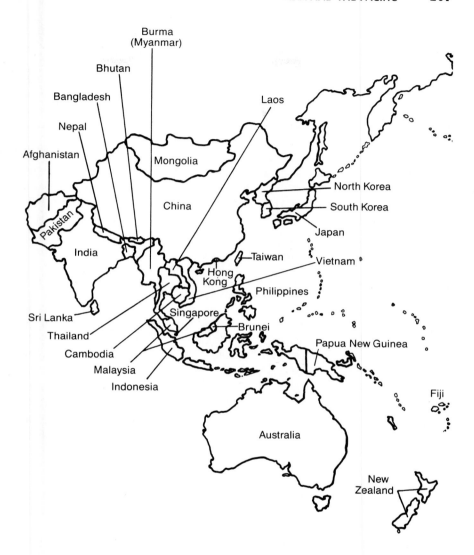

late as 1800. But with a population of some 300 million in 1800, China had around 15 million potential readers.

Beginning in the Ming dynasty (1368–1644), competing publishers issued court news periodicals for sale to literate officials and merchants. Printed from hand-carved blocks, these gazettes lasted into the 1800s. More popular illustrated newspapers carrying sensationalized news appeared occasionally before 1800 (Bishop, 1989, p. 42).

Westerners—including colonial authorities, missionaries, and trading companies—started the first regularly published modern periodicals. In 1616, the Dutch East India Company in Indonesia issued a newsletter called *Mémoires des Nouvelles.* The first general-interest publication, the Dutch-language *Bataviasche Nouvelles,* appeared in 1744; edited by a Dutch official in Indonesia, it lasted only two years. During the remainder of the century, various Dutch journals appeared and disappeared.

In 1780 in India, an Englishman, James Hicky, started a two-sheet weekly called the *Bengal Gazette.* Also known as *Hicky's Gazette,* the paper exposed the private lives of East India Company officials and Governor General Warren Hastings and his wife. In 1782, Hicky was sued for libel and imprisoned in poverty.

The Press in the Nineteenth Century

Papers in indigenous languages appeared later than those in colonists' languages. A British missionary began a monthly magazine in vernacular Chinese in 1815. The first newspapers in Afghanistan, Burma (officially called Myanmar after 1989), and Korea were also in the native language.

An American missionary established the pioneering *Bangkok Recorder* in Thailand in 1844. Other missionaries active in publishing set up a printing press, which had been "reinvented" by Gutenberg and imported back to Asia, in the important port of Malacca (now Melaka, Malaysia).

The first Indian paper owned by an Indian was the English-language *Bengal Gazette,* established by Gangadhar Bhattacharjee in Calcutta in 1816. Raja Ram Mohan Roy, one of India's greatest champions of political and press freedom, published the country's first non-English-language paper, *Mirat-ul-Akhbar,* in 1821. Sometimes called the "father of modern India," he wrote a noted memorial for the repeal of the press ordinance of 1823.

In South and Southeast Asia, a number of existing publications have nineteenth-century roots. Both Singapore's *Straits Times* and Malaysia's *New Straits Times* share common parentage in the original *Straits Times,* founded in 1834 and a daily since 1858. The *Times of India,* the country's oldest English-language daily, was established in 1838 as a commercial biweekly and converted into a daily in 1851. Other long-established Indian papers include the *Amrita Bazar Patrika,* a Bengali-language daily in Calcutta (1868); the *Statesman,* an independent liberal English-language daily (1875); and the *Hindu,* an English-language daily in Madras (1878).

As in India, the press in Sri Lanka has strong British roots. The colonial authorities started the *Government Gazette* for foreign residents in 1802. The first newspaper in a conventional sense was the *Colombo Journal* (1832) in English; the first in Sinhalese was the weekly *Lakminapahana* (1862).

Both the *China Mail* in Hong Kong (1845) and the *North China Herald* in Shanghai (1850, precursor of the renowned *North China Daily News*) were published in English for foreign residents. Other non-Chinese publications—in Portuguese, French, German, Italian, Japanese, and Russian—likewise sprang up to serve the expatriate population in China's port cities.

Hong Kong's first modern Chinese-language newspaper, *Chungwai Hsin-pao* ("Sino-Foreign News"), got its start in 1860 because a group of Chinese rented a font of metal Chinese characters from the English-language *Hong Kong Daily Press* office, which used the font for job printing.

In 1864, noted journalist Wang Tao, who had fled China and settled in the British crown colony, became the editor of the Chinese-language *Hong Kong News*. Using vernacular Chinese, Wang "became an influential reformer and investigative reporter, exposing corruption and giving advice" (Bishop, 1989, p. 45).

In Japan, the first vernacular newspaper started in 1868. At first, the press toed the government line, but by the summer of 1875, reformist demands of Japanese who had studied abroad were finding their way into the press. Both the *Asahi Shimbun* ("Rising Sun Newspaper) and the *Yomiuri Shimbun* ("Read and Sell Newspaper") were established during this era, in the 1870s; the third of Japan's Big Three, the *Mainichi Shimbun* ("Daily Newspaper"), is the successor to a paper established in the 1870s as well.

In the Philippines, journals specializing in commerce, agriculture, and industry appeared earlier than general-interest periodicals. The monthly *Registro Mercantil de Manila* debuted in 1824, while the bilingual (Spanish-English) *Precios Corrientes de Manila* was established in 1839.

The press of the Pacific is generally young, without nineteenth-century roots. Exceptions are the *Fiji Times* (1869) and four of Australia's dailies: the *Sydney Morning Herald* (1831), the *Melbourne Herald* (1840), the *Age* of Melbourne (1854), and the *Daily Telegraph* of Sydney (1879).

The Press in the Early Twentieth Century

In South Asia, the story of the press is intertwined with independence movements. The press in Pakistan is a direct descendant of the Muslim League press of preindependence India, founded primarily to advocate for a separate Muslim state on the Indian subcontinent. By 1925, the Muslim press had grown in size and circulation and comprised about 220 newspapers in nine languages, including Urdu (the first Urdu journal had been founded in 1836), English, and Bengali.

Muhamad Ali Jinnah, who assisted in founding the first Muslim news agency in the 1930s, greatly helped the Muslim national cause. He was involved in establishing a number of publications, including *Dawn*, the official organ of the Muslim League, still one of the most powerful dailies in Pakistan.

Until 1947, when India achieved its independence from the British, the spirit of nationalism stimulated the growth of the press. Social and political reforms and nationalism were considered the press's three main objectives. Mahatma Gandhi, India's most widely known leader in the struggle for freedom, was a journalist for 60 years. He used the press to propagate his ideas and views as editor of four weekly newspapers: *Indian Opinion, Young India, Navajivan,* and *Harijan.* Through these publications, he spread his ideas of freedom and nonviolence throughout India and to Indians in South Africa as well.

Jawaharlal Nehru, the first prime minister of India, advocated complete freedom of the press. "I would rather have a completely free press, [with] all the dangers involved in the wrong use of that freedom, than a suppressed or regulated press," he said (quoted in *India Abroad,* August 25, 1989, p. 13).

Another towering political figure who made use of mass media during a period of revolution was Dr. Sun Yat-sen of China. When the *China National Gazette* of Shanghai was suppressed in 1903, it merely changed its name and registered under foreign ownership. Probably the best paper of the period was the *Eastern Times* of Shanghai (1904).

During the early years of the century, the press of Japan was engaged in circulation battles rather than battles for independence. It adopted some of the worst features of British and American yellow journalism and was well read but often unreliable. During the 1930s, the military forced a restructuring of the press, both to conserve supplies and to make the press easier to control. The 1,200 dailies and 7,700 nondailies of the 1930s were reduced to 55 dailies and weeklies by 1943.

The story of postwar press development and the entire history of broadcasting are covered in the regional discussions in this chapter.

MEDIA OVERVIEW

Table 8.1 (see pp. 212–213) shows that contrasts prevail as well in the indices related to mass media. Newspaper circulation per 1,000 population averages 73 in Asia, far below the "saturation" figure of 200 (one paper for every five people). Indeed, five nations—Kiribati, Nauru, Samoa, Tonga, and Vanuatu—and a number of territories in Oceania as of the early 1980s had no daily newspapers at all. Against the bleak statistical picture for print media in Asia, we should consider that the United States and France ranked below Singapore and that Italy and Spain ranked below Fiji in circulation per 1,000 people.

According to Merrill and Fisher (1980), in the early 1980s, seven Asian newspapers qualified as "great dailies," including three in India alone: the *Hindu* (Madras), the *Statesman* (Calcutta), and the *Times* (main office, Bombay). The other "great dailies" are the *Asahi Shimbun* (Japan), *Renmin Ribao* (China), the *Straits Times* (Singapore), and the *Sydney Morning Herald* (Australia).

In the realm of electronic media, the Asia-Pacific region had 10 radios and 2.5 television receivers per 1,000 people in 1985, both figures exceeding the UNESCO criteria of 5 radios and 2 TV sets. UNESCO has determined that by 1985, all Asian countries except Bangladesh, Bhutan, and Nepal had reached the standard for radios. But averages can mask wide divergences. The figure of 2.5 sets per 1,000 Asians includes media-rich Japan, with 563 sets per 1,000 people, and media-poor Bangladesh, with 1 set per 1,000 people.

Yet despite its diversity, we can isolate patterns that apply to parts of Asia, and even to the entire region. South Asia and parts of the rest of the region, for example, share the Hindu-Buddhist tradition. East and Southeast Asia share the Chinese language. Although in Malaysia and Indonesia, Chinese does not dominate as a language, many media use Chinese; even in Japan, Chinese ideographs are used, despite the dissimilarity of the spoken languages.

According to Tran Van Dinh (1989), mass communication in modern Asia has been shaped by three factors:

1. Western domination, motivated originally by Europeans' desire to reach India for trading purposes but resulting in transplanted technology, media institutions, and popular culture
2. The modernization of Japan, whose use of an "Eastern ethics, Western science" strategy stands as a model that still influences developing Asian nations in the 1980s
3. Independence, resulting in regional rather than colonial alignments for communication systems and individual solutions regarding the role and form of national mass media

One tangible legacy of Western domination, the strong English-language press of Asia, started out as an extension of British rule. It remains strong in former British colonies—India, Pakistan, Malaysia,

TABLE 8.1. COMPARATIVE INDICES FOR 26 ASIAN NATIONS AND HONG KONG

| | Population (millions) | Adult Literacy (%) | Print Media | | Electronic Media | | |
			Number of Daily Newspapers	Government Control of Content	Radios (per 1,000 population)	Television Sets (per 1,000 population)	Government Control of Content
South Asia							
Afghanistan	14.2	24	13	Strong	80	3	Strong
Bangladesh	107.0	33	30	Moderate	8	1	Moderate
Bhutan	1.5	18	N.A.	Strong	8	N.A.	—
India	800.0	44	1,087	Weak	56	3	Moderate
Nepal	17.8	26	29	Moderate	23	N.A.	Strong
Pakistan	104.0	30	106	Moderate	75	11	Strong
Sri Lanka	16.3	87	24	Moderate	N.A.	3	Moderate
Southeast Asia							
Burma (Myanmar)	38.8	78	6	Strong	22	N.A.	Strong
Cambodia (est.)	6.5	75	16	Strong	115	7	Strong
Indonesia	175.0	74	94	Moderate	131	23	Strong
Laos	3.8	84	3	Strong	100	N.A.	Strong
Malaysia	16.1	73	47	Strong	429	88	Strong
Philippines	61.5	86	22	Weak	43	25	Weak
Singapore	2.6	86	12	Moderate	N.A.	172	Strong
Thailand	53.6	91	69	Strong	N.A.	17	Strong
Vietnam	62.2	90	4	Strong	N.A.	N.A.	Strong

	(1)	(2)	(3)	(4)	(5)	(6)	(7)
East Asia							
China	1,062.0	69	53	Strong	22	6	Strong
Hong Kong (est.)	5.7	N.A.	79	Weak	506	229	Moderate
Japan	122.2	100	125	Weak	560	563	Weak
Mongolia	1.9	90	2	Moderate	99	5.7	Moderate
North Korea	21.4	90	11	Strong	N.A.	N.A.	Strong
South Korea	42.1	92	27	Moderate	432	174	Strong
Taiwan	19.6	92	77	Moderate	N.A.	N.A.	Moderate
Pacific							
Australia	16.2	100	63	Weak	N.A.	428	Weak
Fiji (est.)	0.7	86	3	Strong	N.A.	N.A.	Strong
New Zealand	3.3	100	31	Weak	N.A.	289	Weak
Papua New Guinea	3.6	45	N.A.	Weak	N.A.	N.A.	Weak

N.A. = not available. Figures for 1982.

Sources: Population Reference Bureau, *1987 World Population Data Sheet;* United Nations International Children's Fund, *State of the World's Children, 1986* and *1987;* Embassy of Iceland, Washington, D.C.; *UN Statistical Yearbook, 1983–84; UNESCO Statistical Yearbook, 1986;* various U.S. government agencies.

Sri Lanka, and Burma—but would not have survived so long or sprung up in places outside Britain's sphere had it not answered local needs. The United States established the language in the Philippines, while missionary influence and the presence of troops after World War II led to the implantation of other English-language media.

English now functions as a lingua franca in multilingual countries and an international language to serve tourists and business people. Moreover, its alphabetic script presents few typesetting problems and takes up less space than most Asian languages, which saves on newsprint. Older papers have been joined by the *International Herald Tribune* and the *Wall Street Journal*'s Asia edition to provide same-day access to international news.

PRINT MEDIA

South Asia

Among the oldest and freest in South Asia, the press in India is also one of the most influential in the developing world. Its growth has been phenomenal. At the time of independence from British rule in 1947, only 200 newspapers were being published in the country. Forty years later, in 1987, a total of 24,629 newspapers and magazines were published in 92 languages and dialects including English and 15 principal languages enumerated in the Indian Constitution. Of these, 2,151 were dailies, 7,501 weeklies, and the rest biweeklies, monthlies, quarterlies, half-yearlies, and annuals. The Hindi press had a total readership of 14 million, followed by the English with 10 million.

The distribution of print media in India is largely an urban phenomenon, with about 80 percent of circulation confined to cities where only 20 percent of the country's population lives. About 30 percent of newspapers are published in the four major cities of Delhi, Bombay, Calcutta, and Madras.

Despite the low literacy rate of around 40 percent, the English-language press plays an influential role in the country's political milieu. Mostly owned by large business concerns, publications in English reach the educated elite throughout the country as well as abroad and are regarded by the government as a barometer of public thinking. Five newspapers rank as elite papers: the *Times of India*, the *Statesman*, the *Hindustan Times*, the *Indian Express*, and the *Hindu*.

Among multiedition dailies, the *Indian Express*, with 11 editions, was leading in 1987 with 632,199 circulation, followed by the *Times of India*, with 573,552 circulation in six editions. The English-language dailies are serious in content and tone and are widely known for their comprehensive national and international coverage as well as independent views.

The regional-language press constitutes the bulk of mainstream journalism in India and has a much higher readership than the English-language press. It played an active role in the struggle for Indian independence and still remains the most sought-after vehicle to reach the increasingly literate non-Anglophone provincial population. According to the registrar of newspapers in India, regional-language newspapers constitute more than half of the country's newspapers and periodicals. *Ananda Bazar Patrika,* a Bengali paper published from Calcutta, has the highest circulation of any single-edition daily, with a readership of 409,334. The other prominent regional-language newspapers include *Malayala Manorama,* a Malayalam paper published from three centers; the Urdu-language daily *Pratap;* Kerala's daily *Mathribhumi;* and the Oriya daily *Samaj.*

The Hindi-language press leads both in number and in circulation. *Navabharat Times,* a daily newspaper published from both Delhi and Bombay, has a readership of more than 45 percent in the capital. Another Hindi paper, *Punjab Kesri,* published in Delhi, is the second largest single-edition paper in the country.

Among periodicals, the Malayalam-language *Mangalam,* published once a week in the state of Kerala, is the largest, followed by *Malayala Manorama,* another weekly published in Kerala. The third largest is *Kumudam,* a Tamil-language weekly of Madras.

The newsmagazines carrying investigative stories have become especially widespread since the 1970s. One of the most influential is *India Today,* a political news fortnightly published from New Delhi. *Sunday* and *India Week* are the other two serious opinion newsweeklies of quality, which provide insights into the political and social reality of the country. All these newsmagazines, generally modeled after *Time* and *Newsweek,* are ranked along with respected daily newspapers in terms of influencing public opinion. In addition, the *Illustrated Weekly of India,* a pictorial newsweekly founded in 1880, has perked up considerably in recent years to become the largest-circulation magazine.

Magazines in other major Indian languages are also flourishing and becoming increasingly influential in molding public opinion. There has been a magazine boom in the country over the past 15 years. Special-interest magazines, particularly film magazines and women's magazines, have become a booming industry in India, catering to the needs of a dramatically emerging middle class. All top film magazines, including *Cine Blitz, Filmfare, Movie,* and *Star and Style,* have undergone radical facelifts in recent years to appeal to a much wider audience. The most widely read women's magazines include *Femina, Eve's Weekly,* and *Society* in English and *Manorama* and *Mahila* in Hindi.

When Pakistan appeared on the map of the world on August 14, 1947, there were only two English dailies and two Urdu dailies published from Lahore. Soon after independence, the English daily *Dawn* and two Urdu dailies, *Jang* and *Anjam,* all of which were appearing from Delhi, shifted to Pakistan. It took six years for the number of dailies to reach 55, but by 1986 (the latest year for which figures are available), a total of 1,275 newspapers and journals were published, including 121 dailies and 361 weeklies.

Among the major national Urdu-language dailies are *Jang* (largest-circulation daily), *Nawa-i-Waqt,* the government-owned *Mashriq,* and *Hurriyat.* The major English-language dailies are *Dawn,* the *Muslim,* the *Nation,* and the *Pakistan Times.* The *Pakistan Times* is a government newspaper, published by the National Press Trust, a nonprofit organization set up in 1964 by businessmen but now owned by the government. Other newspapers and periodicals are owned by private individual proprietors, joint-stock companies, or trusts.

The English-language papers are mostly read by the elite class, whereas Urdu papers are read by the elite as well as the masses. Most educated people subscribe to at least two papers, one in English and one in Urdu, to get a taste of both the conservative and the liberal viewpoints. The English dailies are mostly conservative, whereas the Urdu dailies are more aggressive in expressing viewpoints.

A majority of newspapers are full of political news and essays and hardly carry any cultural and entertainment news. One unique feature of the Pakistani press is the publication of statements from political leaders. Approximately 70 percent of the news is based on statements made by political leaders. Another characteristic of the Pakistani press is its religious orientation. Practically all newspapers in the country have an insert on religion every Friday. Several newspapers specialize in business news also. *Dawn,* the English-language daily, issues, once a week with its regular edition, a four-page economic and business review.

Weekly newsmagazines are also widely read in Pakistan. *Akhbar-e-Jehan* ("News of the World"), a weekly newsmagazine, owned by the Jung group of publications, has the largest circulation. Other major weekly newsmagazines are *Takbeer* and *Zindagi.* Two major English-language weeklies are *Mag* and *Herald.*

Pakistani periodicals dealing with literary and cultural subjects, religion, sports, films, women, science, medicine, health, trade, and tourism are also quite popular.

In the smaller South Asian nations—Sri Lanka, Bangladesh, Nepal, and Bhutan—prospects for the press have brightened. In Sri Lanka, there has been a tremendous growth of newspapers and other publications over the past two decades, especially since 1977, when President J. R. Jayawardene considerably relaxed the press controls imposed by previous regimes. In 1979 alone, the circulations of Sri Lanka's newspapers increased by more than 30 percent.

The newspaper industry in Sri Lanka is dominated by three major publishing houses, each of which publishes daily and weekly newspapers and several magazines in English, Tamil, and Sinhalese (the official language).

The Associated Newspapers of Ceylon, Ltd., one of South Asia's best-established newspaper publishers, owns the prestigious English-language daily, *Ceylon Daily News*, which received an award for media excellence in 1984 from the International Press Institute. In addition, it owns the largest Sinhalese-language daily, *Dinamina*, and the largest Sunday Sinhalese paper, *Silumina*. It also publishes the largest English-language Sunday paper, *Sunday Observer*, and several other weekly newsmagazines and general-interest magazines in all three languages. A second publishing group, Independent Newspapers, Ltd., publishes the *Sun* and *Weekend* in English, *Dawasa* and *Rivirasa* in Sinhalese, and *Thinapathi* in Tamil. A third major publishing house is Upali Newspapers, Ltd., which also publishes daily newspapers in English and Sinhalese. The *Island* (English) and *Divaina* (Sinhalese) are two of its major daily newspapers. In addition, the Communist Party of Sri Lanka also publishes several dailies and weeklies. Some of the well-known general-interest periodicals are *Ferguson's Ceylon Directory, Reader's Relish, Outlook, Public Opinion,* and *Ceylon Government Gazette* in English, *Sinhala* and *Subasetha* in Sinhalese.

The Bangladeshi press has also grown considerably since martial law ended there in 1979. Today, 62 daily newspapers are published in the country, with an estimated 1.5 million circulation. *Ittefaq* ("Unity") is the largest-circulation daily published in the Bengali language; *Inquilab* ("Revolution") is the second largest. Other well-known Bengali daily newspapers are *Sangbad* ("News"), *Khabur* ("News"), *Dainik Bangla* ("Daily Bangla"), and *Azad* ("Freedom"). The largest and most influential English-language daily is the *Bangladesh Observer*, which for all practical purposes is government-operated. The other well-known English-language papers are the *Bangladesh Times*, the *New Nation*, and the *Daily Life*.

Weekly newspapers are quite popular in Bangladesh. Presently, there are approximately 242 weeklies and 132 monthlies besides several fortnightlies and quarterlies. *Weekly Holiday* is the largest-circulation newsweekly in English, and *Bichitra* ("Unusual") is the largest-circulation Bengali newsweekly. Some of the well-known general-interest periodicals are *Bangladesh Illustrated Weekly, Kishore Bangla* (a children's magazine), *Chitrali* (cinema), *Fashal* (agriculture), and the *Commercial Bulletin* (commerce).

Nepal was isolated from the mainstream of world events for a century (1846–1950) under the Rana regime. Only after 1950 did newspapers come into existence in a real sense. By 1987, there were a total of 448 publications, including 59 dailies, 340 weeklies, and several other biweeklies and fortnightlies.

The oldest and still the major Nepalese-language newspaper is *Gorkhapatra*, owned by the Gorkhapatra Corporation, an autonomous newspaper organization managed by a board of directors consisting of members nominated by the government. Other Nepalese-language newspapers include *Awaj, Dainik Nepal, Hamra Desh*, and *Jana Jivan*.

Among the major English-language newspapers, *Rising Nepal*, the oldest daily established in 1961, is a semiofficial newspaper, also owned by the Gorkhapatra Corporation. Other English-language dailies include the *Commoner*, the *Daily News*, the *Motherland*, and the *New Herald*. The newsweekly *Jagaran* and a host of political mouthpieces, bulletins, and literary magazines are also quite popular.

Bhutan, with just over 1 million population, can now boast of publishing its own national newspaper. *Kuensel* ("The Enlightener"), the country's only newspaper, was sanctioned by the government in 1986 to operate as a weekly. Prior to 1986, it was a small government newsletter. The newspaper is printed in English, Nepali, and Dzongkha, the official language of Bhutan. Circulation is about 8,500. The 12-page tabloid consists of national and international news and features, sports, public notices, and a letters page. It also contains photographs, comics, and a crossword puzzle.

Besides the newspaper, there are two general-interest periodicals in Bhutan, *Kuenphen Digest* and *Kuenphen Tribune*, both of which are published in English.

In Afghanistan, newspapers relay communist propaganda. All news, comments, slogans, and photographs reflect the Marxist-Leninist approach. After the coup of 1978, even the names of Afghanistan's major newspapers were changed to reflect Sovietization. The *Kabul Times*, for example, was renamed the *Kabul New Times*, and the Communist Party's official newspaper, *Jamhoriat*, was changed to *Haqiqat-i-Enqelab-i-Saur* ("Truth about the Saur Revolution") in 1980. Both papers are a carbon copy of the Soviet newspaper *Pravda*. All newspapers are owned by the government. The *New Kabul Times* is the official paper of Afghanistan; *Haqiqat-i-Enqelab-i-Saur* is the state organ of Democratic

Republic of Afghanistan; *Hewad* is the organ of the Council of Ministers, which mainly reports state and government affairs; and *Anis*, the organ of the Fatherland Front, is the mouthpiece of the nation.

All newspapers are published in Dari and Pashtu, and their circulation is restricted to the major cities. Theoretically, each province has its own paper, but none is published on a regular basis. The periodicals are also the mouthpieces of government, dealing mostly with Marxism-Leninism and reflecting the Soviet way of life. For example, *Haqiqate Sarbaz* ("The Truth of the Soldier"), published by the Ministry of Defense, deals with the life of soldiers, inviting them to follow Marxism-Leninism and fight against their own people; *Dousti* ("Friendship") publishes articles and poems praising the Soviet Union and its leadership; and *Zawana* ("Youth") is designed to lead Afghan youth into accepting Soviet ideas.

The Afghan Resistance Group, known as the *mujahideen*, demanding the expulsion of Soviet troops from Afghanistan and the establishment of a free Islamic regime in the country by Afghans, started its own publications after the coup of 1978. In the 1980s, the Afghan press became concentrated outside Afghanistan, operating chiefly from Pakistan or Iran. The Afghan Resistance Group formed its own Afghan interim government, based in Peshawar, and started its own organ, *Subha-Pairozi* ("Dawn of Victory"), which is published weekly by Mujahideen, a party press. Seven groups of guerrillas have formed interim governments, and each one of these groups publishes its own newspapers in two languages, Dari and Pashtu. Some of the well-known publications are *Akhbar-e-Haftagi Jehad* ("Weekly News of Resistance"); *Azadi* ("Freedom"), a publication of the Afghanistan Freedom Society; *De Jehad Ghag* ("Voice of Jehad"); and *Nida-e-Mujaheddin* ("Voice of the *Mujahideen*"), published by Afghan Press International.

Besides the party papers, several other newspapers and periodicals by other organizations appear in English, Dari, and Pashtu. One such organization is the Cultural Council of Afghanistan Resistance, an independent organization, which started publishing a quarterly magazine in 1987, *Afghan Jehad*, devoted to a factual presentation of events related to the Afghan-Soviet war.

Southeast Asia

Just as World War II affected most print media in Asia, so the Vietnam War had a cataclysmic effect on parts of Southeast Asia. As the 1990s begin, a decade and a half after the fall of Saigon in April 1975, some changes are looming on the horizon in Cambodia, Laos, and Vietnam.

In the early 1970s, South Vietnam had more than 40 dailies, published in Vietnamese, Chinese, English, and French. After 1975, a press crackdown left only government-, party-, and army-controlled media. Many journalists who had served in the Thieu regime were arrested immediately, and in the next decade others who were not conforming to policy were rounded up.

Then in 1987, party general secretary Nguyen Van Linh started a column under the byline "NVL" in which he exposed social problems and corruption. Subsequently Linh told journalists that they should be "chasing away darkness," but without "smearing the regime." In addition to sanctioning mild muckraking, the party requires its members to answer accusations leveled in letters-to-the-editor columns within two weeks.

The press in Cambodia and Laos, which had never been important, virtually shut down in 1975. In Laos, after private publishing ceased in 1975, only two government dailies operated. Cambodia has a few periodicals, all party-run. In September 1989 in Cambodia, change began brewing when Vietnam pulled out its forces after more than ten years of occupation, leaving its client regime to battle the Khmer Rouge guerrillas. Cambodian reporters covet front-line assignments because they get three to four times their normal salary, but in so doing they themselves become targets for the Khmer Rouge's bounty on "enemy" journalists.

Burma (Myanmar), a one-party socialist state, represents a whole-hearted but one-sided embrace of Japan's credo, "Eastern ethics, Western science." Eschewing everything from the West, ranging from its science to its media, it has lived in not-so-splendid isolation since a 1962 coup by General Ne Win. The only Western media that Pico Iyer (1989) found for sale in 1985 at Rangoon newsstands were old copies of *Good Housekeeping* and *Reader's Digest.*

All media are government-owned, including two six-page English-language dailies, the *Guardian* and the *Working People's Daily*, that operate with outmoded equipment. In 1983, when North Koreans killed 18 South Korean cabinet ministers in Burma, both newspapers published terse, identical (and erroneous) reports that an exploding bomb had killed three South Koreans.

Burma's neighbor, Thailand, has a private press that practices some self-censorship. By law in this constitutional monarchy, nothing negative may be written about the royal family. Everyone else, however, is treated as fair game. But journalists know that the government sees press freedom as a privilege that can easily be revoked. Some books have been banned as subversive, and in 1987 the Thai-language *Khaosod* was closed for a month. However, the paper simply published under a different name for the duration, using one of the extra publishing permits most Thai papers keep on hand.

Thailand has dozens of daily, weekly, and monthly publications in Thai, Chinese, and English. The prestigious daily *Matichon* belongs to a group with five other publications. Other Thai-language papers are criticized as having too little foreign and hard news, along with too much gossip, sports, and entertainment news. Most influential among English dailies is the *Bangkok Post.*

South of Thailand, Malaysia has a private and varied press, but like Thailand, one subject is taboo. In Malaysia's case, it is forbidden to publish anything that might adversely affect communal relations in this complex society, whose ethnic makeup is Malay (44 percent), Chinese (36 percent), Indian (10 percent), and other groups (10 percent). Publications reflect this diversity, appearing in seven languages.

The largest publishing house, the New Straits Times Group, produces the nation's largest English-language daily, the pro-government *New Straits Times.* The group also includes *Berita Harian*, a Malay-language daily; and the *Malay Mail, New Sunday Times, Sunday Mail,* and *Business Times*, all in English. Three-quarters of the company is owned directly or indirectly by the United Malays National Organization, the political group that dominates Malaysia's coalition government. The Malaysian Chinese Association, a minority partner in the ruling coalition, owns a competing daily, the *Star.*

Malaysia and the city-state of Singapore agreed to break politically in 1965. Singapore occupies an island of only 588 square kilometers on the tip of the Malay peninsula. It has the same ethnic groups as Malaysia, but in different proportions: Chinese (77 percent), Malays (15 percent), and Indians (6 percent). However, by mutual agreement, Malaysian and Singporean newspapers are not distributed in each other's territory.

Thus the daily newspapers being published in Singapore in the late 1980s served a varied readership. Because of a bilingual educational system, many residents read both English and Chinese publications. (Indeed, Prime Minister Lee Kuan Yew encourages the use of English as an integrative force.) Dailies are also published in Tamil and Malay. The number of dailies has fallen since 1980s, mainly because of government action to shut them down. The *Eastern Star, Singapore Herald, New Nation,* and *Singapore Monitor* have all ceased publication.

One company, Singapore Press Holdings, dominates the newspaper scene in the city-state. Its flagship publication, the *Straits Times*, had a circulation of nearly 270,000 in 1988. Founded in 1845 by Robert Carr

Woods, when Singapore had a population of only 40,000, the *Straits Times* served the commercial interests in the seaport. During the Japanese occupation, many staff members were interned.

Today, this "great daily"—indeed, all the press in Singapore—has been tamed by Lee Kuan Yew, who has ruled Singapore since 1959. Few can argue that Yew's strict social control measures and guided economic policies have brought material well-being, with Singapore enjoying a per capita GNP of more than $7,000.

Partly to redress the top-down role of the authoritarian government, the *Straits Times* carries an unusual letters-to-the-editor column. Called the "Forum" page, it enables readers to address a particular person or institution, public or private. Addressees, particularly those in government, reply to these open letters. Most letters, ranging from general topics to specific incidents, contain critical comments.

In addition to the *Straits Times*, the Singapore Press Holdings company publishes four other dailies—*Shin Min Daily*, *Berita Minggu*, the *Business Times*, and *Berita Harian*—in addition to the *Sunday Times*. Furthermore, two other Chinese newspapers, *Lianhe Zaobao* and *Wanbao*, had a combined circulation of 264,000 in 1988.

As if to compensate for frequent closings, new papers spring up frequently. In 1988, the *New Paper*, modeled on *USA Today*, began publishing to appeal to young readers. It promised to avoid politics and offer fun-to-read stories. As if all this were not enough for the city-state's 2.6 million people, some 3,700 publications, including the *Asian Wall Street Journal* and *Time* magazine, are imported into the island.

In Indonesia, despite the multiplicity of ethnic groups, a variety of languages, and geographic and cultural barriers, the press has grown considerably both in quantity and quality in recent years. The country now has 94 daily newspapers, 17 in Jakarta alone. One of the most respected and largest is *Kompas*, a Catholic paper published in Jakarta, with 500,000 circulation. Two other large-circulation Jakarta dailies are *Pos Kota* and *Suara Pembaharuan*. Other influential Jakarta papers, smaller in circulation, are *Sinar Harapan*, a Protestant paper; *Berita Buana*, a sensational paper known for "circus-type" graphics; *Meredka* ("Independence"), a nationalistic paper founded during the struggle for independence in 1945; and *Suara Karya*, the official paper.

The *Indonesian Times*, the *Jakarta Post*, and the *Indonesian Observer* are the three most widely read English-language papers of Jakarta. The first two are government spokespapers of unwavering seriousness, while the *Observer* claims to give Indonesia an international perspective. The English-language newspapers are widely read by government officials, diplomats, the military, and the elite strata of Jakarta and other major cities.

The sole Chinese-language paper, *Harian Indonesia*, is also read widely by the indigenous Bahasa community.

Outside Jakarta, some of the influential dailies are published in West Java, Yogyakarta, North Sumatra, Central Java, East Java, and Bali.

In addition to daily newspapers, Indonesia has several weekly papers that serve provincial and rural areas. In 1979, in its third five-year development, the Indonesian government introduced a rural press program, popularly called *Koran Masuk Desa (KMD)*, "Newspapers for Villages." These newspapers, written in simple language, were designed to help the rural Indonesians become an educated society. In line with the KMD program, the Indonesian Press Council in 1980 limited daily newspapers to 12 pages and to 30 percent advertising content to enable the weeklies to obtain more newsprint and advertising. The government also provides a 3½-cent-per-copy subsidy for the first 5,000 copies of the village editions for the first year of publication. These weekly newspapers generally consist of four pages and usually appear in the local language of the region.

Indonesian newsmagazines are well known for publishing provocative editorials and columns. The most influential are *Tempo, Topik,* and *Stop. Tempo* and *Topik* are satirical, while *Stop* is more cartoonish.

Magazines dealing with fashion, women, men, health, hygiene, and tourism are also quite popular.

In the Philippines, before the declaration of martial law in 1972, newspapers flourished and flaunted their freedom, going so far as calling the president one of the richest, most corrupt leaders in Southeast Asia. With the declaration of martial law, all media establishments were confiscated or closed, with the exception of the *Daily Express* and Kanlaon Broadcasting's radio and television stations, owned by the family and friends of Ferdinand Marcos. In the final years of Marcos's rule, only four daily newspapers were publishing in Manila. Today, under the free-press policy of President Corazon Aquino, newspapers are again proliferating. About 26 dailies and 6 weeklies are presently published in Manila, while 288 papers, mainly weeklies, are published in the provinces. *Manila Bulletin*, with 270,000 daily circulation daily and 310,000 on Sunday, is the nation's largest and most respected serious paper, supporting the Philippines in its nation-building efforts. Other major dailies of Manila include the *Manila Times, Manila Chronicle, Philippines Daily Express, Philippine Daily Inquirer, Philippine Star,* and *Tempo.*

The bulk of the daily newspapers are owned by wealthy entrepreneurs. There are no government-owned newspapers. Yet the newspapers tend to practice self-censorship, and journalists are inclined to be protective of the government in power. Page one news in virtually all of the dailies consists of the president's official statements and actions, and editorials lack any solid stands on politics.

Besides newspapers, general-interest and special-interest magazines are quite popular in the Philippines. Among fashion magazines, *She* and *Style* are at the top, and among women's magazines, *Woman's Home-Companion* and *Women's Journal* are widely read.

East Asia

In May 1989, the mass media of the People's Republic of China made news in non-Chinese mass media all over the world for their coverage of the Tiananmen uprising. Beijing journalists carried aloft banners that said, "Don't believe us—we print lies," and wrote front-page stories sympathetic to the hunger strikers. But after June 4, the official media made a complete about-face, praising soldiers as "model heroes" and condemning the protesters. In a purge that reached even into the journalism schools, supporters of the protest were arrested, discharged, and sent to rural areas or put on "study" leave. Some newspapers were shut down. At the *People's Daily*, the military's propaganda director took over as editor.

To understand the mass media of the world's most populous nation, Robert Bishop (1989) points out that one must understand the forces that shape that media. China, with a physical size slightly larger than the United States, remains to this day a nation of villagers. The 80 percent of Chinese who live in rural areas, many of them isolated due to geographic barriers, have limited access to mass media. There, the extended family "forms a closed, face-to-face, wheel-like system of communication, strongly resistant to outside influences," writes Bishop (p. 9).

Regionalism meant that local dialects developed, a serious barrier to nonprint mass communication. At the same time, print media faced the problem of a low rate of literacy, which in turn resulted from the time required to master several thousand written characters. Both the typesetting problems associated with the writing system and delivery problems have hindered print penetration of the countryside. Thus when we speak of media in China, we are really talking about two Chinas: the cities, especially the port cities, and the rural villages.

The first large-scale mass media audience survey in China took place in 1982 in Beijing. Everett Rogers and his colleagues (1985) discovered that a majority of those surveyed read two or more dailies each week. The local Beijing newspapers had the most readers, with 72 percent of those surveyed reading the *Beijing Evening News* and 71 percent reading the *Beijing Daily*.

However, sizable audiences also existed for the national *People's Daily* (48 percent) and the *Reference News* (40 percent) in this city of about 6 million. Thus Beijing readership combined with readership among all the rest of China's 1.1 billion people explains the high circulation figures of these two publications. Even though the *Reference News* (*Cankao Xiaoxi*) reaches only about 1 percent of Chinese citizens, its circulation is reported at 11 million. The *People's Daily* (*Renmin Ribao*) distributes about 5.3 million copies.

In 1986, China had 2,300 publications—most of them registered after 1980, an average of one every day and a half. The flagship *People's Daily*, founded in 1948, is printed in 20 Chinese cities besides Beijing as well as in Hong Kong and Tokyo. About 1,000 staff members produce the paper, which typically runs eight pages, seven days a week.

As an organ of the Central Committee of the Chinese Communist Party, the *People's Daily* (along with the central broadcasting station and Xinhua, the Chinese news agency) sets the line for all other publications. National, provincial, municipal, and district papers all practice self-censorship, looking to the *People's Daily* for guidance. As an antidote to this top-down communication, the letters section (which received hundreds of letters a day) used to let readers express complaints, but the practice changed after June 1989.

For the major publications in China, readers number many more people than subscribers for several reasons. Members of units (such as rural work teams, factory teams, or offices) that subscribe to a paper all have access to it, and passersby can read papers posted on "newspaper walls." Sometimes study groups meet to read and discuss the news.

The *Reference News* belongs to a special class of publications referred to as "internal." Originally created to keep party officials informed about overseas news, now just about anyone can subscribe for 50 cents a month. A second level of restricted publication is *Reference Material* (*Cankao Ziliao*), a twice-daily foreign news digest for about 1,000 middle- to high-ranking party officials, running 100 pages in the morning and 50 pages in the afternoon.

Surprisingly, the distinction of being the largest newspaper in China and probably the most widely read one in the world goes to a little-known publication, *Chinese Children*, aimed at the under-14 age group. Official statistics for 1982 listed the distribution at 10 million, with a readership of many times more. In China, newspaper reading is highest among those 25 and under because younger people have more education.

In 1981, an English-language newspaper that carries advertising, *China Daily*, began publication. Now, thanks to satellite transmission, the eight-page broadsheet can reach North America and Europe the same day as the home editions. Its physical look reflects the startup assistance of Australian and British journalists, and its style is also clearly Western. For example, its headlines try to capture a story's essence rather than simply state its topic. Compare this headline from the *China Daily:*

China Will Not Turn to Capitalism, Says Deng,

with a headline for the same story from the *People's Daily:*

Deng Addresses the Closing Ceremony of National Science Work Conference.

China Daily did not, however, cover the prodemocracy movement before June 4 with the same passion as the *People's Daily.*

After the 1989 crackdown in Mainland China, massive public protest demonstrations were held in Hong Kong, and the pace of out-migration increased. The uncertainty about the post-1997 years, when Hong Kong will be returned to China, extends to the press as well as to individuals' lives. Hong Kong has the freest Chinese-language papers in Asia, but their future remains uncertain.

In the late 1980s, Hong Kong's 5.5 million people supported about 60 newspapers in Chinese and English. According to a 1988 survey, the journalists who work for these newspapers and for other media are young (84 percent aged 35 and under), single (66 percent), and on the job less than five years (60 percent). About half the journalists are female.

Joseph Man Chan and C. C. Lee (1988) divide the present-day press into four groups. The ultra-leftist group includes *Ta Kung Pao* and *Wen Wei Pao*, both supervised by Xinhua's Hong Kong branch. The centrist group includes advertising-supported papers not linked to any political party, including *Ming Pao, Sing Pao,* and the *Oriental Daily News.* The ultra-rightist group includes the *Hong Kong Times*, established in 1949 as the Kuomintang Party withdrew to Taiwan.

The mainstream rightist group includes the conservative, influential *South China Morning Post*, a Rupert Murdoch holding; it has about twice the circulation as the other English-language daily, the *Hong Kong Standard*. The *Standard* and its stablemates, the *Sing Tao Daily News* and the *Sing Tao Evening News*, are published by Sally Aw Sian.

Hong Kong likewise serves as a central point for incoming satellite facsimile transmissions. Both the Asian *Wall Street Journal* and the *International Herald Tribune* have printing plants in Hong Kong, from where copies circulate throughout the region.

In Taiwan, significant changes occurred in 1987 when martial law was ended and the 1950s-era restrictions on print media were lifted. With the restrictions in force, newspapers had to have licenses to publish and could print only 12 pages. Despite restrictions, the opposition Democratic Progressive Party launched a newspaper in February 1987. All of the early issues were confiscated, but a reported 60,000 copies still slipped into circulation.

Under martial law, the *China Times* and *Central Daily News* (organ of the Kuomintang Party) had more than 80 percent of the nation's daily newspaper circulation and more than 70 percent of newspaper advertising (about $200 million in 1986). After the print media restrictions were lifted, the private *United Daily News,* with a circulation of about 1.5 million, rose to become the largest daily. The United Daily News Group also publishes Taiwan's first business daily, a lifestyle daily, and three overseas newspapers. In 1988, it launched a new daily, the *United Evening News.*

All told, in the first eight months of 1988, 205 new newspapers were approved. Similarly, between mid-1988 and mid-1989, more than 700 new magazines were approved, ranging from *PC World* to *Career Woman Fashion.* Some of these publications are in English, including two dailies that predate the lifting of restrictions. Most reporters for Chinese-language media still produce handwritten copy, but typesetting has been computerized; one system lets typists set 125 Chinese characters per minute.

Striking parallels exist between Taiwan and South Korea, although one should not forget important differences, such as the role of religious (Christian) media in South Korea. Ever since the military takeover in 1961, press freedom has taken on various shades of gray. Martial law in 1980 brought with it the repressive Basic Press Act and the biggest press purge in the history of the nation; 172 publications were closed, and 683 journalists were dismissed.

A dissident Korean poet called 1985 the "most nightmarish" year in Korean cultural history when authorities shut down two magazines. Every day the Ministry of Culture and Information (MOCI) issued daily instructions to the press about what it could not say. In September 1987, Korean CIA forces entered a printing plant to forcibly stop publication of two magazines.

Even as they were doing so, and hastened by public reaction to the incident, according to Kyu Ho Youm (1990), "breathtaking developments" were brewing. In late 1987, a new constitution was put in place and a new press law enacted, followed in February 1988 by President Roh Tae Woo's inauguration. Changes began.

In 1984, South Korea had 25 daily newspapers, including 6 with a nationwide circulation of more than 700,000 each. By the end of April 1989, some 65 dailies were being published, with a total of 3,728 periodicals registered with MOCI—1,492 of them new since 1987. The largest and most prestigious paper, *Dong-A Ilbo*, founded in 1920, maintains many foreign bureaus. Other major dailies include *Chosun Ilbo*, the *Joong-ang Daily News*, and *Hankok Ilbo*. The two English-language dailies are the *Korea Times* and the government-owned *Korea Herald*.

Along with changes in numbers of periodicals came changes in content. More aggressive reporting has led citizens rather than the government to criticize—and even physically attack—journalists whose stories they disliked. And in March 1989, several reporters were arrested for extorting about $40,000 from factory owners whose illegal pollution practices they promised not to expose.

Compared to South Korea, the government-controlled press of North Korea lacks variety, veracity, and vitality. Foreign publications are carefully excluded, although elites can get a digest of world press reports. A major task of the media is to enhance the personality cult of the present leader, Kim Il Sung, and his son, the officially appointed successor; one six-page issue of the party paper *Rodong Sinmum* referred to the two men more than 200 times.

Another mission is to denounce South Korea as a country ruled by a "puppet clique" of U.S. imperialists. In one disinformative campaign, newspapers said the United States had exported AIDS-contaminated blood to South Korea in order to run some tests on unsuspecting South Koreans.

If China draws international power from the sheer size of its population, Japan, the other potent force in Asia, draws power from its economic well-being. As an affluent people with a GNP per capita of $11,300, the Japanese have more than 2,000 periodicals from which to choose—about the same number as in China, but with about one-tenth the number of people to read them (122 million versus 1.1 billion). Daily newspaper circulation of 562 copies per 1,000 people, the highest in the world, means that the average family of four gets more than one paper.

Various explanations have been given for the high figure, such as Japan's homogeneous population, high density, heavily used public transportation, and high literacy—all of which characterize other countries with low readership. The answer may lie in the content of the newspapers, which surveyed readers rank as their most reliable source of news. All of these factors are coupled with a phenomenal circulation system whereby independent contractors work exclusively for one paper, sometimes for three generations. About 97 percent of households get a home-delivered paper.

Of the nation's 125 dailies, the Tokyo Big Three—the *Asahi*, *Yomiuri*, and *Mainichi*—account for 45 percent of daily newspaper circulation. Add in the *Nihon Keizai Shimbun* and *Sankei Shimbun* (both business and economics papers), likewise published in Tokyo, and those five papers account for 62 percent of circulation. The *Yomiuri* had a 1988 circulation of 9.8 million; the *Asahi*, 7.5 million; and the *Mainichi*, 4.4 million (morning editions only).

Why such a centralized system? Tokyo, the political and economic capital of Japan, generates more news than any other region. Second, organizations of all types in Tokyo place bulk subscription orders. Third, 10 percent of the population lives there, representing well over 10 percent of the nation's purchasing power.

The *Asahi Shimbun* ("Rising Sun Newspaper"), founded in 1879 in Osaka, manages to be a quality "great daily" while preserving a mass readership—not an impossible task in a country where 38 percent of high school graduates go on to college. To join the highly competent staff of about 10,000 journalists, applicants must take a test so difficult that only one in 80 passes.

The *Asahi*, like all Big Three dailies, has numerous media and nonmedia holdings, ranging from English-language dailies to baseball teams. (The "sister papers" of the Big Three join the *Japan Times* to provide a choice of four English-language daily publications.) The papers from early on have sponsored projects and events, from art exhibits to Antarctic explorations to the first airplane flight in Japan, making them an integral part of national life—and trying to attract readers in the process.

Yet all is not rosy in the Japanese print media picture. Readers spend fewer minutes with newspapers even as the papers get fatter. Journalism professor Chugo Koito (n.d.) says that the reading public can be divided into two groups: the newspaper (prewar) generation and the television (postwar) generation. By 1985, Japan's adult population was split about 50-50 between the two groups, a fact that does not auger well for newspapers.

Furthermore, more newspaper space is being devoted to comics to appeal to the phenomenal cartoon appetite of Japanese young people. In 1987, an amazing 1.68 billion volumes of *manga* (books or magazines using a cartoon-panel format) were published. The most popular *manga* publication, *Boys Jump*, which has a weekly circulation of about 2 million, sold 4.85 million copies of a special New Year's issue in 1988.

During the 1960s, according to Chugo Koito, college students carried around left-leaning magazines. During the 1970s, teenagers took to reading *manga*, which now college students and adults have taken up. *Manga* run the gamut from science fiction and fantasy to adventure, romance, pornography, and how-to manuals. The *Japan Economic Journal*'s *manga* series on economics, which has sold about 2 million copies since late 1986, is now available in English.

Pacific

Australia appropriately belongs in a chapter on Asia, since in recent years, half of all its immigrants have been Asian, although Asians still make up only 5 percent of the country's population. (Under 2 percent are aborigines.) Before Asians began arriving in the 1970s, waves of immigrants poured in from Europe and the Middle East, such that "white Australia" has now become multicultural Australia. Australia, China, and the United States are all about the same size geographically, making Australia, with only 16 million people, still roomy enough for more newcomers.

Australia's private press now includes a publication for almost every language group. But in the past journalists looked to Britain for its models, so the older prestige press has a British feel. In fact, Australia's "great daily," the *Sydney Morning Herald*, looks something like a composite of the *Times* of London and the *Daily Mail.*

Started in 1831, the *Herald* prides itself on its government watchdog role. It stands as one of those great dailies that have great popular as well as elite appeal, boasting a circulation of 400,000 in a city of 3.4 million. Like most Australian newspapers, the *Herald* is published by a holding company. It belongs to the John Fairfax and Sons group, which also publishes the *Sun, Sun Herald,* and (with David Syme and Company, Ltd.) the *Melbourne Age*. The *Age,* the most serious Australian newspaper, has a strong following among the nation's elite.

Three other groups, whose broad activities include book publishing, newsprint production, magazine publication, and broadcasting, combine with Fairfax to dominate the Australian press scene. The Melbourne-based *Herald* and *Weekly Times* group publishes, besides its namesake newspapers, the popular and unrestrained *Sun News-Pictorial.* Rupert Murdoch's News, Ltd., holds the *Daily Telegraph* of Sydney. Australian Consolidated Press publishes some of the nation's most popular magazines.

Located 1,000 miles east of Australia, New Zealand's population of 3.3 million is 12 percent Maori, but Maoris represent only 1 percent of journalists and say they do not get adequate coverage. Women likewise complain about their press.

As of late 1985, typewriters and pencils were the norm, with not a single VDT in the nation's newsrooms. Of the country's 33 dailies, most have local monopolies. The largest daily, the *New Zealand Herald,* is published in Auckland. Wellington has two dailies, the morning *Dominion* and the *Evening Post*, as does the southern city of Christchurch, with its morning *Press* and its evening *Christchurch Star*. Because of historical and geographic factors, New Zealand has much less influence on the mass media of the Pacific than Australia.

Papua New Guinea, located north of Australia in the Pacific, has a larger population than New Zealand but a much less developed press. Like its economic, military, and technical spheres, the press of Papua New Guinea partly depends on Australia. The *Melbourne Herald* and *Weekly Times* group owns the English-language *Post-Courier*. The island nation's own publishing group, the Word Publishing Company, is owned by five Christian churches. It publishes nondaily periodicals in English and Pidgin.

After a military leader staged a coup in 1987, Fiji's private press was subjected to censorship. Before the overthrow, Suva, Fiji, stood out as the busiest publishing center of the Pacific islands, with the long-established *Fiji Times* battling it out with the newer *Fiji Sun*, founded in 1974.

Elsewhere in the Pacific, weeklies characterize the press scene, with English the dominant language. (Exceptions are Tahiti and New Caledonia, which produce daily newspapers in French.) In some locations, such as tiny Pitcairn Island, only a small monthly is published. Common problems of the island societies include geographic isolation, small populations, and the vestiges of top-down colonial structures. Many of the periodicals are new, having been established within the past 30 years.

In late 1989, Peter Lomas, editor of the magazine *Islands Business*, listed the top three English-language newspapers in the South Pacific as the *Times* of Papua New Guinea, the *Papua New Guinea Post-Courier*, and the *Samoa News* of American Samoa. The best of the northern island papers, in his view, are the *Pacific Daily News* (Guam), the *Marshall Islands Journal*, and the *Marianas Variety*. All six are free of government control.

ELECTRONIC MEDIA

Both radio and television broadcasting began in some parts of Asia soon after being established in the West. The Philippines, an early adopter, had radio service in the 1920s and television by 1953; Thailand, another pioneer, established radio in 1931 and television in 1954. By the mid-1960s, some 18 Asian countries had television, and by 1983, only Nepal, Bhutan, and certain Pacific islands lacked TV service.

Asiavision, which began visual news exchanges experimentally in March 1983, grew out of UNESCO-sponsored symposia. According to Donald Flournoy (1985), the participants feel that news of Asia "gets short shrift" on the global news services (p. 5).

The "free-to-offer, free-to-choose" daily news exchange operates via coordinating centers in Japan and Malaysia. Based on interest in the proposed offerings, each center sends out 10- to 15-minute individualized visual packages of items that other members have produced. By the mid-1980s, Asiavision's two zones approached the volume in news items of Western visual services.

South Asia

Radio remains the principal broadcast medium throughout most of South Asia, and in some places where illiteracy is widespread, it is more important than newspapers. It is particularly well suited to the communication needs of nations where there is a multiplicity of languages and cultures and where the mountainous terrain (including Afghanistan and Nepal) is a formidable obstacle to the use of television. The development of inexpensive battery-operated transistor sets has greatly increased the size of radio audiences everywhere. Some governments have made radio programs more available to rural masses by establishing community listening centers. In India, for example, a scheme of community radio sets was introduced in 1954. Under the rural forum, information on all aspects of rural development is communicated to the villages.

All India Radio (AIR) is one of the largest radio systems in Asia, with 94 stations broadcasting for a total of more than 700 hours a day. The programs, which are radiated from 173 transmitters, cover 93.5 percent of the population spread over 82.2 percent of the country. No other medium in the country has a comparable capacity to reach such a gigantic mass of people. With the recently established satellite radio network, it is possible to take radio signals anywhere in the country.

Radio broadcasting began in India in 1927 with two privately owned transmitters in Bombay and Calcutta. In 1930, broadcasting operations were taken over by the government, which retains them today. AIR is supported mainly by license fees. It also obtains revenue from sales of program journals and related publications, and since 1967, it has been operating as a commercial service.

AIR maintains two distinct services for its domestic and foreign audiences. The domestic service has three main components: the news service, the Vividh Bharati Service, and the general cultural service. The news organization of AIR is one of the biggest of its kind in Asia; it broadcasts 273 bulletins daily for a total duration of over 36 hours in more than 92 languages and dialects. The Vividh Bharati Service broadcasts popular music, including folk and patriotic songs and Western music. The foreign service of AIR, the External Services Division, broadcasts daily programs for 62 hours in several foreign languages for listeners in 54 countries. It recently set up a 12-hour daily service for Sri Lanka. The External Services Division has assumed the role of cultural ambassador in projecting and promoting the Indian image abroad. The programs are also designed to serve as a link with the people of Indian origin living or settled abroad.

In addition, AIR regularly broadcasts programs on family planning, health, hygiene, nutrition, vocational training, farming, industries, and various other aspects of rural life.

Television in India was introduced on September 15, 1959, with $20,000 in UNESCO aid as a one-hour, twice-a-week experimental service to provide social education to the urban slum dwellers in New Delhi. It was reorganized in 1965 and began its regular service. Until 1976, it was managed by All India Radio. In April 1976, television was separated from AIR and formed into an independent unit, Doordarshan ("Distant Vision"), under the Ministry of Information and Broadcasting.

After 30 years of operation, Doordarshan has now grown into a giant network. With a total of 210 transmitters, television today reaches over 70 percent of the population.

Satellite and microwave facilities have further helped in the spread of TV network programs all around the country. In 1975, the one-year Satellite Instructional Television Experiment (SITE) was launched in which more than 2,300 villages experienced television. SITE is often described as one of the biggest communications experiments ever undertaken. Currently, India's national multipurpose satellite (INSAT-IB) is being used for telecommunications, meteorology, and radio in addition to television.

Television turned commercial on January 1, 1976, with the introduction of advertising spots. Currently, in addition to the spots, series of sponsored programs are being telecast. Color transmission began in August 1982, multichannel transmission in 1984. Teletext service in "picture mode," started in 1987, enables viewers to obtain information on a normal receiver without the aid of a decoder.

In its efforts to act as a catalyst for social change, Doordarshan television offers a variety of information, cultural, entertainment, educational, and scientific programs.

Radio Pakistan has been broadcasting programs for the information, education, and entertainment of listeners since it came into existence on August 14, 1947. In Pakistan's multilingual, largely rural society, radio is an extremely powerful communication vehicle that transmits 270 program hours per day in 21 languages. There are 16 radio stations, and the nation had an estimated 9.8 million radio sets in 1987. In cities, three out of every four households have radios, and in villages, two out of three.

The Central News Organization of Radio Pakistan puts out 80 news bulletins daily over its Home Service, External Services, and World Service to keep the listeners abreast of the latest news. The External Services broadcast in 15 foreign languages for 18 hours a day to 64 countries. Their main object is to project Pakistan's views and policies on important national and international matters and to promote good-will between Pakistan and other countries.

Music, drama, and features constitute about 45 percent of the total broadcasting of Radio Pakistan. Religious broadcasts account for 16 percent. Religious programs are broadcast at least twice a day, featuring recitations from the Koran followed by talks and discussions to relate the Koran's teachings to problems of everyday life.

In addition to propagating the Muslim faith and reflecting the official views and policies of the government, Radio Pakistan is used extensively as an educational tool. In 1960, Pakistan started radio broadcasts for schools in five different regional languages. In 1974, a distance-learning educational institution known as the Institute of Educational Technology was established; it uses radio broadcasts for its distance education program.

Radio is also considered an effective medium for farm broadcasting. Introduced on an experimental basis in 1966, farm programs have become an integral part of Radio Pakistan. They are broadcast by all 16 stations twice a day.

Pakistan's television reaches more than 82 percent of the population. Its five production centers provide more than seven hours of transmission daily to over 10 million viewers. Like India, Pakistan also uses television to promote adult literacy. PTV has devised seven major educational programs covering adult functional literacy and formal school and college education. In addition, various programs are produced and televised on religion, culture, and politics that depict national development and support the policies of the government.

Both radio and television are state-owned and are supported by license fees, government subsidies, and advertising. Radio broadcasting is handled by the Broadcasting Corporation of Pakistan, a statutory corporation under the direct control of the Ministry of Information and Broadcasting. Television is administered through the Pakistan Television Corporation, Ltd., a public limited company whose shares are held by the government.

Radio in Bangladesh, as in Pakistan and India, is also a government operation, supported by license fees, government subsidies, and advertising. Radio Bangladesh broadcasts a total of 90 hours daily in Bengali and transmits programs for 6 hours per day in six foreign languages including English. There are six radio stations, and the nation had an estimated 1.2 million radio sets in 1985.

Bangladesh TV (BTV) started in 1965. After the independence of Bangladesh in 1971, a big TV complex was set up at Rampura, in the suburb of Dacca. It transmits programs through ten relay stations. It started color transmission in 1980.

In Sri Lanka, where radio listening is extremely popular, broadcasting is handled by the Sri Lanka Broadcasting Corporation, a public corporation under the Ministry of Information, financed by license fees and advertising revenues. Radio programs are broadcast in six languages: Sinhalese, English, Hindi, Urdu, Tamil, and Arabic. Experimental TV began in 1979 as a private venture and was taken over by the government later that year.

In Nepal, since the Nepalese people were kept in total darkness until 1950 during the Rana regime, even radio sets were not available in the country. Radio Nepal came into existence in 1952, but it was not until the government sanctioned a national communications plan in 1971 that radio developed in a modern sense. With the technical assistance from Great Britain, the United States, Japan, and Australia, Radio Nepal has made considerable progress in recent years. The studio building of Radio Nepal, constructed with U.S. assistance, contains six studios and is outfitted with the latest equipment, provided by the United Kingdom.

Radio is used extensively for educational purposes and for educating the rural masses in agricultural, public health, and family planning programs.

Television in Nepal began in 1982, and the age of satellite communications in the Himalayan kingdom was ushered in October 1982 with the installation of the satellite earth station.

Bhutan Broadcasting Service started as Radio NYAB (National Youth Association of Bhutan) in 1973. It broadcasts local, national, and international news as well as developmental issues and music every day in four languages: English, Nepali, Dzongkha, and Sharchop (Eastern Bhutanese).

Bhutan has no television. The country is presently investing nearly $6 million on its own satellite.

In Afghanistan, Radio Afghanistan broadcasts programs in Dari and Pashtu. The Soviet Union and East Germany have donated radio transmitters and modern technology to enable Radio Afghanistan to broadcast 45 hours of programming on a daily basis.

Television, established in 1978, is used mainly for propaganda.

There is hardly any entertainment. Soviet TV programs and Soviet feature and documentary films are shown on a regular basis. In March 1982, with the inauguration of Shamshad, a modern earth station, television entered a new phase of development.

Southeast Asia

Burma (Myanmar), Cambodia, and Vietnam all have state-run, strictly controlled systems. Burmese radio programs music extensively, with its spoken messages reinforcing the ideological content of the press. Television came to the country in 1980, but the two national stations are on the air only from 7:30 to 9:30 p.m. Television came to Vietnam in 1966, introduced by the U.S. government in the midst of the war. Now it belongs to the Soviet Intersputnik system.

Laos depends greatly on signals from Thailand, which has lively, if chaotic, television programming. The central Thai government authorizes the operation of channels, but channel assignments are not technically standardized and change often. Almost all operators are official entities, such as branches of the military, public universities, and the royal household, but private entrepreneurs often handle the actual program scheduling, then share the profits (Thai television carries advertisements) with the operators.

Content includes both Thai and foreign syndicated material, much of the latter from the United States. In 1985, as many as 40 U.S. programs could be seen in Bangkok, where 90 percent of the households had color sets. Ranging from "The Incredible Hulk" to "Nova," about 80 percent of the shows had been dubbed into the Thai language. Tan and Suarchavarat (1988) found that frequent viewing of U.S. programs influenced Thai students to have stereotypes of Americans as pleasure-loving, athletic, individualistic, and sensual.

During the Vietnam War years, the United States helped Thailand build a radio system that reached previously isolated rural areas. Today, all official radio stations must broadcast government news programs and promote government policies, but many unofficial stations operate clandestinely. For example, from 1962 to 1981, the illegal Communist Party of Thailand broadcast from various locations inside and outside of Thailand.

Similarly, the Khmer Route guerrillas send radio programs throughout Cambodia, often with battle reports rife with inflated numbers of enemies killed and weapons seized. Another clandestine broadcasting operation, that of the Malaysian Communist Party, sends signals from Thailand across the border to Malaysia; the station appeared in 1976 and was still operating in the late 1980s.

Legal broadcasting in Malaysia falls under the purview of the Ministry of Information and is government-operated, with the exception of one private radio company in West Malaysia that charges fees to its subscribers. Radio-Television Malaysia (RTM), which receives revenue from license fees on radio and TV sets and from commercials, operates out of a modern $19 million facility in Kuala Lumpur. Microwave links tie in regional production centers and transmitters in every part of the country, including Sabah and Sarawak. Both radio and television broadcast in Bahasa Malaysia (the national language), English, Chinese, and Tamil.

Residents of southern Malaysia can receive programs from the multilingual Singapore Broadcasting Corp., which broadcasts in Malay, English, Chinese (Mandarin and a number of dialects), and Tamil. SBC, a unit under the Ministry of Culture, receives funding from license fees and advertising. Other than a fee-based private radio service and external services that can be picked up in Singapore, SBC handles all broadcasting. Public affairs programs stress racial tolerance and national unity.

Because Indonesia is made up of isolated islands scattered across thousands of miles and has a low literacy rate, radio is the nation's only true mass medium. The state-owned Radio Republik Indonesia (RRI) is the largest network in the country. It was founded on September 11, 1945, within days of the Dutch colony's declaration of independence.

In 1988, RRI had 49 broadcasting stations consisting of five Nusantara relay stations. There are also 27 RRI stations in each of the 27 provinces, 17 stations in the districts, and 109 regional broadcasters managed by the local administrations. The national service broadcasts an average of 69 hours altogether every day.

The overseas radio service, known as Voice of Indonesia, broadcasts 12 hours daily in Indonesian, English, German, French, Spanish, Arabic, Chinese, Thai, Malay, and Japanese.

The current policy of RRI is directed toward the improvement of broadcast quality, particularly the quality of the Groups of the Rural Broadcasting listeners, which constitute a part of the Groups of Listeners, Viewers and Readers (KLOMPENCAPIR). KLOMPENCAPIR plays an important part in the overall information strategy of the nation to create an equal and balanced flow of information. In addition, it is also designed for educating the rural media audience.

Televisi Republik Indonesia (TVRI), the state-owned television service, was begun on August 24, 1962, with the cooperation of the Japanese government in preparation for the Fourth Asian Games. Thirty-two percent of the budget comes from the 15 percent of time devoted to advertisements, 65 percent from license fees, and the remainder from a government subsidy. By 1988, there were ten television broadcasting stations in major towns and 240 transmitters in various provinces that enabled the population at the border areas and remote places to watch national television programs. In addition, the government has made available ten mobile production units in ten provinces to expand its TV broadcasting network.

TVRI national broadcasting service programs are on the air for an average of 8.34 hours daily, and the regional services broadcast an average of 2 hours daily. With programs from regional stations and mobile units, TVRI has been able to produce almost all of its programs in-house.

National television programs can now be viewed in all the capitals of Indonesia's 27 provinces as well as in almost all district capitals.

The official network follows policies laid down by the Ministry of Information and makes every effort toward building a unified society. Therefore, programs that might offend any religious or ethnic groups are avoided.

In November 1988, a new privately owned special television network, Rajawali Citra Televisi Indonesia (RCTI), was started in Jakarta.

Indonesia has its own domestic communications satellite system, Palapa, launched in 1976. As a result, television is received in the most isolated villages. The Palapa satellite has united Indonesia through one communications and information system and has enabled the cultures of smaller minority groups to be telecast nationally. The satellite is also being used for the Packet-switched Public Data Network, which is connected to international data centers in Europe, Japan, and the United States. Indonesia is the first country in the world to use a domestic satellite for such a network.

The Philippine broadcasting media had enjoyed the same freedoms as the press before martial law. With the declaration of martial law in 1972, a number of radio and television studios were sealed, and several others were placed under military control. During that time, editorials, opinion, and commentary were forbidden over the air, and all radio and television stations were required to "broadcast accurate, objective, straight news reports of the government to meet the dangers and threats that occasioned the proclamation of martial law, and the efforts to achieve a 'new society.' "

Currently, with the "free access" policy of the new government, radio stations and television channels are multiplying. There are five main television channels. Only one channel is owned by the government. Ownership is mainly in the hands of private companies. A majority of broadcasting programs stress national development and Philippine culture and history.

East Asia

Although estimates of the number of *working* TV sets in China vary, statistics culled from multiple sources put the 1987 figure at about 60 million. Curiously, Japan has just about the same number. But there similarities end; Japan's highly developed, diverse television culture evolved step by step in the years after World War II, whereas China's is a recent creature of exponential development in the years after the Cultural Revolution. Now its estimated 600 million viewers form the largest TV audience in the world.

Japan's Nihon Hoso Kyokai (NHK) radio service, unabashedly modeled on the BBC when it was established in 1926, became a military propaganda tool during World War II. After the war, in 1950, the Occupation forces approved the licensing of private, commercial radio stations, giving Japan the mixed system it has today. NHK's radio coverage now far exceeds that of commercial broadcasters, but it has about an equal number of television facilities.

Television began in 1953 after the Occupation ended. The autonomy of NHK derives partly from its ability to set and collect its own fees, although the legislature does review fee proposals. Moreover, NHK has complete freedom in programming; the government can in no way dictate content. However, the prime minister does appoint NHK's board of 12 governors.

According to Sydney Head (1985), "Japan has a rich artistic heritage that lends itself readily to television" (p. 22). A typical weekday in the late 1980s offered viewers in the Kanto (Tokyo metropolitan) area a choice of two NHK channels (educational and entertainment); five commercial channels (Nihon TV, TBS, Fuji TV, TV Asahi, and TV Tokyo); and six UHF channels with in-school programs and local news.

For overseas coverage, Japan's electronic media make frequent use of satellites and have numerous overseas correspondents (Japan has a larger corps of correspondents in Washington, D.C., than any other country). However, Anne Cooper (1989) found NHK's news reporting to be the most insular of five countries studied. During one week in 1986, only 22.6 percent of the stories on NHK were on international topics.

In entertainment TV programming, Japan imports major movies from abroad but has virtually stopped importing regular series, meaning that it must shoulder its production burden alone (about 150 hours a week for most stations). The well-researched Japanese audience prefers Japanese programs; even "Dallas," which succeeded elsewhere, failed in Japan. Animated cartoons constitute Japan's main programming export.

If Japan's uniquely non-Western television culture impresses the outsider as sophisticated, modern, and highly developed, China gives the visitor a chance to witness historical change in the making. The USSR was just helping China start its state-run television system in 1958 when the two countries had a falling out; the Soviet advisers went home, leaving radio as the prime means of instant communication through the Mao years.

Radio uses a three-layer system: (1) the national Central People's Broadcasting Station (in China, the English word *broadcasting* refers to radio, not television), (2) about 100 regional, provincial, and municipal networks, and (3) grass-roots stations that send national programs and local announcements by wires to loudspeakers in communes, market-places, fields, and homes. During the Cultural Revolution, loudspeakers blared everywhere, but in the 1980s, government policy favored over-the-air stations. With the wired radio layer included, radio reaches about 95 percent of China's people.

Figure 8.1 shows the astounding growth in TV set ownership in the 1980s. Today a set, according to Nancy Rivenburgh (1988), ranks as one the "four big things" that the Chinese desire (the others are a refrigerator, a washing machine, and a cassette player). At U.S. $370 for a black-and-white set or $700 for a domestic color set, the prices are no

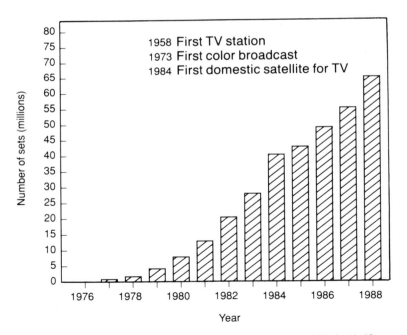

Figure 8.1. Growth in Chinese TV Set Ownership, 1976–1988 (est.) (*Source:* Nancy Rivenburgh, ''China: The Television Revolution,'' paper presented at the Association for Education in Journalism and Mass Communication convention, Portland, July 1988.)

bargains. Even so, purchasers may have to get on a waiting list or do business with smugglers, who, according to Bishop (1989), make regular runs from Hong Kong.

Because of China's size and terrain, it has enthusiastically turned to satellites to increase the reach of Chinese Central Television, which now serves all 29 provinces, including Tibet and Xinjiang. In addition to domestic satellites launched in 1984 and 1986, CCTV leases space on *Intelsat V.* The country hopes to build 5,000 receiving stations in the next few years.

The first U.S. series, "The Man from Atlantis," which was chosen for its bargain price rather than its ideological content, aired in 1979. In 1983, CCTV began taking 64 hours of programming from CBS. In choosing a color system, however, China chose not to follow the U.S. model (National Television Standards Committee, or NTSC), which had also been adopted in Japan, the Philippines, and South Korea. Instead, it opted for the German PAL (Phase Alternate Line) system.

Residents of Hong Kong can receive signals from China in addition to their own commercial services, two in Cantonese (Asia Television and the Jade channel) and two in English (Asia Television and the Pearl channel). From 1957 to 1967, the only television available in the crown colony came via cable from a local subsidiary of Britain's Rediffusion International.

In 1967, HKTVB began over-the-air broadcasts on the Jade and Pearl channels but was subject to government regulation. For example, advertisements must take up no more than 10 percent of programming time. Commercial radio, which began in 1959, must likewise limit the time devoted to ads. In addition, the government runs an educational channel.

Although only 400 miles square, Hong Kong serves as a major radio and television production center for overseas Chinese-language media from Taiwan to California. Its TV exports emphasize kung fu and other action fare, while its Cantonese-language radio programs range from storytellers to serial dramas.

Taiwan's three competitive, commercial TV networks offer both modern-dress and costume-opera dramatic series, as well as game shows, variety shows, news, and public affairs. The drama series proved so popular that government regulations now limit the number of episodes in a series and the number of series in any one evening.

With the end of martial law in 1987, restrictions on television eased somewhat. Taiwanese can now legally purchase satellite dishes for receiving signals from Japan in Japanese, a language that many young Taiwanese study and that all Taiwanese who went to school before 1945 can understand. (Japan ruled Taiwan as a colony from 1898 to 1945.) In prior years, pirate cable operators fed Japanese programs illegally to small subscriber groups. In 1989, the government even agreed to consider a request from the three networks to drop the ban on direct satellite transmissions from mainland China.

Despite its small population (20 million), Taiwan ranks as one of the world's leading markets for videocassette recorders. Other Asian countries with high VCR penetration include Japan, Australia, Singapore, and Malaysia.

Financing and ownership of the three TV networks involves a complex arrangement among government, military, party (the Kuomintang), private, and overseas interests. Radio ownership shows a similar mixed pattern. The KMT does fully control two overseas radio services, the Voice of Free China and a second service aimed specifically at the mainland. The English-language radio station formerly operated for U.S. forces was converted into a service for foreign residents after the United States broke diplomatic relations with the island.

Television penetration in South Korea stands at nearly 100 percent. The government-run KBS network has 51 affiliated stations, while the Munwa Broadcasting Company (partly government-owned) has 21.

The American Forces Korean Network (AFKN) runs six stations, which reach the entire Korean population without Korean official interference. AFKN, which began its TV service in 1957, broadcasts nothing but U.S. programs, including satellite transmissions from the United States. Kang and Morgan (1988) found in 1984 that Korean women who viewed AFKN held liberal, nontraditional views, while males who viewed a great deal of AFKN showed a "backlash effect" whereby they feared an erosion of traditional Korean values.

During the 1988 Olympic Games, the media played a role in already strained U.S.-Korean relations. After NBC repeatedly played footage of a Korean trainer assaulting an American boxing referee, the Korean media heavily covered the arrest of two U.S. swimmers who stole a Korean ceremonial mask. Despite these incidents, the Olympics bore witness worldwide to the sophistication and maturity of Korean telecommunications.

South Korea has about four times the TV set penetration of North Korea. Both entities, which are still officially in a state of war, send radio broadcasts to each other. In fact, North Korea's external service in eight languages rivals the BBC's. But little South Korean content gets through to the North, since all radios have dials fixed to prevent such reception.

Pacific

Geography practically ordained that Australia would, from broadcasting's earliest days, have a mixed system. The concentration of two-thirds of Australia's people in the southeastern coastal region made commercial broadcasting, which started in 1924, attractive in that region. However, only a publicly supported system was feasible in the thinly populated outback. Today, Australia has about as many private as government stations.

The Australian Broadcasting Corp. (ABC), established in 1932, has much in common with the BBC. Its board guards ABC's independence from government interference, although the ABC relies on Parliament to transfer over the license fee funds collected from the public.

In the 1960s, ABC began losing audience numbers to the commercial broadcasters. In the 1970s, two dramatic changes transformed broadcasting on the island continent. First, immigrant groups and aborigines who felt unconnected to Australia's European roots began lobbying for multicultural media. Using an access station set up in 1976, these groups started radio programs in 26 languages. In 1980, the government set up a multicultural TV service.

Second, using a communications satellite loaned by NASA, Australia experimented with sending programs to the remote areas in the 1970s. With the launching of *Aussat* in 1985, homes and institutions could now receive television, radio, and phone service via low-cost satellite ground stations.

Aussat also provides television service to Fiji and Papua New Guinea and assists telephone service in New Zealand. New Zealand depends even more on broadcasting than Australia to unite, inform, and entertain its small, scattered, agricultural population. The country even has a minister of broadcasting in the ruling cabinet.

New Zealand adopted the BBC model in 1932 but preserved the government monopoly many years longer than the mother country did. Because of competition from offshore pirate radio stations in the 1960s, the New Zealand Broadcasting Corp. (NZBC) finally began licensing private radio stations, but by 1982, only 17 had been authorized.

NZBC waited until 1960 to begin two television networks and until 1984 to approve an independent, nongovernment TV network. The two government networks, however, run commercials on certain days of the week, relying on advertisements for 85 percent of their budgets. TV-2, which emphasizes entertainment fare, has in the past run many American situation comedies but now tries to emphasize local production.

Radio came to the Pacific Islands in 1935 when service started in Fiji. However, more than half of the services are much more recent, dating from after 1960. They show the influence of nearby Australia and distant colonial powers, with American influence strong in Micronesia and American Samoa and British (BBC) influence in Fiji. In the 1970s, local staffs for the most part replaced the expatriates who managed many media enterprises in the islands.

Despite problems with funding, government interference, low

salaries, inadequate training, outdated equipment, and multiple languages, radio serves as the only timely link between many islands and the rest of the world. Even those that lack a daily newspaper have a radio system; Nauru, for example, the smallest republic in the world, has one 200-watt AM station to serve its 8,000 citizens. Papua New Guinea, which has the Pacific's most extensive system, inherited a service that Australia began in 1946; it broadcasts in 33 languages.

Of the more than 20 broadcasting systems in the region, 10 had television as of the mid-1980s. Guam joined the television age in the mid-1950s; other early adopters, in the 1960s, include New Caledonia, Tahiti, and American Samoa. Except for funding problems, virtually all Pacific nations and dependencies could link into Intelsat, even if lack of facilities and staff limited local productions. In the meantime, in the absence of television, videocassette systems are thriving in places such as the Cook Islands. A cassette circulation network poses a creative alternative to television in places that cannot or choose not to go the TV route.

NEWS SERVICES

The existence of myriad news services in Asia holds both hope for better information availability and the specter of managed news flows. The various patterns found in Asia include the presence of a government agency only, government and private agencies operating side by side, private agency or agencies only, private agencies subject to indirect government control, and regional cooperation of various kinds.

The Asian News Network, created in 1981, answered a need for an exchange of development and other regional news. However, it is still dwarfed by the regional services of the Big Four international services. Likewise, Asiavision complemented but in no way replaced the international news film and videotape services of Visnews and WTN (World Television News).

Worldwide, 56 percent of countries (a total of 90) have a government news agency, whereas 50 years ago, only 28 countries had one. Freedom House found that in 1987, fully 89 percent of the nations with the lowest civil liberties rating operated a government news agency. The pattern holds for Asia even more strikingly.

Only six Asian countries have no national government news agency: Australia, Bhutan, Fiji, Taiwan, Japan, and New Zealand. Of these, Australia, Japan, and New Zealand have the highest civil liberties ranking (1); indeed, in all of Asia, only these three have attained that rank.

The national agencies in Asia range from those that act solely as gatekeepers (e.g., the Korean Central News Agency of North Korea, which controls domestic consumption of news from regional and international sources) to those that do active local reporting to those that rival the Big Four international agencies in the scope of their overseas staffs. Kyodo News Service of Japan approaches true world agency status, but Xinhua (the New China News Agency) and the Press Trust of India have an impressive reach as well. Kyodo is free of government control, while Xinhua is the state-owned agency of the People's Republic of China. The Press Trust of India will be discussed in the next section.

South Asia

Among South Asian countries, India has a diverse national news agency system, including four major agencies and several other specialized agencies. The most widely known is the privately owned Press Trust of India (PTI), which has been called the backbone of daily journalism in the country. It was established in 1947 and operates as a nonprofit company. In addition to providing services to the newspapers and periodicals, it provides TV screen news in capsule form round the clock to hotels, airports, ministries, and public-sector undertakings. In 1986, PTI launched its TV operations under the banner of PTI-TV, and in 1987, it started a photo service on a nationwide scale. PTI has news bureaus in London and New York and has correspondents in 30 world capitals. It has news exchange agreements with 100 countries.

PTI's main rival is the United News of India (UNI), established in 1961. It has news bureaus and correspondents in 25 world capitals. UNI also has a photo service of its own and supplies news clips and features to the television station.

The other two news agencies, *Hindustan Samachar* and *Samachar Bharati*, are multilingual.

All four agencies were merged by the government during the emergency in 1975 into a single agency called Samachar, which was used as a vehicle for government propaganda. After a change in governments in 1977, the four agencies were restored to their former positions, but the agencies' operations continue to be heavily influenced by the government.

In Pakistan, there are two major news agencies: the Associated Press of Pakistan (APP) and Pakistan Press International (PPI). APP, founded in 1947, supplies national and international news to the newspapers, radio and TV stations, government departments, and other commercial subscribers. PPI, formerly known as the Pakistan Press

Association (PPA), was established in 1956 as a private joint-stock company. Both APP and PPI have bureaus in all major cities of Pakistan and exchange agreements with major news agencies of the world.

Bangladesh has three news agencies: Bangladesh Sangbad Sangstha (BSS), a news service in English, owned by the government; Eastern News Agency (ENA), privately owned; and United News of Bangladesh (UNB), a computerized news service with the latest equipment established in 1988.

Sri Lanka has two news agencies: Press Trust of Ceylon and Sandesa News Agency.

Nepal's news agency, the Rashtriya Samachar Samiti (RSS), was founded in 1962 in Kathmandu. It has correspondents in all 75 districts and exchange agreements with AP, Agence France-Presse, and Xinhau.

Bhutan has no news agency.

Afghanistan's Bakhtar News Agency (BNA) has signed agreements with many socialist states for the exchange of news. BNA is equipped with Soviet cameras, laboratories, materials, and paper. In 1980, it opened a direct radio service in English for Asia, Europe, the Middle East, North and West Africa, and socialist countries. With the assistance of TASS, the Soviet news agency, BNA is able to transmit international news to 27 different countries.

Southeast Asia

With UNESCO's encouragement, a number of countries established national news agencies in the 1970s. As of 1987, Burma (Myanmar), Cambodia, Laos, Indonesia, Malaysia, the Philippines, Singapore, and Vietnam all had government news agencies. Cambodia's pro-Vietnamese news agency, SPK, employs more than 100 reporters, making it that nation's largest single news operation. Thailand's Thai News Agency is an exception in its freedom from direct government control.

One of the largest, Bernama of Malaysia, was established in 1968 under the Ministry of Information. It derives most of its income from government subscribers, including the state-controlled radio and television services. Like many Third World agencies, it shares news directly with a number of other national agencies and indirectly by belonging to the Non-Aligned News Agency Pool. Bernama does not act as the sole media gatekeeper for information coming into Malaysia, since the international agencies can sell directly to customers.

Indonesia has three national news services. Antara (meaning "between" in Bahasa Indonesian) is the major agency. Founded in 1937 to distribute news about the independence movement with a nationalist interpretation, Antara became an official agency in 1962 and is governed through a council composed of representatives from government and the private sector. The oldest surviving and biggest Indonesian news service, Antara provides news, feature, and photo services to newspapers, radio stations, foreign embassies, and commercial institutions. In addition to bureaus in all 27 provinces of Indonesia, it has bureaus or correspondents in several major cities of the world and exchange agreements with several major agencies of the world. It is also an active member of the confederation of ASEAN journalists, the Non-Aligned News Pool, and the Organization of Asian News Agencies (OANA).

Two other major news agencies besides Antara are the PAB (Armed Forces News Agency) and the Independent KNI (National News Agency). PAB (Pusab Pemberitaan Angkatan Bersendjata), formed in 1965, handles primarily army news but is in the business of general news reporting as well. KNI (Kantorberita Nasional Indonesia), formed in 1966 by 11 Djakarta newspapers, is an independent service free of government or political ties. In 1970, KNI started an English "KNI Daily Bulletin," specializing in economic issues, for its foreign readers. KNI has bureaus or correspondents throughout Indonesia.

In the Philippines, with the restoration of press freedom in 1987, the government-owned Philippine News Agency was discontinued.

East Asia

North Korea, South Korea, and Mongolia all have government news agencies, but they are dwarfed in scope by Xinhua. Xinhua, which celebrated its 50th anniversary in 1981, has hundreds of employees in 90 overseas bureaus; correspondents are classified as diplomats and enjoy diplomatic immunity. With a total staff of more than 5,000, it transmits about 50,000 words daily to the Chinese media and about 60,000 words overseas in six languages. Furthermore, it monitors all incoming news and culls from that flow the 10 million–circulation *Reference News*.

In Hong Kong, according to Chan and Lee (1988), Xinhua's role goes far beyond that of a news agency, with only 30 of its 500 staff members working in the news division. Instead of having a news agency structure, Xinhua's divisions were changed in 1983 to coincide with those of the Hong Kong government. As Beijing's surrogate presence in Hong Kong, Xinhua organizes and supervises the committees that are designing Hong Kong's post-1997 future.

Kyodo, a private cooperative agency formed in 1945, has bureaus in some 40 countries. For its large domestic clientele, it produces more than 200,000 Japanese characters a day, while for overseas clients it sends out about 40,000 words a day in English; the English service has recently responded to increased demands for news about Japanese sports.

Jiji Press, a business-oriented private agency, was also born in 1945. Like Kyodo, it produces domestic Japanese and overseas English files but also sends out about 12,000 words a day in Chinese.

Pacific

The nongovernmental New Zealand Press Association and, especially, the Australian Associated Press (AAP) serve not only their home countries' media but Pacific communities as well. From its headquarters in Sydney, the AAP supplies both Fiji and Papua New Guinea with a file that it culls from major agencies and its own members' news output.

GOVERNMENT-MEDIA RELATIONS

Worldwide, 25 percent of all countries have generally free broadcast and print media, but in Asia only 15 percent of the countries do (the Philippines, Japan, Australia, New Zealand, and Papua New Guinea). Generally speaking, the laws of Asian countries establish sweeping powers for controlling media.

In 1987, John Merrill interviewed 58 information and press officers posted in the United States regarding nations' inclinations to control the press. Of the ten Asian nations studied, China ranked with those having the most severe controls, or a "control inclination index" (CII) score of 24. Australia and Japan had the lowest (freest) scores, 11 (compared to the United States with 8). India scored 12; the Philippines, 14; Bangladesh, Indonesia, and South Korea, all 18; Malaysia, 20; and Pakistan, 19 (Merrill, 1988).

Control mechanisms on the press include annual licensing of publications, exorbitant security deposits, confiscation, cutting allowable circulation, control of newsprint and official advertising, and outright closure. Journalists themselves can be punished under sedition, libel, security, or martial law provisions.

South Asia

In most of South Asia, governments try to restrain the press by promoting a "guidance" concept to be used in conjunction with national development aims. Media must cooperate, according to the guidance concept, by stressing positive, development-oriented news and by supporting government policies and plans for national development. The guidance comes in the form of supplying news releases and actual stories to the media, providing public speeches by officials on the desired role of the press in a developing society, and telephone calls from government officials offering advice. In Pakistan, Bangladesh, Sri Lanka, Nepal, and sometimes even in India, telephone guidelines are provided by the government in power. Official speeches in practically all South Asian countries are published verbatim on front pages. For fear of displeasing the government, journalists most often practice self-restraint and avoid investigative reporting. For years now, Tamil journalists in Sri Lanka have been keeping quiet about terrorism, willingly censoring their own stories.

Besides promoting a guidance concept, most governments use direct censorship, suspend offending newspapers, and arrest journalists who do not conform to the official policy. Direct censorship is prevalent in Sri Lanka, Pakistan, Bangladesh, Nepal, and Afghanistan.

In Sri Lanka, direct censorship is permitted under the antiterrorism law, and parliamentary privileges can be invoked to shield parliamentary discussion. As a result of direct censorship, Sri Lanka's mainstream publications do not contest the government's viewpoint directly or probe its activities deeply. On a recent Tamil ethnic problem, much of the press fully backed the government's military campaign, presenting it as a justified, patriotic war.

The Bangladesh government closed two Bengali-language daily newspapers in February 1988 on the grounds that they had published "objectionable news" and that they had attempted to undermine the sovereignty and independence of the country.

In Pakistan, there was no mention or glimpse of opposition figures in the media for years. Under the leadership of a new prime minister, in a dramatic reversal of the 11-year blackout on the activities of the Pakistan People's Party, opposition politicians now get a share of airtime.

Nepal functions under the guidelines of the Press and Publications Act, which prohibits publication of material detrimental to the national interest, peace, law and order, and the power of the king.

In Afghanistan, after the coup in 1978, all private printing houses were forbidden to operate. Newspapers cannot publish anything that disobeys government laws or discloses state secrets or defames the Islam religion.

Suspension of newspapers and harassment and arrest of journalists occur when officials or others in positions of power and influence do not like what is written about them. Though India's press is among the freest in Asia and there is no direct censorship, the Indian government has not hesitated at times to use its enormous powers over the press. In June 1989, the *Indian Post* of Bombay, an independent newspaper known for its investigative reporting, was emasculated overnight when its editor, Vinod Mehta, was asked to resign by its owner because the paper had published critical reports involving some power brokers close to the prime minister. However, the press in India is still holding its own despite pressure. The resignation of the *Post*'s editor generated much concern in the journalistic community in India. Several journalists issued a statement warning that the resignation of the editor "reveals disturbingly the perils of press freedom in the country today." The Editors' Guild of India immediately set to investigating reports of pressures put on the *Post*'s editor by the management.

More recently, the 84-year-old editor of a Hindi daily in the state of Bihar was dragged from his house to a police lockup, where he was physically assaulted because he had written an editorial over an instance of alleged police brutality. According to the Indian Federation of Working Journalists, more than 50 such attacks were reported in 1988, from almost every state. Media analyst and former *Times of India* editor M. V. Desai, however, sees otherwise: "These attacks also go to show that the press is doing its job in exposing misuses of authority in institutions answerable to society" (quoted in *India Abroad*, August 25, 1989, p. 12).

The press in India and Sri Lanka has recently also been the target of rebel groups, who have sought to intimidate and assassinate journalists and disrupt newspaper distribution. Because of the Hindu-Sikh communal strife, journalists and others associated with the press in India are risking their lives to keep the flag of a free press flying. In May 1989, three persons were killed by terrorists when the Hind Samachar group of publications ignored the warnings of terrorist organizations to shut down their widely circulated papers in Punjab. In Sri Lanka, Tamil militant groups have from time to time used both threats and violence against journalists writing articles that the rebels found displeasing. In January 1988, Tamil rebels bombed the home of the editor of *Divaina*, the largest-circulation Sinhalese daily, and later tried to cripple the operation of Associated Newspapers of Ceylon, Ltd., the country's leading publishing house. The newspaper distribution systems have also been attacked by rebels time and again in Sri Lanka.

Liberty of the press must constantly be fought for in most South Asian countries, where the governments allocate newsprint, distribute advertising, stipulate registration rules, and operate the broadcast media.

In India, Pakistan, Bangladesh, Sri Lanka, and Nepal, governments control newsprint and advertising quotas. In India, quality newsprint must be imported through the State Trading Corp., a government agency, since domestic producers are unable to meet even a quarter of the annual requirement. The government recently announced a 30 percent increase in the price of newsprint. As a result, two daily newspapers in the state of Kerala folded in June 1989, and others are becoming more and more dependent on government advertisements for their survival. The newspapers see the rising cost of newsprint as an attempt to punish the newspapers for their role in exposing corruption at the highest level. In Pakistan, newsprint controls and government advertisements account for about 70 percent of advertising revenue. Although the new government of Prime Minister Benazir Bhutto has announced new guarantees of press freedom, journalists still feel that the press cannot be really free until the state monopoly on newsprint allocation is lifted. Arif Nizami, editor of the *Nation,* said: "The real checks on publishing remain. . . . They [Government authorities] can still strangle a newspaper financially by removing advertisements or delivering their patronage to a newspaper that publishes the Government's views" (quoted in Goldenberg, 1989, p. 7). In Nepal, government is the country's largest advertiser. Hence, advertisements are placed lavishly only with government newspapers.

Since the broadcast media in the entire region of South Asia are owned and operated by the government, the broadcasts are usually replete with official news and views. In India, during the regime of late prime minister Indira Gandhi, media coverage of All India Radio was government-oriented to such an extent that some critics labeled it "All Indira Radio"; now, under the leadership of Rajiv Gandhi, critics call it "All India Rajiv." Pakistan's state-controlled television network was recently criticized by some viewers for the celebration of what would have been the birthday of Prime Minister Bhutto's father, Zulfikar Ali Bhutto, who was executed under the Zia regime. Government-controlled broadcasting in Sri Lanka presents a narrow range of views. The success of Sri Lanka's radio is usually measured in terms of how convincingly it presents the government policies and projects to the people.

Southeast Asia

In Burma (Myanmar), Cambodia, Laos, and Vietnam, where the mass media are run as an arm of the government, one can discuss press philosophies more readily than relations *between* media and government. Freedom House considers all four of these countries to have highly controlled print and broadcast systems. The other countries in the region, as Table 8.1 shows, have at least some degree of freedom, except Malaysia.

Malaysia's highly publicized run-ins with the *Asian Wall Street Journal* (which the government accused of having an "anti-Malaysia bias" in its investigative reporting) resulted in a three-month publishing ban imposed on the paper in 1986 and the expulsion of two reporters. "We gave them a publishing permit, but why haven't they said anything good about us?" asked an official. In addition, under provisions of the Official Secrets Act, a reporter for the domestic *New Straits Times* was fined U.S. $4,000 in 1985; a reporter for the *Far Eastern Economic Review* was fined the next year.

In Thailand, according to *Asia Magazine*, "the right to publish is a right wholly defined by the government, as is the right to revoke the right to publish" ("The Press in Asia," 1987, p. 42). As one newspaper editor told the magazine, "It's not right that we can be shut down by an unhappy man whose emotions may have gotten the better of his judgement." Indeed, in 1987, the sensational Thai-language daily *Khaosod* was ordered closed. However, that had been the first closure in some time and was not seen as a precursor of a major press curb. (After a month, *Khaosod* resumed publication under a different name.)

In Singapore, critics claim that the threat of government action has effectively tamed the press. Some local journalists have been arrested, but recently foreign publications have been more frequent targets. In 1986, *Time* and the *Asian Wall Street Journal* had the number of allowable copies cut—*Time*'s from 18,000 to 2,000 and the *AWSJ*'s from 5,000 to 400.

The Indonesian Press Law, enacted in 1966 and amended in 1982, bars censorship. However, it requires a balance between press freedom and responsibility and stipulates that the press should not publish materials that violate the national ideology (*pancasila*). Four vital and sensitive issues that are considered to be in violation of the national ideology are *suku* (ethnic group) issues, *agagma* (religious) issues, *ras* (racial) problems, and *antar-golongan* (intergroup) conflicts. These four issues, known as SARA, from the first letters of the four points, are practically taboo because any mention of such issues could stir up a given situation, leading to chaos and political instability. Indonesian journalists who want to stay in the profession recognize the limitations on their freedom and are careful to avoid reporting anything that could be construed as dissent. The law also requires a license to publish.

The government is as sensitive about the foreign press as it is about its own. A supplement to the Press Act of 1966, enacted in 1972, regulates the foreign press and journalists in Indonesia. Foreign publications have to obtain government permission to circulate. All foreign publications are screened carefully, and those that harm or endanger society or are considered to be contrary to the national ideology (*pancasila*) are banned. Foreign journalists writing about such sensitive issues are barred from entry into the country. Barbara Crossette of the *New York Times* was ousted and later barred entry in 1987 for writing a piece that had displeased President Suharto. Earlier, Australian journalist David Jenkins had written a piece in the *Sydney Morning Herald* that likened Suharto to ousted Philippine president Marcos. The story described how Suharto had built a $2 billion business empire fashioned out of banking, manufacturing, steel, shipping, and real estate. The Indonesian government barred not only Jenkins but all Australian journalists, banned the Australian newspaper, and even refused entry to Australian tourists.

In the Philippines, the debate over press freedom and press responsibility seems to have intensified under Aquino's presidency. Despite Aquino's proclaimed commitment to a free press "even to the extent that its exercise may take destructive forms" (Aquino pledged to uphold press freedom at a meeting with trustees of the Press Foundation of Asia), she has expressed concern over some media reporting and at times has denied interviews to reporters.

Perhaps because of the aftereffects of Marcos's dictatorship, newspapers in the Philippines still hesitate to displease the government, hence they tend to practice self-censorship. Editorial criticism is often muted in a majority of newspapers or recast as constructive criticism. Moreover, newspapers tend to be supportive of the developmental efforts of the country. The *Manila Bulletin*, for example, calls itself the "exponent of Philippine progress," and the *Manila Times* carries the national flag on the front page with the inscription "Rally to the Flag!"

East Asia

China, North Korea, and Mongolia follow the Marxist-Leninist concept of total integration of press and government. In Taiwan and South Korea, as in other parts of Asia, the press has until recently followed the concept of guidance, which means extensive use of government news releases, avoidance of investigative reporting, and downplaying of opposition. Telephone calls from and speeches by officials clarify what is expected.

However, by 1987, most print media in South Korea could publish without restraint. In 1988, two journalists who had been previously purged established the nation's first major independent newspaper; half of its staff had likewise been purged.

In Taiwan, as the 1986 municipal election approached, action against opposition publications increased. Censorship incidents against opposition magazines increased from 33 in 1984 to 302 in 1986. By early 1987, only 3 of 15 opposition magazines were still publishing. Between 1984 and early 1987, six opposition journalists were jailed for libel. The situation in the post-martial-law years (after 1987) is still fluid but shows signs of increased freedom.

The 1946 constitution of Japan guarantees freedom of expression unconditionally, unlike the previous constitution, which added the insidious phrase "within the limits of the law." The self-censorship that still occurs in Japan derives partly from the rigid official censorship that prevailed until the end of the Occupation; the imperial family, for example, is treated with kid gloves. Furthermore, the newspapers' huge circulations tend to dampen initiative, since editors fear that outspoken writing might antagonize large numbers of readers.

As in most democratic states, Japanese citizens may sue the mass media for libel after publication, but relatively few do so. According to Kyu Ho Youm (1989, p. 20), the "low rights consciousness of Japanese as individuals" and a respect for the media as important social institutions discourage such suits. Indeed, the Japanese courts have tended to expand rather than contract protected expression over the past 30 years.

Pacific

Australia's and New Zealand's print media are among the freest in the world, but New Zealand's tough libel law requires provable truth as a defense in defamation cases. More state control exists over broadcast media. For example, the Australian Broadcasting Tribunal can regulate program content and advertising and has set a maximum standard of 30 percent for foreign-produced TV programs (to encourage indigenous productions). New Zealand's customs agents censor objectionable videocassettes at points of entry.

Elsewhere in the Pacific, media suppression does not reach the magnitude seen on the Asian continent. In Papua New Guinea, for example, critical viewpoints are allowed on the government-controlled radio system. The exception is Fiji, where in 1987 a military coup resulted in censorship and severe control.

CONCEPTS OF MEDIA FREEDOM

Article 19 of the United Nations Declaration of Human Rights reads: "Everyone has the right to freedom of opinion and expression; this right includes the freedom to hold opinions without interference and to seek, receive and impart information and ideas through any media and regardless of frontiers." Many peoples and governments in Asia do not agree with these ideas. At least three concepts of the mass media's role can be found, in addition to the Western model as practiced in Australia and New Zealand. Often these traditional concepts seem at odds with nontraditional business practices, but for the moment, Eastern ethics and modern techniques coexist, if somewhat uneasily.

Authoritarian Concept

According to Hachten (1981), as mentioned in Chapter 1, more people have lived under authoritarian press systems than any other. He defines this concept as constant direct or implied control from above, with consensus and standardization as a goal and dissent an "annoying nuisance" (p. 17). As long as the press (broadcast media are more likely to be under direct government control) operates within mutually understood boundaries, the government does not intervene. However, to portray the press as a would-be adversary just barely reined in would be inaccurate.

Singapore's government and tamed press both regard the media as the government's partner in development. One official explained his distaste for James Bond–style journalists who attack national leaders at will, and the progovernment *Straits Times* agreed; it warned Westerners in an editorial not to apply the American ideal of press freedom to a multiethnic society such as Singapore. Similarly, a Malaysian official warned against applying Western-style individual liberties in a non-Western context. In Taiwan, a government spokesman called the Taiwanese approach "management" rather than control.

The partnership arrangement means that the mass media do not broach certain subjects. In Taiwan, for example, three topics have long been taboo: Taiwanese independence (the idea of two Chinas, which grants de facto legitimacy to the mainland); communism or mainland China (if treated favorably), and the private lives of political leaders. In Malaysia, one must not write about racial disharmony. In Thailand, one must not show disrespect for the royal family.

Modified Libertarian Concept

In Japan, too, self-censorship reigns in discussion of the imperial family. When Emperor Hirohito died in January 1989 after 62 years of rule, Japanese television showed scenes of Japanese military action from the 1930s and 1940s. However, the programs did not show footage of the Rape of Nanking (in Japan called "the Nanking incident") or discuss in any depth the occupation of Korea. The emperor was portrayed as peace-loving but manipulated, with no alternative explanations offered.

Investigative journalism has never been the strong suit of Japan's mass media. Accuracy and insight distinguish the material that the media produce, but much of reality simply does not appear. Many persons knew about a kickback scandal involving the Lockheed aviation firm's Japanese contracts, for example, but no one broke the story until a former prime minister referred to it in a speech. Then teams of reporters went to work.

Journalism professor Hideo Takeichi says that the characteristics of Japanese corporate life apply just as much to corporations that happen to be newspapers ("The Press in Asia," 1987, p. 19). Once an employee passes the entry gate, the newspaper assumes that the employee will work there all his or her life. Much like bureaucrats, journalists work their way up the promotion ladder, following majority opinion and directives from above rather than risk antagonizing lifelong colleagues. Since few free-lance journalists exist in Japan, an outcast reporter literally has nowhere to go.

A blend of Eastern practices and Western libertarian trappings also marks the press of India. Except during the emergency rule imposed by Prime Minister Indira Gandhi in 1975, when direct censorship dampened journalistic ardor, the press in India has been one of the freest in Asia. "For 28 years there were no real constraints on the press till the Emergency came," states Kuldip Nayar (*India Abroad*, August 25, 1989, p. 12), a former editor of the *Statesman* and the *Indian Express.* With the lifting of the emergency, the Indian media reverted to what is generally considered a free-press philosophy in the Western tradition. Even though the government has never quite accepted the concept of the adversarial relationship of the press and authority (according to Prime Minister Rajiv Gandhi, the fostering of an adversarial relationship between the press and the government is not always conducive to good governance), the press in India does play a significant watchdog role. Newspapers and newsmagazines are constantly engaged in aggressive, yet responsible, journalism in exposing corruption, malfeasance, and nepotism on the part of the authorities. Almost all leading papers have been critical of the government in power. Most papers write strong editorials criticizing the acts of government. The *Statesman* has an "insight" investigating team. So has Bombay's *Free Press Journal.* The *Economic Times* and a host of other newspapers have a similar "insight" page as well.

The *Indian Express,* under the editorship of Arun Shourie, has been an especially consistent critic of the government. Shourie was named International Editor of the Year for 1982 for exposing corruption and malfeasance in the highest councils of the late Indira Gandhi's ruling party, resulting in the ouster of one of her most powerful allies and in changes in police, judiciary, and other institutions. Another journalist, C. R. Irani, managing director of the *Statesman*, won the Freedom House Award for his opposition to government attempts to control the press. Not long ago, journalists, editors, and publishers of various newspapers engaged in a nationwide protest against the Defamation Bill of 1988 that resulted in the successful withdrawal of the bill from the Parliament by the Indian government. The bill had been introduced into the lower house of Parliament without any prior consultation of the press. It was widely perceived as an effort to intimidate the press into submission. The withdrawal of the defamation bill is a perfect example of victory for the press freedom. Moreover, the Press Council of India safeguards freedom of the press. Being a statutory body, the council has sufficient scope to act independently of the government pressures.

In the Philippines, dramatic changes in press philosophy have occurred over the past two decades as a result of the political changes. Prior to the declaration of martial law in 1972, the Republic of the Philippines had the most libertarian press in Asia. After martial law, the press was completely under authoritarian control. Under the present leadership, the press claims to be free once again. According to the Constitution of the Republic of the Philippines, ratified in 1987, "No law shall be passed abridging the freedom of speech, of expression, or of the press, or the right of the people peaceably to assemble and petition the government for redress of grievances."

Communist

According to Hachten (1981), the communist concept holds that a free press, divisive by its very nature, gets in the way of the key job of nation building; by contrast, state-owned media can pursue in unison their tasks of agitating, propagandizing, and organizing. News is any information that serves the state.

From the early days of Mao Tse-tung's revolution, communicating through media has been crucial. The Maoist dictum "Thought determines action" means that people must receive correct information in order to think and in turn act "correctly." Mao incorporated all channels in this task, from traditional *tatsupao* ("big character posters") to national newspapers, but did not pay as much attention as he might have to television.

According to Godwin Chu (1978), the mass media provide dos (such as profiles of model workers) and don'ts (bad news from overseas), while omitting ideas that contradict party policies or bad news that might depress the spirit of the people. In July 1976, an earthquake in Tangshan, China, killed an estimated 800,000 people, but the print media did not carry any news of the disaster until August. Casualty statistics, which erroneously listed the death toll as 242,000, were not released until 1979.

Because television developed in the post-Mao era, it followed a different pattern from that of the press. Advertising has appeared on the air since 1979. The news, free of harangues and stories long on ideology, draws high viewership. According to Nancy Rivenburgh (1988), television functions less for political consolidation and more as an entertainment medium.

However, when cataclysmic bad events happen, time lags occur while party officials decide how to portray the incidents. For example, viewers did not see anything about the 1987 Tibet uprising until three days after it started. Monumental but brief changes occurred in May 1989, including a televised session when prodemocracy student leaders were shown lecturing Premier Li Peng. But by June the patterns of the past had returned. An army documentary showed how "hooligans" had attacked soldiers, while the news showed "criminals" who admitted their guilt. On June 24, the dismissal of party General Secretary Zhao Ziyang, who had supported the students, was aired.

MEDIA ECONOMICS AND SPECIAL PROBLEMS

The mass media in Asia derive revenues from subscriptions, user fees (in the case of cable television), advertising (private or government), government or institutional subsidies, and allied enterprises. Where a healthy advertising base exists, mass media can turn huge profits; in 1984–1985, for example, New Zealand's major papers reported profits ranging from 34 to 72 percent. In China, state-controlled media now run ads from private firms.

By the 1980s, concentrated ownership characterized much of the Asian press. The Singapore-based *Straits Times*, for example, has bought into media in more than ten countries. In Japan, the Big Three (*Asahi*, *Mainichi*, and *Yomiuri*) have myriad editions that blanket the nation. Sing Tao Ltd. of Hong Kong, in addition to a stable of publications worldwide, has now expanded into real estate and pharmaceuticals.

But no one has reached beyond the Asia-Pacific area as dramatically as Australian Rupert Murdoch, although, ironically, his first Asian purchase (Hong Kong's *South China Morning Post*) did not occur until 1988. Murdoch's News Corporation Ltd., which has newspapers in Fiji and Papua New Guinea, expanded outside Australia in 1968, moving into Britain and later the United States. In 1987, when he bought the *Herald* and *Weekly Times* group of Australia, his corporation became the world's largest publisher of English-language newspapers.

Like English, the Chinese language has spread throughout the world, such that Chinese publications exist from Manila to New York and Taiwan to Vancouver. In order to confront common problems, Sally Aw Sian founded the International Chinese-Language Press Institute in Hong Kong.

Other issues now confronting Asian media include the difficulty of serving rural (often illiterate) populations, the fear that imported film and TV fare may smother local cultures, and apprehension about the effects of television (especially on young people).

In countries less developed than Japan and Singapore, the profitability and accessibility of an urban base have accentuated a tendency for newspapers to serve city dwellers. The gradual penetration of television into rural areas does not overcome the need for print media and literacy.

Global marketing of television has resulted in a one-way flow of programming, most of it entertainment fare from the United States. Pricing structures mean that nations can import programming for a fraction of production costs, thus expanding their broadcasting hours. For example, in 1985–1986, a half-hour episode from the United States cost U.S. $600 to $850 in Hong Kong or $500 to $600 in India, whereas in Japan it would run $6,000 to $7,000.

Does imported programming have adverse effects? It does discourage local production, but the more subtle effects on attitudes are harder to measure. Some nations, such as Australia, have put limits on the amount of imported programming that can be shown domestically.

Does television itself, even domestic programming, have detrimental effects? The case of Japan may shed some light on this crucial question. As Table 8.1 shows, Japan has the highest TV penetration in Asia, 563 sets per 1,000 people; that means that only two people ever need to share the same set. In fact, Japan is second only to the United States, which has 793 sets per 1,000 people. Yet at the same time, Japan has the highest ratio of newspaper readers, with 562 copies per 1,000 people—in other words, newspapers and TVs are about equally available. Compare that picture with the United States, which has only 268 newspapers per 1,000 people. Our easy arguments about television's displacing the reading habit just don't seem to hold up.

JOURNALISM EDUCATION AND TRAINING

Many journalists in Asia and the Pacific still get their training on the job. Despite this tradition, Asia has more institutes and academic programs in communications than any other region in the world except North America—an estimated 250 in the mid-1980s. About half of these follow the U.S. pattern, offering a degree in communication or journalism that combines academic study with practical experience.

The first schools began in the 1920s and 1930s, but real expansion in training for mass media jobs did not occur until after World War II. The pioneer programs include three departments of journalism in China—at St. John's University in Shanghai (1920), Yenching University in Beijing (1924), and Fudan University in Shanghai (1929); the Department of Journalism in the Faculty of Letters at Jochi (Sophia) University, a Jesuit institution in Tokyo (1932); a B.A. in communications at a branch of Far Eastern University in Manila (1934); and a program at Chengchi University, founded in mainland China (1935) but now located in Taiwan.

Because of the growth of such programs, especially in the 1970s, fewer practitioners and teachers will need to go overseas to study in the future. The descriptions that follow highlight a few examples, but many other notable programs exist.

South Asia

One of the best training institutions in South Asia is the Indian Institute of Mass Communication, which was set up in New Delhi in 1965 as a center for advanced study and research in mass communication. The institute conducts teaching and training programs, organizes seminars, and contributes to the creation of an information infrastructure suitable for India and other developing countries. The institute also provides its expertise and consultancy services to other institutions in the country as well as other developing countries of the world.

The tradition of journalism education and training in India began in 1941 with the establishment of a department of journalism at Panjab University in Lahore (now Pakistan), which was transferred to Delhi in 1947 and finally to Chandigarh in 1962. Madras University also established its journalism department in 1947, followed by the universities of Calcutta, Mysore, Nagpur, and Osmania in the 1950s. In the next two decades, many universities throughout the country started offering programs in journalism and mass communication.

Today, more than 40 universities and 20 private coaching institutions, plus 20 agricultural universities, annually train approximately

1,000 students in various specialized areas including print journalism, broadcast journalism, and films. Yet the vast infrastructure of national education from schools to universities built up so far is not enough to cope with the needs of so populous a country. Realizing that mass communication is an essential catalyst for national development and social change, the University Grants Commission has recently undertaken to set up six centers for education and training in mass communication in six universities of the country. The Centre for Mass Communication Research, established at Jamia Millia Islamia University in Delhi in 1983, is the first such center, featuring a wide range of sophisticated and modern audio, video, and film equipment for its studios. The university offers a two-year master's degree in mass communication involving theoretical and practical instruction in radio, audiovisual, television, and film production.

Some newspapers, including the *Times of India,* the *Hindustan Times,* the *Hindu,* and the *United News of India,* have their own in-service training programs. All India Radio also trains its own employees at its staff training school in New Delhi. For training in the art of filmmaking, the Film and Television Institute of India at Poona is the largest of its kind in Asia. Established by the Ministry of Information and Broadcasting in 1961, the institute offers courses in film direction, motion picture photography, sound recording, film editing, and television production.

Journalism education at the university level in Pakistan also dates back to 1941, when a one-year diploma in journalism was offered at the University of Panjab at Lahore. Later, Karachi University and other universities began diploma and degree programs in journalism and mass communication. The University Grants Commission has recently recommended that all universities in Pakistan offering programs in journalism upgrade their two-year M.A. journalism courses to four-year courses in mass communication leading to the degree of M.S. in mass communication. In the field of broadcast journalism, the Pakistan Broadcasting Academy conducts in-service courses for the professional training of producers, news editors, and broadcast engineers.

In Bangladesh, Dacca University offers diplomas in journalism. The Bangladesh Press Institute, run by the government, also provides journalistic training. A majority of journalists, however, receive in-service training at the newspapers.

The University of Sri Lanka and Kabul University in Afghanistan have also established journalism programs for the training of their journalists.

However, these specialized courses in journalism and mass communication in a majority of South Asian countries are academically oriented and do not provide sufficient practical training. A majority of journalism and mass communication programs in universities lack the resources needed for purchasing equipment and training material or offering practical experience for students. Very few universities have their own radio, television, or film studios or even possess basic facilities for producing a student newspaper. The Indian Institute of Mass Communication is perhaps the only center in South Asia that is well equipped and offers training in all the media. The institute has a press and highly developed audiovisual facilities that cater to the training and publication needs of the center. The institute publishes a quarterly research journal, *Communicator* in English and *Sanchar Madhyam* in Hindi, among other publications. As the concept of developmental journalism gains a much wider meaning in developing countries, the institute is emphasizing the study and practice of communication relevant to developmental needs and resources.

Most other universities in India as well as Pakistan, Bangladesh, Nepal, Sri Lanka, and Afghanistan have not adopted an integrated approach to mass communication. Moreover, a majority of universities are inadequately financed and therefore lack a trained staff to prepare students adequately to enter the media profession. In several countries, there is a shortage of local university teachers with an academic background in mass communication. As a result, the universities resort to part-time teachers, who are often less committed to the profession than full-time teachers. This runs hand in hand with a lack of concern with research activities. Scholarly research in communication is almost nonexistent in most universities. There is a grave shortage of suitable textbooks written with the local or national perspectives of individual countries. As a result, most students depend on American and British textbooks and reference books.

Despite these pitfalls, South Asian countries have advanced more than others in mass communication education. Mass media owners are now beginning to recognize the importance of formal training and to employ more graduates in journalism and communication.

Southeast Asia

Malaysia exemplifies the tremendous growth that can occur in a short time when a society decides to pursue mass media education wholeheartedly. The nation's first courses were offered in 1971 at the Universiti Sains Malaysia. The next year, the School of Mass Communication at the MARA Institute of Technology was established; it now ranks as the largest such school in Malaysia. By the late 1980s, some 800 students were enrolled in programs at five universities and colleges.

With support from the Friedrich-Ebert Foundation, the government of Singapore created the Asian Mass Communication and Research Center (AMIC). This regional mass media center sponsors research, offers training, and holds conferences.

In Indonesia, professional journalists have now started to replace some of the former politicians and experienced journalists who learned their trade mostly through association with the independence movements. In the late 1950s and early 1960s, several universities started offering the equivalent of the master's degree in mass communication. The earliest program was started in 1948 at the Gadjah Mada University in Yogyakarta as the Department of Information. Thereafter, several universities started offering five-year programs leading to a master's degree.

Several private institutions also train journalists. For example, the Newspaper Publishers' Association offers a five-year program leading to a master's degree. The Indonesian Institute for Press Training and Consultancy and the Surabaya Journalism Academy also offer extensive courses. The most notable is probably the Perguruan Tinggi Publisistik, which is both a private teaching institution, giving instruction up to the master's degree level, and an institute for mass communication research. In addition, several organizations offer short courses and seminars for working journalists. For instance, the Indonesian Journalists' Association, in cooperation with the government, offers one- to two-week courses and seminars on special subjects for working journalists. The Ministry of Information offers training for its own personnel through the Academy of Information. TVRI also operates a training center for its employees, known as Pusat Latihan TVRI. Another organization, Pendidikan Periklanan Jakarta, offers short courses in advertising and public relations.

Yet many working journalists have little or no college education or any special education. Marsden Epworth (1988), who recently worked as a journalist in Indonesia for two years, observed: "If [journalists] can read and write, if they can get a security clearance, and if they can tell what news bolsters the regime and what news does not, they've got a job" (p. 42).

In the Philippines, at least one out of every three colleges or universities offers training in journalism. Postgraduate degrees in journalism and mass communication are offered at the University of the Philippines, University of Santo Tomas (Manila), and Silliman University with a focus on population communication, development communication, and community press, respectively. The University of the Philippines Institute of Mass Communication offers a joint doctoral program with U.S. universities.

The Asian Institute of Journalism in Manila offers a graduate course in media management and a master's degree in journalism in addition to short-term seminars and workshops for practicing journalists. Moreover, the institute, in cooperation with the Communication Foundation of Asia, also promotes the writing and publishing of communication books by Asians. A communication research journal was also founded recently.

The Philippine Press Institute, another organization, frequently holds a series of training sessions for reporters and editors around the country. In addition, Nieman fellowships are available to permit Philippine journalists to study abroad.

East Asia

The Japanese mass media tend to follow recruitment patterns similar to those of other Japanese corporations, with the most prestigious institutions hiring (for lifetime jobs) students from the most prestigious universities. The newspapers or broadcasting firms then handle their own training. For example, NHK pursues both training and research, as does the Japan Newspaper Publishers and Editors Association.

Korea, by contrast, has followed the United States model. Since the mid-1970s, it has established a network of 20 programs at four-year colleges, in addition to ten master's and eight doctoral programs. According to Jin Hwan Oh (1985), foreign influence on journalism education is "tremendous," resulting in a field "equipped with Japanese technology, armored with American theory and reinforced by philosophy from Germany" (p. 22). But by the late 1980s, the picture was changing, as Korean-educated "second-generation" faculty began to teach in South Korean schools.

In China, a lecture series on journalism began in 1918, but little development in education occurred until after World War II. In the 1950s, Soviet influence was pervasive, but it later retreated from mass media education. By the mid-1980s, 26 universities had journalism departments, but only about 6 percent of journalists had specialized degrees. In fact, less than half had had any college training. With more than 1,200 mass media outlets, China will need an estimated 90,000 journalists by the year 2000.

Five important journalism schools in China today exist at Fudan University, whose prestigious program incorporated the department at St. John's University; People's University in Beijing (1950), which incorporated the department at Yenching; the Beijing Broadcast College (1959); Xiamen University (1981), located in a coastal city on the Taiwan Straits; and Jinan University in Guangzhou, which trains overseas Chinese to work at newspapers outside China. In addition, the Chinese Academy of Social Sciences in Beijing (1979) carries out mass media research and trains graduate students.

Pacific

In the late 1980s, Australian universities had no full professorships in mass media studies. The nation's 15 degree-granting programs were scattered over 18 universities and 50 colleges and institutions, with little uniformity in academic content. Much mass media research goes on in the social sciences and other departments rather than in journalism schools.

In New Zealand, by tradition, new employees joined newspapers out of high school and received on-the-job training. Now a number of training programs exist, but they are specialized short courses for high school graduates lasting less than a year.

PROSPECTS FOR THE FUTURE

The 1989 prodemocracy uprising in China dramatized the information-gathering potential of citizens armed with technology. In the aftermath of the uprising, facsimile machines were used to bypass government controls, carrying newspaper stories into China about events within China. Photocopying machines then multiplied the contraband stories so that they could be distributed widely. In China and elsewhere, camcorders in the hands of citizens have permitted amateurs to record scenes that authorities claim never happened or would have slipped quietly into history without being officially mentioned.

The vehemence of the June 1989 crackdown could mean that Chinese citizens may not gain the right of free expression for another 15 to 20 years. More immediately, the force with which the Chinese government brought the media into line raised questions about the media on Hong Kong, due to revert to China in 1997. Self-restraint has been evident since 1984, some journalists say.

By contrast, a pattern of expanded rights seems on the horizon for other countries. A free, well-developed media system does not need to precede or even accompany economic development. Taiwan, South Korea, and Singapore, with their partly free media and booming economies, have taught the world this lesson. They may yet teach the world that civil liberties—including free, developed, and diverse media—can follow as well as precede economic development, presenting a model quite different from that of the West.

Asia and the Pacific, like the rest of the world, partake in global culture. As Pico Iyer notes in *Video Night in Kathmandu* (1989), the "most remarkable anomalies in the global village today are surely those created by willy-nilly collisions and collusions between East and West" (p. 10). Iyer found bands in Burma (Myanmar) playing the Doors' song "L.A. Woman" to perfection, a million people in Beijing rushing to see *First Blood* within ten days of its opening, and a copy of *Best Disco '84 Vol. 2* for sale in Tibet.

Iyer questions the assumption that the West is corrupting the East, "both because corruption often says most about those who detect it and because the developing world may often have good reason to assent in its own transformation" (p. 13). It is hoped that our discussion has underscored the difference between modernization and Westernization and has helped readers appreciate the strength and variety of Asia's cultures and the depth of its media's roots.

CHAPTER 9

Latin America and the Caribbean

Michael B. Salwen, Bruce Garrison, and Robert T. Buckman

The 1980s ended as Latin America's "lost decade," with many economies in turmoil and living standards decreasing. When it began, the decade had been hailed as the "decade of democracy." Military dictatorships throughout the region were giving way to democratically elected governments. But today, the economic, political, and social direction of the region remains unclear. Demonstrations and strikes, spurred by austerity measures to deal with hyperinflation and growing national debts, broke out in Argentina, Colombia, Brazil, Bolivia, Guatemala, Uruguay, and elsewhere. Under such conditions, issues dealing with human rights and personal freedoms, including freedom of the press, were forced to take a back seat.

The state of affairs in Argentina, though worse than most, illustrates the situation. When former Argentine president Raul Alfonsín took office in 1983 after the seven-year rule of one of the hemisphere's most brutal dictatorships, he was hailed as a new breed of Latin American leader committed to liberal values, moderation, democracy, and human rights. He restored press freedom and other freedoms crushed under the dictatorship. Although he succeeded in restoring democracy, he left office in disgrace in 1989 five months before his term expired. Alfonsin's inability to deal with rampant inflation was his downfall. When he left his offices in the Casa Rosada, the Argentine equivalent of the White House, he was met by jeers, eggs, and, as one local newspaper delicately phrased it, "gross epithets that questioned the honorableness of the chief executive's mother."

In Peru, the democratic government of President Alan Garcia had to deal with both hyperinflation and rampant terrorism. The government imposed measures to silence news media sympathetic to the Sendero Luminoso ("Shining Path") guerrillas. In 1988, Luis Arce Borja, a former editor of the leftist newspaper *El Diario*, was arrested for publishing an antigovernment pamphlet. Four months earlier, Arce was arrested for publishing an interview with the leader of the Sendero Luminoso, Abimael Guzmán, known as "Chairman Gonzalo." Even Colombia, regarded as one of the continent's more stable democracies, was so wracked by drug-related terrorism that it passed an antiterrorist statute in January 1988. One of its articles that may affect the press sets penalties for anyone who has contacts with armed groups and refuses to reveal their whereabouts.

Perhaps journalists and communication scholars can be accused of making too much about press freedom. Critics of that Western notion correctly assert that the banner of press freedom is often waved by wealthy media owners who simply want to be left alone to rake in profits. This has been particularly true in the Latin American context, where many media owners have sided with the most conservative, even reactionary, elements who foot the media's advertising bills. Bolivian press scholar Luis Ramiro Beltrán summed up this view:

> The state is not the only enemy of democratic freedom in modern Latin America. Conservative and exploitative interests, native and from outside the region, have built a private and commercial mass communication system that, on several counts, falls short of being democratic. (From preface to Fox, 1988, p. 1)

If supporters of a free and unencumbered press put too much faith in private ownership of the press, some supporters of "benign" state intervention in the news media tend to overlook the possibility for governments to extend and abuse their powers. A free press can alert the public about government abuses of power. As Marvin Alisky (1981), a longtime observer of the Latin American press, wrote:

> Press freedom in Latin America does not guarantee that problems will be solved, but the converse holds that when press freedom is lacking both leaders and citizens do not face problems openly or solve them in ways that are equitable for all citizens. (p. 4)

Although economic troubles threaten Latin America's democracies and press freedom, the 1980s ended with greater press freedom. Paraguay, in the wake of a 1989 coup against Gen. Alfredo Stroessner, appears to be restoring democracy and press freedom. The nation's leading daily newspaper, *ABC Color*, which Stroessner closed in 1984, is publishing again.

Even in Chile, considered one of Latin America's last bastions of *caudillo* (strongman)-style military dictatorships. Chileans voiced their disapproval against Gen. Augusto Pinochet's continued rule by voting no in a yes-no plebiscite in 1988. The plebiscite made it possible for the press to express its anti-Pinochet feelings. Formerly underground publications that opposed Pinochet became openly available in kiosks, and many Chilean journalists took strong, aggressive stands against Pinochet's continued rule. The "no" faction received support in the form of televised segments from well-known Chilean entertainers as well as Jane Fonda and Christopher ("Superman") Reeves and in a music video by rock star Sting, who sang "They Dance Alone." The title referred to the widows of the "disappeared" during the early years of Pinochet's rule. A democratically elected president was sworn into office in Chile in March 1990. In December 1989, Patricio Aylwin, a centrist Christian Democrat, easily defeated Pinochet's hand-picked candidate in the first presidential election since 1970.

During the 1960s and 1970s, Fidel Castro's Cuba was lauded as an alternative political model, demonstrating how a small nation could assert its independence and achieve progress. By the early 1990s, however, the once-revolutionary Cuba was now viewed as an old-guard, conservative communist regime. This defect in the Cuban model was especially glaring in comparison with Soviet leader Mikhail Gorbachev's attempts to show "the human side of socialism" through *glasnost* (openness). Castro remains firmly committed to central planning and strengthening the authority of the Communist Party. In a number of speeches and interviews, Castro described his commitment to Marxist policies as "a sacred international mission." In 1989, the Cuban government took the unusual step of banning two Soviet publications, the weekly *Moscow News* and the monthly *Sputnik*, claiming that the publications justified "bourgeois democracy as the highest form of popular participation."

HISTORICAL HIGHLIGHTS

Compared to most regions of the world, Latin American nations were early adopters of print and, later, broadcast media. The reason for this early adoption was the willingness of a wealthy class to invest in media technologies and the lack of government involvement in the media policies. The laissez faire attitude of governments combined with the freewheeling nature of media entrepreneurs resulted in complaints that media were not operating for the public good.

In 1539, Mexico was the first nation in the hemisphere with a printing press, turning out books and pamphlets. From Mexico, the printing press was exported to Peru. The printing press, however, was not used for anything resembling journalism for almost two centuries. Reliable documentation on the first newspapers in the region are sparse, leading to a number of debates among historians as to which nation had the first newspaper: Brazil, Peru, Chile, or Mexico, depending upon what criteria is used to define a newspaper and which historian you believe. It is clear, however, that Latin America had an active press addressing important political issues by the early and mid nineteenth century.

From its earliest days, the Latin American press was in the hands of the hemisphere's wealthiest families. The family names associated with the operation of the press were the same names associated with politics, banking, agriculture, and various industries. These families frequently operated the press as their personal fiefdoms to advance their political views and aspirations. The editorial direction, not surprisingly, was usually conservative and sometimes downright reactionary.

In Peru, where the economic disparity was perhaps greater than anywhere else in the hemisphere, five major dailies controlled by leading families operated the press up to the eve of the 1968 revolution. During the 1930s, *El Comercio*, operated by the powerful Miro Quesada family, ran editorials praising Hitler and European fascism. *La Crónica*, in the hands of the Prados family, turned out four presidents. *La Prensa* was in the hands of Pedro Beltrán, a member of a planter family descended from conquistadors. As premier of the republic during the late 1950s, the conservative economist trained at the London School of Economics was credited with saving the crumbling economy by eliminating food subsidies, restricting credit, and enforcing tax collection. His achievement was praised by the nation's wealthy but earned him the animosity of the poor, who had to sacrifice their already low standard of living for the economic good of the nation. Beltrán appeared to brag when he once said, "I am the most hated man in Peru."

During the early twentieth century, mobs of peasants frequently attacked the leading Peruvian newspapers because they correctly viewed them as mouthpieces of the wealthy. In 1968 reform-minded generals took power in a military coup, and in 1974 they used police force to take control of the principal newspapers. Despite protestation from the Inter American Press Association and Western journalists, most of the Peruvian public appeared to support the takeover. During the 1970s, military dictatorships came to power throughout the region. Many newspapers, including many conservative newspapers, improved their tarnished reputations by defying these dictators.

Latin American nations were quick to adopt radio during the 1920s and 1930s and television during the 1950s. In most cases, the broadcast media, too, quickly fell into the hands of wealthy entrepreneurs. These entrepreneurs were interested in earning profits, so the majority of content tended to emphasize light entertainment over news. Investments from media organizations in the United States during the early days of Latin American broadcasting also ensured broadcast media's growth in the region.

New World Information and Communication Order

In Part I, we followed the development of the New World Information and Communication Order (NWICO) in UNESCO during the 1960s. NWICO was created to address the need to increase the quality and quantity of the flow of news around the world.

From the outset, many Latin American media organizations reacted coolly, if not hostilely, to the NWICO. Latin American news media have a long tradition of private ownership and subscribe to the concept of an independent press. Despite this, UNESCO's "experts" saw Latin America as the first region to implement many NWICO policies. The UNESCO-sponsored First Intergovernmental Conference on National Communication Policies in San José, Costa Rica, in 1976, attended by 20 Latin American nations, unanimously recommended national communication policies. The declaration was staunchly condemned by many Western participants and Latin American publishers and broadcasters.

Supporters of the NWICO in Latin America point to Latin America's "dependence" on Western news agencies in the United States and other nations. Such reliance on "alien cultures" for vital information, they argue, is tantamount to "media imperialism" and "cultural imperialism," modern-day forms of imperialism that rest on mass media propaganda rather than military force.

Most observers view the uneven news flow as a by-product of economic conditions favoring the Western media organizations with well-developed media systems and markets (i.e., economies of scale). According to this view, Western news agencies depend primarily on domestic audiences for the bulk of their revenue. Not surprisingly, then, the news media serve the interests of their Western audiences first. It costs little more money for the Western agencies to send the news they already gathered for their Western clients to developing nations.

Some Latin American intellectuals from the dependence school reject the explanation that the uneven news flow is a consequence of economies of scale. Many of these intellectuals maintain a "conspiracy view," which suggests that the uneven news flow is an intentional effort by Western news media, in collusion with Western governments, to dominate developing nations. Beltrán (1978) gave the most succinct summary of this view when he wrote that "cultural imperialism through communication is not an occasional and fortuitous event. . . . It is a vital process for 'imperial' countries to secure and maintain economic domination and political hegemony over others" (p. 185).

The alleged dangers of the dissemination of foreign information in Latin America is directed not only at news information. Entertainment and advertising also are singled out. NWICO supporters argue that as a result of Latin America's great disparities of poverty and wealth, entertainment television and advertising from the Western nations may contribute to the "rising tide of frustrations" by permitting the poor and lower classes to comprehend how bad off they are relative to the middle and upper classes. Advertising, in particular, may create desires for imported luxuries when Latin American nations need to reduce imports to deal with their economic problems. Many Latin American nations have lax advertising rules, allowing foreign firms to sell products and make product claims in Latin America that they cannot sell or claim in their home countries. In recent years, Argentina and Brazil have established self-regulatory advertising bodies to deal with these abuses.

PRINT MEDIA

Newspapers

Latin America has a number of regionally and even internationally prestigious newspapers of many political leanings. Traditionally, many large Latin American newspapers are associated with leading families and decidedly political views. There is a discernible trend, however, toward fewer political newspapers. Most of the best newspapers are published in the largest nations, including Mexico, Brazil, and Argentina. A number of them have earned reputations for defiantly challenging autocratic governments. But by and large, most of them are driven by market demand and are interested in providing their readers with both news and entertainment and earning profits, just as in any other industry.

Business and Management. Ownership of Latin American newspapers has yet to feel the same effect of the "grouping" of most major newspapers in the United States, where inheritance laws have discouraged family-owned newspapers and magazines from being passed down from generation to generation. Tradition in Latin American newspaper and magazine companies holds that sons or daughters continue to manage and direct the business and policymaking as a generation passes. However, some of the owners today are large national and international companies.

It is not unusual for a son or daughter to be groomed as publisher, editor, or general manager today. For example, at the prestigious *El Mercurio* in Santiago, Chile, the Edwards family has run the newspaper since 1880. It is currently managed by Agustín E. Edwards (publisher and editor) and his son Agustín J. Edwards (consultant to the newspaper).

Latin American owners and publishers have long been educated at the best universities in the United States and in Europe. But some of the leading companies are beginning to recruit managers from universities and colleges within their own countries.

Production Technology. Some of the leading Latin American newspapers and magazines have traditionally sought to be at the forefront of publishing technology. These publications, mainly the major dailies and international or "pan-American" magazines, have been financially successful and have had the resources to do so.

Others, desiring to make technological progress as new equipment and production techniques are developed, simply have not had the resources and have had to depend on secondhand equipment. In some countries, the government has severely restricted availability, ownership, and use of new technologies such as satellite earth stations. The smaller regional newspapers and magazines use equipment obtained on the resale market from the United States and elsewhere in the Americas.

The adoption of new technologies to advance the newspaper industry is a high priority for leading Latin American newspapers. Professor Bruce Garrison of the University of Miami reported the results of a 1984 survey of the adoption of technology at major Latin American newspapers. He found that two-thirds or more of the papers responding had adopted new technologies relating to electronic editing and reporting systems, computerized phototypesetting, and platemaking equipment. Presses and mailroom (distribution) equipment was also high on the modernization list. Furthermore, from one-quarter to one-third of the newspapers were adding information-retrieval and storage capabilities, new darkrooms, and even first-generation pagination systems.

El Mercurio in Santiago, Chile, is typical of modern plants in South America. Its spacious new facilities at the edge of the city are the envy of visiting North American journalists. With state-of-the-art production equipment in a large, modern building, the company produces its flagship newspaper and 13 other newspapers totaling more than 520,000 circulation daily and 643,000 on Sunday. Mexico's *El Norte*, in Monterrey, is also a leader in technological innovation and is currently developing databases and satellite technology.

Prestige Newspapers.   In each Latin American country, a handful of newspapers has emerged to form the prestige or elite press of that nation. These newspapers have varying political orientations and are at times in and out of favor with their governments. Some attain degrees of prestige despite sensational formats because of investigative journalism or quality business sections. John Merrill (1968) says that elite newspapers "represent the serious, informed, and influential journalism of their respective nations" (p. xiii). Merrill rated two of Latin America's newspapers as world-caliber: Mexico's *Excelsior* and Argentina's *La Prensa*. Merrill said an elite international press should be complete in foreign coverage, concerned with interpretation, graphically dignified, serious and lacking sensationalism, impartial, and imaginative, among other criteria.

Although circulation by itself is not an indicator of prestige, this factor cannot be overlooked. Unfortunately, gauging circulation estimates in Latin America is not always easy. The circulation figures being presented here may vary from those reported elsewhere. Since Latin American newspapers usually do not subscribe to formal audits, the figures should be taken as no more than estimates.

Argentina

Economic troubles since the late 1980s have seriously hampered the work of Argentine newspapers. Only the strongest have been able to survive the national economic crisis. During 1989, *El Heraldo* of Buenos Aires, established in August 1988 and managed by the prestigious English-language *Buenos Aires Herald*, shut down. The final edition's banner headline told the story: HYPERINFLATION SWALLOWED EL HERALDO. According to the story, the paper could not recoup the costs for ink, newsprint, photo supplies, and other materials, which increased 430 percent during April and May. During the same period, the paper increased its cover price 300 percent, and circulation fell rapidly.

Argentina's *La Prensa* and *La Nación* are widely rated as among the best in the region. *Clarín* is sometimes also included in this list. The three are part of nearly 50 daily newspapers publishing in Argentina. *La Prensa* was founded in 1869 by Domingo Faustino Sarmiento, one of the nation's most revered literary figures, who also was elected president. It is an independent family-owned newspaper that has the motto "Truth, honor, freedom, progress, civilization." It refuses any government

subsidies and has fought against the likes of former dictator Juan
Domingo Perón to stop censorship and seizures over the past century.
Perón closed the newspaper from 1951 to 1955 and forced its editor,
Alberto Gainza Paz, into exile in Uruguay. Though some authorities
believe that *La Prensa's* hemispheric influences have waned, it remains
influential with national and hemispheric political and economic decision makers. *La Nación* was founded in 1870 by Bartolomé Mitre, a
former president of Argentina.

   Clarín, established in Buenos Aires in 1945, has become a leading
force in the nation, even though it is a sensational tabloid. *Clarín* is the
nation's largest-circulation newspaper, with a 600,000-circulation
morning tabloid that features business news.

   The brutal military dictatorship that ruled from 1976 to 1983 led to
severe press restrictions. *La Prensa* and *La Nación* were forced into
docility during this period, and other newspapers were frequently closed
for periods of a few days as sanctions for having printed objectionable
news about the government. One paper, *La Opinión*, was seized outright for allegedly collaborating with leftist guerrillas. The paper was
turned into a government mouthpiece and its editor, Jacobo Timerman,
was jailed, tortured, and held under house arrest without charges for two
years before being allowed to emigrate to Israel in 1979.

Brazil

With 224 daily newspapers in 1985, Brazil has the fifth largest landmass
in the world and the largest population in Latin America—most of it
concentrated in urban areas such as São Paulo and Rio de Janeiro. In fact,
Diario de la Tarde, headquartered in Curitaba, has a combined daily
circulation of 2.25 million. *Tribuna de Imprensa*, an evening daily in
Rio de Janeiro, has a combined circulation of 2 million copies.

   However, *Jornal do Brasil*, *O Estado de São Paulo*, and *O Globo* are
often rated as the three best newspapers in Brazil. *O Estado de São Paulo*
is considered one of the region's most outstanding newspapers. *Journal
do Brasil* and *O Globo* are based in Rio de Janeiro; *O Estado* is published
in São Paulo. *O Estado*, owned by the Mesquita family, has long boasted
a reputation for journalistic independence. It was closed for opposing
the dictatorship of Getulio Vargas in the 1940s and was placed under
prior censorship in the 1970s by the military government.

The Caribbean

The most influential newspapers in the Caribbean and the West Indies
are located in Jamaica and Puerto Rico. The *Daily Gleaner*, of Kingston,
Jamaica, is one of the elite of the Caribbean. The very name Gleaner is

synonymous with newspapers on the island. The Gleaner Company Limited, its owner, also produces the *Star*. The morning *Gleaner* circulates 40,000 daily and 89,000 on Sundays. The *Star* circulates 55,000 afternoons and 105,000 for the *Week-End Star*. *El Nuevo Dia* and *El Vocero de Puerto Rico*, both published in San Juan, Puerto Rico, battle for circulation supremacy in the U.S. territory. Both print about 200,000 copies daily.

Chile

Santiago's *El Mercurio* was founded in Valparaiso in 1827. It claims to be the oldest Spanish-language newspaper published in the world today. It was acquired by Agustín Edwards in 1880, who built the paper into the nation's most prestigious daily. In 1900, Edwards launched a Santiago edition. It had an unbroken record of continuous publication until the Marxist Allende government closed it for one day on June 16, 1973. It is published today by the third and fourth generations of Agustín Edwardses, father Agustín E. Edwards and son Agustín J. Edwards. El Mercurio Newspapers, now a total of at least 14 newspapers, including *El Mercurio de Valparaiso*, has a daily combined-edition circulation of 520,000 and a Sunday combined-edition circulation of 645,000.

The conservative *El Mercurio* was once recognized as one of the best daily newspapers in the Southern Hemisphere. Its image has been severely tarnished over the years, however, because of its close association with the Pinochet government and the disclosure that it took money from the United States' Central Intelligence Agency during Salvador Allende's last days to resist the government's economic pressure.

After the overthrow of Allende, the Pinochet government immediately suspended the publication of daily newspapers and magazines that had been supportive of Allende. For more than a decade, the only dailies published in Santiago were those owned by the Edwards and Picó families, who were generally supportive of Pinochet. The Picó family own the nation's largest-circulation newspaper, the tabloid *La Tercera de la Hora*, as well as a spin-off, *La Cuarta*.

By the 1980s, Pinochet gradually began to relax his grip on the press. In 1987, he permitted Emilio Filippi, a respected journalist who had resigned as editor of the news magazine *Ercilla* in 1976 because of its support of Pinochet, to publish *La Epoca*, an opposition daily. It became an instant success. Filippi earlier had founded the opposition news magazine *Hoy* in 1977. A smaller, less professional opposition daily, *Fortín Mapocho*, was also allowed to publish in 1987. Since Pinochet's defeat in a 1988 plebiscite and the subsequent election of a civilian president, Chilean press freedom has been essentially restored to its pre-Allende levels.

Colombia

Drug wars have become a major concern of the Colombian press. Wealthy and dangerous drug lords often murder or injure journalists to express disagreement with stands taken or displeasure with unwanted publicity. The drug lords bomb newspaper offices, causing millions of dollars in total damages. In 1989, the Colombian government cracked down on the cartel, which then declared "all-out war" on Colombian institutions, including journalists who, according to the declaration, "have attacked and insulted us. . . . We will not respect the families of those who have not respected our families." A short time after the declaration was issued, Bogotá's *El Espectador*, which vigorously called for action against the cartel, was bombed. The editor of *El Espectador*, Guillermo Cano, was slain in an ambush in 1986.

Hard-hitting coverage of the cartel, however, is not the norm in Colombia. Such coverage has been largely limited to a few leading dailies in Bogotá. Many Colombian journalists have been intimidated into self-censorship. A leading Colombian human rights group, the Permanent Committee for the Defense of Human Rights in Colombia, polled 1,500 journalists and reported that 78 percent censored their work in some way. Many drop their bylines from stories, and editors regularly do not use their own reporters' controversial articles when similar stories are available from the foreign press.

Two of Bogotá's daily newspapers, *El Tiempo* and *El Espectador*, often rank among the nation's best newspapers and have built reputations for challenging the cartel. Each of the newspapers has a daily circulation of about 200,000. *El Tiempo*, though strongly conservative today, was founded by members of the Liberal Party in 1911. Its one-time publisher Eduardo Santos was also president of the country from 1938 to 1942. A Conservative president, Laureano Gomez (1950–1953), founded his party's daily newspaper, *El Siglo*. The politically prominent Pastrana family of the Liberal Party established a new daily, *La Prensa*, in 1988.

Cuba

Cuba has no privately owned press; its official newspapers and magazines are owned and operated by the government, although a few crude newsletters and magazines are occasionally published. *Granma*, the official newspaper of the Communist Party, is Havana's morning daily and Sunday newspaper, with an estimated daily circulation of 650,000. The newspaper is small (in terms of number of pages printed daily) compared with other Latin American and Caribbean newspapers.

Granma also publishes an English edition (as well as ones in other languages) and is available in some U.S. libraries.

Cuba's largest afternoon newspaper is *Juventud Rebelde*. It is published by the Union of Cuban Youth, and its content focuses on young people. Its circulation is around 250,000. Havana's third largest newspaper, *Las Trabajadores*, circulates 120,000 daily. It is operated by the Cuban Federation of Labor.

Ecuador

There were 16 daily newspapers in Ecuador in 1985. *El Comercio*, of Quito, is the most highly regarded. With a circulation of 135,000 daily and Sunday, *El Comercio* is Quito's largest newspaper. The largest-circulation newspaper in Ecuador is Guayaquil's *El Universo*, with a circulation of 190,000 mornings and Sundays. *El Universo* leans more toward entertainment and sports content.

El Salvador

The nation's largest newspaper is the morning tabloid *La Prensa Gráfica*, with 96,000 copies printed daily. It was started in 1903. *El Diario de Hoy* is published mornings and Sundays and circulates 74,000 copies daily and 77,500 Sundays. Both newspapers are published in the capital, San Salvador, and are owned by conservative families.

Guatemala

With a history of poverty, illiteracy, dictatorship, political instability, and guerrilla warfare, Guatemala has not been fertile ground for a strong independent press. One success story, however, was *El Imparcial*, which was founded in 1922 by Alejandro Córdoba. Córdoba was assassinated in 1944 during the political turmoil that brought about the downfall of the enigmatic dictator Jorge Ubico. *El Imparcial* survived six decades of political turbulence and was considered the country's newspaper of record until it folded because of financial problems in 1984.

For more than three decades, the country's dominant daily has been the conservative but reasonably professional *Prensa Libre*, established in 1951 by Pedro Julio García and three other maverick reporters from *El Imparcial*. A third major player in the daily newspaper market, *El Gráfico*, was founded in 1963 by the Carpio Nicolle brothers, Jorge, Roberto, and Mario, who introduced offset printing to Guatemala.

Until the late 1980s, Guatemala had experienced only one decade of genuine press freedom—from the overthrow of Ubico in 1944 to the ouster of the pro-Marxist elected government of President Jacobo Arbenz in a CIA-engineered coup in 1954. The military continued to rule Guatemala through a series of rigged elections until a group of reform-minded officers seized control in 1982.

The period of right-wing military dictatorship gave rise to a guerrilla movement, which reached a violent crescendo in the late 1960s and early 1970s. The Guatemalan press, then as now, was highly politicized, and journalists found themselves under attack both from the government, which sought to control information either through intimidation or *fafas* (bribes), and from the guerrillas, who regarded the newspapers as part of the establishment. Approximately 40 journalists were slain during this period. Among the victims was *Prensa Libre* cofounder Isidoro Zarco, who was gunned down by leftists in 1970. As recently as 1982 and 1983, two *Prensa Libre* editors were kidnapped and released after the newspaper paid a total of $1 million in ransom, a financial blow from which the paper has yet to fully recover. Its editorial offices are still guarded by shotgun-wielding sentries.

In 1985, Guatemalans had their first free elections since 1951. The winner was Christian Democrat Vinicio Cerezo. As an example of the continued politicization of the press, Cerezo's leading challenger on the right was *El Gráfico* publisher Jorge Carpio Nicolle; incredibly, Carpio Nicolle's brother Roberto was elected Cerezo's vice president in the same election. In a curious twist for Latin America, a left-of-center civilian president has been the target of intense criticism from two conservative dailies. Cerezo has not been above using legal measures, including Guatemala's right-of-replay law, to harass *Prensa Libre* and *El Gráfico.* Cerezo's only editorial voice has been the government-owned daily, *Diario de Centroamerica,* a dull tabloid traditionally compiled from government handouts. As Guatemala enters the 1990s, persistent economic problems and political unrest raise questions about the continuing existence of its democracy and its new press freedom.

Mexico

Mexico, along with Brazil and Argentina, has developed into a cultural and political center in Latin America, so, not surprisingly, some of its newspapers are considered among the best in the region. However, as a result of active government attempts to compromise journalists with bribes and control over newsprint supplies, among other methods, many newspapers have been compromised and are seen as publicity agents for politicians and agencies. The provincial newspapers are thought to be even more accommodating to the government than Mexico City's newspapers.

The daily *Excélsior* of Mexico City is still regarded as among Mexico's best newspapers, but its competition is catching up. *Excélsior* has been compared to the *New York Times* and the *Times* of London by some experts, primarily because of its role as the country's "newspaper of record." Inter American Press Association assistant director Julio Munoz believes that in the past 20 years, *Excélsior* has been equaled in influence by newcomers such as *El Norte* in Monterrey. *El Norte* has made its reputation in the 1980s as a technological leader that has grown rapidly in circulation. As it has improved its quality in production, it has also improved in reporting quality as well.

Excelsior, which calls itself the "newspaper of national life," was founded in 1917 and has a circulation of about 175,000 copies daily. Two other Mexico City newspapers, *Novedades* and *Uno Mas Uno*, also enjoy some national prestige.

Novedades, founded in 1934, is owned by Romulo O'Farrill, Jr. O'Farrill is president and publisher of Novedades Editores, S.A., in Mexico City, which publishes eight newspapers. However, he is also chairman of the board of Televisa, Mexico's major media conglomerate, which owns 156 television stations throughout the country. O'Farrill also owns the *News*, *Novedades de Acapulco*, *Novedades de Baja California*, and four other newspapers.

Another prominent media empresario is Mario Vásquez Raña, who in the late 1970s purchased the *El Sol* newspaper chain from the government. The government had taken over the financially troubled chain, then sold it when it proved unable to turn a profit. Vásquez Raña not only made the chain profitable but expanded it into a media empire that now totals more than 50 papers throughout Mexico. In 1986, Vásquez Raña purchased 90 percent interest in the financially troubled UPI but surrendered operational control a year later.

The Mexican government has started its own national version of *USA Today*, a daily called *El Nacional*. Produced using satellite technology to ensure availability in several cities on the same day, *El Nacional* has built a circulation of 120,000 daily. One advantage *El Nacional* has over other privately held newspapers is newsprint supply. Since the Mexican government owns the only newsprint plant, *El Nacional* does not find newsprint availability a problem, as many other Mexican newspapers sometimes do.

One individual who successfully defied the government's newsprint monopoly is Julio Scherer García, who in 1976 was ousted as editor of *Excélsior* in an in-house coup inspired by then-President Luis Echeverría. The president, himself a moderate leftist, had found himself outflanked on the left by *Excélsior's* increasingly caustic editorial criticism of his administration. Scherer García sought to launch his own magazine, *Proceso,* but the state-owned PIPSA (Producer and Importer of Paper) refused to sell him the necessary paper. Scherer García then bought the paper at full price on the open market, *Proceso* appeared on schedule, and it has remained one of the country's most successful magazines. Scherer García subsequently founded an equally successful daily newspaper, *Unomasuno.*

The case of *Proceso* and *Unomasuno* are aberrations, however, as the government and the long-dominant ruling party, the PRI, have managed to keep most editorial criticism mild, either through intimidation or through the time-honored practice of granting *mordidas,* or bribes, to notoriously underpaid journalists. Those journalists who have defied the government have frequently found themselves in physical danger. The best known such case was that of Manuel Buendía, who wrote an acerbic front-page column for *Excélsior* in the style of Jack Anderson. Long a burr under the saddles of three presidents and their government ministers, Buendía was assassinated in 1984. In 1989, the former head of the national police force was charged with masterminding the murder. Journalists in northern Mexico who take on the powerful drug traffickers—for whom it is widely believed corrupt political and police officials are working—have been killed at an alarming rate. Jesús Michel Jacobo, who often condemned drug traffickers in his column in the daily *El Sol de Sinaloa,* was assassinated in December 1987. Two months later, Manuel Burgueño Orduño, a columnist for *El Sol del Pacífico* in Mazatlán who also focused on crime and the drug traffic, was shot to death at home by masked men. Héctor Félix Miranda, who used the pen name "El Gato" ("The Cat"), wrote a satirical column for the iconoclastic weekly *Zeta* in the state of Baja California; he was gunned down on his way to work in April 1988, ostensibly because he was about to link the state attorney general to drug traffickers. A former policeman was convicted of the murder in 1989 and sentenced to 27 years in prison. President Carlos Salinas de Gotari, who assumed office in 1988, has shown unprecedented tolerance for the PRI's opposition parties, and observers are waiting to see whether this new attitude will extend to aggressive journalists as well.

Nicaragua

Because Nicaragua never has had a democratic tradition, its newspapers never have been allowed to operate in a climate free of intimidation. In 1936 Anastasio Somoza established a dynastic dictatorship that would last for more than 40 years. The Somoza family controlled one daily newspaper, *La Prensa Gráfica*, while the Chamorro family owned the country's only true opposition paper, *La Prensa*. *La Prensa* was closed several times, both by the elder Somoza, who was assassinated in 1956, and by his son, Anastasio Jr., who came to power in 1967.

On January 11, 1978, the editor of *La Prensa*, Pedro Joaquín Chamorro, Sr., was assassinated on his way to work. Somoza sought unconvincingly to disavow any connection with the murder, and the previously ambivalent middle class turned against Somoza and toward the Sandinista rebels who were seeking to overthrow him by force.

After the Sandinistas took power in July 1979, they nationalized the Somoza paper and another privately owned daily, *Novedades*. In their place appeared *Barricada*, the official organ of the Sandinist National Liberation Front, or FSLN. Because the slain Chamorro was a genuine martyr of the anti-Somoza struggle and because his widow, Violeta, was briefly a member of the first Sandinista junta, *La Prensa* was allowed to remain in the family's hands. However, its criticism of the government's Marxist policies led to frequent harassment and closure. A third daily, *El Nuevo Diario*, began publication in 1980 as an independent, pro-Sandinista voice. Interestingly, all three papers are edited by members of the Chamorro family. Reprisals against *La Prensa* reached their height in mid-1986 when the paper was ordered closed. The order was finally lifted 16 months later because of pressure on President Daniel Ortega from other Central American presidents to liberalize his regime, and *La Prensa* outpaces the two progovernment papers in circulation. *La Prensa*'s publisher, Violeta Barrios de Chamorro, widow of the martyred Pedro Joaquín, scored an upset victory over Ortega in the February 1990 presidential election and became president in April 1990.

Panama

Once a highly competitive industry, the Panamanian press has suffered severe repression under the military-dominated governments that have ruled the comparatively prosperous country since 1968. Gen. Omar Torrijos, who came to power in a coup that year, used judicial trickery to seize two newspapers, *El Panamá América* and *Crítica*, from the underage heirs of their late founder, Harmodio Arias. Torrijos converted them and a new daily, *Matutino*, into government mouthpieces. Torrijos also jailed Tomas Gabriel Altamirano Duque, owner of the country's leading daily, *La Estrella de Panamá*, which was established in 1853. Altamirano Duque was released on the condition that his family's paper adhere to the government line, which it did for more than 20 years.

As a concession to U.S. president Jimmy Carter, with whom Torrijos was negotiating a new treaty by which Panama would assume control of the Panama Canal in 1999, Torrijos agreed to end human rights abuses and restore press freedom. The result was Law 11 of 1978, which outlined a broader, if not unlimited, degree of press freedom. Taking the new law at its word, Roberto I. Eisenmann, a businessman who had been exiled by Torrijos for three years, established a publicly owned daily, *La Prensa*, in 1980. The paper was a persistent critic of Torrijos and, after Torrijos' death in a 1981 plane crash, his eventual successor, Gen. Manuel Noriega. Despite years of harassment, including acts of vandalism, libel suits, and beatings of its reporters, *La Prensa* quickly passed *La Estrella* and the government-owned dailies in circulation.

As the excesses of the Noriega regime led to mounting public unrest, two other dailies, *El Siglo* and *Extra*, joined the opposition camp in 1986. As part of a general crackdown against dissent, Noriega closed the three opposition papers in July 1987 and, except for a five-week reappearance in early 1988, they remained idle until the U.S. invasion of Panama in December 1989. Eisenmann and *La Prensa's* most widely read columnist, Guillermo Sánchez Borbón, lived in exile in Miami because of death threats from 1986 until the U.S. invasion. With the fall of Noriega and the restoration of a democratically elected government under President Guillermo Endara, Panamanian press freedom essentially has been restored. The Arias family regained control of its family's confiscated papers, and *La Estrella* now expresses unwavering support for the Endara regime.

Paraguay

Paraguay, with a population of about 3 million, experienced much change at the end of the 1980s. The major newspaper, *ABC Color*, resumed publication in 1989 after dictator Gen. Alfredo Stroessner was ousted in a coup. The paper was established by Aldo Zuccolillo, an Italian immigrant and an acquaintance of Stroessner, in 1967. Published in Asunción, with a daily circulation of about 75,000, *ABC Color's* battles with the government in the late 1970s and early 1980s generated international attention.

The provisional president promised to bring democracy, including freedom of expression, and vowed not to arrest journalists for carrying out their duties. One of his first actions was to permit *ABC Color* to reopen, exactly five years to the day after it was shut down.

Another leading paper, *Hoy*, is published by Humberto Domínguez Dibb, Stroessner's former son-in-law. And the newspaper *El Diario* was established by Nícholás Bo, a wealthy businessman and television station owner.

Peru

As a result of the wide disparity of poverty and wealth, Peru has developed a small, elite press associated with the nation's leading families. The nation has 30 daily newspapers, 16 in Lima alone, where most of the nation's wealth is concentrated. For almost a century, Peru boasted two of South America's most respected dailies, *El Comercio* and *La Prensa*. The conservative *El Comercio*, a morning (140,000 copies circulation) and Sunday (200,000 copies) daily, celebrated its 150th birthday in 1989.

As a result of a 1968 coup by a group of reform-minded army officers, the government attempted to shift the mass media into the hands of various "social sectors" in society. *El Comercio* became the organ of the Indian peasants. *La Prensa* became the organ of the labor sector. Other newspapers reflected the views of educators, lawyers, and so forth. This unique experiment captured substantial attention in journalistic circles around the world but ultimately failed because the daily newspapers became political organs with little credibility.

One result of the expropriation was the growth of weekly newspapers, some of them established by the same families whose newspapers had been confiscated. After 12 years, the military acknowledged its failure and held presidential elections in 1980. The winner was Fernando Belaunde Terry, the same president who had been ousted in the 1968 coup. His first act upon taking office was to sign a decree restoring the confiscated newspapers to their original owners. However, *La Prensa* folded in 1983 because of financial losses.

Most of Peru's newspapers reflect the conservative views of their conservative owners. A politically moderate newspaper is *La República*, the mouthpiece of the American Popular Revolutionary Alliance (APRA), whose candidate Alan Garcia won the presidency in 1985. *El Diario* is a leftist tabloid that not only reports but praises the Sendero Luminoso guerrillas.

Although Peruvian journalists enjoy considerable press freedom, the practice of journalism has become risky in Peru, as it has in neighboring Colombia. Journalists are frequently the targets of guerrilla attacks and often get caught in the cross fire while covering military operations.

Uruguay

El Diario, with a circulation of about 170,000 daily, is the largest newspaper in Uruguay. However, *El Día* is regarded as one of the best newspapers in the nation. *El Día* was founded in 1886 as the Colorado

Party organ. *El Espectador* is the mouthpiece of the Blanco Party, which won the 1989 presidential election.

Venezuela

Most of Venezuela's 69 daily newspapers are closely associated with political parties or are outright political organs. *El Universal*, published in Caracas, is regarded as one of the nation's best dailies. It was founded in 1901 and draws its reporting strength from stories on energy and iron ore. *El Universal* circulates 160,000 copies mornings and 200,000 copies on Sundays, but it is not the nation's largest newspaper. The largest is *Meridiano*, with 300,000 copies daily and Sunday, followed by *Ultimas Noticias*, with 285,000 mornings. Both *Meridiano* and *Ultimas Noticias* are published in Caracas.

Magazines

In every major city in Latin America, small kiosks dot the street corners. Hanging from the sides and inside walls of these tiny businesses are literally dozens of Latin America's newspapers and magazines. Both newspapers and magazines depend on these street-corner vendors for circulation. This sales system is reminiscent of the news stalls of Paris or Madrid and takes advantage of the fact that Latin Americans tend to go into the streets of their cities more than do North Americans.

Mail-delivered magazines and newspapers, as well as home-delivered newspapers, are the exception rather than the rule in most of Latin America. Kiosks, instead, are the heart of the magazine business in this region. Irregular mail service and higher costs are two reasons for the success of the kiosks in Latin America.

There are numerous magazines that are originally written, edited, and produced in the urban centers of Latin America. Even though some companies in the United States and Portugal produce Spanish-language and Portuguese-language editions of popular U.S. and European magazines, most magazines are published and distributed within each country.

For example, *Buen Hogar/Good Housekeeping*, *Cosmopolitan en Español/Cosmopolitan*, and *Mecánica Popular/Popular Mechanics* are written and edited in the United States, printed in Mexico, and shipped back to the United States for distribution throughout Latin America.

Part of the reason for this complex form of production and distribution is related to costs. But the strict laws affecting content that exist in each country also make elaborate production planning necessary. And because these laws vary greatly from nation to nation, it is legally and logistically complicated to publish magazines from outside a country and to import them each week or month.

Though a number of major Latin American magazines are distributed in just one country, numerous "pan-American" magazines also exist. In addition to those already mentioned are *TV y novelas, Business Week, Ideas para su Hogar, Cogneta, Time, Geomundo,* and *tu.*

One of the leading publishers of pan-American magazines is the Spanish conglomerate Anaya. Anaya, based in Madrid, is one of Spain's largest publishers. Anaya was founded in 1959 by German entrepreneur Sánchez Ruiperez, Anaya's president. In 1989, Anaya purchased Editorial America from the Venezuelan-based Bloque de Armas publishing company. Anaya now controls 40 book and magazine publishing companies.

Anaya's subsidiary, Editorial America, is headquartered in Miami and employs several thousand persons—300 in Miami alone. Editorial America publishes *Vanidades, Cosmopolitan, Buen Hogar, Mecánica Popular, TV y novelas,* and 35 other magazines that are read in 23 countries. It maintains offices in Chile, Colombia, Ecuador, Peru, Mexico, and Venezuela. Editorial America was founded in 1961 in New York by Cuban exiles.

In addition to the regionwide magazines, there are a number of highly respected national news and feature magazines. One of the most professional is Brazil's *Manchete,* a full-size news-photo magazine in the style of *Life;* in fact, the magazine has ties to Time-Life. Probably the most influential newsmagazine in Brazil is *Veja,* which resembles the U.S. newsmagazines in format. Other journalistically professional magazines that mix news and photo features include *Siete Días* in Argentina; *Cromos* in Colombia; and *Bohemia* in Cuba, one of the few holdovers from the prerevolutionary period. High-quality national newsmagazines include *Tiempo* and *Proceso* in Mexico; *Ercilla, Hoy,* and *¿Que Pasa?* in Chile; *Somos* in Argentina; *Resumen* in Venezuela; and *Caretas* and *Oiga* in Peru.

Some magazines, in political and economic battles with their governments, do not last long under one name. Instead, some fold and are resurrected under a new name. After the failed assassination attempt on Chilean dictator Augusto Pinochet in 1986, the foreign editor of *Análisis,* which was critical of Pinochet, was abducted and murdered.

Some magazine publishers have battled their conservative national governments and the Catholic church over content. Though most battles are over political or social content, the content does not have to be politically or socially sensitive to cause conflict. Attempts at censorship or even closings have involved invasion-of-privacy matters or have centered on nudity or sexually explicit content.

ELECTRONIC MEDIA

Latin America's broadcasting systems are generally more advanced and sophisticated than those elsewhere in the developing world. However, the variation in radio and television development within the region is such that it is impossible to examine Latin America as a homogenous unit. Popular access to the electronic media ranges from 37 radio receivers and five television sets per 1,000 population in Haiti to 1,100 radios in Chile and roughly 200 television sets per 1,000 population in Argentina, Chile, and Panama.

Cuba, the third nation in Latin America to adopt television, developed a sophisticated television system run by profit-minded entrepreneurs during the 1950s. The brothers Goar and Abel Mestre built CMQ-TV into a network of stations that rivaled those in New York for their technical quality.

The Mestres already had established a reputation for broadcasting creativity years earlier through CMQ radio. In 1948, they established a station called Radio Reloj (Radio Clock), believed to have been the world's first 24-hour, seven-day-a-week, all-news station. The station and its fast-paced format of short news segments accompanied by the sound of a ticking clock became a fixture in Cuban popular culture that survives to this day.

CMQ-TV proved it was a major network to be reckoned with when, in 1953, the station carried the first live television broadcast from one nation to another. The station sent a DC-3 airliner over the south Florida Keys equipped with two antennae and an RCA radio transmitter to pick up the signal of the World Series broadcast and relay it back to Cuba, where it was then transmitted throughout the island. The event received wide attention in Cuba, where baseball is a popular sport. According to Abel Mestre, active in 1990 in the Cuban exile community in Miami and looking back on the historic event 37 years later, the event caused nervous tension in the CMQ organization because the airliner had a limited amount of fuel. If the games ran too long into extra innings, the plane might have to land, ending the broadcast and turning what was meant as a publicity event to promote the station into a public relations disaster. In September 1961, the Cuban government took over the CMQ broadcasting system, the last independent broadcasting outlet in Cuba. Goar Mestre went on to establish stations or program distribution centers in Argentina, Venezuela, and Peru.

Ownership Patterns

Traditionally influenced by both U.S. and European culture, Latin America has steered a middle course between the U.S. model of private ownership of broadcast media with an emphasis on entertainment and the European tradition of public ownership, which places more value on educational and cultural programming. Most Latin American countries have a true mixed economy in which most broadcasting stations are in private hands. Governments, however, retain ownership of a few key stations or even networks and wield regulatory power over the privately owned media. In some countries, such as Mexico, Peru, and Uruguay, the public sector pioneered radio or television broadcasting, only later allowing private stations to enter the field. In others, such as Argentina and Chile, entrepreneurs led the way, and the governments established rival stations to ensure some degree of educational and cultural programming.

As with the overall level of sophistication, the degree of private versus state control varies from country to country. In Cuba, the broadcast media are totally controlled by the state or the Communist Party. In Costa Rica and Ecuador, there is almost complete private ownership. In Colombia, there are several private radio networks and one government network, but the government holds a monopoly on television broadcasting. Virtually all private radio stations and networks in Latin America are commercial. Privately owned television, of course, is also commercial, but some government-owned stations rely on subsidies in the European manner, while others accept advertising to allay expenses; a few employ both methods of financing.

Broadcast Media as Political Weapons

In addition to ownership of broadcast media by both governments and private business, it is not uncommon in Latin America for political parties, universities, labor unions, the Catholic church, and various Protestant sects to control broadcasting facilities, usually radio. Perhaps the best-known model of university control of broadcasting is in Chile, where four of the country's five TV stations and their repeaters are owned by universities; the government owns the fifth.

The broadcast media have frequently been used as pawns in the struggle for political power in the region. Whenever there has been a military coup, radio and television stations have been among the first targets seized. Dictatorships have either controlled the broadcast media outright or relied on censorship or intimidation to keep privately owned stations in line. For those that refuse to do so, forcible closure has been common. The most celebrated recent case is Radio Católica in Nicaragua, the Catholic station that was shut down by the Sandinista government for more than a year.

Other instances of forcible closures include Radio Nanduti in Paraguay, which was closed by the Stroessner dictatorship but resumed broadcasting after his overthrow in 1989, and several stations in Panama whose owners defied the dictatorship of Manuel Antonio Noriega in 1988. Cuba maintains a powerful shortwave station that transmits throughout Latin America in several languages. Guerrilla movements, meanwhile, such as those in Salvador, Peru, and Colombia, operate clandestine radio stations for propaganda purposes. Radio is an especially potent medium in Latin America because (1) receivers are relatively inexpensive and do not require an outside power source, (2) programming is less expensive to produce than for television, and (3) medium-range and short-range signals can reach the most isolated communities in the rugged, inaccessible regions of such countries as Brazil, Bolivia, Peru, and Colombia.

Though television is not as pervasive as radio, it is still a highly influential medium in most Latin American countries and it, too, is often used as a political weapon in the volatile politics of the region. Both broadcast journalism and entertainment production have frequently suffered at the hands of repressive regimes. Argentina and Chile are cases in point. Because journalists and people in the creative arts in Latin America tend to lean toward leftist causes, the right-wing military coups in Chile in 1973 and in Argentina in 1976 resulted in death, imprisonment, or exile for much of the talent in the nascent television industries in those countries.

In Peru, the military government seized power in 1968 and decreed 51 percent public ownership of the broadcast facilities, which had been controlled by a few wealthy families. Although the socially conscious generals intended to transform the radio and television industries into instruments of national development, the salaries they paid were so low that writers, directors, technicians, journalists, and entertainers voluntarily left for countries such as Colombia and Venezuela, where they could command higher pay.

Because of the powerful impact of television on the public of any given country, the independent stations do not even have to be critical of dictatorial regimes for journalists to engender suspicion and hostility. Even objective news reporting can lead to censorship or closure, and investigative reporting can be hazardous. An extreme case of television's sociopolitical impact occurred in Haiti in 1986 during the autocratic dictatorship of Jean-Claude Duvalier. The state-run television station carried a program that depicted Madame Duvalier's shopping spree at some of Paris's most exclusive shops. The program sparked spontaneous rioting by Haiti's deprived masses—most of whom had access to television only in storefronts—and within days the Duvaliers were forced to flee the country, ending a dynastic dictatorship that had lasted nearly 30 years.

Although the Brazilian military government of 1964–1985 was

more enlightened than the Argentine or Chilean dictatorship in allowing creative expression in the entertainment field, it showed little tolerance for aggressive television journalists. Several were arrested or harassed, and at least two died in police custody. The former Noriega government in Panama closed down independent TV stations for reporting on opposition rallies. In countries with ongoing insurgencies, such as Salvador, Colombia, Guatemala, and Peru, journalists are frequently caught in the cross fire between government and antigovernment forces.

Broadcasting and National Development

Aside from their use as a political tool and their traditional function as a source of entertainment and information, the broadcast media in general, and radio in particular, have been used increasingly in Latin America as instruments for national development. Although literacy is relatively high in Latin America, there are pockets where illiteracy remains a serious social problem. Radio has been especially important as a development tool among illiterate and isolated peasants.

In addition to Spanish or Portuguese, programs are aired in the native Indian languages in Guatemala, Peru, Bolivia, and Paraguay, carrying information on animal husbandry, agricultural techniques, family health, and birth control. Catholic-owned Radio San Gabriel in Bolivia airs literacy classes in the Aymara language during the week, and the "students" meet once a week at regional community centers to take exams.

Moreover, radio has fostered cultural identity by broadcasting traditional music: the ranchero sounds of Mexico, the salsa music of the Indies and the Caribbean basin, the reggae of the English-speaking Caribbean islands, the exotic sambas of Brazil, the tangos of Argentina that were once the rage in Europe and North America, the haunting Andean flute music of Bolivia and Peru, and the lilting harp music of Paraguay. To be sure, the rock music of Europe and North America has found a willing audience in Latin America, and it permeates the airways, though it has yet to supplant the traditional sounds. In some countries, such as Paraguay, the government requires that radio stations air a certain percentage of indigenous music.

The development of television in Latin America closely followed the medium's advent in the United States, with Mexico, Cuba, and Brazil leading the way. The medium was slower to develop than radio because of the need for outside capital and technological know-how. Consequently, Latin American television programming until the 1970s was characterized by a heavy dependence on foreign—especially U.S.—

financing, technical assistance, and program imports such as "I Love Lucy" and a host of other situation comedies and adventure shows. Some countries, such as Haiti, Honduras, Bolivia, and Paraguay, still have relatively primitive TV systems, but more affluent countries have increasingly produced programs locally for domestic consumption and even export. The most popular such program export is the Latin American genre, the *telenovela*, a prime-time soap opera that has successfully held its own against such North American imports as "Dallas" and "Dynasty."

The level of sophistication of TV production still varies from country to country, but Brazil's mammoth TV Globo Network is now reputed to be the world's fourth largest (after three U.S. networks), and Mexico's dominant Televisa network (the fifth largest network) has become a major exporter of programs throughout Latin America and is the parent company of Univision, formerly SIN, the Spanish-language network of the United States. The growth of a regionwide television industry was made feasible as countries switched from microwave to satellite transmission. Virtually all Latin American countries are members of Intelsat (Cuba belongs to the Soviet bloc's Intersputnik system), and the technological leaders—Argentina, Brazil, Mexico, Colombia— have their own communications satellites in orbit. Satellite uplinks are especially vital for countries with vast land areas and mountainous terrain and have helped foster national unity and culture.

Major National Broadcasting Systems

Argentina. Radio broadcasting was inaugurated in Argentina in 1923, only three years after the first regular broadcasting began in the United States. Already affluent by Latin American standards, Argentina experienced an economic boom in the 1920s that expanded the middle class and fueled the development of the new electronic medium, with the private sector leading the way.

Radio held its own despite the Great Depression, and by 1938 there were more than 40 stations and two national networks. Programming was similar to that of the United States, except that the tango took precedence over the Big Band sound. Soap operas were popular, and radio drama was responsible for the rise of an actress named Eva Duarte, later the mistress and wife of Juan Domingo Perón. Perón and his wife skillfully employed radio to sway the masses of "shirtless ones," as had Perón's role model, Benito Mussolini. Eva Perón died in 1952, and her husband was ousted in a military coup in 1955.

Initially established by the government during the Perón era, television alternated between public and private ownership for several years, just as the government itself oscillated between civilian and military control. Television came into its own during the early 1960s when a number of private entrepreneurs—including Cuban Goar Mestre—built a thriving television system. Perón returned to power in 1973 and died ten months later, bequeathing the presidency to his second wife and vice president, Isabel. Her brief rule was marked by mismanagement and guerrilla warfare, which led to her ouster by the military in 1976.

Broadcasting was among the victims of the repression employed by the military during the so-called Dirty War aimed against perceived subversives. Argentina experienced a drain of journalistic and artistic talent, to the extent that between 1972 and 1981 the number of hours of imported TV programming actually doubled, from 20 to 40 percent of total airtime, according to a six-nation study by Livia Antola and Everett Rogers (1984). With the return to civilian rule in 1983, exiles began returning, and the country experienced a renaissance in its cinema and television industries.

One legacy of Perón is the considerable role of the public sector in broadcasting, which has persisted to the present under a succession of governments of varying political philosophy. Radio is predominantly private, with 75 independent stations, but the national government still retains 37; provincial governments own another four, municipal governments own three, and three others are university-owned.

Brazil. Radio in Brazil, as in Argentina, was ushered in in 1923, but with a curious twist: The first stations were private yet noncommercial. Early radio stations were actually clubs or associations supported by listeners' membership fees. In fact, the government precluded advertising until 1932, and programming stressed education and culture over entertainment. Brazil was dominated from 1932 to 1945 by Getulio Vargas, a fascistic dictator who imposed strict censorship on radio broadcasting. Like Argentina's Perón, Vargas employed radio as an effective propaganda tool. There was a relaxation of censorship during the period of democratic rule between the fall of Vargas in 1945 and the military coup of 1964.

Television was inaugurated during this democratic epoch. A communications entrepreneur, Assis Chateaubriand, established the first station in 1950 and correctly envisioned a bright future for the new medium in that mammoth market. As elsewhere in Latin America, however, early Brazilian television depended heavily on imported technology. Programming during the 1950s was mostly domestic, however, and appealed to an elite audience. Once dubbing into Portuguese began in the early 1960s, the Brazilian networks became increasingly dependent on U.S. program fare. As the country's middle class expanded during this same period, a mass TV audience evolved.

Sergio Mattos explains that a landmark in Brazilian TV development occurred in 1962 when Roberto Marinho, owner of the successful Rio de Janeiro daily *O Globo*, established TV Globo. He signed an agreement with Time-Life whereby the U.S. media giant would provide financial and technical assistance in return for 45 percent of future profits. By 1968, TV Globo had emerged as the largest of the five TV networks. The rival networks, however, took Marinho to court, alleging that the deal with Time-Life violated Article 160 of the military-imposed constitution of 1964 that forbade foreign ownership of Brazilian media. TV Globo was forced to terminate its agreement and repay the loans, but by then its dominance in Brazilian television was secure and remains so at present.

TV Globo also spearheaded the drive toward "Brazilianization" of television programming. Professor Joseph Straubhaar (1984) found that by the 1980s, fully 80 percent of TV Globo's audience hours were domestically produced programs, 90 percent of them by the network itself. The TVS–Silvio Santos network had 60 percent domestic programming, and the Bandeirantes network 55 percent. The Brazilian networks and production companies also have tapped into the lucrative foreign market. Popular programs are exported to Portugal and to Portuguese-speaking African nations. In the early 1980s, TV Globo began dubbing its programs into Spanish for export to other Latin American countries and to the U.S. Spanish-language network. Even Italy has begun importing Brazilian programs. Television journalism followed the U.S. model, such as TV Globo's popular hourlong newscast "Hoje" ("Today"), but aggressive reporting was discouraged and even punished until the return to civilian rule in 1985.

Brazil has developed one of the largest and most sophisticated broadcasting systems in the world, with more than 2,400 mostly private radio stations and 188 television stations grouped into six networks. The newest entry to the field is TV Manchete, established in 1981 by the owners of the popular magazine of the same name. Its broadcast journalists, however, are still feeling their way in the new climate of free expression.

Chile. In no Latin American country did radio and television develop along more contrasting lines than in Chile, a relatively prosperous country with a highly literate and educated population and, until the 1970s, a strong democratic tradition. Early radio was almost entirely a private, commercial enterprise, with the government entering the field afterward to guarantee educational and cultural representation on the airways. Political parties, religious groups, universities, and even miners' unions also took advantage of Chile's wide-open marketplace of ideas to operate their own stations.

Television, however, did not come to Chile until 1961, later than almost any other large Latin American country. It began not at the behest of the government or of private investors but as an experiment by technicians at the University of Chile and the Catholic University of Santiago. Interestingly, the conservative administration of President Jorge Alessandri decided against the addition of private commercial television in 1963, leaving the two universities in control of the country's only two stations. The medium experienced little growth until the Christian Democratic administration of Eduardo Frei implemented the Broadcast Law of 1970 before it left office that year. Under this law, the government established a third television station, which Frei had intended to use to promote the Christian Democrats.

However, leftist candidate Salvador Allende was elected president the same year, and both radio and television became embroiled in the ideological tug-of-war that prevailed in Chile during Allende's three-year Popular Unity regime. Allende was overthrown and died in the coup of 1973, but the right-wing military government of Augusto Pinochet that succeeded him left the government-university system of TV ownership essentially intact, with two more universities establishing stations. In addition to government subsidies, the 1970 statute authorized advertising on both the government and university stations but confined commercials to six minutes per hour between but not during programs. In his study of the Chilean broadcast system, Valerío Fuenzalída (1988) reports that the Pinochet government later allowed advertising during programs and greatly centralized control over all the television stations.

By the mid-1980s, there were more than 300 radio transmitters in Chile, including five shortwave, 149 medium-wave, and 167 FM. The five television stations—the government's Television Nacional on Channel 7, the University of Chile's Channel 11, Catholic University's Channel 13, Catholic University of Valparaiso's Channel 4, and Universidad del Norte in Antofagasta—are in reality networks with repeater stations throughout the country. TV Nacional alone has 108 repeaters. Because of the country's peculiar narrow but 2,500-mile-long shape from north to south, satellite transmissions have gradually replaced the old microwave system.

Broadcast journalism, which was freewheeling and often less than objective before the 1973 coup, was placed under severe constraints until the 1980s but enjoyed considerable freedom during the later days of the Pinochet government. For example, radio and television reported widely on the notorious incident in which two youths allegedly were set on fire by soldiers following an antigovernment demonstration and on the 1987 assassination attempt on Pinochet. Journalists have been allowed to return from exile. Whether Chilean broadcast journalism will be restored to its pre-1973 status in the post-Allende period is a question that has yet to be answered.

Colombia. For more than 50 years, Colombian broadcasting has been caught up in a violent struggle among the country's various political factions. Private investors pioneered radio in Colombia and successfully thwarted an attempt at expropriation in 1936. The frictions between the Liberal and Conservative parties erupted into a low-grade civil war in 1948 that lasted ten years and led to a temporary suspension of all radio licenses and imposition of strict censorship of news, especially political reporting. Today, there are nearly 500 licensed radio stations, with the government's Radio Cadena Nacional (RCN) operating a network of 144 stations. There are five private networks, the major ones being Circuito Toledar de Colombia, with 74 stations, and Cadena Radial Colombiana (CARACOL), with 44 stations.

Colombian television, meanwhile, developed quite differently from radio. TV broadcasting began in 1954 during the five-year dictatorship of the charismatic Gustavo Rojas Pinilla, who made the new medium a state monopoly called Intravision. When the Liberals and Conservatives united to oust Rojas in 1958 and established the two-party democracy that exists to this day, they agreed to retain state control of television. Under the Colombian model, however, Intravision operates two commercial channels and one educational. Not only do the two commercial networks carry advertising, but the government "sublets," or brokers, airtime to independent programmers.

Cuba. No country in Latin America has undergone a more dramatic shift in media policy than Cuba. Radio and television both developed in Cuba not only as private ventures but with heavy U.S. influence. Prior to the 1959 revolution that brought Fidel Castro to power, the Cuban broadcasting system was described as "the most freewheeling private commercial system in the hemisphere" by University of Miami professor Sydney W. Head (1985, p. 27).

In this virtually unregulated broadcasting environment, Cuba became the first nation in the world where television signals were available to everyone in the nation. Some broadcasting stations carried almost as much advertising as nonadvertising programming. Within two years after coming to power, Castro had expropriated all privately owned broadcast stations and had turned them into propaganda organs.

Today, the government controls nearly 200 radio transmitters grouped into five national networks. Radio Musical Nacional carries classical music; Radio Enciclopedia carries traditional music; Radio Progreso airs music and entertainment; Radio Rebelde emphasizes news, music, and sports; and Radio Reloj has a 24-hour, all-news format. Radio Habana aims shortwave broadcasts to the United States, the Caribbean, and Latin America in Spanish, English, French, Creole, Portuguese, Quechua, and Guaraní.

From the moment he seized power, Castro has used television as a powerful forum to exhort his followers, much as Perón employed radio. Cuban television today consists of two national networks with 73 transmitters. Despite recent reforms in other communist nations toward greater freedom for broadcast journalists, Castro has shown little interest in loosening his grip on Cuba's airways.

Mexico. Along with Brazil and Argentina, Mexico initiated radio broadcasting in 1923. Despite the socialist principles embodied in the Mexican constitution of 1917, a succession of governments allowed private broadcasters, notably the Azcarraga family, to operate parallel with the state's own educational, cultural, and propaganda outlets. The Law of General Ways of Communication of 1940 was the first definitive effort to regulate broadcasting. It resembled the U.S. Federal Communications Act of 1934 in many respects. The airways were declared to be in the public domain, and foreign ownership of radio stations was prohibited. Basically, the law treated radio more as a public utility than as an instrument of social importance.

During the administration of the conservative President Miguel Alemán from 1946 to 1952, the government sold several of its stations to private interests and granted new licenses to others. It was also during Alemán's administration that Mexico pioneered Latin American television broadcasting in 1950 as a private venture. Alemán remained active in private television broadcasting after he left office and was a principal figure in the rise of Televisa. Today, radio remains overwhelmingly in private hands; there are more than 800 commercial stations and fewer than 50 noncommercial. There are at least a dozen commercial networks.

Whereas the role of the public sector in radio diminished over time, television began exclusively as a private enterprise. The Law of Radio and Television of 1960 recognized the social value of the new medium and authorized the government to ensure that television stations fulfill certain social functions and adhere to such nebulous concepts as "moral principles" and "human dignity." Television is charged with enhancing the country's cultural level, preserving customs and traditions, and fostering the principles of democracy and national unity.

In her study of the Mexican broadcast system, Elizabeth Mahan (1985) relates that although television was firmly in private hands, a "fiscal time" agreement negotiated during the 1964–1970 administration of President Gustavo Díaz Ordaz required station owners to make 12.5 percent of broadcast time each day available to the government to air programs produced or financed by the General Directorate of Radio, Television, and Cinema. The government became directly involved in television broadcasting in the late 1960s when it nationalized the bankrupt Channel 13 in Mexico City under the terms of the 1960 law.

Another station in the capital, Telesistema Mexicano (TSM), also was facing financial difficulties, but it sidestepped nationalization by accepting an offer from entrepreneur Romulo O'Farrill, Jr., to merge with his station, Television Independiente de Mexico (TIM). This merger in January 1973 gave birth to Televisa, which has become one of the most powerful international media empires in the world. Like Brazil's TV Globo, Televisa broke the dependence on U.S. program imports. Two of Televisa's Mexico City stations still air U.S. programs almost exclusively, but programming on its two other stations is virtually 100 percent Mexican. Moreover, Televisa exports *telenovelas* and other programs throughout Latin America and is the parent company of Univisión, the U.S. Spanish-language network. Televisa currently controls 70 of Mexico's approximately 120 TV stations, only eight of which are state-owned cultural stations.

However, the government remains an active player in the television industry through a complex bureaucratic structure. The powerful secretary of government, who is essentially a deputy president, oversees not only the agencies that produce government programs but also those that regulate commercial television. The secretary can prosecute stations that violate the principles set forth in the 1960 broadcast law, though this is seldom done. Though there are formal channels established between the government and private broadcasters, especially Televisa, it is more common for the two players to reach agreements and resolve disputes informally. For example, the two cooperated on the financing and installation of Mexico's 80 satellite earth stations, though ownership is in government hands. In addition to their airing of government-produced programs, private station owners also cooperate with the government in the production of educational or cultural programs and have even agreed to incorporate some of the government's high-priority social issues into the scripts of *telenovelas*.

Because of the enormous power the government wields over even a giant like Televisa, it is not surprising that government pressure has prevented Mexican broadcast journalism from becoming as forthright as it has in some other Latin American countries. Major events, especially foreign ones, are reported objectively and critically, but the approach to news that could be embarrassing to the Mexican government is less forthright. This was particularly evident during the administration of President Luis Echeverría from 1970 to 1976, but the administration of Carlos Salinas de Gotari, who was sworn in in 1988, has shown an unprecedented tolerance toward opposition to the Institutional Revolutionary Party (PRI), which has dominated Mexico since 1929. Observers of Mexico are waiting to see whether this climate of openness will extend to aggressive broadcast journalism as well or whether the sword of Damocles will continue to dangle.

Peru. The first radio station in Peru was established by the government in 1925, but it was sold to the Marconi Company because of financial losses. The succession of military and civilian governments in the following years adopted a laissez faire attitude toward radio broadcasting. The same pattern was repeated for television.

By 1968, the year a reform-minded junta toppled the civilian government, Peruvian radio and television broadcasting were concentrated in the capital of Lima in the hands of some of the wealthiest families. The nation's interior, with its predominantly Indian population, was largely unserved by the broadcast media.

In 1971, the military issued a telecommunications law mandating a 51 percent government share in broadcast stations. The law also prohibited foreign ownership of broadcast stations and required reductions in imported programming and advertising in favor of locally produced educational and cultural programming. The junta's attempts to redistribute Peru's wealth ended in failure. In 1980, with a new democratically elected president, the broadcast media were returned to private hands.

The government still controls Radio Nacional de Peru, a network with transmitters in Lima and 21 cities in the interior. Peru's other 270 stations, however, are in private hands. Two television stations are controlled by the government, and five are privately owned. All the television stations are in Lima.

Venezuela. Broadcasting developed in Venezuela much as it did in Peru. Radio developed in the 1930s as a private venture virtually unfettered by government regulation—except for news censorship during periods of dictatorship. The state eventually entered into radio ownership, but even today, the state-owned Radio Nacional operates only eight stations, two of them with cultural formats. Meanwhile, there are about 150 private stations.

Television was promulgated by the government in 1952 during the autocratic rule of Marcos Pérez Jiménez. Television development followed the pattern of early dependence on U.S. program imports. During the early years of their development, the three Caracas stations were underwritten by investments from the large U.S. networks.

An economic boom in the 1970s, sparked by the demand for Venezuela's oil, contributed to the growth of Venezuela's broadcast industry. Between 1972 and 1981, audience hours devoted to imported TV programming declined from 50 percent to 33 percent, and Venezuela joined Mexico, Brazil, and Argentina as exporters of *telenovelas.*

Concurrent with the move toward greater domestic programming came efforts to provide increased cultural programming. This move initially met with fierce opposition from the owners of private stations and some politicians. But in 1980, the Social Christian administration of Luis Herrera Campins enacted a law requiring programs aired on the three state-owned stations to be screened 48 hours in advance to ensure that they meet educational and cultural criteria.

NEWS SERVICES

The large Western news agencies have been singled out by supporters of the NWICO as the primary culprits for Latin America's dependence on the Western news media. Critics charge that the Big Four international news agencies—Associated Press (AP) and United Press International (UPI) of the United States, Reuters of the United Kingdom, and Agence France-Presse (AFP) of France—dominate international news coverage in Latin America. In addition, large international television film news agencies are also immensely powerful and influential in Latin America and the Caribbean.

The Big Four international news agencies, and later television news services, derive their power and influence from a long history of international news reporting that dates back to the nineteenth century. But more than just experience in journalism accounts for their dominance in Latin America: The cartels we read about in Chapter 2 meant that peoples in various regions of the world effectively had access to only one foreign news organization's news.

Many Latin Americans and Latin American news organizations were particularly angered by the cartel's restrictive policies during the First World War. According to the cartel agreement, the now-defunct French agency Havas was the exclusive provider of cartel news to Latin

America. A number of South American newspapers questioned the credibility of Havas accounts, suspecting that the French agency had a pro-French, anti-German bias. Some South American newspapers asked AP to provide them with news because the United States was officially neutral at the outbreak of the war. AP refused because it did not want to endanger its valuable alliance with the cartel by competing against another cartel member.

AP's refusal to break the cartel agreement allowed another fledgling U.S. agency, the United Press (which later became UPI), to serve South American newspapers and gain a foothold in the region. AP's initial refusal to serve Latin American newspapers, however, was a move the agency later regretted. While AP is clearly the dominant U.S. agency in the world today, UP's early entry into Latin America allowed it to become the dominant agency in the region during the following decades. UPI prides itself as the "General Motors of Latin America."

Though the international news cartel no longer exists, a large proportion of the international news disseminated in Latin America today still originates from the Big Four international agencies. As a result, there are charges that Latin America is still a victim of "media imperialism," and a number of Latin American governments have joined UNESCO in calling for the establishment of regional news agencies to counter the power of the international news agencies.

Many Latin American media organizations, as well as governments, also support the development of regional agencies, although their conservative owners do not subscribe to the rhetoric of the dependence and media imperialism theories that underlie many of the calls for the establishment of regional agencies. But even Latin American publishers would like to see privately run agencies with a special focus on events in the region.

One outcome of the UNESCO-sponsored San José conference in 1976 was the need to establish a regional news agency that might more appropriately be described as an intergovernmental news exchange. Representatives from nine Latin American and Caribbean nations met in Mexico City and approved the formation of the Agencia Latinoamericana de Servicios Especiales de Información (ALASEI). ALASEI was established in 1983, with its headquarters in Mexico City. ALASEI has a negative reputation among many media professionals in the region as representing government views on news rather than objective reporting. In 1984, IAPA rejected an offer to serve on ALASEI's board of directors, charging that "news agencies in whose management governments or international entities such as UNESCO intervene directly or indirectly [are] dangerous to the free flow of information."

In 1971, the Agencia Latinoamericana de Información (LATIN) was established as a cooperative, privately owned by various newspapers in the region. It was established with the support of UNESCO and the valuable assistance of Reuters. Since LATIN was established without government involvement, it enjoyed more credibility than most other news agencies in the developing world. LATIN, however, experienced financial problems and by 1978 was nearly bankrupt. As a result, LATIN and Reuters integrated their operations, although they remained legally separate.

IPS and CANA

Two of the more successful Latin American regional agencies are Inter Press Service (IPS) and the Caribbean News Agency (CANA). IPS, which has its headquarters in Rome, was founded in 1964 by Latin American and European journalists as a means of creating an "information bridge" between Latin America and Europe. By the late 1970s, it had expanded from its Latin American base to other regions.

By 1984, IPS had correspondents and bureaus in 63 nations, 24 of which were in Latin America and the Caribbean. The rest were in Europe, the Middle East, Asia, and North America. Despite its expansion outside Latin America, IPS still has a strong Latin American focus. By early 1983, it was estimated that IPS had grown to the world's sixth largest news agency in total communication links, behind the Big Four and the Soviet Union's TASS.

Though IPS has no direct connections with governments, it has not totally escaped political controversy. A number of Western media organizations have complained about an anti-Western bias in IPS. A U.S. State Department cable once described IPS as having "a standard anti-imperialist line." IPS management has conceded that some of its reporters hold leftist political views. IPS, however, makes no apologies for its sympathy toward developing nations. It explicitly states that its editorial policies "are in line with the ideals of 'decolonization of information.'"

In contrast to some attempts to establish regional news agencies, CANA has met with both financial success and relatively little political controversy. CANA has frequently been praised as a Third World model. It was established in the Caribbean basin in 1976 by stockholders from private and public media in the region, with UNESCO assistance. The additional assistance of Reuters was particularly important. By the late 1980s, CANA had succeeded in quadrupling the volume of news exchanged among the English-language media in the Caribbean.

From the outset, CANA's management was determined to maintain the organization's credibility by not permitting governments to influence the agency's policies or reporting. To this end, CANA was successful and has gained a reputation for quality and credibility even among Western news organizations that is unusual among Third World news agencies.

In 1983, Ken Gordon ("Pressures on the Press," 1983), managing director of the *Trinidad Express* and chairman of CANA, told the *Caribbean West Indies Chronicle* magazine that there is a connection between development and a free, independent, and critical press:

> Development in the real sense means not only a high per capita income, it means developing people, resources, environment, culture. And once you get into the bag of placing controls on the press, those controls never remain static. They are exercised in accordance with the inclinations of the party in power. . . . In my view, dissent is an important part of development. Without dissent, you cannot really test ideas, and without that a society cannot really grow. (p. 6)

Other News Agencies Serving Latin America

Between the international news services and Latin America's regional news services are the "second-tier" news agencies from Western European nations that operate in Latin America and the Caribbean. These include Deutsche Presse-Agentur (DPA) of West Germany, Agenzia Nazionale Stampa Associata (ANSA) of Italy, and Efe of Spain. Efe is widely used in some Latin American nations. A study of Latin American prestige newspaper use of news agency services in Brazil, Argentina, and Mexico reported by Jere Link in 1984 found that Efe was used in Mexico City's prestigious *El Universal* and *Excelsior* almost as often as UPI, AP, and AFP. In Argentina, *La Crónica* used Efe reports more than any other news agency. Since Brazil is a Portuguese-speaking nation, the Spanish agency Efe was rarely used. These second-tier agencies entered the Latin American market during the 1960s and 1970s. According to Jonathan Fenby's thorough 1986 study of the world's news agencies, the competition of international, second-tier, and regional news agencies in South America "gave the continent the widest choice of news services of any area outside Western Europe" (p. 206).

In addition, a number of Latin American nations have national news agencies, many of them government-operated and, not surprisingly, progovernment in their coverage. Overall, their impact on international news flow has been negligible, but they have had some influence within their respective nations.

The functions of national news agencies differ. They frequently act as exchange services, exchanging national news with other national and international agencies as well as receiving, editing, and distributing news from government agencies and the international agencies to local media. In some cases, such as Venezuela's Venpres, the national agencies promote government policies. Venpres openly promotes Venezuela's tourism industry and is housed in the Ministry of Information and Tourism. Some of the larger nations in the region, such as Argentina, Brazil, and Mexico, have several state-owned agencies that are sometimes cited by journalists in their correspondences and treated as official views of their representative governments.

GOVERNMENT-MEDIA RELATIONS

As in other regions, tensions occasionally arise between governments and the press in Latin America, but most Latin American nations have been reluctant to institute outright controls of the press. Even Nicaragua, when the Sandinistas were in power, was no paradigm of Marxist press theory. The Sandinistas felt compelled to insist to their Central American neighbors that they permitted an opposition press in the form of *La Prensa*. The Cuban model, which closely adheres to Marxist-Leninist tenets of the press, is an aberration in Latin America that has not been copied elsewhere.

This is not to suggest that Latin American news media operate with little or no government control. However, the fact that governments appear apologetic for their attempts to control the press suggests that Western notions about freedom of the press, in the form of a privately owned and commercially operated press, are ingrained in Latin America.

As a result of the reluctance of many Latin American governments to institute outright controls on the media, a number of subtle measures of press control exist. The best-known measures consist of government control over newsprint and other materials to operate the media. In Mexico, the government has successfully created a system that effectively permits it to wield strong control over the press. The legal control results from the government's near monopoly on the import, distribution, sale, and manufacture of newsprint since 1935 through the state-owned PIPSA (Producer and Importer of Paper) organization. The Mexican government keeps the broadcast media in check by means of regulations that go beyond simple allocation of frequencies. The Mexican government mandates that as a public service, a portion of airtime be devoted to government reports.

Alejandro Junco de la Vega (1989), publisher of *El Norte* in Monterrey, Mexico, claims that he saw sharp reductions in his government
quota of newsprint as a result of his newspaper's aggressive reporting
about the government. He noted that the government can turn on and
off the control of newsprint to reward its friends and punish its enemies:

> It would have been unreasonable at the height of the Watergate
> scandal for Katharine Graham [publisher of the *Washington
> Post*] to be obligated to purchase newsprint from Richard
> Nixon. We Mexican publishers have been doing the equivalent
> of that for a long time. (p. 6)

Another potential weapon wielded by Latin American governments against recalcitrant publications or broadcast stations is the
withholding of government advertising. In Mexico, Argentina, and
Brazil, which have quasisocialist or mixed economies, major industries
are controlled by the public sector. The advertising of their products is
extensive, and lost advertising often hurts the news media, and may
sometimes lead to insolvency.

Despite what might appear as a legal, political, and social structure
that would make criticism of the government and authorities difficult,
Latin American media exist in spirited political and economic interaction with the national and local governments of the countries in which
they publish. Before the return to democracy in the 1980s, many
governments legally or illegally used extreme measures, such as long-
term closings and even violence against writers and editors. During the
1980s, with the return to democracy combined with economic crises,
many newspapers and magazines closed as a result of the economic
situations. It wasn't necessary for Argentina to have a dictatorship to see
widespread newspaper closings during the rule of democratic President
Raul Alfonsin.

With many newspapers and magazines in Latin America taking
strong political positions, life as a journalist in South and Central
America is not for the weak. Threats to journalists come not only from
governments but from terrorist groups, drug lords, and quasigovern-
mental hit squads as well. Numerous news organizations have been
bombed, ransacked, and destroyed by opponents. Dozens of Latin
American journalists have been murdered for their beliefs or for writing
articles that contain those beliefs. Colombia is widely regarded as
among the most dangerous nations in the world in which to practice
journalism.

The overt violence, subtle pressures, and even nonviolent threats
often lead to self-censorship, or *autocensura*, as it is known in demo-

cratic Venezuela, where the practice is thought to be widespread. Self-censorship is a decision Latin American journalists are often forced to make when faced with threats of physical violence or economic pressure. It has occurred in other countries such as Argentina, Colombia, Nicaragua, Panama, Chile, and Peru.

The Partisan Press

The partisan political press remains in Latin America today. Some efforts have been made to develop newspapers that are not owned by or affiliated with political parties. Some U.S. media practitioners would like to see the Latin American press become more "professional," meaning that it should subscribe to notions such as "fairness," "neutrality," "detachment," "balance," and "objectivity." For instance, many U.S. media professionals would look askance on an example of political reporting provided by Professor John Lent (1987), of Temple University, a longtime observer of the Caribbean mass media, describing how a partisan newspaper in St. Kitts ran a photograph of former Premier Lee Moore sprawled on the ground. The caption described Moore as so "knocked out with liquor that he vomited like a whale, urinated like a dog, exposed himself like a jackass and wallowed in his muck like a pig." The paper also ran a response from Moore: "Let us start from the assumption that I was drunk. . . . Who money I drunk wid? Is my money. So why I have to explain to anybody if I drunk?" (p. 249).

Some critics of this trend to greater neutral reporting, especially critics from Latin America's dependence school, argue that this notion of professionalism amounts to imposing a foreign (i.e., Western, especially American) journalistic standard on the Latin American news media. They note that it is not necessary to adhere to such standards to have a free "marketplace of ideas" where all ideas can be discussed.

JOURNALISM EDUCATION AND TRAINING

Journalism education in Latin America is experiencing rapid growth. In 1950, there were only seven journalism programs in Latin America; by 1985, there were almost 200. During the late 1950s, the United Nations Educational, Scientific, and Cultural Organization (UNESCO), an organization within the United Nations that has advocated restructuring the "world communication order," discussed the creation of regional journalism education centers in Latin America. As a result, UNESCO founded the International Center of Advanced Studies in Journalism for

Latin America (CIESPAL) in Quito, Ecuador. Today, CIESPAL is regarded as one of the leading journalism research centers in the region.

Journalistic organizations helped launch journalism programs in universities throughout the region, ostensibly as a means of promoting "professionalism" in journalism. Over the years, the universities and other organizations were able to persuade many Latin American governments to legally require practicing journalists to belong to professional organizations known as *colegios* whose members had to possess journalism degrees from recognized national universities. This suited the professional organizations because it provided a means of restricting entry into the field—a method that, if successful, would keep journalists' skills in demand and salaries higher than they would otherwise be.

The roots of *colegio* laws in Latin America stem from the poor lot of local journalists. They have traditionally been underpaid, overworked, and given little job security. Mexican journalists are often encouraged by their employers to solicit advertisements from their sources and are rewarded with commissions. Many Mexican journalists have found it necessary to hold two jobs to survive. The starting pay for a journalist in Mexico City in 1986 was estimated at U.S. $120 a month. The journalists' other jobs to supplement their incomes have frequently been with government agencies, raising serious conflict-of-interest questions. Mexican politicians have exploited the poor lot of journalists. They frequently hire journalists, expecting favorable news coverage in return. As a result, a number of observers have criticized the state of journalism in Mexico. Professor Robert Pierce (1979) wrote that Mexico's "mass media are held in widespread disdain by citizens at all levels of life" (p. 97).

Controversy over *Colegios*

Latin America's *colegio* laws have become a controversial issue in the Americas. The controversy has reached the halls of the United Nations and is a regular part of discussions during professional meetings of U.S. journalists. U.S. and many Latin American news organizations view *colegio* laws as government attempts to manipulate the press. The laws are regularly condemned during meetings of the Inter American Press Association (IAPA), the major media watchdog group in the Western Hemisphere, as covert attempts to establish government licensing of journalists. UNESCO supports *colegio* laws. The various political groups that have gotten involved in the debate have framed the issue of *colegio* laws solely in political terms, dealing with such heady matters as national and cultural sovereignty, the free flow of information, and journalistic autonomy. But as Professor Jerry Knudson (1987) of Temple

University has observed, Latin American journalists have traditionally viewed the matter of *colegios* largely in economic terms as a form of job protection.

As of 1987, at least 11 Latin American nations had *colegio* laws on their books: Bolivia, Brazil, Costa Rica, Dominican Republic, Ecuador, Guatemala, Haiti, Honduras, Panama, Peru, and Venezuela. Although the laws are unevenly enforced, critics, such as Professor Mary Gardner (1967) of Michigan State University, claim that *colegio* laws provide governments with a legal means to clamp down on the press. She points out that *colegio* laws have more often been instituted and enforced under authoritarian governments than democratic ones.

One notable exception to Gardner's observation is Costa Rica, where it is widely agreed that the press enjoys a considerable amount of freedom. Costa Rica also has the region's most famous *colegio* law as a result of a failed legal challenge brought against the law by an American journalist practicing in Costa Rica. Costa Rica's Colegio de Periodista ("Association of Journalists") was formed in 1969 to "raise the standards of journalism." To qualify as a member of the Colegio, a member is required to graduate from the University of Costa Rica's Journalism School. Anyone else who practices journalism faces a two-year prison sentence.

The notoriety of Costa Rica's Colegio stems from a lengthy legal battle waged by American reporter Stephen Schmidt, who, in 1983, was convicted by the Costa Rican supreme court for the "illegal practice of the profession." The officers of the University of Costa Rica brought pressure on the government to prosecute Schmidt, who had been working as a reporter for several years for the English-language *Tico Times* and Spanish-language *La Nación* without membership in the Colegio. Schmidt raised the ire of the Colegio by flaunting the fact that he was not a member. At a 1980 meeting of the IAPA in San José, Schmidt declared: "I'm covering this meeting illegally. Let me work or sue me."

Schmidt won his case in a lower court but lost on appeal to the Costa Rican supreme court, which sentenced him to a suspended three-month jail term. Schmidt appealed to the Inter-American Commission on Human Rights, where he lost in a 5–1 decision, with Costa Rica abstaining. Only the United States supported Schmidt. A subsequent nonbinding investigation by the IACHR sided with Schmidt and held that a *colegio* could not restrict the practice of journalism, although it did not rule against the practice of *colegios* in general. The nonbinding decision was hailed by critics of *colegios* as a landmark decision.

It would be incorrect to interpret the Schmidt decision only in terms of freedom of the press. A good deal of economic self-interest was involved on the part of all parties, except perhaps Schmidt himself. The University of Costa Rica and the nation's journalists, through their professional organizations, supported the law. They had obvious financial interests in doing so. Their claim that the *colegio* would promote professionalism in journalism, however, should be regarded with suspicion.

Richard Dyer, the publisher of the *Tico Times*, naturally sided with Schmidt. Dyer claimed that the law limited a publisher's autonomy to hire employees. It should be obvious, however, that Costa Rican publishers had more to gain from a Schmidt victory than just hiring autonomy. If publishers do not have to hire members of the *colegio*, the labor market of journalists would be larger, and journalists could be paid lower salaries. Nevertheless, Dyer was correct in asserting that the *colegio*'s house organ, *Primera Plana*, hardly met high professional standards. As an example, he cited a banner headline in the February 1988 edition of *Primera Plana* that read: "THE NORTH AMERICAN PRESS IN THE HANDS OF JEWS."

The fear that *colegio* laws could be invoked by governments to deal with outspoken media seemed to be borne out by the Honduran government, which in 1983 expelled a United Press International correspondent who had reported about government torture and the presence of Nicaraguan rebel bases in the nation. The government justified the expulsion on the grounds that he was not a member of the nation's *colegio*. A reporter from the Spanish news agency Efe was expelled a short time later by the Honduran government on similar grounds.

PROSPECTS FOR THE FUTURE

Many Latin American nations made the successful transition from military dictatorship to constitutional democracy during the 1980s. The news media contributed to and profited from these transitions. Although some Latin American nations continue to exert pressure on the press to provide favorable coverage of the government, the trend is toward better and more independent reporting and increased professionalism in journalism. In addition, Latin America has several regional news agencies and large newspapers, magazines, and broadcast networks. With this growing media power, Latin American media have reduced their reliance on the international news agencies.

The dangers of foreign debt and hyperinflation, combined with increased terrorism against journalists and others, poses a threat to these achievements. In addition, the perennial problems of poverty and overpopulation endure. Before the transition to democracy, many Latin Americans tolerated, if not supported, military dictatorships to achieve economic and social stability at the cost of decreased political freedom. The press and other institutions suffered as a result. Though recourse to a military dictatorship seems distasteful, it is always possible that such a solution will be considered if a given situation does not improve. The possibility of left-wing solutions seems unlikely, however, given the image of Fidel Castro's Cuba as a failed political and economic model rejected even by other communist nations.

As we enter the 1990s, most Latin American nations continue to hang their hopes on democracy rather than quick-fix solutions with dictatorships. But the economic problems must be addressed. The news media must determine what role they can play in creating and maintaining democracy and improving the social situation of the public.

CHAPTER 10

North America

Paul Adams and Catherine McKercher

"Let the people know the facts, and the country will be safe," Abraham Lincoln once said. His sentiment could sum up the philosophy of the press in North America, where the right to free expression is basic to the Canadian and American systems of government.

The number of journalistic organs available to citizens of the two countries is awesome: almost 1,800 daily newspapers, more than 8,000 weeklies, and thousands of magazines of every type and hue. There are more than 10,000 radio stations to listen to, and broadcast networks or cable channels give TV viewers dozens of things to watch 24 hours a day.

Among these media are some of the world's most influential and powerful: the *New York Times* and the Associated Press, to name only two. And American television programming literally reaches to the far corners of the world.

The mass media of North America also drive the engines of commerce. They carry not only news and entertainment but also millions of advertising messages. Advertising literally pays the bills of day-to-day journalism—well over $100 billion is spent to reach North American consumers each year.

As the news business enters the 1990s, both technology and competition challenge the journalism establishment in North America. Though progress has sparked enormous growth in the media, it also has brought about a different kind of journalism in both countries.

For one thing, the business of journalism at the end of the twentieth century is vastly different from what it was at the beginning. Gone are the days when newspapers were locally owned and towns of any size or consequence had at least two. Chain ownership of newspapers and the single-newspaper town are the pattern in the United States and Canada.

And particularly in the United States, the business of broadcasting involves giant corporations and conglomerates. Television news is a high-tech, high-pressure, high-cost, and high-profit enterprise. In the magazine field, the 1989 merger of Time Inc. and Warner Communications created the largest media enterprise in the world.

Big is, of course, not necessarily bad. Large media firms are far more able than small ones to weather dips in the economy or threats from angry local advertisers. And the best newspapers in Canada and the United States are generally among the largest. But concentration of ownership raises questions about accountability and concentration of content: Critics say concentration risks narrowing the free flow of viewpoints, opinions, beliefs, and entertainment forms that make the media a marketplace of ideas. Such concepts are at the core of a free press.

Communication technology has advanced at a breathtaking pace in recent decades. For broadcasters, this means that instantaneous coverage of events is not only possible but routine. Events that aren't covered, meanwhile, can be re-created with startling realism. Dramatic reenactments of events have become a favorite television tool, ranging from gruesome simulations of murder and mayhem on tabloid TV shows to sophisticated reenactments on prestigious network news and current affairs shows. But the blurring of reality and fiction in these reenactments raises some troubling questions: What are the ethics of broadcasting "neo-events," and what impact do they have on traditional journalistic values?

In the print media, new technology allows for almost unlimited variations on a standard page layout. And the growing field of graphic design lets newspapers and magazines show their readers the sequence of events in a disaster—the explosion of the space shuttle, for example, or the anatomy of a train wreck. The new technology also allows newspapers to alter the content of photographs.

For print and electronic media, the new technologies are seen as ways of gaining or maintaining a competitive edge. In a business where ratings and advertising revenues are the measure of success and where potential audiences are swamped with choices, newspapers and broadcasters face constant pressure to outdo their rivals.

The political climate within which the North American media operate has also changed in recent years, particularly in Canada. Canada in the late 1970s had a Liberal government wrestling with questions of nationalism and U.S. domination of its industry and culture. The

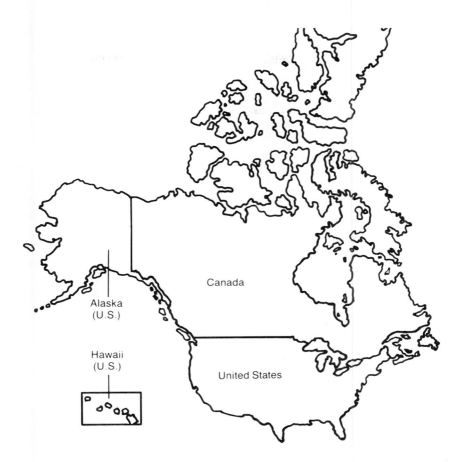

Progressive Conservative government of the late 1980s wrestled with another set of questions: how to get the most out of proximity to the giant U.S. economy. The answer it found was a free-trade agreement with the United States. The agreement, which came into effect on January 1, 1989, over the opposition of large numbers of Canadians, was described by former U.S. President Reagan as a "new economic constitution for North America."

Supporters of the agreement say it preserves Canada's cultural sovereignty because it explicitly excludes "cultural industries"—including book, newspaper, and magazine publishing, radio and television broadcasting, and the film, video, and music business. It does, however, allow either country to take "measures of equivalent commercial effect" to retaliate against action it believes to be anticompetitive. This means that if Canada enacted new legislation to protect its magazine industry, the United States could retaliate by imposing a duty on some other Canadian product—lumber, for example, or minerals. Critics of the deal say that it has a second, broader impact on culture: placing it directly in the realm of commerce and treating it as a commodity, to be bought and sold.

One small point in the deal is of particular interest—and concern—to journalists. In a section dealing with relaxed immigration laws for temporary work in the other country, journalists are defined as having a baccalaureate and three years of professional experience. A very small number of journalists would ever be affected by the clause, but many in the media oppose it as a matter of principle. They feel that the state has no business defining what makes a journalist and that the existence of a definition might be a first step down the slippery slope toward licensing. Canadian and U.S. officials are considering deleting the provision.

It is unlikely that there will be any moves to break up media corporations in North America. Certainly there will be no turning back in technology. The tenor of the times, domestically and internationally, is one of increasing concentration in all areas of business. Technology provides the tools in a fast-changing world.

HISTORICAL HIGHLIGHTS

The first newspapers in the United States and Canada followed the traditions of British journalism. An exiled London publisher, Benjamin Harris, printed the continent's first newspaper, *Publick Occurrences, Both Foreign and Domestick*, in Boston in 1690, but it was immediately banned by the colonial governor. Nevertheless, the ground had been broken, and journalism flourished as civilization thickened across North America.

United States

Eighteenth Century: The Political Years. During the early years, as the nation sought to establish itself, newspapers were caught up in politics—first the war, then partisan wranglings. Postmaster John Campbell of Boston published the first continuously appearing paper in America, the *Boston News-Letter*, in 1704. Campbell's "news" was primarily clippings from English newspapers and had to be cleared for publication by the governor.

The crusading James Franklin did not pretend to have anyone's authority when he published his *New England Courant* in 1721—and went to jail for it. His younger brother, Benjamin, took over as publisher. But by breaking the influence of licensing on the American press, James Franklin had established an important precedent for later journalists.

By mid-century newspapers had sprung up in all the colonies, but almanacs and pamphlets were common, and magazines were emerging. The most widely read almanac was Ben Franklin's *Poor Richard's Almanack.* The first magazine in America was Andrew Bradford's *American Magazine* on February 13, 1741, beating by three days Ben Franklin's *General Magazine.*

During the war period, courageous editors were influential in molding opinion through the use of their news columns. Writers such as Samuel Adams and Thomas Paine fanned the flames of revolution.

After the Constitutional Convention, Alexander Hamilton, James Madison, and John Jay wrote the *Federalist Papers* in an attempt to sway public opinion toward ratification of the Constitution. The series of articles first appeared in the *New York Independent Journal.*

Opinion dominated newspapers, which had a difficult time adjusting from their role as political advocate after the war. Newspapers supported government, and government supported "viewspapers" through political patronage.

But alternatives were offered by the many magazines that came into being late in the century. The *Saturday Evening Post*, for example, featured fiction, poems, and essays.

Nineteenth Century: Growth to Maturity. Journalism spurted, then accelerated, then boomed as the nation grew. At the start of the century, Philadelphia had six dailies. Most large cities had at least one, but newspapers were also following settlers into new areas, spurred by the development of a national postal system.

Partisanship and political patronage continued for many papers until mid-century, but as the new nation's economy and population changed, so did demand for newspapers.

The first true mass-circulation paper, the *New York Sun*, was begun by Benjamin Day in 1833. By shifting costs to advertisers, he priced his paper at one cent—launching the "penny press." The *Sun* had 8,000 circulation within six months. Not printers now, but publishers, such as James Gordon Bennett and Horace Greeley, joined in.

The new papers emphasized news instead of opinion and sent out true reporters to gather facts. Important papers like the *New York Times* and the first news cooperative, the Associated Press, were born during this era.

Technology helped newspapers expand, and with the demand for news about the Civil War, railroads, steamships, the telegraph, and new types of presses were harnessed to expand mass communication throughout the country. Reporters flocked to battle scenes for firsthand accounts, and a photographer, Matthew Brady, captured the war for posterity.

Big business was booming, and so was big journalism, as literacy, population growth, and more leisure time fostered the growth of newspaper chains and dynasties. By the late 1800s, the number of newspapers had more than doubled. As competition intensified, newspaper barons like William Randolph Hearst and Joseph Pulitzer exploited events for maximum circulation. Their sensationalized fare was branded "yellow journalism" after a cartoon character of mindless simplicity.

Twentieth Century: Competition and Change. The challenges of the modern era were met by a more sober brand of mass communication, which itself underwent profound changes. Newspapers had essentially the same content and form as today, but the number of papers began to decline after peaking at over 2,000 in 1910.

Magazines showed the serious side of journalism with what President Theodore Roosevelt called "muckraking." Exposés by writers Lincoln Steffens, Ida Tarbell, and others attacked big business and big institutions—and brought results. The first newsmagazine, *Time*, was introduced in the 1920s, and so were *Reader's Digest* and many other magazines.

The first radio station, KDKA, began broadcasting from Pittsburgh in 1920, and by 1927, the major networks were formed. Radio was highly popular during the Great Depression, giving the nation a varied diet of programming. President Franklin Roosevelt used radio to communicate directly to the people. During World War II, radio kept the world posted from abroad through reporters such as Edward R. Murrow in London.

Television came into mass availability after the war and soon became the dominant medium, primarily through its entertainment fare. It also enabled news events to come into people's homes, with such items as political conventions, the first presidential debate, men walking on the moon, and the Vietnam War. Television became the major source of news for two-thirds of the population, the sole source for half.

Television's effects on the other media were profound. Newspapers began running more colorful graphics and in-depth and feature material while struggling to attract mass readers again. Radio became a supplementary medium and an adjunct to the recording industry, although it remained a news and information medium during early morning hours. General-interest magazines such as *Life* and *Look* began dying off as television usurped the national audience in the mid-1950s. Magazines became increasingly fragmented to cater to special-interest audiences.

But television itself underwent changes in the late 1980s. Cable television spread rapidly, and satellites broadened programming competition. Network dominance was eroded by consumers' use of home video recorders, coupled with the growth of independent stations. Like newspapers a century earlier, television came under fire for its often trivial and sensational content.

Canada

Eighteenth Century: The Founding Newspapers. In August 1751, Bartholomew Green, Jr., the grandson of the first printer of the *Boston News-Letter*, brought a printing press from Boston to the brand-new city of Halifax, Nova Scotia. Green planned to establish a newspaper but died a few months after the press arrived. As a result, his former partner, John Bushell, who came to Halifax to take over the shop, earned the distinction of being Canada's pioneer journalist when he published the first issue of the *Halifax Gazette* in March 1752. Like most colonial newspapers in North America, it was an adjunct of a commercial printing venture, and its existence depended on government patronage.

Over the next 50 years, newspapers were begun in each of the six most easterly provinces of Canada. The first in the former French colony of New France was the bilingual *Quebec Gazette*, established in 1764 by two Philadelphia printers, William Brown and Thomas Gilmore. Quebec City, founded in 1605, was one of the oldest European settlements in North America, but no newspapers had been established under the French colonial regime, largely due to French opposition to the introduction of printing presses in the colony. The *Quebec Gazette* appeared just one year after the signing of the Treaty of Paris, which ceded New France to Britain. During the American Revolution, the Philadelphia Congress encouraged Fleury Mesplet to set up a printing shop in Montreal. He was jailed in 1776 for attempting to persuade Quebec to join the revolution. He was soon released and in 1778 launched *La Gazette du Commerce et Littéraire*.

The *Royal Gazette and Nova Scotia Intelligencer*, set up by Loyalist editors in 1783, became New Brunswick's pioneer newspaper more or less by default: It was located in a part of Nova Scotia that was detached to form the new province of New Brunswick in 1784. The journal was quickly renamed the *Royal St. John Gazette*. Prince Edward Island's first newspaper was the *Royal American Gazette and Weekly Intelligencer*, founded in 1787. In what is now the province of Ontario, the *Upper Canada Gazette or American Oracle* began publication in 1793 at Newark, now Niagara-on-the-Lake. Newfoundland's first newspaper was the *Royal Gazette and Newfoundland Advertiser*, set up in 1807.

Government announcements, proclamations, and orders accounted for much of the content of early Canadian newspapers. Foreign news was next in importance, even if it was months old by the time it crossed the Atlantic.

Nineteenth Century: Growth and Diversification. During the next 50 years, as Canada's population grew and its political and economic structure evolved, weekly newspapers developed rapidly in the six eastern provinces. By 1857, there were 291 news-sheets in British North America.

These newspapers were quite different from the early gazettes, which in effect had constituted an official press. The new, free-enterprise newspapers relied more on advertising and subscriptions, and they were increasingly political in content. Newspapers were allied—often financially as well as editorially—with political parties or factions within the parties. By the middle of the nineteenth century, most of the important journals were identified with either the Reform Party or the Conservatives, and most towns big enough to support one newspaper supported two, one for each party.

But not all nineteenth-century publications were tied to political parties. By the 1830s, a country press, catering to local interests, was developing. There were also a number of commercial news-sheets, particularly in the cities, as well as religious journals, satirical publications, and a "class" press.

The daily newspaper was a later arrival in Canada than in the United States. The first was Montreal's *Daily Advertiser*, which was founded in 1833 and went bankrupt a year later. The first penny newspaper was the *Morning News* of Saint John, New Brunswick, which began as a triweekly in 1839. Ontario's first successful daily was the *British Whig* of Kingston, in 1849. By 1873, there were 47 dailies in Canada; by 1900, there were 112.

The press moved west in Canada in 1858, when two San Francisco journalists came to British Columbia and founded the *Victoria Gazette and Anglo-American*. The most enduring British Columbia pioneer was the *British Colonist*, which survives today as the *Times-Colonist* of Victoria. Journalism in Manitoba began in 1859 with the *Nor'Wester* at Fort Garry. Saskatchewan's first newspaper was the *Saskatchewan Herald* of Battleford, founded in 1878. In Alberta, the *Edmonton*

Bulletin, founded in 1880, preceded the formation of the province by 25 years.

Although partisanship was a key feature of late-nineteenth-century newspapers, their reliance on political parties for finances declined. In part this was due to rising literacy rates and technological developments that made mass media possible. Mass audiences were a perfect target for merchants, and advertising became an increasingly important source of income for newspapers.

From Confederation into the Twentieth Century. Canadian historian Paul Rutherford (1978) has called the 60 years between Canada's Confederation and the Great Depression the golden age of the press. Print journalism was unchallenged by other media, and Canadians became loyal fans of newspapers. In Toronto in 1872, each family bought, on average, one newspaper; 11 years later, two newspapers. And a comparison of circulation and census figures shows that by 1931, there were roughly four newspapers and periodicals per household in Canada.

The number of Canadian dailies peaked in 1913 at 138. But the recession of that year, followed by wartime inflation and postwar economic instability, put intense pressure on the newspaper industry. Between 1914 and 1922, some 40 dailies disappeared. Many simply ceased publication; others merged with stronger competitors.

With the return to prosperity in the early 1920s, the number of dailies began to rise again. But a number of factors—including the economic travails of the Great Depression and World War II and the growth of broadcasting, which broke print's monopoly on advertising— kept the number of dailies below the 138 published in the peak year of 1913. In 1953, only 89 dailies were in business in Canada. By the end of the 1980s, this number had risen to about 110. However, only a handful of Canadian cities are served by separately owned daily newspapers.

PRINT MEDIA

Newspapers and magazines are the key media for information, opinion, and ideas in North America. Newspapers are also the largest advertising medium in both countries. Nearly two-thirds of North American adults read a newspaper on an average weekday. The print media, including magazines, have long histories but are facing new challenges in serving readers and maintaining economic health.

United States

Newspapers. In 1988, a total of 1,643 daily newspapers were being published in the United States. Each issue of a daily is read by slightly more than two people, so the 1988 circulation figure of 63 million translates to about 134 million readers every day.

Daily papers are published in 1,516 U.S. cities. Evening-delivery, or p.m., papers are the most common at 1,150, with a circulation of 23 million. Morning papers, although numbering only 525, have more circulation, at 40 million. Both a.m. and p.m. totals include 32 "all-day" papers, which are published for delivery or newsstand sales throughout the day.

The circulation of daily newspapers ranges from less than 5,000 to almost 2 million copies a day. About 85 percent are under 50,000 in circulation. Four U.S. papers circulate more than 1 million copies a day: the *Wall Street Journal* at 1.9 million, *USA Today* at 1.3 million, the *New York Daily News* at 1.3 million, and the *Los Angeles Times* at 1.1 million.

The number of daily newspapers peaked at 2,600 in 1909 and has been declining ever since. Circulation has grown, but it has not kept pace with population. Sunday newspapers have been the healthiest segment of the industry, showing continued growth: 22 percent more circulation since 1970.

A total of 7,606 weekly papers were published in 1989. They had an average weekly circulation of 6,959 but a combined total of about 53 million. Suburban papers, published in a variety of formats and often given away, expanded rapidly in the 1980s.

In addition to the suburban press, alternative weekly papers are thriving in many cities by taking aim at young readers. They range in circulation from 5,500 to 160,000 and run more in-depth and provocative stories than the dailies.

Six nationally distributed supermarket tabloids, including the largest, the *National Enquirer*, account for $13 million in sales and 50 million readers. Their content centers around celebrities and the four S's: sleaze, sensationalism, sex, and scandals.

Many other papers serve the diverse population of the United States. The black press grew slightly during the 1980s. The *1988 Editor & Publisher International Yearbook* listed 184 black newspapers. One Indian journalist estimated that Native American newspapers made a 20 to 30 percent jump in the 1980s. Ethnic newspapers are published in languages ranging from Albanian to Yugoslavian. The Spanish press is the largest foreign-language press in the United States, with 51 newspapers.

Advertising takes about 60 percent of the space in U.S. dailies. This figure has remained steady for many years. Advertising revenue pays about three-fourths of the cost of publishing a newspaper.

The typical daily newspaper reader spends 44 minutes a day reading one or more newspapers. In the United States, 67 percent of the adults read a daily every weekday; 72 percent do on Sunday. Readership is highly correlated with education and income—which fact has kept newspapers popular with advertisers.

Many fine newspapers are published in the United States. At the top of the list are those that excel in coverage of local, state, national, and international news, that carry news that has an impact, and that emphasize good writing and clear graphics.

- *New York Times.* The *Times*, as the nation's paper of record, sets the national news agenda. "Page One of *The Times* is the barometer of what's truly important in the world," says *Los Angeles Times* media writer David Shaw (1989, p. 60). The *Time*'s extraordinary standards of coverage, writing, and editing make it a model for U.S. journalism. It leads a group of 35 regional newspapers, several magazines, and broadcast properties owned by the New York Times Company. Circulation is 1 million.
- *Washington Post.* Coverage of the nation's capital in its back yard makes the *Post* the nation's second most influential paper. It is noted for its political investigative stories. Circulation tops 770,000. The Washington Post Co. also owns *Newsweek* magazine, television stations, a cable company, and a feature syndicate.
- *Wall Street Journal.* The *Journal* is the nation's premier financial paper. It is marked by exemplary writing and business news coverage. It is distributed nationally via satellite to 18 locations and also publishes international editions. The *Journal* is published by Dow Jones & Company, Inc., a giant in financial information.
- *Los Angeles Times.* A strong financial history has enabled the *Times* to concentrate on its news coverage. Regional coverage is especially strong, and its long stories give much detail. It is the flagship of the Times Mirror Company, which owns several large U.S. newspapers, a cable company, and several book and magazine publishing companies.
- *Chicago Tribune.* The *Tribune* is renowned for its political coverage, blockbuster series, and editorial writing and cartoons. It is owned by the Tribune Company, which includes several news-

papers, newsprint and forest products, and entertainment enterprises. Circulation is 715,000.

- *Miami Herald.* One of the nation's most aggressive newspapers, the *Herald* is noted for its coverage of Latin America. It also is strong in local and sports news. Both it and the *Philadelphia Inquirer* are part of the Knight-Ridder Inc. group. Circulation tops 400,000.
- *Philadelphia Inquirer.* Great coverage of the city marks the *Inquirer.* It is known for its exhaustive and relentless pursuit of local, state, and regional news. Circulation is 500,000.
- *USA Today.* Although its content resembles a magazine more than a newspaper, the paper's influence on American journalism has been profound. Its use of color and snappy graphics has been copied extensively. *USA Today* is published by the Gannett Company and distributed via satellite to 33 U.S. printing sites.

Numerous other excellent papers are published in the United States, including the *Boston Globe*, the *Dallas Morning News*, the *Milwaukee Journal*, the *St. Petersburg Times*, the *San Jose Mercury News*, the *Louisville Courier-Journal*, the *St. Louis Post-Dispatch*, the *Christian Science Monitor*, the *Atlanta Constitution*, the *Baltimore Sun*, and *Newsday*.

Magazines. Magazines rounded the corner into the twentieth century as the nation's first national advertising medium. But they began to change when network radio grabbed much of the national advertising and when movies pulled readers away from romance and adventure. Many magazines began looking for their own market and their own circle of readers—their "niche."

Henry Luce found one among educated readers hungry for news, with his *Time* magazine. *Reader's Digest* went without fiction, pictures, or ads with a little magazine for the busy reader. *The New Yorker* aimed at a metropolitan upscale audience with quality writing. *Life* used vivid photography—and market research.

The magazine industry exploded during the 1960s, blasting specialized audiences into fragmented ones. Four new magazines appeared for every one that folded. By the late 1980s, some 1,200 titles were available.

Today's magazines employ research and marketing techniques as never before. The theoretical goal in the 1990s is a single-reader magazine designed by computer and delivered by satellite.

Competition from other media is formidable, but the result has been healthy. Magazine revenue went from $1.3 billion in 1975 to $5.9 billion in 1988, ad page sales from 81,000 to 167,000.

Most magazines are sold by subscription. Only about 11 percent of magazines are sold at retail outlets, mostly supermarkets. Advertising rates in magazines are based on size, use of color, times of insertion, location, edition, and production costs. A one-time, full-color, full-page ad in *The Atlantic* sold for $17,700 in January 1989.

Magazines have more freedom of expression than newspapers or television. Today, readers are finding different kinds of reporting. Some magazines are taking stands on complex issues: the homeless, AIDS, pollution, gun control.

The large number of magazines makes it difficult to generalize about them, but they can be grouped into loose categories.

- *News weeklies. Time, U.S. News and World Report,* and *Newsweek* report on a range of events—not only the national and international scene but also news of science, business, and so on. They have faced keen competition from Sunday newspapers, television talk shows, news programs, and public broadcasting. In response, they have improved graphics, added new departments, and altered content.

  Of the three, *Time* is the oldest and the healthiest. In 1988, it led all magazines in advertising revenue, with $350 million. *Time* gives more analysis and interpretation to the news than the other two. *U.S. News and World Report* emphasizes stories on education, health, and finance—"news you can use." *Newsweek* aims its stories at a modern, urban set of readers in their thirties and forties. It aggressively makes last-minute cover changes to beat the competition.

- *Women's magazines.* For many years the sole audience of these magazines was the housewife, who was served by the so-called seven sisters: *Ladies Home Journal, McCall's, Good Housekeeping, Better Homes and Gardens, Family Circle, Redbook,* and *Woman's Day.* But the changing role of women has in turn given birth to new magazines—25 mainstream titles in recent years.

- *Fashion magazines.* The top fashion magazines are *Vogue, Harper's Bazaar, Elle, Glamour, Mademoiselle, Cosmopolitan,* and *Lear's.*

- *Men's magazines.* Only two mainstream men's magazines exist: *Esquire* and *GQ.* Numerous titles serve two special interests that unite men: sex and sports.

- *Readers' magazines.* Graphics give way to text in these magazines, but otherwise tastes are varied. They include *The New Yorker, The Atlantic,* and *Harper's. Reader's Digest,* with 39 editions in 15 languages and 100 million circulation worldwide,

circulates 16.3 million in its U.S. edition (a Hispanic edition has 130,000 circulation).
- *Entertainment and culture magazines.* Titles include *Rolling Stone, People, Vanity Fair,* and *TV Guide,* which has 106 regional editions and a circulation of 15.8 million.
- *Business magazines.* The top three are *Fortune, Forbes,* and *Business Week.*
- *City and regional magazines.* A niche relating to geography has been carved out by magazines such as *Texas Monthly, Los Angeles,* and *Washingtonian.*
- *Institutions. National Geographic* and *Smithsonian* are top-rated magazines that tend to cover a wide range of topics with quality writing and photography. *Consumer Reports* carries no advertising to keep its independence in rating products.

Canada

Newspapers. There was a time earlier this century when the daily newspaper was the major—at times the only—medium through which Canadians got the news and information they needed. The arrival of radio and television toppled the newspaper from its position of prominence, but the daily remains a strong and profitable element of the media business.

On the average weekday, 8 million Canadians read a daily newspaper. They can choose from among approximately 110 dailies, with an average total circulation of 5.7 million. And for advertisers, the daily newspaper is still the prime medium: Newspaper advertising revenue was $1.96 billion in 1988.

Ownership of Canadian newspapers is highly concentrated. Some major Canadian newspaper companies are also involved in magazines, cable television, or book publishing. And for the largest chains, such as Thomson Corp., the newpaper holdings are but a small component of an economic empire.

During the 1980s, Canadian publishers found new ways to diversify their product and increase profits. One was the development of online databases, which can be accessed from computers in businesses and home offices. Another was the growth of the Sunday newspaper. Sunday newspapers run counter to newspaper tradition in Canada, where the Saturday paper is the week's biggest edition and carries the color comics and weekly inserts. In recent years, a number of large dailies have begun Sunday editions that are different in style, tone, and design from papers produced during the rest of the week.

The editors of most Canadian dailies see their prime responsibility as reporting on the local scene. Many newspapers, however, serve larger audiences—and mandates—through their thorough coverage of provincial, national, and international affairs.

- *Toronto Star.* With daily circulation of more than 562,000 (806,000 on Saturday and 533,000 on Sunday), the *Toronto Star* is the largest daily in Canada. It is owned by Torstar Corp., an information and entertainment company. The paper has a colorful history: Canadian journalism historian W. H. Kesterton (1967) notes that early in the century, the newspaper's love of stunts earned it a reputation as "the last home of razzle dazzle journalism." Today, the newspaper is known for both the breadth and the depth of its news coverage.
- *Globe and Mail.* This Toronto newspaper describes itself as "Canada's national newspaper." It targets Canada's political and economic elite and has long been known as one of the country's top newspapers of record. A national edition is distributed across Canada, and sales outside Toronto account for a substantial portion of the *Globe and Mail*'s 326,000 daily circulation. The newspaper joined FP Publications in 1965 and became part of the Thomson newspaper empire when Thomson bought out FP in the 1970s. The newspaper has a strong reputation for quality reporting, and its daily "Report on Business" is virtually required reading for the business community.
- *Toronto Sun.* Toronto's brash and breezy *Sun* tabloid is a newcomer in Canadian journalism—and a vastly successful one. It was founded in 1971, when 62 people put out of work by the closing of the *Toronto Telegram* decided to set up their own paper. They chose the tabloid format—easy to read on the city's subway and bus system—and developed a formula of simple writing, large headlines, and lots of sports coverage. The first press run was 60,000; today, weekday circulation is just under 300,000. In 1973, the *Sun* added a Sunday edition whose circulation now tops 460,000. The *Sun* is owned by Toronto Sun Publishing Corp., which is in turn controlled by Maclean Hunter, Inc.
- *Ottawa Citizen.* The leading newspaper in Canada's capital has a circulation of close to 211,000 (249,000 on Saturday and 170,000 on Sunday). The *Citizen* is a major holding of Southam, Inc., which produces several other leading Canadian dailies, including both Vancouver dailies (the *Sun* and the *Province*) and the *Calgary Herald*, *Edmonton Journal*, and *Montreal Gazette*.
- *Vancouver Sun.* With a daily circulation of 227,000 (280,000 on

Saturdays), the *Vancouver Sun* is the largest newspaper west of Toronto. Vancouver journalism earlier this century was marked by a hotly contested competition for readers between the *Sun* and the *Vancouver Province.* A series of mergers, however, has brought the two papers under the ownership of the Southam newspaper chain.

- *Winnipeg Free Press.* This newspaper's reputation as the prestige paper of the prairies can be traced back to John W. Dafoe's 40 years as editor. The paper is now owned by Thomson Newspapers Company, Ltd. Its circulation is 169,000 daily, 145,000 on Sunday.

- *Le Devoir.* Despite its relatively small circulation—27,000 daily and 31,000 on Sunday—Montreal's *Le Devoir* has long been one of the most influential dailies in Canada. It was founded in 1910 with an eye toward serving the French-Canadian intellectual elite and has been a strong voice for federalism.

- *La Presse.* With ten times the circulation of *Le Devoir, La Presse* (circulation 221,000 daily, 327,000 on Saturday, and 184,000 on Sunday) is the leading French-language newspaper in the city of Montreal, the province of Quebec, and, indeed, the country as a whole. The newspaper is owned by Paul Desmarais's Gesca, a subsidiary of Power Corp., one of the major conglomerates in Canada.

- *Le Journal de Montréal.* Montreal's largest-circulation daily (328,000 daily, 355,000 on Saturday, and 348,000 on Sunday) began publication in 1964 when a strike at *La Presse* left the market open for a popular French-language daily. The tabloid is owned by Quebecor, Inc., which also owns the *Winnipeg Sun,* the *Journal de Québec,* close to 60 regional weeklies, four popular weeklies, several magazines, and a book publisher.

- *Halifax Chronicle-Herald and Mail-Star.* The leading newspaper of Canada's Maritime Provinces is the result of a series of mergers. Halifax Herald Ltd. publishes the morning *Chronicle-Herald* (circulation 88,000) and the evening *Mail-Star* (circulation 60,000).

Weekly Newspapers.   The weekly newspaper has been a major component of Canadian journalism for more than 200 years. Approximately 950 are in business, and advertising revenue tops $600 million. During the 1980s, there was rapid growth in chain ownership of weekly papers. Desktop publishing also arrived, which has meant major savings on production costs. An increasing number of weeklies are distributed free of charge to readers.

Magazines. Canada's magazine business has never been as healthy as some other sectors of the print media. There are many reasons for this, including a small and linguistically divided domestic market and an overwhelming influx of foreign magazines, particularly from the United States.

Canada has tried on occasion to stem the tide of American magazines flowing into Canada. In 1931, R. B. Bennett's Conservative government imposed a content tax on U.S. magazines. As a result, about 50 American magazines moved their printing into Canada. When the tax was abolished a few years later, the American magazines moved home.

Interest in news and information magazines rose strongly during World War II, and some American magazines, including *Time*, began producing Canadian editions, while others relied on exports to Canada. By 1960, fully 75 percent of the general-interest magazines bought in Canada were American. Only five Canadian general-interest consumer magazines were in business, and two of them were in poor economic shape.

Royal commissions in the 1960s and 1970s made recommendations on ways to help the Canadian magazine industry. In 1975, the federal government changed the tax laws, adding a strict definition of what makes a magazine Canadian for tax purposes. *Time* closed its Canadian edition in 1976, and American publishers continue to fight the Canadian tax law. They won a measure of success in the Canada-U.S. Free Trade Agreement when Canadian negotiators agreed that if a magazine meets the other criteria for being Canadian, it could be typeset and printed in the United States.

Maclean Hunter Ltd. was one of the biggest beneficiaries of the 1975 tax change. With *Time Canada* out of the way, the field was open for a weekly Canadian newsmagazine. A revamped and redesigned *Macleans's* hit the newsstands in 1978. Its circulation is now 645,000. Maclean Hunter also produces the country's leading women's magazine, *Châtelaine*, with separate English and French editions. Circulation of the English-language *Châtelaine* is 1 million; the French, 285,000.

Saturday Night, one of the oldest Canadian magazines, is back on an upswing after some hard times in the 1960s and 1970s (it ceased publication for six months in 1974 and 1975). It is owned by Conrad Black's Hollinger, Inc., and circulation is 140,000.

Other magazines of note are the popular science magazine *Equinox* (circulation 163,000) and the consumer and environmentalist bimonthly *Harrowsmith* (circulation 155,000). Both are owned by Telemedia Publishing, Inc., of Toronto.

Alternative Media. The alternative press continues to struggle for survival in Canada, but several magazines and periodicals managed to keep their heads above water in the conservative mainstream of the 1980s. *Canadian Forum*, for 70 years Canada's leading political monthly, resumed publication in 1989 after a shutdown that lasted more than a year. Other leading alternative publications include *This Magazine, Now, Probe Post, Briarpatch*, and *New Maritimes*.

Ethnic Press. Canada is truly a nation of immigrants and has a long tradition of foreign-language periodicals aimed at preserving ethnic culture. The *1988 Editor & Publisher Yearbook* lists about 75 foreign-language periodicals in Canada, produced in more than 30 languages.

ELECTRONIC MEDIA

The electronic media represent North America's commercial and entertainment marketplace. Radio and television signals don't stop at the border. Entertainment and news programs have become multicultural. Besides radio and television, cable operations have become a major distributor of programs, and videocassette recorders provide an alternative to radio, television, and cable.

United States

The first regular network in the United States was started by the National Broadcasting Company (NBC), a subsidiary of the Radio Corporation of America, in 1926. It had 24 stations. A year later, the Columbia Phonograph Record Company began the Columbia Broadcasting System (CBS). NBC operated two networks, a red and a blue, but sold the blue network, which became the American Broadcasting Company (ABC). The three networks have been the prime providers of radio and television programming for seven decades.

Network affiliation means that stations may—but are not required to—carry network programming. In return, the networks pay the local stations to carry their programs. The increased audience numbers enable the networks to charge advertisers more.

Since the number of people watching programs not only indicates their popularity but also how much ads cost, broadcasters check audiences through ratings services.

The A. C. Nielsen Company, the nation's largest ratings firm, uses a scientific sample of about 2,000 households in its national research. It collects information from "people meters," which indicate which viewers in a household are watching when a set is on. Nielsen also employs a "black box" to record when a set is on and to relay the information to a computer. Some viewers are asked to fill out diaries about the programs they watch.

A program's *rating* indicates the percentage of sets tuned to it. A *share* reflects the percentage of turned-on sets turned to a program.

Broadcasting in the United States is regulated primarily through the Federal Communications Commission. It was created in 1934 with the prime mission of putting order into the use of radio frequencies. Assigning frequencies and stations are still major FCC responsibilities. A third is regulating existing stations. It issues licenses and monitors the content of both radio and television. The FCC has no jurisdiction over the networks.

Radio. Radio is everywhere. Eight of every ten Americans listen to it every day, and the other two hear it by the end of the week. They receive it on the average of 5.6 radios in their homes. They hear it in one of their 131 million cars with radios or the 37 million trucks, vans, and recreational vehicles. Or they might be one of the 21 million Americans who carry a radio with them on walks.

In 1988, a total of 10,337 U.S. radio stations beamed signals over the airwaves. Of these, 4,913 broadcast over the AM (amplitude modulation) band. AM is the traditional wavelength, and today its programming leans toward sports and information. A total of 4,085 stations broadcast over the FM (frequency modulation) band, which came into use in the 1960s. The FM is a short-range, line-of-sight signal that provides excellent clarity. FM stations tend toward music programming, much of it in stereo. FM's better sound quality has given it about three-fourths of the radio audience. Noncommercial radio stations total 1,339 and are found primarily on the FM dial.

Radio is pervasive, but not in the same sense as a half century or so ago, when it was the prime mass medium in the country. Millions of people sat in their living rooms in the 1930s and 1940s and listened to drama, comedy, news, mysteries, big bands, and soap operas (so named because they were sponsored by soap companies).

But the advent of television burst radio's balloon, and it took two decades after 1950 for radio to pump itself back up in a different form. Radio has changed from a mass medium into a more specialized, personal companion. Stations try to attract a specific kind of audience by restricting programming to a narrow format. Adult contemporary, country, and rock music are the three most popular formats, but two dozen others also exist.

Because of its immediacy, news has been a staple of radio since its infancy. Today, radio is the typical American's major source of news in the mornings and during urban commuting periods, when it brings traffic reports and weather forecasts.

Television. Television is the most popular and influential mass medium in the United States. Americans spend more time watching television than doing just about anything else. It is their confidant, companion, and family member. Broadcasting over the airwaves still provides most of the material viewers watch, but cable and videocassette recorders are muscling onto the TV screen.

More than 175 million television sets dot the United States. Over 90 million homes—98 percent—have at least one; 63 percent have two or more. Almost every home has a color set. The average household, including those that have cable, can receive 27 channels, and only 7 percent can get fewer than six, according to the 1989 Nielsen report.

Commercial broadcast TV stations numbered 1,064 in 1988. Of these, 545 operated at very high frequency (VHF) on channels 2–13, and 519 are ultra high frequency (UHF), broadcasting over channels 14–82. The number of UHF stations doubled during the 1980s. In addition, 334 noncommercial television stations broadcast in the United States.

Americans spend 6 hours, 55 minutes a day watching television, Nielsen reports. That is one hour more than in 1970 and two hours more than in 1960. However, viewing time peaked at 7 hours, 10 minutes in 1985 and has been declining incrementally since. The television audience is highest during the so-called prime-time hours of 8 to 11 p.m. Situation comedy is the most popular type of program, followed by feature films and general drama.

News and public affairs programming has long been a constant in TV programming. Early on, the network's evening news shows were 15 minutes long, but they produced some memorable documentaries, led by Edward R. Murrow on CBS. In the mid-1960s, the evening news shows were expanded to 30 minutes. Weekend and morning news programs and prime-time "magazines" were also added. The three network evening news shows each attract at least 9 million viewers.

Initially, news cost more to produce than it returned in revenue, but the situation changed as it attracted more viewers. CBS's "60 Minutes" was a top-rated program throughout the 1980s. The Cable News Network carries news around the clock. Polls have consistently shown that television is the preferred source of news for most Americans, who consider TV news more believable and trustworthy. The increased audiences, and revenue, from news programs keep the networks investing millions in celebrity newscasters. In the 1980s, network budget woes forced a cutback in their news staffs. Technology now allows many local stations to dispense with network news and pick up advertising revenue for their own news shows.

Cable. Cable television started in 1948 as a means to carry local signals to remote or isolated areas. Cable service exploded in the 1970s as satellite communications allowed national distribution of programs. In the 1980s, the number of subscribing households tripled. In 1989, as many as 53 percent of the homes in the United States had cable, and 29 percent also subscribed to one of the pay cable services, according to the Television Bureau of Advertising.

The average subscriber has access to about 35 channels of entertainment and information programming, according to the National Cable Television Association. Some offerings are merely national relays of independent stations in major cities, such as WTBS from Atlanta, with the second largest number of subscribers. Most, however, reach special-interest audiences. These include the top-selling Entertainment and Sports Network, number 3 Cable News Network, and others carrying rock videos, cultural programming, minority programs, live coverage of government, and so on. Their proliferation is based on the idea of "narrowcasting"—targeting a specific audience for advertisers. The largest pay service is Home Box Office.

The largest cable multiple system operator (MSO) is Tele-Communications, Inc., followed by American Television and Communications Corp. Each has more than 4 million subscribers. About a third of cable systems have ties with broadcast interests, 20 percent with program producers, and 18 percent with newspapers. Cross ownership is common. At the local level, cable companies operate without competition. Federal law prevents their being regulated as a utility.

Subscribers spend about $15 monthly for basic services and about $10 more if they want pay cable offerings. The local cable companies then pay the cable networks a fee based on the number of subscribers. The cable companies nationwide have total revenue of about $15 billion. About half comes from basic services, a fourth from pay cable, and the rest from other services.

Videocassette Recorders. Almost two-thirds of U.S. homes have a VCR attached to a television set. One study found VCR users renting almost five movies a month and thus cutting into both broadcast and cable use. Nielsen data show that VCR recording occurs throughout the day, although 40 percent is done during prime time and 25 percent during the daytime. Two-thirds of the taped material comes from the networks, according to the Television Information Office. That's good news to the networks; the bad news is that the VCR's remote control devices enable viewers to scroll past commercials in programs they have taped.

Canada

Canada's broadcasting system is a unique mix of public and private, commercial and noncommercial, that reflects its historical ties to Britain and its geographic, cultural, and economic ties to the United States.

The public radio and television network, the Canadian Broadcasting Corporation (CBC), traces its roots to the British Broadcasting Corporation. But in style, content, and presentation, much of Canadian radio and television is virtually indistinguishable from American broadcasting. And through cable and satellite transmission, Canadians from Windsor to well north of Whitehorse receive large, undiluted doses of American television, including round-the-clock pickups of the major U.S. networks.

The prospect of Canadian voices being drowned out by the overwhelming chorus from the south is a perennial and long-standing concern. It prompted the appointment of a royal commission in 1928, charged with developing policies to ensure Canadian control of broadcasting from Canadian sources. In the ensuing six decades, reports by about a dozen commissions, committees, and task forces have addressed the same question. Gerald Caplan and Florian Sauvageau, the cochairs of the most recent task force, said in their 1986 Task Force on Broadcasting Policy report that they were appointed in circumstances strikingly similar to those facing the 1928 royal commission.

Caplan and Sauvageau cite a recurring set of issues confronting policymakers: Canadian programming versus American, public ownership versus private, the responsibilities of the public broadcaster versus those of the private sector, the subsidizing of culture versus protection of commercial interests, the commercial needs of private stations versus freedom of expression, federal authority versus provincial, annual funding of the CBC versus longer-term financing, and technology versus programming as the driving force of the system.

The stream of task force studies and reports has had the effect of protecting and promoting an indigenous broadcasting industry. Nonetheless, the level of foreign domination of Canadian television is striking: Of the 52,000 hours of English television programming available to the average Canadian annually, fewer than 400 hours are Canadian drama; of the 27,000 hours of French-language programming available to the average Francophone viewer, 630 hours are Canadian drama. More than 70 percent of English-speaking Canadians tune their

TV dial to American shows during the peak viewing hours of 7 to 11 p.m. And in French Canada, where language has been relied on to protect against American influence, teenagers spend more than half their viewing time watching foreign programs.

The broadcasting regulatory body is the Canadian Radio-television and Telecommunications Commission (CRTC), which is charged with regulating and supervising all aspects of the Canadian broadcasting system in line with the policies contained in the 1968 Broadcasting Act. The CRTC was founded as the Canadian Radio-Television Commission by that act, replacing the 10-year-old Board of Broadcast Governors. In its early years, the CRTC took a hands-on approach to broadcast regulation, making rules on the amount of Canadian content stations and networks must carry and developing cable TV and FM policy. In recent years, however, the CRTC has been less of an activist. In part this is because of extra demands placed on it in 1975, when its mandate and name were expanded to cover telecommunications. In part, however, it is also due to a change in government philosophy, which emphasizes marketplace considerations over government regulation.

Radio. Radio developed in Canada in much the same way as in the United States, but at a slower pace. The result was that by the late 1920s, American radio dominated the airwaves in Canada. The newly formed U.S. radio networks sent their programming north, either directly from stations across the border or from Canadian stations that served largely as relays. In addition, Canadian stations experienced interference from unregulated U.S. stations.

The 1928 royal commission headed by Sir John Aird recommended that Canada adopt a British or European model of public broadcasting rather than the commercial form that was developing in the United States. Parliament passed an act creating the Canadian Radio Broadcasting Commission in 1932, and replaced it with the stronger Canadian Broadcasting Corporation in 1986. The CRBC was given broad powers—it was to regulate and carry on broadcasting, originate programming, and lease or build stations. Its goal was full public ownership of all Canadian broadcasting. The money was never provided to reach this goal, however, and in most cities, network programming was broadcast on privately owned stations. This mixed system of publicly owned CBC stations and privately owned affiliates is still the pattern today for CBC radio and television.

CBC radio operates four radio networks: mono and stereo in both English and French. Programs are distributed through owned-and-operated stations, affiliates, or rebroadcast transmitters. CBC radio programming is noncommercial, and shows are produced regionally or nationally. CBC also operates the Radio-Canada International shortwave service and the Northern Service, which broadcasts news and entertainment programming in English, French, and seven native Canadian languages. CBC radio is a leader in news and public affairs reporting in Canada. Its productions include the prestigious magazine show "Sunday Morning" and the nightly "As It Happens."

Although the CBC is Canada's best-known radio broadcaster, there are roughly 325 private AM radio stations and 120 on the FM band. As in the United States, FM radio is increasingly popular, while AM has been in relative decline. Annual revenue taken in by private radio totals about $550 million, virtually all of it from advertising.

Networking of private radio stations is a relatively new phenomenon. Until recently it was the domain of the public sector. In the fall of 1989, Canada's only private all-news national radio network, CKO, ceased operation. CKO, which operated in nine Canadian cities, had lost $55 million since its formation in 1976. CKO's licenses were returned to the CRTC. In Quebec, unlike in English-speaking Canada, private AM radio is dominated by two major networks, Télémedia and Radiomutuel.

Television. Television arrived in Canada in 1952. As with radio, plans for the CBC to control both programming and distribution were scrapped due to a lack of money. Unlike the BBC in Britain, CBC TV would not be self-sufficient. Some stations would be owned and operated by the CBC, but in many areas, private license holders would distribute the network's national programs.

CBC TV operates two networks: English and French. Unlike commercial-free CBC radio, CBC TV carries advertisements. Advertising revenue—about $300 million in 1987–1988—is, however, a relatively minor source of income. About 80 percent of the corporation's revenue comes from government appropriations. The CBC is a major originator of TV programming, and Canadian shows now account for 82 percent of prime-time CBC TV programming. (News, current affairs, and sports programming are strong components of the prime-time schedule.) However, a major budget cut announced by the federal government in 1989 has forced the CBC to postpone plans to "Canadianize" 95 percent of its network prime-time schedule.

Despite the budget cut, the corporation opened a 24-hour, all-news cable TV channel in 1989. The channel is modeled in part after the U.S. Cable News Network, which is carried by many cable systems. CBC's "Newsworld" is part of basic cable TV service across Canada. CBC is also a shareholder with seven other Canadian partners in the Canadian branch of the international French-language consortium TV5.

The CBC's leading news show is "The National," which is immediately followed by the current affairs show "The Journal." In central Canada, the package begins at 10 p.m., an hour ahead of the major news broadcast by the private network, CTV.

CTV began operation in 1961 and competes nationally with the CBC. In Ontario, both compete for audiences with a regional private network, Global Television. The French-language TVA, which has ten affiliates in Quebec and competes with French-language CBC, is also being challenged by the small, new Quatre Saisons network, which operates in the major regional markets of Quebec. Private networks in Canada are subject to CRTC regulation, including Canadian content requirements. The content rules for private broadcasters are less stringent than those for the public CBC.

Regionally, some provinces finance and operate their own TV services. Radio-Québec, the Access Network in Alberta, TV Ontario (which offers French and English service), and, on a smaller scale, British Columbia's Knowledge Network of the West, all produce a number of educational and cultural programs, and many attract substantial general audiences.

Cable. With cable television available to 80 percent of Canadian households, Canada is the second most cabled country in the world, after Belgium. Three-quarters of households to whom cable is available subscribe, which means that 67 percent of households are connected.

The high penetration level of cable was achieved almost entirely through the sale of basic cable service rather than pay or specialty services. In 1983, before pay and specialty services were approved, the number of subscribers was only 5 percentage points below what it is now.

Cable in Canada is regulated by the CRTC. Since cable operates as a series of local monopolies, without competition among firms for subscribers, the CRTC plays a major role in setting a rate structure. The CRTC also sets regulations on the services that cable firms must provide, including a requirement that all but the smallest cable systems must set aside a community channel. In many communities, local council meetings are broadcast on cable. Community channels also provide opportunities for programming by ethnic groups. The CRTC also has regulations on simulcasting, or the use of two channels to carry an identical signal. This practice ensures a wider audience for Canadian advertisers.

Canadian cable television operators took in $870 million in revenue in 1987. About 500 companies provide cable service, but the industry is dominated by three firms—Rogers Telecommunications

Ltd., Télécable Vidéotron Ltée., and Maclean Hunter Ltd.—which between them account for more than 50 percent of cable subscriptions.

National Film Board. Finally, no entry on Canadian journalism would be complete without a mention of the documentary filmmaking work of the National Film Board. The NFB, founded in 1939, was a pioneer in the film documentary, and its productions have won awards around the world.

NEWS SERVICES

Not all the news and information carried by North America's mass media is provided by their own employees. Much of the content comes from news agencies set up to provide information from outside local areas. Full-service agencies provide news, photos, and graphics. They also collect news from their clients and distribute it worldwide. Supplemental news agencies offer stories from individual newspapers or groups. The media also receive feature and entertainment material from national feature syndicates.

United States

In Chapter 2, we were introduced to the leading agencies, the Associated Press and United Press International. For additional news, many U.S. media receive supplemental stories from foreign news agencies, although they are full-service agencies in their home countries. British-based Reuters operates 14 bureaus in the United States and serves about 200 North American newspapers. Agence France-Presse directly serves several U.S. papers with an English-language version of its international news report and its photographic service.

Several U.S. news services offer material that augments the full coverage of AP and UPI. Supplemental agencies give news media a choice of domestic stories as well as additional features, in-depth stories, and analyses. Stories average about 800 words each.

Most supplemental services are arms of individual newspapers or newspaper groups. These include the Los Angeles Times/Washington Post News Service, the New York Times News Service, the Scripps Howard News Service, the Knight-Ridder/Tribune News Information Service, the Copley News Service, the Christian Science Monitor News Service, and the Newhouse News Service. Selling stories helps the papers recoup some of the costs of reporting. In turn, buyers can get stories from top-name reporters and prestigious newspapers.

Syndication companies, a type of news agency, supply most U.S. newspapers' feature and entertainment material, including comic strips, columns, and editorial cartoons. A writer or artist creates the material, and the syndicate produces, markets, and distributes it to individual newspapers for a slice of the fee. Fees are on a sliding scale. At one paper they may be only a few dollars, but the syndicates' object is to multiply the users. Popular offerings such as "Garfield" appear in 2,000 papers.

Eight major syndicates dominate the market: Creators Syndicate, Inc.; King Features Syndicate; Los Angeles Times Syndicate; New York Times Syndicate Sales Corp.; Tribune Media Services; United Media; Universal Press Syndicate; and the Washington Post Writers Group.

Canada

In Canada, the major national wire service is the Canadian Press, which serves 109 daily newspapers and offers domestic and international news in English and French, as well as business news, sports, and photographs. Like AP, CP is owned and operated cooperatively by the newspaper publishers and has about 550 staff in eight bureaus in Canada. CP operates bureaus in Washington, New York, London, and Moscow but gets most of its international news from the Associated Press, Reuters, and Agence France-Presse.

CP was founded largely as a business necessity. At the turn of the twentieth century, Canadian Pacific Telegraphs acquired the rights to distribute Associated Press reports, which were transmitted in bulk— and at low rates—to Canadian newspapers. When a handful of Canadian newspapers set up the Western Associated Press and tried to circulate Canadian news, Canadian Pacific Telegraphs charged them commercial rates, which worked out to be about four times higher than the AP package. The newspapers protested, and the telegraph company eventually withdrew, clearing the way for a domestic news agency. In 1917, the prime minister, Robert Borden, decided that the national interest would justify a subsidy of $50,000 a year to allow the creation of a national service. The subsidy ended in 1923.

CP provides news for broadcasters through Broadcast News Ltd., which operates both wire and audio services for private broadcasters, and Press News Ltd., which provides news for the CBC and has a range of other clients.

United Press International provides some competition for CP, although its role has diminished since the demise of United Press Canada, which was founded by the *Toronto Sun* and UPI in the late 1970s and operated until 1985. About ten Canadian dailies now subscribe directly to UPI. In the private radio market, UPI has an arrangement with Standard Broadcasting, which competes with CP's Broadcast News subsidiary.

Both Southam and Thomson operate news services that supplement the CP wire. Southam News has five domestic and seven foreign bureaus filing news reports and columns for the Southam chain. (Some non-Southam dailies also subscribe.) Thomson columnists and reporters provide copy for about 45 smaller Thomson newspapers.

Canadian dailies also subscribe to the services of major U.S. newspapers, including the New York Times News Service and the Los Angeles Times/Washington Post service.

Among specialized agencies operating in Canada are Canadian University Press, which provides a news exchange among college and university papers, and Agence de Presse Francophone, a small, new agency that provides news to French-language newspapers outside of Quebec.

GOVERNMENT-MEDIA RELATIONS

Thomas Jefferson once said he would prefer newspapers without government to government without newspapers. But Jefferson never really had that choice, and neither do the modern-day citizens of the United States and Canada. Both government and media exist in a relationship where rights and responsibilities are continually evolving.

United States

In the United States, press freedom stems from the First Amendment to the Constitution, which prohibits Congress from making laws curtailing the freedom of the press. But while the mass media have great freedom, they are by no means completely free. Through legislation, regulation, and judicial interpretation, the government exercises controls over both the content of information and access to it.

Control over Content. The U.S. Supreme Court established early in the twentieth century that the press was free to carry what it wished, within limits. Overall, the press has been accorded freedom from prior restraint, or censorship, in coverage of public affairs.

Only in wartime has the government overtly censored the media, and the press usually cooperated and even acquiesced to government dictates. A strong challenge to prior restraint came during the 1970s, when the *New York Times* and the *Washington Post* were prevented for

14 days from publishing secret papers about the Vietnam War and a radical magazine was barred from carrying a story about how to make an atomic bomb.

The guiding principle has been that if the press has the information, little can be done to stop dissemination—but the press can face penalties afterward.

After-publication actions have centered on libel, or the communication of defamatory information. In these cases, individuals are permitted to sue the press in the civil courts to seek damages and, occasionally, punishment. U.S. Supreme Court rulings have made it difficult for government officials, politicians, and celebrities to win a libel suit because they must show that the media published the story knowing that it was or might be false. Plaintiffs today may also seek redress from the press by claiming an invasion of privacy.

Outside the area of news and public affairs, the First Amendment can be stretched quite thin. It only partly covers student journalists and advertising, and it does not cover obscene material at all.

In 1988, the Supreme Court ruled that educators in public schools (but not public colleges) could exercise editorial control if it were based on legitimate pedagogical concerns. Complaints about school censorship immediately rose 25 percent.

Advertising that concerns "matters of clear public interest" enjoys First Amendment protection, but not if it is false, deceptive, or misleading. Monitoring of advertising has fallen to various government agencies such as the Federal Trade Commission.

Obscenity has been a nebulous concept hinging on a definition that never quite sits still. Publications often complain that it is impossible not to run obscene material if no one but the Supreme Court knows what it is beforehand.

Content of the electronic media, both broadcast and cable, falls under the jurisdiction of the Federal Communications Commission, which requires broadcasters to "serve the public interest." In effect the FCC has ultimate control over content—the power to revoke a broadcaster's license. Although the FCC is forbidden by law from censoring programs, it uses programming as a criterion of public service.

The most pervasive FCC regulation affecting broadcasting was the fairness doctrine, which required broadcasters to cover controversial issues and to air opposing viewpoints. The FCC dropped the fairness doctrine in 1987 as part of a broadcast deregulation effort. Congress tried to make the regulation a law, but President Reagan vetoed the legislation.

Still in effect are regulations affecting political campaigns. The so-called equal-time rule says that if a candidate uses a station, the station must afford an equal opportunity to all other candidates for that office, and the station has no power over the content of the material. News coverage is exempted, however.

Content of the electronic media is restricted in other ways, often from a moralistic point of view. For example, the FCC has given broadcasters a 25-word definition of what it considers "indecent" material, which it prohibits except between midnight and 6 a.m., when children are not likely to be in the audience.

Control over Access. In terms of restrictions on content about public affairs, the press has fared relatively well, with some exceptions for the electronic media. In recent years, the government has shifted to the area of access. Government seems to follow the theory that if the press can't be stopped once it has the information, it must be prevented from getting it. *Media Law Reporter* recorded only seven access cases in 1977 but 200 in 1985, and the annual tally has continued at about that level.

Journalists generally argue that the press, as the eyes and ears of the public, has special rights under the First Amendment. However, the U.S. Supreme Court has ruled that journalists do not enjoy special privileges under the First Amendment to gather information unavailable to other citizens. At the local level, however, journalists are often accorded special rights and access through tradition.

Two areas where the press complained of government interference in the 1970s concerned confidential sources and newsroom searches. Most states have since passed "shield laws" that give journalists some protection from having to reveal their sources. In 1980, Congress made it necessary for police to obtain a subpoena before conducting a search of a journalist's home or office for criminal evidence.

A significant impediment to news gathering has been the tendency of government toward secrecy. Where most documents were open a half century ago, now they are closeted away. Reporters—indeed, all citizens—are denied access to records and files, not just at the federal but also the state and local levels, which tend to follow the federal pattern.

The cornerstone of open government at the federal level is the Freedom of Information Act, which gives "any person" access to all records of all federal agencies unless they fall within one of nine categories of exemptions. But over the years, the law has been continually eroded.

The courts have been a particularly difficult area for access, stemming from a conflict between the First Amendment and the Sixth Amendment, which guarantees a fair trial. Judges, who rule when a conflict arises, have been prone to close courtrooms, pretrial proceed-

ings, and court files and to issue "gag orders," which prohibit participants in a trial from talking to the press. Almost all the states allow
photographic coverage of court proceedings. Five states and the federal
court system do not.

Canada

Constitutional Protection. Press freedom is guaranteed in the Canadian
Charter of Rights and Freedoms. Section 2(b) of the Charter lists
"freedom of thought, belief, opinion and expression, including freedom
of the press and other media of communication," as fundamental
freedoms in Canadian society. Section 1 of the Charter guarantees these
fundamental freedoms, subject only to "such reasonable limits pre-
scribed by law as can be demonstrably justified in a free and democratic
society."

This written guarantee of freedom of expression is, however,
relatively new. The Charter has been in effect since 1982, when the
British Parliament enacted legislation giving Canada control over its
own constitution. (Until that time, Canada's chief constitutional docu-
ment, the 1867 British North America Act, was an act of the British
Parliament and could only be amended there.)

The preamble of the 1867 act that created the Canadian Confederation says Canada's constitution is "similar in principle" to that of the
United Kingdom. This means that the basic ideas of British democracy,
including freedom of the press, are basic to Canadian democracy as well.

Robert Martin and G. Stuart Adam, in their 1989 *Sourcebook of
Canadian Media Law*, note that the philosophical underpinnings of
Canada's support for freedom of expression are complex. Canada draws
on liberal democratic theory that emphasizes the primacy of the rights
of the individual, but it also draws on the collectivist conception that
freedom of expression is essential to the success of democracy and not
merely a commodity possessed by individuals.

The Canadian Charter of Rights and Freedoms dramatically extends the scope of judicial review and the authority of the Supreme
Court of Canada, giving the Court powers similar to those of the U.S.
Supreme Court. Martin and Adam say the post-Charter rulings of the
Supreme Court of Canada have made it clear that the Charter's provisions will be made to apply only to the state and its institutions. This
means that while the court will strike down legislation that contra-
venes the "fundamental freedom" of expression, it is unlikely to
interfere if a private individual—a publisher, for example—interferes
with a journalist's right to free expression.

Control over Content. Freedom of expression in Canada has never been absolute. There are laws prohibiting the importation or distribution of obscene material and hate propaganda, and provinces have the authority to operate film censorship boards. At various times, broader levels of censorship have been imposed.

During both world wars, Canada invoked the War Measures Act, which gives the government sweeping powers to suspend the freedoms of Canadians. Telephone and telegraphic communication was censored, and the government banned associations and publications that were viewed as hostile to government policy or actions. The War Measures Act was also invoked during the so-called October Crisis of 1970, triggered by the two political kidnappings by members of the Front de Libération du Québec. In 1988, the War Measures Act was replaced by the Emergencies Act. Its provisions could also drastically limit freedom of expression.

In the area of criminal law, codified and uncodified laws restrict what can be published. The 1985 Young Offenders Act prohibits publication of the names of juveniles charged with or convicted of criminal offenses. There are also restrictions on the kinds of information that can be published about adults charged with criminal offenses. Newspapers cannot, for example, publish a prior criminal record or any other information that might prejudice prospects for a fair trial.

The major form of after-publication action against the press in Canada is libel. Journalists sued for libel have several possible defenses; the most common ones are proving that the statements at issue are true or that they are fair comments made in good faith on matters of public interest. Most libel cases are civil matters, although there is provision in Canada for defamatory or criminal libel.

Parliament claims the right to protect against false, unfair, or defamatory accounts of its proceedings. In theory, Parliament could imprison an offending journalist, although such an action is extremely unlikely to occur. In 1975, however, the House of Commons took the unusual step of calling a Montreal newspaper before a special committee to defend a news report.

Control over Access. The Canadian counterpart to the U.S. Freedom of Information Act is the 1983 Access to Information Act. The difference in the titles is more than simply symbolic: The Canadian legislation is considerably less powerful than the American. It has 5 mandatory and 12 discretionary exemptions. Its greatest gap as far as journalists are concerned is that it does not apply at all to the cabinet system. Canada's information commissioner, who handles complaints about problems with access requests, has said the rule of thumb for some bureaucrats seems to be "only disclose information when you can't find a way to exempt it."

The flip side of the access coin is Canada's Official Secrets Act. Although the intent of the act is to combat spying, it could be used to prosecute almost anyone releasing or receiving information that is classified "secret official" by the government. It has been used against a newspaper only once, in 1978, and that prosecution was unsuccessful. In a more recent case involving leaked documents, a television reporter was charged under the Criminal Code in 1989 with possession of stolen goods after broadcasting details about the federal budget that had not yet been made public.

Canada has no "shield laws" for journalists.

The Press and Politics. Reporting on the federal government is done from the Parliamentary Press Gallery, which has been called the most powerful instrument of political communication in the country. The gallery combines the jobs done in the United States by the White House press corps and the Congressional press corps and is the key Canadian institution for disseminating government initiatives and commenting on them.

The parliamentary system ensures that journalists have relatively easy access to the country's top political leaders. The House of Commons is the forum for debate, and reporters covering the House meet with party leaders or government ministers en masse in "scrums" or individually in interviews in the corridors of the Parliament buildings. Formal news conferences by the prime minister, by contrast, are relatively uncommon.

The intensity of contact between press and politicians soars during Canada's highly compressed election campaigns. Parliament is dissolved for the campaign, and the leaders ricochet around the country, trailed by reporters, photographers, and TV cameras. The campaigns are heavily stage-managed and aimed at a TV audience.

In the 1980s, media polling became a major tool for covering election campaigns. During the seven-week 1988 federal election campaign, TV networks and newspapers commissioned 24 major polls—twice the number conducted during the 1984 campaign, and three times the number in 1980 and 1979. Supporters of media polling say the technique makes for better journalism, providing reporters with insights into how the voters feel about the party leaders' policies and campaign performance. Critics of the practice argue that continuous polling places too much emphasis on the horse-race aspects of campaigns and may help create the very consensus the polls are said to reflect.

CONCEPTS OF MEDIA FREEDOM

The concept of media freedom in Western societies has changed and evolved as the societies and the media developed. In North America as elsewhere, the social, political, economic, and governmental forces at work have all affected the development of the mass media.

In the earliest days of European settlement, colonial authorities kept a tight lid on publishing. In the United States, Benjamin Harris's *Publick Occurrences, Both Foreign and Domestick* died in 1690 after one issue, killed by Massachusetts licensing restrictions. In Canada, the earliest newspapers depended on the patronage of the colonial government and served more or less as an official press.

As we saw in Chapter 2, the development of libertarian principles—based on the ideas of Mill, Milton, and Locke and the philosophical climate of the Enlightenment—led to a new view of society and the role of the press. These philosophers argued that fulfillment of the individual is the ultimate goal of society, and the role of government is to provide the proper environment. Each individual has a right, although not a duty, to speak out. The most rational ideas will emerge and be accepted.

The role of the press in a libertarian society is to provide access to other people's ideas—part of this being to inform and to entertain. Financial independence is assured through the sale of advertising. The idea of objective reporting, of trying to cover all sides of an argument so that the truth will emerge, fits in well among libertarian concepts. The press also carries an important duty to serve as a watchdog over government, and although some government constraints, such as postal regulations or taxes, are acceptable, the press should operate free of prior restraint.

The deficiencies of libertarian theory become increasingly apparent when applied to modern society. The content of the electronic media is outside the realm of public affairs, and regulation of broadcasting frequencies naturally brings in the government. In addition, the concentration of ownership in the media industry raises serious questions about how open the marketplace is to the ideas of others.

The key idea in the social responsibility theory that evolved out of the Hutchins Commission Report in the 1940s is that if the press does not operate to the benefit of society, some outside agency should step in. The problems in applying the theory focus on the kind of responsibility, who should monitor it, and what controls should exist. The operators of the mass media, recognizing the importance of what they provide the public and aware that any outside regulation would impinge on their freedom, have developed ways of regulating themselves. The American Society of Newspaper Editors established in 1923 its Canons of Journalism, which exhorted newspapers to perform in the public interest. The Society of Professional Journalists issued a code of ethics in 1926. Radio, television, and film organizations also set up codes, generally proscribing what the electronic media may *not* do. But the problem with voluntary codes is that they frequently lapse into platitudes and provide no way to enforce violations.

Individual media have policies to guide employees through ethical thickets and to avoid the public perception of conflict of interest. Violations can result in the suspension or dismissal of an individual journalist. About 40 newspapers in Canada and the United States have appointed ombudsmen, or readers' representatives, to try to make the papers more responsive and accountable. Critics contend, however, that the ombudsmen make the paper's reporters and editors more isolated, not less.

Some journalists have joined with public representatives in the formation of press councils, which consider complaints against the media and then seek to have results publicized. In Canada, the Ontario Press Council and the Alberta Press Council were founded in 1972, the Quebec Press Council a year later. (A media council covering broadcasters as well as newspapers was founded in the Ontario city of Windsor even earlier, in 1971.) Today, press councils cover newspapers in all provinces except Saskatchewan. Canada is now moving toward the creation of a Canadian Broadcast Standards Council that would act in part as a press council for broadcasting.

In the United States, the National News Council was established in 1973. It acted on 200 complaints about media fairness and accuracy but was opposed by virtually all the American press, with the *New York Times* leading the opposition. It died in the 1980s for lack of support. The strongest existing organization in the United States is the Minnesota News Council. It serves as an appeals body for news organizations, even from outside Minnesota. It has 24 members, half of them not connected with the news business.

Numerous outside groups monitor the media, particularly television. Media critics say that television is so pervasive, powerful, and commercial-oriented that it is in a separate class from other media. Such groups include Action for Children's Television, which strives to raise the quality of children's programming, and the Christian Leadership for Responsible Television, a coalition of Protestant and Catholic church leaders who threaten to boycott advertisers that sponsor TV network programs featuring sex, violence, or profanity. Their efforts have had some effect, since advertisers want to protect their image from association with anything "impure."

Other groups—representing Roman Catholics, women, Arabs, Israelis, homosexuals, and so on—monitor the media for perceptions of how members of their group are portrayed. They attempt to pressure the media through letter-writing campaigns or boycotts of advertisers. Critics say that these groups themselves try to muffle other groups' free expression.

With no objective standards by which to judge the media, the social responsibility theory comes full circle. Rather than allow an outside agency to set the standards, media are letting the marketplace do it. Standards of commerce are the criteria by which much media performance is judged. Networks use ratings for a program's success, movies employ box office receipts, magazines use audience demographics, and newspapers watch advertising revenue.

Thus a mercantile theory appears to be supplanting earlier ones. Audience pressure on the advertiser changes television programming, advertiser pressure on the print media forces target marketing, and so on. Concentration in the media industry abets the entire process.

Finally, there is a growing body of communications research in the United States and Canada (as well as in Europe and Latin America) that looks at the mass media from a critical approach. These scholars, drawing on a substantial body of neo-Marxist research in economics, political science, and sociology, take as their starting point the view that Western mass media serve to promote the dominant political and economic ideology of society. News organizations, acting as watchdogs, may attack individuals or institutions that deviate from the system but do not question the validity of the system itself. Some alternative ideas are presented in the media, but they are the ideas of entrenched but competing elites. And by presenting variations on the dominant ideology, the media reinforce that ideology. In this view, freedom of the press is seen as a property right of media owners.

MEDIA ECONOMICS AND SPECIAL PROBLEMS

The mass media are part of the economic fabric of the United States and Canada. Their products, information, and institutions are integral threads in the free-enterprise system. The media invigorate the commercial marketplace and stimulate the consumer by carrying millions of advertising messages every day. The media also convey information to government, industry, and labor and contribute a flow of ideas that keeps the economic stream flowing strong and deep.

But the media are a product themselves of the economic system and are subject to its forces. Factors that stimulate business in general—markets, inflation or recession, competition, global commerce, mega-companies—also affect media institutions and influence the practice of journalism across North America.

United States

Advertising. Advertising literally pays the bills of the mass media. Without it, journalism would not exist—at least not in its present form. About three-fourths of the mass media's revenue comes from advertising.

Advertisers spend billions of dollars each year—$118 billion in 1988—to inform consumers and to persuade them to purchase their products and services. A little more than half of these dollars go for national advertising, to get people to buy certain products and services. The rest goes for local advertising, to get people to buy at certain stores.

Television is the dominant medium for national advertising. In 1988, advertisers spent $24.5 billion, 20.7 percent of all U.S. ad dollars, on broadcast television. About 70 percent of all television billings come from the national networks or from "spot" advertising placed directly with stations by national advertisers. The rest is spent at the local level.

For the other broadcast medium, radio, the pattern is reversed. Advertisers bought $7.8 billion worth of advertising in 1988, 6.5 percent of the total, but three-fourths of it was local.

The third segment of the electronic media, cable, gets only about 1 percent of the U.S. total. It draws less than 25 percent of its nearly $2 billion each year from advertisers—national, local, and spot. But that figure is climbing.

The top medium in local advertising is newspapers, which gather almost 90 percent of their $31.2 billion each year at the local level. Because of strong local sales, newspapers are the nation's largest advertising medium, with television second.

Among other advertising media, direct mail has shown the most growth—almost 25 percent in the 1980s—to account for 17.9 percent of all advertising expenditures. Americans receive 100 million pieces of third-class mail each day. Although many consider it "junk mail," its personal nature has made the effort pay off for advertisers. They spent $21.2 billion in 1988 on direct mail, ranking it third overall as an advertising vehicle.

Magazines are another medium carrying primarily national messages, although many regional and local magazines have helped bring in local advertising too. Magazines get 5.1 percent, or $6.1 billion, of total U.S. advertising expenditures.

Other advertising media include farm publications, business publications, outdoor, and miscellaneous advertising. Together, they account for $26.6 billion, or 22.2 percent of total expenditures.

Advertising's success has led to its biggest problem in recent years. One expert estimated that the number of advertising messages doubled from 1970 to 1985 and would double again by the end of the century. Not only have the vehicles for advertising increased, but the length of the messages has decreased. The 15-second television ad now accounts for more than a third of those on the networks. As a result, viewer recall of commercials has dropped off significantly. Many viewers don't watch ads at all. Others zap to another channel with their remote control or tape a program on their VCR and zip through its commercials.

But as the volume of ads buoys the media, it buries the advertiser. In today's highly competitive and complex economy, advertisers are finding buyers harder to reach. Some have concluded that mass marketing is no longer the most efficient way to sell. They want to reach specific segments of the population. And they want their advertising messages to stand out amid the clutter.

Network television offers a good example of the problem. Network advertising revenue fell in the 1980s as advertisers cut spending. At the same time, costs of network advertising skyrocketed. A 30-second prime-time announcement averages $100,000, twice what it was a few years earlier.

Added to this is a decrease in network viewers. The networks' share of the prime-time audience dipped from 91 percent in 1978 to 68 percent in 1988. Cable television, independent stations, syndicated shows, and videocassette recorders have offered more choices and have taken a solid bite out of the network audience.

Many advertisements are placed in the media by advertising agencies, which receive a commission of 15 percent of the advertisement's price. Advertisers also pay for the cost of materials and supplies. What they get in return is the agency's research, creativity, and experience. Agencies vary in size from local shops run by one person to international conglomerates employing thousands.

Media Concentration. The U.S. economy in recent years has spawned larger and larger business entities, including the mass media. Giant businesses have come to dominate every element of mass communications. Not only do newspapers own other newspapers and television companies own other stations, but newspapers and TV companies own each other. And corporations own them all.

Media critic Ben Bagdikian (1987) estimates that 29 corporations control most of the country's 25,000 media outlets. For example, three-fourths of U.S. dailies are owned by groups, and the rest are independently owned, a reversal of the situation just after World War II. The groups control more than 80 percent of the nation's circulation. Bagdikian's figures show 15 groups dominating the newspaper industry. In television, the three networks still dominate. But ABC is owned by a newspaper chain, and General Electric owns NBC. Six corporations dominate the magazine industry. Ten control books, and four film. Bagdikian contends that if present trends continue, one massive company could control all of the major media by the end of the century.

Proponents of consolidation say that it is only in response to the economic climate and is the only way to compete in a global marketplace. They say that it provides a medium with greater resources, better management, and stronger resistance to pressure from government and advertisers.

Critics of concentration, however, counter that the pressure for profits results in irreparable damage. The late publisher C. K. McClatchy called chains "cash cows," which measure success by the rate of return, not public service. Detractors say that when a chain moves in, it first cuts staff, then alters content to attract more and different kinds of advertising.

The same kinds of forces are said to be at work when products are featured in movies or on television or when the TV networks will run ads for products but not for controversial ideas. The networks acknowledge that prime-time news shows can be profitable and thus are willing to pay millions for a well-known personality. But they cut the news budget in the process.

At the heart of critics' arguments is the fear that concentration will limit the nation's free flow of information, that big corporations, inspired by the profit motive, will take over control of the supply of information to suit their own purposes. Bagdikian says that concentration of the media in the hands of a few corporations gives the public no real choices for its entertainment, news, and information—and the idea of media accountability in a free society flies out the window.

Competition has been a worry for years, especially among newspapers, the nation's chief supplier of news and information. A total of 43 cities have two or more separately owned, competing newspapers, but this includes 18 in joint-operating agreements. The special federal law for newspapers permits two in a city, when one is in danger of failing, to merge all noneditorial operations and share profits. Thus, of the 1,516 U.S. cities with daily newspapers, only 25 have papers that are truly in competition.

Canada

Advertising. In Canada, daily newspapers are the dominant advertising medium. Newspaper ad revenue was $1.96 billion in 1988, almost one-quarter of the $8 billion in net advertising revenues for Canadian media in 1988. Television, with ad revenues of $1.2 billion, ranked second, and magazines, with $1 billion in ad revenue, were third.

As in the United States, however, television tends to be the medium of choice for national advertisers, while local advertisers choose newspapers. Just under 80 percent of television ad revenue in 1988 came from national advertising, and just over 20 percent from local commercials. This picture was reversed in daily newspapers: National ad revenue accounted for 21.5 percent of the $1.96 billion in revenue. Local ads and classifieds accounted for the rest. The single largest advertiser in Canada is the federal government. Other major buyers of advertising space and time are food companies, breweries, and car manufacturers.

Advertising is regulated in Canada on a number of fronts and at a number of levels. The philosophy behind the regulations combines consumer protection with promotion of fair competition in the marketplace. The result is a mixture of direct government regulation and self-regulatory codes drawn up by the Canadian Advertising Advisory Board and its Advertising Standards Council in conjunction with government and manufacturers.

Advertisements aired on radio and television are regulated more strictly than those in the print media. A number of regulations prohibit or restrict advertisements for specific products, such as liquor and cigarettes. It is up to the provinces to decide which alcoholic beverages can be advertised and where the ads can be carried. None permits broadcast advertising of hard liquors, and four forbid commercials for beer or wine. The advertising of tobacco products, meanwhile, is being phased out. The advertising of children's products is also regulated.

Canada's income tax laws state that advertisements aimed at a Canadian audience and placed in Canadian media outlets—newspapers, magazines, and radio and television stations—qualify as tax-deductible business expenses, whereas ads placed in foreign outlets do not. This section of the tax law was brought in during the 1970s to promote and protect the Canadian media.

Concentration. A long-simmering concern about concentration of ownership in the Canadian media boiled over one day in 1980 when the Southam Company shut down the *Winnipeg Tribune* and the Thomson organization pulled the plug on the *Ottawa Journal.* The simultaneous closings left the two corporations in an enviable position: Thomson's *Winnipeg Free Press* now had a monopoly in Winnipeg, and Southam's *Ottawa Citizen* became the only English-language daily in Canada's capital.

Within a week, the Liberal government of Pierre Trudeau set up a Royal Commission on Newspapers, headed by former journalist Tom Kent. The commission subjected the chains to public scrutiny and proposed the creation of a Canada Newspaper Act that would, among other things, prohibit further concentration and correct the "worst cases" of concentration existing at the time. But no action has been taken on the proposed act.

In some respects, Kent covered ground that was already familiar to media critics. In 1970, a Special Senate Committee on Mass Media, headed by Senator Keith Davey, proposed the creation of a review board to discourage concentration of ownership of papers and periodicals. At the time of the Davey report, 77 of Canada's 116 dailies were owned by groups or chains. Ten years later, the degree of concentration had increased. Independents controlled only 25.7 percent of English-language circulation, down from 39.6 percent in 1970. In French Canada, the decline of independents was even more dramatic: down to 10 percent of circulation from 50.8 percent a decade earlier. Kent found that three chains controlled nine-tenths of French-language circulation. Three others controlled two-thirds of English-language circulation. In seven provinces (all but Ontario, Quebec, and Nova Scotia), two-thirds or more of provincial circulation was controlled by a single chain.

Media scholars have argued that Kent's biggest contribution was to put the Toronto-based Thomson Newspapers Ltd. on notice that the government would not tolerate continued expansion at the pace of the preceding decade. In the decade that followed the Kent report, Thomson Newspapers Ltd. bought large numbers of dailies in the United States and now is the largest newspaper chain in that country in terms of numbers of newspapers, though not in circulation. In 1989, it owned close to 160 dailies and 41 weeklies in Canada and the United States. The holdings of another Thomson company, International Thomson Ltd., included 119 weeklies in Britain, plus several hundred consumer, trade, and technical publications in the United States. In 1989, family head Ken Thomson announced plans to merge the two companies, which had combined sales of U.S. $4.7 billion and combined profits of $380 million, into a new company, Thomson Corp.

Southam, Inc., whose dailies control 20 percent of Canadian newspaper circulation, underwent a turbulent time of reorganization and spending cuts following a takeover attempt in 1985. That bid failed when Southam entered into a controversial share swap with the giant Torstar Corp. The terms of that deal expired in June 1990. Torstar, publisher of Canada's largest-circulation daily, the *Toronto Star*, describes itself as a broadly based information and entertainment company. Its holdings include 18 community newspapers, a direct mail and catalog publishing firm, and Harlequin Enterprises, the world's largest publisher of romantic fiction.

Ownership of the magazine press is also highly concentrated. The major players are Southam, Inc., which produces more than 50 business publications, and Maclean Hunter Ltd., which publishes more than 100 Canadian periodicals, including the country's major newsmagazine, *Maclean's*, more than 55 periodicals in the United States, and 90 in the United Kingdom and Europe. Maclean Hunter also has major holdings in cable television and is the majority owner of the Toronto Sun Publishing Corp., which publishes the *Sun* newspapers in Toronto, Ottawa, Calgary, and Edmonton. Sun subsidiaries print four other Canadian dailies and close to 50 weeklies in Canada and 40 in the United States. The Sun corporation has also recently bought a commercial printing firm outside Washington, D.C., and in 1987 it purchased the *Financial Post* from its parent corporation, Maclean Hunter. The *Post* became a daily in 1988.

Ownership is less concentrated in private radio and television. Only two companies own 20 or more private radio stations. The largest radio group, CHUM, has 24 stations, or 5.4 percent of the total. In television, 21 groups own two or more stations. The nine largest groups own less than 50 percent of all stations.

JOURNALISM EDUCATION AND TRAINING

Most journalism education in North America is conducted at the university level, although many secondary schools may offer mass communication classes and some student media experience. The first journalism courses were set up at Washington and Lee University in the 1870s. The first journalism degree program in Canada began at Carleton University in 1945. Today, journalism is offered at many universities, with a wide choice in career paths. Mid-career journalists also have numerous opportunities for professional development.

United States

More than 300 U.S. universities offer courses for a bachelor's degree in journalism. Of these, 90 are accredited by the Accrediting Council of the Education in Journalism and Mass Communication, which assesses journalism programs periodically to ensure high standards of education.

In 1988, a fellow at the Gannett Center for Media Studies rated 11 university journalism programs as exemplary, based on teaching, research, and opportunities for students. They were Florida, Illinois, Indiana, Maryland, Minnesota, Missouri, North Carolina, Northwestern, Stanford, Syracuse, and Texas.

Departments and schools of journalism offer degrees with areas of specialization in news-editorial, broadcast, advertising, photography, public relations, and magazine journalism. The most popular is broadcasting, with about 23 percent of the graduates in 1987. Advertising was next, with about 20 percent; news-editorial, 19 percent; public relations, 18 percent; and others, about 20 percent. Graduate degrees also are available at many institutions. In recent years, advertising has shown the highest growth among undergraduates, news-editorial the least.

The number of journalism students is high but appears to be leveling off. In 1987, more than 25,000 students graduated with degrees in journalism and mass communication. About 10 percent were minorities, and more than 60 percent were women. In 1987–1988, the enrollment increase of only 0.13 percent was the smallest in 50 years.

In addition to beginning and advanced courses in their journalism sequence, students take such courses as introduction to mass communication, mass media and society, history, press law, ethics, management, and graphics. Outside the major, students are required to delve deeply into the liberal arts and sciences, for not only must they have the requisite skills, but they must also possess the knowledge to function successfully. In accredited programs, students must take 90 semester-hours outside journalism, in nonskills courses such as psychology, history, economics, government, science, and literature.

Universities also offer opportunities for students to gain experience on campus newspapers, television and radio stations, or advertising and public relations agencies. In addition to on-campus work experiences, internships are widely available, and 75 percent of journalism students take advantage of them. The *Student Guide to Mass Media Internships* lists 3,000, almost all salaried.

In recent years, the media have made special efforts to support minority journalism education through grants, scholarships, and summer internships. Universities have also attempted to recruit minority students.

Nearly all faculty members at university schools and departments of journalism have professional media experience, primarily in newspapers, public relations, or television. About half have doctoral degrees, and a third have master's. Only 20 percent are women; about 5 percent are members of minorities.

Working journalists can apply for fellowships offered by two dozen institutions. These are usually connected with a university. As a fellow of the Nieman Foundation, for example, a dozen journalists each year pursue courses of their own choosing at Harvard University. Some journalists pursue advanced degrees in journalism or another area.

Many mass media encourage professional development among their staff by forming such things as writers groups. They also call in writing coaches and other consultants. Additional training occurs through workshops and meetings sponsored by professional groups like the Society of Professional Journalists.

Several publications serve the profession, including *Editor & Publisher, Broadcasting, Advertising Age*, and *The Quill*.

Canada

University training for journalists is a postwar phenomenon in Canada. Although there had been talk of the university's potential in journalism training since the turn of the twentieth century, Canada was far slower than the United States in developing schools of journalism. The University of Western Ontario offered a few courses in the 1920s, but Canadians who wished to pursue a program in journalism had to go abroad.

The situation changed at the end of World War II, when Carleton University in Ottawa and the University of Western Ontario in London, Ontario, began offering degree programs in journalism. They were joined a few years later by Ryerson Polytechnical Institute in Toronto. These three schools continue to be the leaders in journalism education in Canada.

The 1970 report of the Special Senate Committee on Mass Media deplored the fact that journalism training was limited to central Canada and recommended that courses be instituted in all regions of the country. This has more or less happened. Programs are in place at a number of universities, including the University of King's College in Halifax, Nova Scotia; Concordia University in Montreal; Université du Québec in Montreal; Laval University in Quebec City; the University of Regina in Saskatchewan; and the University of Moncton in New Brunswick.

The journalism programs offered and the degrees accorded vary widely among the Canadian universities, from bachelor of arts degrees with a minor or major in journalism to master of journalism degrees. Carleton runs a four-year bachelor of journalism with honors program and a master of journalism program that lasts one or two years, depending on the student's background. Western's program is exclusively at the master's level. Ryerson runs large undergraduate programs in journalism and radio and television, as well as a two-year graduate program. The degree earned at Ryerson is known as a bachelor of applied arts.

None of the Canadian universities offers a Ph.D. program in journalism studies, although Carleton is moving in that direction. There are three Ph.D. programs in the field of communication, as well as a number of undergraduate programs in mass communication. In addition to programs at universities, there are about 25 college-level programs in journalism or related areas, including broadcasting and film production.

Professional development programs have been slower to develop in Canada but have gained some ground in recent years. The Canadian Daily Newspaper Publishers Association has an editorial division that organizes workshops and circulates material to members. In Quebec, the Fédération Professionnelle des Journalistes du Québec holds seminars and colloquia on professional issues.

The Centre for Investigative Journalism, founded by reporters and editors in 1978, is active on both the local and national levels. It has chapters across Canada that organize seminars and discussions for reporters. It also holds an annual convention that focuses on issues facing the profession, produces a magazine, and hands out annual prestigious reporting awards. More than a dozen other programs give awards for outstanding journalism.

The Southam Fellowship for Journalists, the oldest and best-known fellowship program in Canada, provides an academic year of study at the University of Toronto for up to five senior journalists. Also noteworthy are the Michener Awards Foundation's study-leave fellowships and the Atkinson Fellowship in Public Policy. The latter funds a journalist for a one-year research project.

PROSPECTS FOR THE FUTURE

Technology and intense competition will undoubtedly mutate traditional mass media in North America in the coming decades. Hybrid media, spawned by technology and abetted by increasing concentration among communication firms, will offer new opportunities to business and consumers and pose new challenges to government regulators. Although the pace of technological change makes predicting the future difficult, several trends are evident in the United States and Canada.

Perhaps the most significant impact of technology will be in integrating information delivery systems. At one time, telecommunications and broadcasting were separate and distinct industries, and it made sense to develop separate regulatory systems for them. But with computers, satellites, and optical-fiber cable, the distinctions blur. Fiber optics can carry virtually an infinite number of electronic signals— television, cable, telephone—over a single wire. However, conversion is expensive; estimates are that in the United States, conversion could cost $300 billion and take up to 20 years.

Satellites will also be more powerful in the future. Today, they are used to transmit primarily between commercial points—business to business. But future signals will be powerful enough to be picked up in homes on antennas the size of a briefcase.

Facsimile transmission machines are becoming inexpensive and ubiquitous. In 1989, a space agency newsletter was faxed to astronauts in the shuttle *Discovery*. Several newspapers already use fax machines to distribute limited news products.

Videotex appears to be making a comeback as newspapers experiment with new uses for computer-based receiving systems in the home. Videotex trials in the early 1980s proved too expensive and too complex. But as the decade ended, newspapers in Canada and the United States were keeping an eye on two new Canadian videotex systems, including one being developed by the country's largest telephone company, Bell Canada. Meanwhile, three dozen newspapers established local services in the late 1980s that combined the telephone and the computer. The material delivered this way is specific, such as classified ads and sports results.

Conventional telephone lines will become more widely used to distribute information and photos. The seven Bell regional operating companies in the United States are barred from generating such information as Yellow Pages, weather, commercial information, and home shopping. They are being forced to allow greater access to their lines by other media.

Several countries are feverishly working on high-definition television, which creates a picture with 1,125 horizontal lines instead of 525. The image will be as large as a television projection screen and as sharp as a color snapshot. A high-definition system requires a reconfiguration of the broadcasting bandwidths in the United States and Canada.

Despite its promise, high-definition, nondigital television might be outdated by the time it arrives on the market. U.S. firms are working to integrate the computer and the television set. The unit would receive and process signals like a compact disk, handle more information quicker, and have a high-quality digital picture.

What kind of content will these information machines deliver? William J. Donnelly (1986) says that by the year 2000, images will "float down like cheap confetti." To get the right consumer's attention, the media will narrow markets even further. Computers, with databases containing exhaustive information about individuals, will select information, entertainment, and advertising for each audience member.

Hybrid media will be common. Newspapers, television, radio, and magazines will be interlinked via fiber optics and satellites. Most of them will share joint-operating ventures. They will also work with the phone company to deliver such things as classified ads by voice, text, and pictures.

What of society? Donnelly says that the "cultural segmentation" resulting from more targeted media will dissolve the nation's common social ground. People will become increasingly isolated from one another and from their institutions.

Many people will be unable to afford the new technological equipment. The rich will be information-rich as well, and the poor will be increasingly information-poor. For governments and policymakers, one of the major challenges in the coming decades will be to prevent the high-tech information society from widening the gap between rich and poor and thus creating a permanent underclass.

Selected Bibliography

GENERAL

Abshire, David M. *International Broadcasting.* Newbury Park, Calif.: Sage, 1976.

Batscha, Robert. *Foreign Affairs and the Broadcast Journalist.* New York: Praeger, 1975.

Boyd-Barrett, Oliver. *The International News Agencies.* Newbury Park, Calif.: Sage, 1980.

Browne, Donald R. *International Radio Broadcasting.* New York: Praeger, 1982.

Buzek, Antony. *How the Communist Press Works.* New York: Praeger, 1964.

Casmir, F. L., ed. *Intercultural and International Communication.* Washington, D.C.: University Press of America, 1978.

Cherry, Colin. *World Communication: Threat or Promise?* New York: Wiley, 1978.

Cooper, Kent. *Barriers Down: The Story of the News Agency Epoch.* Port Washington, N.Y.: Kennikat Press, 1942.

Cooper, Thomas W., Clifford G. Christians, Francis Forde Plude, and Robert A. White. *Communication Ethics and Global Change.* White Plains, N.Y.: Longman, 1989.

Curry, Jane, and J. Dassin, eds. *All the News Not Fit to Print: Press Control Around the World.* New York: Praeger, 1982.

Dake, Anthony C. A. *Impediments to the Free Flow of Information between East and West.* Paris: NATO, 1973.

Davison, W. Phillips. *International Political Communication.* New York: Praeger, 1965.

Dizard, Wilson P. *The Coming Information Age,* 3rd ed. White Plains, N.Y.: Longman, 1989.

Desmond, Robert. *The Information Process: World News Reporting in the Twentieth Century.* Iowa City: University of Iowa Press, 1978.

————. *Windows on the World.* Iowa City: University of Iowa Press, 1980.

Emery, Walter B. *National and International Systems of Broadcasting.* East Lansing: Michigan State University Press, 1969.

Fascell, Dante B., ed. *International News: Freedom under Attack.* Newbury Park, Calif.: Sage, 1979.

Fenby, Jonathan. *The International News Services.* New York: Schocken Books, 1986.

Fischer, H. D., and J. C. Merrill, eds. *National and International Communication.* New York: Hastings House, 1976.

Fisher, Glen. *American Communication in a Global Society.* Norwood, N.J.: Ablex, 1979.

Gastil, Raymond D. *Freedom in the World: Political and Civil Liberties, 1988–89.* New York: Freedom House, 1989.

Green, Timothy. *The Universal Eye: The World of Television.* Briarcliff Manor, N.Y.: Stein & Day, 1972.

Hachten, William. *The World News Prism: Changing Media, Clashing Ideologies,* 2d ed. Ames: Iowa State University Press, 1987.

Hardt, Hanno. *Social Theories of the Press: Early German and American Perspectives.* Newbury Park, Calif.: Sage, 1979.

Head, Sydney. *World Broadcasting Systems: A Comparative Analysis.* Belmont, Calif.: Wadsworth, 1985.

Hohenberg, John. *Foreign Correspondence: The Great Reporters and Their Times.* New York: Columbia University Press, 1964.

International Encyclopedia of Communications. New York: Oxford University Press, 1989.

Kim, Soon Jin. *EFE: Spain's World News Agency.* Westport, Conn.: Greenwood Press, 1989.

Koszyk, Kurt, and Hugo Pruys. *Handbuch der Massen Kommunikation.* Munich: K. G. Saur, 1981.

Kurian, George, ed. *World Press Encyclopedia* (2 vols.). New York: Facts on File, 1982.

Lahav, Pnina. *Press Law in Modern Democracies: A Comparative Study.* White Plains, N.Y.: Longman, 1985.

Lehman, Maxwell, and T. J. M. Burke, eds. *Communication Technologies and Information Flow.* Elmsford, N.Y.: Pergamon Press, 1981.

Lendvai, Paul. *The Bureaucracy of Truth: How Communist Governments Manage the News.* Boulder, Colo.: Westview Press, 1981.

Lull, James, ed. *World Families Watch Television.* Newbury Park, Calif.: Sage, 1988.

Mankekar, D. R. *One-Way Flow: Neo-Colonialism via News Media.* New Delhi: Clarion Books, 1978.

Martin, L. John, and Anju Grover Chaudhary, eds. *Comparative Mass Media Systems.* White Plains, N.Y.: Longman, 1983.

Martin, L. John, and Ray Eldon Hiebert. *Current Issues in International Communication.* White Plains, N.Y.: Longman, 1990.

McCavitt, William E. *Broadcasting around the World.* Blue Ridge Summit, Pa.: Tab, 1981.

Merrill, John C. *The Elite Press: Great Newspapers of the World.* New York: Pitman, 1968.

———, and Harold A. Fisher. *The World's Great Dailies.* New York: Hastings House, 1980.

Mowlana, Hamid. *Global Information and World Communication.* White Plains, N.Y.: Longman, 1986.

Murphy, Sharon, E. Atwood, and S. Bullion, eds. *International Perspectives on News.* Carbondale: Southern Illinois University Press, 1982.

Nascimento, C. A. *The World Communication Environment.* Georgetown, Guyana: Ministry of Information, 1981.

Nimmo, Dan, and Michael Mansfield. *Government and News Media: Comparative Dimensions.* Waco, Texas: Baylor University Press, 1982.

Nordenstreng, Kaarle. *The Mass Media Declaration of UNESCO.* Norwood, N.J.: Ablex, 1984.

Pelten, Joseph. *Global Talk.* Brighton, U.K.: Harvester House, 1981.

Picard, Robert G. *The Press and the Decline of Democracy: The Democratic Socialist Response in Public Policy.* Westport, Conn.: Greenwood Press, 1985.

———. *The Ravens of Odin: The Press in the Nordic Nations.* Ames: Iowa State University Press, 1988.

Richstad, Jim, and Michael Anderson, eds. *Crisis in International News.* New York: Columbia University Press, 1981.

Righter, Rosemary. *Whose News? Politics, the Press and the Third World.* New York: Times Books, 1978.

Robinson, Gertrude A. *News Agencies and World News in Canada and the United States and Yugoslavia.* Fribourg, Switzerland: University Press of Fribourg, 1981.

Siebert, Frederick S., Theodore Peterson, and Wilbur Schramm. *Four Theories of the Press.* Urbana: University of Illinois Press, 1956.

Smith, Antony. *The Geopolitics of Information: How Western Culture Dominates the World.* New York: Oxford University Press, 1980.

Stevenson, Robert L. *Communication, Development, and the Third World.* White Plains, N.Y.: Longman, 1988.

———, and Donald L. Shaw, eds. *Foreign News and the World Information Order.* Ames: Iowa State University Press, 1984.

Tan, Alexis. *Mass Communications in the Third World.* Norwood, N.J.: Ablex, 1983.

Terrou, Fernand, and Lucien Solal. *Legislation for Press, Film, and Radio.* New York: Arno, 1972.

CHAPTER 1: GLOBAL MEDIA PHILOSOPHIES

Altschull, J. Herbert. *Agents of Power: The Role of the News Media in Human Affairs*. White Plains, N.Y.: Longman, 1984.
Commission on Freedom of the Press. *A Free and Responsible Press*. Chicago: University of Chicago Press, 1947.
Hachten, William. *The World News Prism: Changing Media, Clashing Ideologies*. Ames, Iowa: Iowa State University Press, 1981; 2d ed., 1987.
Head, Sydney. *World Broadcasting Systems: A Comparative Analysis*. Belmont, Calif.: Wadsworth, 1985.
Lowenstein, Ralph L., and John C. Merrill. *Macromedia: Mission, Message, and Morality*. White Plains, N.Y.: Longman, 1990.
Merrill, John C. *The Dialectic in Journalism: Toward a Responsible Use of Press Freedom*. Baton Rouge: Louisiana State University Press, 1989.
————. *The Imperative of Freedom: A Philosophy of Journalistic Autonomy*. New York: Hastings House, 1974.
————, and Ralph L. Lowenstein. *Media, Messages, and Men: New Perspectives in Communication*. New York: David McKay, 1971; 2d ed., White Plains, N.Y.: Longman, 1979.
Picard, Robert G. *The Press and the Decline of Democracy: The Democratic Socialist Response in Public Policy*. Westport, Conn.: Greenwood Press, 1985.
Siebert, Frederick S., Theodore Peterson, and Wilbur Schramm. *Four Theories of the Press*. Urbana: University of Illinois Press, 1956.
Sussman, Leonard. *Power, the Press & the Technology of Freedom: The Coming of ISDN*. New York: Freedom House, 1989.

CHAPTER 2: THE COLLECTION AND FLOW OF WORLD NEWS

Boyd-Barrett, Oliver. *The International News Agencies*. Newbury Park, Calif.: Sage, 1980.
Branscomb, Anne W. *Toward a Law of Global Communications Networks*. White Plains, N.Y.: Longman, 1986.
Cooper, Kent. *Barriers Down*. New York: Farrar & Rinehart, 1942.
Dizard, Wilson P., Jr. *The Coming Information Age*, 3d ed. White Plains, N.Y.: Longman, 1989.
Editor & Publisher 64th Annual Directory of Syndicates. New York: Editor & Publisher, 1989.
Fenby, Jonathan. *The International News Services*. New York: Schocken Books, 1986.
Head, Sydney W. *World Broadcasting Systems: A Comparative Analysis*. Belmont, Calif.: Wadsworth, 1985.
Mott, Frank Luther. *American Journalism*. New York: Macmillan, 1941.
Mowlana, Hamid. *Global Information and World Communication*. White Plains, N.Y.: Longman, 1986.

Rosewater, Victor. *History of Cooperative News-gathering in the United States.* Norwalk, Conn.: Appleton & Lang, 1930.

Sennitt, Andrew G., ed. *World Radio & TV Handbook 1989.* Amsterdam: Billboard Publications, 1989.

Stevenson, Robert L., and Donald L. Shaw, eds. *Foreign News and the New World Information Order.* Ames: Iowa State University Press, 1984.

Storey, Graham. *Reuters: The Story of a Century of News-Gathering.* New York: Crown, 1951.

Television Cable and Fact Book, vol. 57. Washington, D.C.: Warren Publishing, 1989.

CHAPTER 3: THE WORLD'S MEDIA SYSTEMS: AN OVERVIEW

Altschull, J. Herbert. *Agents of Power: The Role of the News Media in Human Affairs.* White Plains, N.Y.: Longman, 1984.

American Electronics Association. *High Definition Television (HDTV): Economic Analysis of Impact.* Washington, D.C., 1988.

Antola, L., and E. M. Rogers. "Television Flows in Latin America." *Communication Research,* 11 (1984): 183–202.

Bagdikian, Ben H. "The Lords of the Global Village." *Nation 250* (1989): 805–820.

British Broadcasting Corporation. *Annual Report and Accounts, 1988–89.* London, 1989.

Boyd, Douglas A., Joseph D. Straubhaar, and John A. Lent. *Videocassette Recorders in the Third World.* White Plains, N.Y.: Longman, 1989.

Center for Communication. *USA/USSR SPACEBRIDGE: The Role of the Media in Current Relations.* New York, 1987.

Chu, L. L. "An Organizational Perspective on International News Flow: Some Generalizations, Hypotheses, and Questions for Research." *Gazette,* 35 (1985): 3–18.

Editor & Publisher International Yearbook. New York, annual.

Fisher, Desmond. *The Right to Communicate: A Status Report.* Reports and Papers on Mass Communication, No. 94. Paris: UNESCO, 1982.

Freedom House. "*1989 Freedom around the World*" issue of *Freedom at Issue* January-February 1989.

Gannett Center for Media Studies. *The Cost of Technology: Information Prosperity and Information Poverty.* Undated conference report.

Gardner, P. Dale, Jr., and Robert L. Stevenson. "Communication Development in Venezuela and Mexico: Goals, Promises, and Reality." *Journalism Monographs,* 108 (1988).

Gastil, Raymond D. *Freedom in the World: Political and Civil Liberties, 1988–89.* New York: Freedom House, 1989.

Gerbner, George, and Marsha Siefert, eds. *World Communications: A Handbook.* White Plains, N.Y.: Longman, 1984.

Giffard, C. Anthony. *Unesco and the Media.* White Plains, N.Y.: Longman, 1989.

"Global Report: Telecommunications," Financial World, April 18, 1989, pp. 32–62.

Guback, Thomas, and Tapio Varis. *Transnational Communication and Cultural Industries.* Reports and Papers on Mass Communication, No. 92. Paris: UNESCO, 1982.

Hachten, William A. *The World News Prism: Changing Media, Clashing Ideologies,* 2d ed. Ames: Iowa State University Press, 1987.

Hancock, Alan, ed. *Technology Transfer and Communication.* Monographs on Communication Planning, No. 4. Paris: UNESCO, 1984.

Hornik, Robert C. *Development Communication: Information, Agriculture, and Nutrition in the Third World.* White Plains, N.Y.: Longman, 1988.

Katz, Elihu, and George Wedell. *Broadcasting in the Third World: Promise and Performance.* Cambridge, Mass.: Harvard University Press, 1977.

Kidder, Rushworth M. *An Agenda for the 21st Century.* Cambridge, Mass.: MIT Press, 1987.

Lerner, Daniel. *The Passing of Traditional Society: Modernizing the Middle East.* New York: Free Press, 1958.

Levy, Leonard W. *Emergence of a Free Press.* New York: Oxford University Press, 1985.

Lowenstein, Ralph L., and John C. Merrill. *Macromedia: Mission, Message, and Morality.* White Plains, N.Y.: Longman, 1990.

Merrill, John C. *The Dialectic in Journalism: Toward a Responsible Use of Press Freedom.* Baton Rouge: Louisiana State University Press, 1989.

———. *"Governments and Press Control: Global Views,"* Political Communication and Persuasion, 4 (1987): 223–262.

———. *The Elite Press: Great Newspapers of the World.* New York: Pitman, 1968.

———, and Harold A. Fisher. *The World's Great Dailies.* New York: Hastings House, 1980.

Mowlana, Hamid, and Laurie J. Wilson. *Communication Technology and Development.* Reports and Papers on Mass Communication, No. 101. Paris: UNESCO, 1988.

Mowlana, Hamid, and Laurie J. Wilson. *The Passing of Modernity: Communication and the Transformation of Society.* White Plains, N.Y.: Longman, 1990.

Murdock, Graham, and Noreene Janus. *Mass Communications and the Advertising Industry.* Reports and Papers on Mass Communication, No. 97. Paris: UNESCO, 1984.

Ogan, Christine L., and Bonnie J. Brownlee. *From Parochialism to Globalism: International Perspectives on Journalism Education.* Columbia, S.C.: International Division of the Association for Education in Journalism and Mass Communication, 1986.

Picard, Robert G. *The Press and the Decline of Democracy: The Democratic Socialist Response in Public Policy.* Westport, Conn.: Greenwood Press, 1985.

Pool, Ithiel de Sola. *Technologies of Freedom.* Cambridge, Mass.: Belknap Press/Harvard University Press, 1983.

Rogers, Everett. *Communication Technology: The New Media in Society.* New York: Free Press, 1986.

Salvaggio, Jerry L., ed. *Telecommunications: Issues and Choices for Society.* White Plains, N.Y.: Longman, 1983.

Schiller, Herbert I. *Information and the Crisis Economy.* New York: Oxford University Press, 1986.

Singleton, Loy A. *Telecommunications in the Information Age,* 2d ed. Cambridge, Mass.: Ballinger, 1986.

Stevenson, Robert L. *Communication, Development, and the Third World.* White Plains, N.Y.: Longman, 1988.

————, and Donald L. Shaw. *Foreign News and the New World Information Order.* Ames: Iowa State University Press, 1984.

Toffler, Alvin, and Heidi Toffler. "Avoiding Global Future Shock." *World Monitor: The Christian Science Monitor Monthly,* October 1988, pp. 48–52.

UNESCO. *A Documentary History of a New World Information and Communication Order Seen as an Evolving and Continuous Process, 1975–1986.* Communication and Society No. 19. Paris, n.d.

Varis, Tapio. *International Flow of Television Programmes.* Reports and Papers on Mass Communication, No. 100. Paris: UNESCO, 1985.

World Press Freedom Committee. *The Media Crisis.* Miami, 1980.

CHAPTER 4: GLOBAL COMMUNICATIONS CONTROVERSIES

Boyd-Barrett, Oliver. *The International News Agencies.* Newbury Park, Calif.: Sage, 1980.

Browne, Donald. *International Radio Broadcasting.* New York: Praeger, 1982.

Desmond, Robert W. *The Information Process: World News Reporting in the Twentieth Century.* Ames: Iowa State University Press, 1978.

Fenby, Jonathan. *The International News Services.* New York: Schocken Books, 1986.

Garbo, Gunnar. *A World of Difference: The International Distribution of Information: The Media and Developing Countries.* Documents on Communication and Society, No. 15. Paris: UNESCO, 1985.

Gerbner, George, ed. *Mass Media Policies in Changing Cultures.* New York: Wiley, 1977.

————, and Marsha Siefert, eds. *World Communications: A Handbook.* White Plains, N.Y.: Longman, 1984.

Hachten, William. *The World News Prism: Changing Media, Clashing Ideologies,* 2d ed. Ames: Iowa State University Press, 1987.

Head, Sydney W. *World Broadcasting Systems: A Comparative Analysis.* Belmont, Calif.: Wadsworth, 1985.

Horton, Philip C., ed. *The Third World and Press Freedom.* New York: Praeger, 1981.

Howell, W. J., Jr. *World Broadcasting in the Age of the Satellite.* Norwood, N.J.: Ablex, 1986.

International Commission for the Study of Communication Problems. *Many Voices, One World.* New York: Unipub, 1980.

Jamieson, Dean T., and Emile G. McAnany. *Radio for Education and Development.* Newbury Park, Calif.: Sage, 1978.

Katz, Elihu, and George Wedell. *Broadcasting in the Third World: Promise and Performance.* Cambridge, Mass.: Harvard University Press, 1977.

Katz, Elihu, and Tamas Szecsko, eds. *Mass Media and Social Change.* Newbury Park, Calif.: Sage, 1981.

Lee, Chin-Chaun. *Media Imperialism Reconsidered.* Newbury Park, Calif.: Sage, 1980.

Martin, L. John, and Anju Grover Chaudhary, eds. *Comparative Mass Media Systems.* White Plains, N.Y.: Longman, 1983.

Martin, L. John, and Ray Eldon Hiebert. *Current Issues in International Communication.* White Plains, N.Y.: Longman, 1990.

McPhail, Thomas L. *Electronic Colonialism: The Future of International Broadcasting and Communication,* 2d ed. Newbury Park, Calif.: Sage, 1987.

Mowlana, Hamid. *International Flow of Information: A Global Report and Analysis.* Reports and Papers on Mass Communication, No. 99. Paris: UNESCO, 1985.

Mowlana, Hamid. *Global Information and World Communication.* White Plains, N.Y.: Longman, 1986.

Murphy, Sharon, E. Atwood, and S. Bullion, eds. *International Perspectives on News.* Carbondale: Southern Illinois University Press, 1982.

Nordenstreng, Kaarle. *The Mass Media Declaration of UNESCO.* Norwood, N.J.: Ablex, 1984.

———, and Herbert I. Schiller. *National Sovereignty and International Communication.* Norwood, N.J.: Ablex, 1979.

Picard, Robert G. "Discipline of Foreign Correspondents," *FOI Center Report,* 448 (1981).

———. "Private Mass Communications Development Aid: An Analysis of Projects of Three Western Organizations." In Mekki Mtewa, ed., *Perspectives in International Development,* pp. 229–239. New Delhi: Allied Publishers, 1986.

Righter, Rosemary. *Whose News? Politics, the Press and the Third World.* New York: Times Books, 1978.

Rogers, Everett. *Communication of Innovations,* 3d ed. New York: Free Press, 1985.

Smith, Anthony. *The Geopolitics of Information: Problems of Policy in Modern Media.* London: Macmillan, 1978.

Schiller, Herbert I. *Communication and Cultural Domination.* Armonk, N.Y.: Sharpe, 1976.

Sreberny-Mohammadi, Annabelle, Kaarle Nordenstreng, Robert L. Stevenson, and Frank Ugboajah. *Foreign News in the Media: International Reporting in 29 Countries.* Reports and Papers on Mass Communication, No. 93. Paris: UNESCO, 1985.

Twentieth Century Fund Taskforce on the International Flow of News. *A Free and Balanced Flow*. Lexington, Mass.: Lexington Books, 1978.

Wiio, Osmo A. *Open and Closed Mass Media Systems and Problems of International Communication Policy*. Tokyo: Studies of Broadcasting, NHK, 1977.

Wildman, Steven S., and Stephen E. Siwek. *International Trade in Films and Television Programs*. Cambridge, Mass.: Ballinger (American Enterprise Institute Trade in Services Series), 1988.

World Press Freedom Committee. *The Media Crisis*. Miami, 1980; 2d ed., Washington, D.C., 1982.

CHAPTER 5: EUROPE

Curry, Jane L. *The Black Book of Polish Censorship*. New York: Vintage Books, 1984.

Duesenberg, Albert. *The Press in Germany*. Bonn: M. Scholl, 1960.

Emery, Walter B. *Five European Broadcasting Systems*. Monograph 1. Austin, Texas: Association for Education in Journalism, 1966.

Freiberg, J. W. *The French Press*. New York: Praeger, 1981.

Gustafsson, Karl, and Hadenius, Stig. *Swedish Press Policy*. Stockholm: Swedish Institute, 1976.

Inkeles, Alex. *Public Opinion in Soviet Russia*. Cambridge, Mass.: Harvard University Press, 1950.

Harasymiw, Dohdan, ed. *Education and the Mass Media in the Soviet Union and Eastern Europe*. New York: Praeger, 1976.

Kaplan, Frank. *Winter into Spring: The Czechoslovak Press and the Reform Movement, 1963–1977*. Boulder, Colo.: East European Quarterly, 1975.

Kottyan, A. *Newspapers in the USSR*. New York: USSR Research Council, 1955.

Markham, James W. *Voices of the Red Giants*. Ames: Iowa State University Press, 1967.

McNae, L. C. J. *Essential Law for Journalists*. London: Granada, 1979.

Mickiewicz, E. P. *Media and the Russian Public*. New York: Praeger, 1981.

Olson, Kenneth E. *The History Makers: The Press in Europe from Its Beginnings through 1965*. Baton Rouge: Louisiana State University Press, 1966.

Picard, Robert G. *The Ravens of Odin: The Press in the Nordic Nations*. Ames: Iowa State University Press, 1988.

Rice, Michael. *Reporting U.S.-European Relations*. Elmsford, N.Y.: Pergamon Press, 1982.

Robinson, Gertrude A. *Tito's Maverick Media: The Politics of Mass Communications in Yugoslavia*. Urbana: University of Illinois Press, 1977.

Sandford, John. *The Mass Media of the German-speaking Countries*. London: Oswald Wolff, 1976.

Schlesinger, Philip. *Putting 'Reality' Together: BBC News*. Newbury Park, Calif.: Sage, 1979.

Schneider, Maarten. *The Netherlands Press Today*. Leiden: E. J. Brill, 1951.

Schulte, Henry F. *The Spanish Press, 1470–1966.* Urbana: University of Illinois Press, 1968.
Smith, Anthony. *The British Press since the War.* Plymouth: Latimer Trend, 1974.
Thorsen, Svend. *Newspapers in Denmark.* Copenhagen: Det Danske Salskab, 1953.
Weber, Karl. *The Swiss Press: An Outline.* Bern: H. Lang, 1948.
Williams, Francis. *Dangerous Estate.* London: Longmans, Green, 1957.

CHAPTER 6: MIDDLE EAST AND NORTH AFRICA

Baker, Simon. "The Tale of Arabsat." *Cable & Satellite Europe*, January 1989, 58–63.
Boyd, Douglas A. *Broadcasting in the Arab World: A Survey of Radio and Television in the Middle East.* Philadelphia: Temple University Press, 1982.
Caspi, Dan. *Media Decentralization: The Case of Israel's Local Newspapers.* New Brunswick, N.J.: Transaction Books, 1986.
Dakroub, Hussein. "Did the News Media Help Ignite Lebanon's Civil War?" *Middle East Times*, 5–11 September 1989: 1, 18.
Head, Sydney. *World Broadcasting Systems: A Comparative Analysis.* Belmont, Calif.: Wadsworth, 1985.
Kirat, Mohamed. *The Algerian News People: A Study of Their Backgrounds. Professional Orientations and Working Conditions.* Bloomington, Ind.: Indiana University, 1987.
"Newspaper Industry Faces Tough Time." *The Turkish Times*, 11 August, 1989: 5.
Ochs, Martin. *The African Press.* Cairo: The American University in Cairo Press, 1986.
Peretz, Don. *The Middle East Today*, 4th ed. New York: Praeger, 1983.
Rugh, William A. *The Arab Press*, 2d ed. Syracuse, N.Y.: Syracuse University Press, 1979.
Shinar, Dov. *Palestinian Voices: Communication and Nation Building in the West Bank.* Boulder, Col.: Lynne Rienner Publishers, 1987.
Tehranian, Majid. "Communications Dependency and Dualism in Iran." *Intermedia* 10 (3, 1982): 40–42.
Varis, Tapio. "The International Flow of Television Programs." *Journal of Communication* 34 (1, 1983): 143–152.
Welford, Ross. "Shift of Ads from Video to TV?" *TV World*, March–April 1986: 33.

CHAPTER 7: AFRICA

Africa South of the Sahara, 1989. London: Europa Publications, 1988.
Ainslie, Rosalynde. *The Press in Africa: Communications Past and Present.* New York: Walker, 1968.
Ansah, Paul, Cheric Fall, Bernard Chindji Kouleu, and Peter Mwaura. *Rural Journalism in Africa.* Paris: UNESCO, 1981.

Barton, Frank. *The Press of Africa: Persecution and Perseverance.* New York: Africana, 1979.

Boyd-Barrett, Oliver. *The International News Agencies.* Newbury Park, Calif.: Sage, 1980.

Commonwealth Broadcasting Association. *Handbook, 1985/86.* London, 1985.

Editor & Publisher International Yearbook, 1989. New York, 1989.

Encyclopaedia Britannica. *1989 Britannica Book of the Year.* Chicago, 1989.

Gastil, Raymond D. *Freedom in the World: Political Rights and Civil Liberties, 1988–1989.* New York: Freedom House, 1989.

Giffard, C. Anthony. "The Impact of Television on South African Daily Newspapers." *Journalism Quarterly* 57, (2, Summer 1980): 216–223.

Hachten, William A. *Mass Communication in Africa: An Annotated Bibliography.* Madison: University of Wisconsin Center for International Communication Studies, 1971.

————. *Muffled Drums: The News Media in Africa.* Ames: Iowa State University Press, 1971.

Head, Sydney W. *Broadcasting in Africa.* Philadelphia: Temple University Press, 1974.

Katz, Elihu, and George Wedell. *Broadcasting in the Third World: Promise and Performance.* Cambridge, Mass.: Harvard University Press, 1977.

Kurian, George. *World Press Encyclopedia.* New York: Facts on File, 1982.

Mwaura, Peter. *Communication in Kenya.* Paris: UNESCO, 1980.

Mytton, Graham. *Mass Communication in Africa.* Denver: Arnold, 1983.

Ochs, Martin. *The African Press.* Cairo: American University in Cairo Press, 1987.

Pinch, Edward T. *The Third World and the Fourth Estate: A Look at the Non-Aligned News Agencies Pool.* Washington, D.C.: Senior Seminar on Foreign Policy, 1977.

Rosen, Philip T. *International Handbook of Broadcasting Systems.* Westport, Conn.: Greenwood Press, 1988.

Rowlands, Don, and Hugh Lewin. *Reporting Africa: A Manual for Reporters in Africa.* Harare, Zimbabwe: Thomson Foundation and Friedrich Naumann Foundation, 1985.

Stevenson, Robert L., and Donald Lewis Shaw. *Foreign News and the New World Information Order.* Ames: Iowa State University Press, 1984.

Tomaseli, Keyan, et al. *Studies on the South African Media: The Press, Broadcasting, Resistance, Community, 1987.* London: St. Martin's Press, 1987.

United States Information Agency. *Country Data Papers: Africa.* Washington, D.C., 1989.

Wilcox, Dennis L. *Mass Media in Black Africa: Philosophy and Control.* New York: Praeger, 1975.

CHAPTER 8: ASIA AND THE PACIFIC

Note: "AEJMC" refers to "Association for Education in Journalism and Mass Communication."

Abbas, Razia. "Radio and Distance Learning in Pakistan." *Media Asia*, 14 (1, 1987): 13–14.

Bain, David Haward. "Letter from Manila: How the Press Helped to Dump a Despot." *Columbia Journalism Review*, May–June 1986, 27–36.

Basu, Tarun. "Papers Hold Their Own Despite Attacks." *India Abroad*, 25 August, 1989, 12.

Bishop, Robert. *Qi Lai! Mobilizing One Billion Chinese: The Chinese Communication System*. Ames: Iowa State University Press, 1989.

Boyle, Kevin, ed. *Article 19 World Report 1988*. New York: Times Books, 1988.

Chan, Joseph Man, and Chin-Chuan Lee. "Shifting Journalistic Paradigms: Editorial Stance and Political Transition in Hong Kong." Paper presented at the AEJMC convention, Portland, Oregon, July 1988.

Chu, Godwin. *Radical Change through Communication in Mao's China*. Honolulu: University of Hawaii Press, 1978.

Chu, Leonard. "Changing Faces of China's TV." *Asian Messenger*, Winter–Spring 1980–1981.

"Circulation of Indian Press Touches New High," *India News*, August 1989.

Cohen, Margot. "Letter from the Philippines." *Columbia Journalism Review*, November–December 1987, pp. 46–48.

Cooper, Anne. "Televised International News in Five Countries." *International Communication Bulletin*, 24 (1–2, 1989): 4–8.

Dahlan, M. Alwi. "The Palapa Project and Rural Development in Indonesia." *Media Asia*, 14 (1, 1987): 28–29, 32–36.

Dameyer, Christina. "Covering Afghanistan, Part 2." *Columbia Journalism Review*, March–April 1987, pp. 44–47.

Dinh, Tran Van. "Asia: Twentieth Century." *International Encyclopedia of Communications*. New York: Oxford University Press, 1989: 143–146.

Domingo, Ben. "Rural Press Development in the Philippines, 1976–1986." *Media Asia*, 14 (2, 1987): 81–88.

Eapen, K. E. "News Agencies: The Indonesian Scene." *Gazette* 19 (1973): 1–12.

Elmi, Yusuf, ed. *Afghanistan: A Decade of Sovietisation*. Peshawar, Pakistan: Golden Printing Press, 1988.

Epworth, Marsden. "Why Chernobyl Was a Nonstory and Other Tales of Indonesian Journalism." *Columbia Journalism Review*, September-October 1988, pp. 41–45.

Flournoy, Donald. "Asiavision: A satellite news exchange." Paper presented to the National Association of Educational Broadcasters convention, Las Vegas, 1985.

Ghorpade, Shailendra. "Retrospect and Prospect: The Information Environment and Policy in India." *Gazette*, 38 (1986): 5–28.

Goldenberg, Suzanne. "Pakistan: Media Exuberant in Post-Zia Revival." *IPI Report*, March 1989, pp. 6–7.

Gupta, V. S. "Rural Press Development in India: Status, Factors Affecting Its Growth and Future Prospects." *Media Asia*, 14 (2, 1987) 67–72.

Hachten, William. *The World News Prism*. Ames: Iowa State University Press, 1987.

Head, Sydney. *World Broadcasting Systems.* Belmont, Calif.: Wadsworth, 1985.

Hopkins, Mark. "Watching China Change." *Columbia Journalism Review,* September-October 1989, pp. 35–40.

Indonesia 1989: An Official Handbook. Djakarta: Republic of Indonesia Department of Information, 1989.

Irani, Cushrow. "India: To Toe the Line, or Not to Toe the Line." *IPI Report,* August 1989, p. 8.

Iyer, Pico. *Video Night in Kathmandu.* New York: Vintage, 1989.

Kamath, M. V. "Sex: Handle with Care." *Probe,* October 1989, 73–76.

Kennedy, George. "Newspapers in New Zealand." *presstime,* May 1986, pp. 23–25.

Koito, Chugo. "The Newspaper and Its Rivals in Japan." In *Journalism Theory.* Tokyo: Sophia University, n.d.

Lansipuro, Yrjo. "Asiavision News Exchange." Paper presented to the Seminar on the Communication Revolution in Asia, New Delhi, India, 1986.

Lent, John A. "Mass Communication in Asia and the Pacific: Recent Trends and Developments." *Media Asia,* 16 (1, 1989): 16–24.

———. "Press Freedom in Asia: The Quiet, but Completed, Revolution." *Gazette* 24 (1978): 41–60.

———. "To and from the Grave: Press Freedom in South Asia." *Gazette* 33 (1984): 17–36.

Li, Xiaohong. "*Peking Review*'s Coverage of the 1976 Tangshan Earthquake in China." Paper presented at the AEJMC convention, Washington, D.C., July 1989.

Mankekar, D. R. *Media and the Third World.* New Delhi: Indian Institute of Mass Communication, 1979.

Merrill, John C. "Inclination of Nations to Control Press and Attitudes on Professionalization." *Journalism Quarterly* 65 (4, 1988): 839–845.

———, and Harold A. Fisher. *The World's Great Dailies.* New York: Hastings House, 1980.

Oh, Jin Hwan. "Foreign Influence on Korean Journalism Education." *Journal of the Korean Society for Journalism and Communication Studies* 20 (1985): 19–33.

"The Press in Asia." *Asia Magazine,* June 14, 1987, pp. 10–19; June 28, 1987, pp. 42–46.

Rai, L. Deosa. "Nepal's Communication Policy Then and Now." *Media Asia,* 14 (3, 1987): 149, 152–153.

Ramanathan, Sankaran, and Katherine Frith. "Mass Comm. Education Young and Growing in Malaysia." *Journalism Educator* 42 (4, 1988): 10–12.

Rampal, Kuldip R. "Adversary vs. Developmental Journalism: Indian Mass Media at the Crossroads." *Gazette* 34 (1984): 3–20.

Rao, B. S. S. "All India Radio: The New Challenges." *Gazette* (1986): 101–113.

Rawanake, Chitra. "Roundtable." *Media Asia,* 14 (3, 1987): 150–151.

Ray, Shantanu. "The Heart of Mainstream Journalism: Growing Regional Language Press No Longer a 'Poor Cousin.'" *India Abroad,* August 25, 1989, 4.

Rivenburgh, Nancy. "China: The Television Revolution." Paper presented at the AEJMC convention, Portland, Oregon, July 1988.

Rogers, Everett, Xiaoyan Zhao, Zhongdang Pan, and Milton Chen. "The Beijing audience study." *Communication Research* 12 (2, April 1985): 179–208.

Saelan, Ahmad. "Rural Press Development in Indonesia: A Case Study of Pikiran Rakyat." *Media Asia*, 14 (2, 1987): 76–80.

Sankhdher, N. *Press, Politics and Public Opinion in India.* New Delhi: Deep Publications, 1984.

Schramm, Wilbur, and Erwin Atwood. *Circulation of News in the Third World: A Study of Asia.* Hong Kong: Press of the Chinese University of Hong Kong, 1981.

Shamsuddin, M. "Constraints on the Pakistan Press." *Media Asia*, 14 (3, 1987): 166–173.

Siebert, Frederick S., Theodore Peterson, and Wilbur Schramm. *Four Theories of the Press.* Urbana: University of Illinois Press, 1956.

Sinaga, Janner. "The Pancasila Press System." Djakarta: Republic of Indonesia Department of Information, 1987.

Singh, Nihal S. "Soul Searching Time." *India Today*, May 15, 1989, p. 167.

———. "Wages of a Free Press." *India Today*, August 15, 1989, p. 118.

Sinha, Arbink K. "Communication and Rural Development: The Indian Scene." *Gazette*, 38 (1986): 59–70.

Soley, Lawrence, and Sheila O'Brien. "Clandestine Broadcasting in the Southeast Asian Peninsula." *International Communication Bulletin* 22 (1–2, 1987): 13–20.

Stevenson, Robert L. *An Atlas of Foreign News.* Research Review Monograph No. 3. Chapel Hill: University of North Carolina School of Journalism, 1984.

Tan, Alexis, and Kultida Suarchavarat. "American TV and Social Stereotypes of Americans in Thailand." *Journalism Quarterly* 63 (1988): 648–654.

Youm, Kyu Ho. "Libel Law and Freedom of the Press: Judicial Interpretation in Japan." *Journalism Quarterly*, in press, 1990.

———. "Press Freedom in 'Democratic' South Korea: Moving from Authoritarian to Libertarian?" *Gazette* 43 (1989): 53–71.

Zhang, Jingming, and Jianan Peng. "Chinese Journalism Education: Slow Progress since 1918." *Journalism Educator* 41 (1986): 11–18.

CHAPTER 9: LATIN AMERICA AND THE CARIBBEAN

Alisky, Marvin. *Latin American Media: Guidance and Censorship.* Ames: Iowa State University Press, 1981.

Antola, Livia, and Everett M. Rogers. "Television Flows in Latin America." *Communication Research* 11, no. 2 (April 1984): 183–202.

Atwood, Rita, and Emile G. McAnany, eds. *Communication and Latin American Society.* Madison: University of Wisconsin Press, 1986.

Beltrán, Luis Ramiro. "Communication and Cultural Domination: USA–Latin America case." *Media Asia*, 5 (1978): 183–192.

Boddewyn, J. J. "Developed Advertising Self-regulation in a Developing Country: The Case of Brazil's CONAIR." *Inter-American Economic Affairs* 38 (3, 1984): 75–93.

Brown, Aggrey, and Roderick Sanatan. *Talking with Whom? A Report on the State of the Media in the Caribbean.* Kingston, Jamaica: Caribbean Institute of Mass Communication of the University of the West Indies, 1987.

Brownlee, Bonnie. "The Nicaraguan Press: Revolutionary, Developmental, or Socially Responsible?" *Gazette* 33 (1984): 155–172.

Buckman, Robert. "The Editor and the Dictator." *Quill,* 76 (1988): 14–21.

Chamorro, Jaime Cardenal. *La Prensa: The Republic of Paper.* New York: Freedom House, 1988.

Cifrino, David A. "Press Freedom in Latin America and the Emerging Right to Communicate." *Boston College Third World Law Review* 9 (1989): 117–144.

Cuthbert, Marlene. "The Caribbean News Agency: Third World Model." *Journalism Monographs,* 71 (1981).

Dassin, Joan R. "The Brazilian Press and the Politics of *Abertura.*" *Journal of Interamerican Studies and World Affairs* 26 (1984): 385–414.

Fejes, Fred. "The Growth of Multinational Advertising Agencies in Latin America." *Journal of Communication* 29 (1979): 36–49.

———. *Imperialism, Media, and the Good Neighbor: The New Deal Policy and United States Broadcasting to Latin America.* Norwood, N.J.: Ablex, 1986.

———. "The U.S. in Third World Communications: Latin America, 1900–1945." *Journalism Monographs* 86 (1983).

Fenby, Jonathan. *The International News Services.* New York: Schocken Books, 1986.

Fox, Elizabeth. *Media and Politics in Latin America: The Struggle for Democracy.* Preface by Luis Ramiro Beltrán. Newbury Park, Calif.: Sage, 1988.

Fuenzalída, Valerio. "Television in Chile: A History of Experiment and Reform." *Journal of Communication* 38, no. 2 (Summer 1988): 49–58.

Gardner, Mary A. *The Inter-American Press Association.* Austin: University of Texas Press, 1967.

Garrison, Bruce. "Estudio muestra nivel de modernización técnica de los periódicos del continente [Study of New Technology Adaptation among Latin American Newspapers]." *El Boletín* 217 (10, 1984): 1–8.

———, and Julio E. Muñoz. "Commentary: The Free and Not-So-Free Press of Latin America and the Caribbean (Report No. 3). "*Newspaper Research Journal* 7 (4, 1986): 63–69.

Gilbert, Dennis. *Sandinistas: The Party and the Revolution.* New York: Basil Blackwell, 1988.

Gilbert, Dennis. "Society, Politics, and the Press: An Interpretation of the Peruvian Press Reform of 1974." *Journal of Interamerican Studies and World Affairs* 21 (August 1979): 369–393.

Goldman, Francisco. "Sad Tales of *La Libertad de Prensa:* Reading the Newspapers of Central America." *Harper's,* August 1988, pp. 56–62.

Head, Sydney W. *World Broadcasting Systems: A Comparative Analysis.* Belmont, Calif.: Wadsworth, 1985.

Hinds, Harold E., Jr., and Charles M. Tatum, eds. *Studies in Latin American Popular Culture,* vol. 6. Tucson: University of Arizona, Department of Spanish and Portugese, 1986.

Hole, M. Cadwalader. "The Early Latin American Press." *Bulletin of the Pan American Union* 9 (April 1926): 323–352.

Junco de la Vega, Alejandro. "Publishing in Mexico is a Perilous Business." *IAPA News,* April 1989: 6.

Kartheiser, Robert, Jr. "De Facto Government, State of Siege Powers, and Freedom of the Press in Argentina." *University of Miami Inter-American Law Review* 18 (1986–1987): 243–269.

Knudson, Jerry W. *The Chilean Press during the Allende Years, 1970–1973.* Buffalo: State University of New York, 1984.

———. "Journalism Education's Roots in Latin America Are Traced." *Journalism Educator* 41 (1987): 22–24, 33.

Lent, John A. "Mass Media in the Leeward Islands: Press Freedom, Media Imperialism, and Popular Culture." In *Studies in Latin American Popular Culture,* vol. 6, ed. Harold E. Hinds, Jr., and Charles E. Tatum. Tucson: University of Arizona Department of Spanish and Portugese, 1987.

———. "Cuban Mass Media after 25 Years of Revolution." *Journalism Quarterly* 62 (1985a): 609–704.

———. "Mass Media and Socialist Governments in the Commonwealth Caribbean." *Human Rights Quarterly* 4 (1982): 371–390.

———. "Mass Media in Grenada: Three Lives in a Decade." *Journalism Quarterly* 62 (1985b): 755–760, 762.

———. *Third World Mass Media and Their Search for Modernity: The Case of the Commonwealth Caribbean, 1717–1976.* Lewisburg, Pa.: Bucknell University Press, 1977.

Link, Jere H. "Test of the Cultural Dependency Hypothesis." In *Foreign News and the New World Information Order,* ed. Robert L. Stevenson and Donald Lewis Shaw. Ames: The Iowa State University Press, 1984.

Mahan, Elizabeth. "Mexican Broadcasting: Reassessing the Industry-State Relationship." *Journal of Communication* 35, no. 1 (Winter 1985): 60–75.

Malcolm, R. Bruce. *To License a Journalist: A Landmark Decision in the Schmidt Case.* New York: Freedom House, 1986.

Mattos, Sergio. "Advertising and Government Influences: The Case of Brazilian Television." *Communication Research* 11, no. 2 (April 1984): 203–220.

Merrill, John C. *The Elite Press: Great Newspapers of the World.* New York: Pitman, 1968.

Montalbano, William. *Improving Latin American News Coverage.* Miami: Latin American and Caribbean Center, Florida International University, 1985.

Nichols, John Spicer. "Cuban Mass Media: Organization, Control and Functions." *Journalism Monographs,* 78 (1982).

Pierce, Robert N. *Keeping the Flame: Media and Government in Latin America.* New York: Hastings House, 1979.

"Pressures on the Press." *Caribbean and West Indies Chronicle,* October–November 1983: 6, 8.

Reyes Matta, Fernando. "The Latin American Concept of News." *Journal of Communication* 29 (1979): 164–171.

Salwen, Michael B., and Bruce Garrison. "Press Freedom and Development: U.S. and Latin American Views." *Journalism Quarterly* 66 (1989): 87–92.

Sidel, M. Kent. "New World Information Order in Action in Guyana," *Journalism Quarterly* 61 (1984): 493–498.

Skinner, Joseph. "Octopus of the Airwaves." *Monthly Review*, September 1987, pp. 44–49.

Soderlund, Walter C., and Carmen Schmitt. "El Salvador's Civil War as Seen in the North and South American Press," *Journalism Quarterly* 63 (1986): 268–274.

Soderlund, Walter C., and Stuart H. Surlin, eds. *Media in Latin America and the Caribbean: Domestic and International Perspectives.* Windsor: Ontario Cooperative Program in Latin American and Caribbean Studies, University of Windsor, 1985.

Straubhaar, Joseph D. "Brazilian Television: The Decline of American Influence." *Communication Research* 11 (2, 1984): 221–240.

Thomas, Erwin K. "Mass Media in Guyana: A Critical Appraisal." *Gazette* 29 (1982): 173–178.

CHAPTER 10: NORTH AMERICA

Audley, Paul. *Canada's Cultural Industries.* Toronto: Canadian Institute for Economic Policy/James Lorimer, 1983.

Bagdikian, Ben H. *The Media Monopoly.* Boston: Beacon Press, 1987.

Bird, Roger, ed. *Documents of Canadian Broadcasting.* Ottawa: Carleton University Press, 1988.

Bogart, Leo. *Press and Public.* Hillsdale, N.J.: Erlbaum, 1981.

Broadcasting/Cablecasting Yearbook, 1988. Washington, D.C., 1988.

The Canadian Encyclopedia, 2d ed. Edmonton: Hurtig Publishers, 1988.

Commission on Freedom of the Press. *A Free and Responsible Press.* Chicago: University of Chicago Press, 1947.

Compaine, Benjamin M. *Who Owns the Media?* New York: Harmony Books, 1979.

De Fleur, Melvin L., and Everette E. Dennis. *Understanding Mass Communication.* Boston: Houghton Mifflin, 1988.

Desbarats, Peter. *Guide to Canadian News Media.* Toronto: Harcourt Brace Jovanovich, 1989.

Donnelly, William J. *The Confetti Generation.* New York: Holt, Rinehart and Winston, 1986.

Eaman, Ross A. *The Media Society: Basic Issues and Controversies.* Toronto: Butterworths, 1987.

Editor & Publisher Yearbook, 1988. New York, 1988.

Emery, Edwin, and Michael Emery. *The Press and America.* Englewood Cliffs, N.J.: Prentice-Hall, 1978.

Government of Canada. *Report of the Task Force on Broadcasting Policy.* Ottawa: Minister of Supply and Services, 1986.

——. *Royal Commission on Newspapers.* (Kent Commission Report.) Hull: Minister of Supply and Services, 1981.

——. *Special Senate Committee on Mass Media.* (Davey Commission Report.) Ottawa: Queen's Printer, 1970.

Halberstam, David. *The Powers That Be.* New York: Knopf, 1979.

Head, Sydney W., and Christopher H. Sterling. *Broadcasting in America.* Boston: Houghton Mifflin, 1982.

Kesterton, W. H. *A History of Journalism in Canada.* Toronto: McClelland & Stewart, 1967.

Levy, Harold. *A Reporter's Guide to Canada's Criminal Justice System.* Ottawa: Canadian Bar Foundation, 1986.

Lorimer, Rowland, and Jean McNulty. *Mass Communication in Canada.* Toronto: McClelland & Stewart, 1987.

Martin, Robert, and G. Stuart Adam. *A Sourcebook of Canadian Media Law.* Ottawa: Carleton University Press, 1989.

Pember, Don R. *Mass Media in America.* Chicago: Science Research Associates, 1983.

Peterson, Theodore. *Magazines in the Twentieth Century.* Urbana: University of Illinois Press, 1964.

Prichard, Peter. *The Making of McPaper.* Kansas City, Mo.: Andrews, McMeel & Parker, 1987.

Robertson, Stuart M. *Media Law Handbook.* Vancouver: International Self-counsel Press, 1982.

Rutherford, Paul. *The Making of the Canadian Media.* Toronto: McGraw-Hill Ryerson, 1978.

Shaw, David. "All the News, Hard and Soft." *Insight* (8 May 1989): 60.

Vipond, Mary. *The Mass Media in Canada.* Toronto: James Lorimer, 1989.

Weaver, David H., and G. Cleveland Wilhoit. *The American Journalist.* Bloomington: Indiana University Press, 1986.

Westell, Anthony, and Carman Cumming. "Canadian Media and the National Imperative." In *Government and the News Media: Comparative Dimensions,* ed. Dan Nimmo and Michael W. Mansfield. Waco, Texas: Baylor University Press, 1982.

Woodrow, R. Brian, and Kenneth B. Woodside, eds. *The Introduction of Pay-TV in Canada: Issues and Implications.* Montreal: Institute for Research on Public Policy, 1982.

About the Contributors

Paul Adams is associate professor of journalism at California State University, Fresno, where he teaches advanced reporting and editing classes, desktop publishing, and graduate courses. He received both an M.A. and a Ph.D. from the University of Texas at Austin. He has been a copy editor, op-ed page editor, regional editor, and features editor at the *Portland Oregonian,* news reporter at the *Lawton* (Okla.) *Constitution,* and writer for the magazine *Outdoor Oklahoma.* He also has worked as an editor for a federal agency in Washington, D.C.

Adams has taught at the University of Texas, Baylor University, the University of Portland, and Louisiana State University and has published articles in several national journals and periodicals. His scholarly interests include mass communication effects, research methodology, and computer technology.

Robert T. Buckman is assistant professor of communication at the University of Southwestern Louisiana in Lafayette, specializing in news writing and international communication, with a focus on Latin America. He worked as a reporter for the now defunct *Fort Worth Press* before becoming an editor with the Foreign Broadcast Information Service, a U.S. government agency. He saw field duty in Panama and Paraguay.

Buckman covered the Texas legislature for the *Fort Worth News-Tribune,* a weekly, while working on his doctorate in journalism at the University of Texas at Austin. A major in the U.S. Army Reserve, he serves annual assignments as a Latin American affairs instructor for the John F. Kennedy Social Warfare Center and School at Fort Bragg, North Carolina, and has served five tours of duty with the U.S. Southern Command in Panama. Several of his articles have appeared in *The Quill,* journal of the Society of Professional Journalists. His B.A. degree in journalism and government and M.A. in government are from Texas Christian University. He has traveled extensively in Mexico, Guatemala, Panama, Chile, and Argentina.

Anju Grover Chaudhary is assistant professor in the Department of Journalism at Howard University, where she teaches courses in comparative journalism and news reporting and writing. She has been a free-lance writer and editor, was an editorial assistant with *Design* magazine in India, and worked at the *Washington Star* as a copyreader.

Chaudhary is the coeditor of *Comparative Mass Media Systems* and author of several articles that have appeared in *Journalism Quarterly* and *Gazette,* among other journals. A Ph.D. candidate in public communication at the University of Maryland, Chaudhary also holds two master's degrees—in journalism and in history. She is a member of the Society of Professional Journalists and the Association for Education in Journalism and is listed in *International Who's Who in Education* and *Outstanding College Students of America.*

Anne Cooper Chen, associate professor in the E. W. Scripps School of Journalism at Ohio University, heads the school's Foreign Correspondence Internship Program. She earned an A.B. in English from Vassar College, an M.A. in Japanese studies from the University of Michigan, an M.S. in mass communication from Virginia Commonwealth University, and a Ph.D. from the University of North Carolina at Chapel Hill.

During more than a decade of professional experience, Cooper Chen has worked for the *Asahi Evening News,* an English-language daily in Tokyo; for a Japanese book publisher; and for several publications in the United States. She is coauthor of *Idols, Victims, Pioneers: Virginia's Women from 1607* and has been listed in *Outstanding Young Women of America* and *Who's Who of American Women.* In the 1970s, she received several writing awards from Sigma Delta Chi and the National Federation of Press Women.

Bruce Garrison is associate professor of communication at the University of Miami in Coral Gables, Florida. He has a variety of research and teaching interests, including Latin America, public opinion, reporting and editing, and sports journalism. He is author of *Professional News Writing, Professional Feature Writing,* and *Sports Reporting.* Garrison has published articles in numerous mass communication journals, including *Journalism Quarterly, Newspaper Research Journal, Mass Communication Review,* and *Journalism History.*

Garrison earned his Ph.D. in journalism from Southern Illinois University of Carbondale in 1979 and his M.S. in communication from the University of Tennessee in 1973. He has worked as a reporter and copy editor for daily newspapers in Kentucky, Tennessee, Mississippi, Texas, Massachusetts, Wisconsin, and Florida.

Albert L. Hester is professor of journalism and mass communication at the University of Georgia. He is also director of the Center for International Mass Communication Training and Research at that university and head of the

Journalism Department of the Henry W. Grady College of Journalism and Mass Communication. He teaches international communication, reporting, editing, and magazine writing. His professional experience includes 13 years of work as reporter, assistant city editor, and city editor of the *Dallas Times Herald*. He has also taught journalism on a Fulbright instructorship at the Autonomous University in Guadalajara, Mexico, and has directed workshops and short courses for journalists in the Dominican Republic, Egypt, Guatemala, Jamaica, Jordan, Lesotho, Malta, Nigeria, Qatar, Saudi Arabia, Tunisia, Venezuela, and Zambia.

Hester is editor of *The Handbook for Developmental Journalists* and coeditor of *The Handbook for Third World Journalists*. He has contributed many articles to scholarly journals on international communication and has published more than 100 magazine articles. He received his Ph.D. in mass communication from the University of Wisconsin, Madison, where he also received his M.A. in journalism. His B.A. in journalism is from Southern Methodist University. He has taught at the University of Georgia since 1971.

Catherine McKercher is assistant professor of journalism at Carleton University in Ottawa, Canada, teaching basic, in-depth, and municipal affairs reporting to undergraduate and graduate students. She received a B.A. from Carleton University and an M.J. from Temple University in Philadelphia.

McKercher's professional experience includes work as a reporter for the now-defunct *Ottawa Journal*; as an editor and reporter for the Canadian Press, Canada's national news cooperative, in Toronto and Washington; and as assistant city editor for the *Whig-Standard* in Kingston, Ontario.

She has also done free-lance work in radio and print and is on the editorial board of *content*, the magazine for Canadian journalists. Her scholarly work focuses on the effects of new technology on Canadian newspapers.

L. John Martin is professor emeritus at the University of Maryland, where he taught courses in comparative journalism, international communication, public opinion, and research methods. He also served for some years as director of graduate studies. A former foreign correspondent and reporter on the Near East, he has worked for dailies in Michigan, New York, Kentucky, and Minnesota. In the 1960s, he was a research administrator in the U.S. Information Agency.

Martin is author of *International Propaganda* and coeditor of *Comparative Mass Media Systems*, among other books. He has been editor of the *International Communication Bulletin* and associate editor of *Journalism Quarterly*. His Ph.D. in political science and his M.A. in international relations are from the University of Minnesota, and his B.A. is from American University in Cairo, Egypt. He is widely traveled, especially in Africa, where he has lectured extensively.

John C. Merrill, editor of this volume, is professor of journalism at Louisiana State University and professor emeritus at the University of Missouri, where he taught for 14 years. He has degrees in English, journalism, and philosophy, and his Ph.D. in mass communication is from the University of Iowa.

Merrill has worked in various capacities on several newspapers and taught in universities for 40 years. He has lectured and conducted seminars and workshops in some 80 countries and has written, coauthored, and edited 24 books. Five of these books have been in the area of international communication, the first being *A Handbook of the Foreign Press* (in the early 1950s).

Whitney R. Mundt is associate professor of journalism at Louisiana State University, where he teaches courses in international mass communications, media ethics, and media law.

He earned his Ph.D. in English with a minor in journalism from Louisiana State University, and he is a graduate of the information officer and broadcast officer courses at the U.S. Army Information School, Fort Slocum, New York. He served in the U.S. Army as chief of the 95th Civil Affairs Group Civil Information Team, preparing area studies of world trouble spots, and as 95th Civil Affairs Group information officer. He also worked as a municipal reporter for the *Lake Charles* (La.) *American Press*. He has taught at Marietta College in Ohio as well as at LSU.

Mundt has traveled in India, East and West Germany, Austria, South Korea, and the USSR. He has published chapters or articles in the *World Press Encyclopedia, Encyclopedia Americana*, the *Dictionary of Literary Biography*, and the *Biographical Dictionary of American Journalism*, as well as in a number of other books and journals.

Christine Ogan is associate professor of journalism at Indiana University, where she teaches classes in international communication, communication and national development, communication technologies, reporting, and media management. She has lived and worked in Turkey and traveled in the Middle East. She has taught at North Carolina Central University; Hacettepe University and Ankara Koleji, both in Ankara, Turkey; and Ithaca College.

Ogan conducts research and writes about the role of new technologies in the development process and has published several recent articles on international video in *Media Development, Journal of Broadcasting and Electronic Media, Journal of Communication*, and *Telecommunications Policy*. She is also the author of a chapter in the 1989 book *The VCR Age*, edited by Mark Levy.

She has served as head of the International Division of the Association for Education in Journalism and Mass Communication and is presently vice head of the Intercultural/Development Communication Division of the International Communication Association. She holds a Ph.D. in mass communication research from the University of North Carolina at Chapel Hill.

Manny Paraschos, professor of journalism and mass communication at Emerson College in Boston, received his Ph.D. from the University of Missouri. His dissertation was titled "National Security and the People's Right to Know." He has taught at the University of Missouri and at the University of Arkansas at Little Rock, where he also chaired the Department of Journalism and founded the *Journal for Arkansas Journalism Studies* and the state's Urban Journalism Workshop for Minorities. In 1986–87, he was a Fulbright scholar in Scandinavia, where he taught at the Norwegian Institute of Journalism and lectured at universities in Norway, Sweden, and Denmark.

Paraschos was a reporter and United Nations correspondent for *Ethnikos Kyrix* of Athens, Greece, as well as a reporter, translator, and critic for *Embros* and *Diaplasis ton Paidon,* also of Athens. He has worked for the *North Little Rock* (Ark.) *Times* and the *Fayette* (Mo.) *Democrat-Leader* and was editorial page editor of the *Columbia Missourian.*

Robert G. Picard is professor of journalism at California State University at Fullerton. He holds a Ph.D. from the University of Missouri School of Journalism, an M.A. in communication from California State University at Fullerton, and a B.A. in communication from Loma Linda University.

A specialist on international public communication policies and media economics, he is the author of numerous books, including *Media Economics: Concepts and Issues, The Ravens of Odin: The Press in the Nordic Nations,* and *The Press and the Decline of Democracy: The Democratic Socialist Response in Public Policy.* He is editor of the *Journal of Media Economics* and associate editor of *Political Communication and Persuasion.*

Picard was formerly publications editor of the Freedom of Information Center (the national research center on controls of information), an editor of the *Ontario* (Calif.) *Daily Report,* editor of the *Riverside* (Calif.) *Community News,* and a reporter for the *Morning Advocate* in Baton Rouge, Louisiana.

Michael B. Salwen is assistant professor of communication at the University of Miami in Coral Gables, Florida. His research interests include the social effects of mass media, international communication, and public opinion. He has published articles in several journals, including *Journalism Quarterly, Newspaper Research Journal, Gazette, Communication Research Reports, The Quill,* and *Terrorism.*

Salwen earned his Ph.D. in mass media from Michigan State University and his M.A. in journalism from the Pennsylvania State University. For several years he worked as a reporter for newspapers in Pennsylvania and New Jersey.

Lowndes F. (Rick) Stephens is a professor in the College of Journalism and Mass Communications, University of South Carolina, where he was named one of the university's outstanding teachers in 1988. Stephens, who has served as head of two divisions (International, and Mass Communication and Society) of the Association for Education in Journalism and Mass Communication, has traveled extensively in Europe and Asia.

His research, supported by the Rockefeller and Gannett foundations, the American Newspaper Publishers Association, the U.S. Office of Education, and the U.S. Department of Defense, has appeared in more than a dozen scholarly journals and in the *New York Times* and other major newspapers. He recently codirected a Gannett-sponsored News Media and Terrorism Project with Robert Picard of Emerson College. He appears in *Who's Who in America* and the *Directory of American Scholars.*

Index

Abidine ben-Ali, Zine el-, 149
Abrams v. *United States* (1919), 14
Academy of Information (Indonesia),
   263
Access to Information Act (Canada),
   342–343
Action for Children's Television,
   345
Adam, G. Stuart, 341
Adams, Samuel, 20, 315
Advancing theory, 22
Advertising, 311, 319, 334, 344
   in Africa, 185
   agencies, 62, 69–70
   in Canada, 350
   government control through, 251,
      305
   in Latin America, 273
   and media content, 95
   in the Middle East, 136–137
   pan-European practices in, 116
   and press freedom, 339
   in Saudi Arabia, 140
   taxes on, to support press
      subsidies, 97
   in the United States, 347–348

Advertising Age, 354
Advertising agencies, 62, 69—70
Advocacy journalism in Africa, 161
Afghanistan, 218–219, 235–236, 246,
   249, 261
AFP. *See* Agence France-Presse (AFP)
Africa, 155–204
African American Institute, support
   for education in journalism, 200
African Press, The (Ochs), 150
Agence Belga news service
   (Belgium), 111
Agence de Presse Francophone, 338
Agence France-Presse (AFP), 34, 36,
   75, 110
Agence Havas, 32–34, 110
Agencia EFE (Spain), 77, 111, 303
Agencia Latinoamericana de
   Información (LATIN), 301–302
Agencia Latinoamericana de
   Servicios Especiales de
   Información (ALASEI), 301
Agencies. *See also* News services
   Agence France-Presse (AFP), 34,
      36, 75, 110
   ALASEI, 301